Ireland and the Americas

Ireland and the Americas

Culture, Politics, and History
A Multidisciplinary Encyclopedia
VOLUME I

EDITED BY

James P. Byrne

Philip Coleman

Jason King

Transatlantic Relations Series

Will Kaufman, Series Editor

A B C ☗ C L I O

Santa Barbara, California   Denver, Colorado   Oxford, England

Library of Congress Cataloging-in-Publication Data
Ireland and the Americas / edited by James P. Byrne, Philip Coleman, and Jason King.
   p. cm. — (Transatlantic relations series)
  Includes bibliographical references and index.
  ISBN 978-1-85109-614-5 (hard copy : alk. paper) — ISBN 978-1-85109-619-0
(ebook : alk. paper) 1. America—Relations—Ireland—Encyclopedias. 2. Ireland—
Relations—America—Encyclopedias. 3. America—History—Encyclopedias.
4. Ireland—History—Encyclopedias. 5. North America—History—Encyclopedias.
6. Latin America—History—Encyclopedias. 7. South America—History—
Encyclopedias. 8. America—Politics and government—Encyclopedias. 9. Ireland—
Politics and government—Encyclopedias. I. Byrne, James P., 1968– II. Coleman,
Philip Michael Joseph, 1972– III. King, Jason Francis, 1970–

E18.75.I74 2008
327.730417—dc22

                                 2007035381

12 11 10 09 08   1 2 3 4 5 6 7 8

Senior Production Editor: *Vicki Moran*
Editorial Assistant: *Sara Springer*
Production Manager: *Don Schmidt*
Media Editor: *Jason Kniser*
Media Resources Coordinator: *Ellen Brenna Dougherty*
Media Resources Manager: *Caroline Price*
File Management Coordinator: *Paula Gerard*

ABC-CLIO, Inc.
130 Cremona Drive, P.O. Box 1911
Santa Barbara, California 93116-1911

This book is also available on the World Wide Web as an ebook.
Visit www.abc-clio.com for details.

This book is printed on acid-free paper ∞
Manufactured in the United States of America

CONTENTS

ADVISORY BOARD

Maureen E. Mulvihill, Fellow, Princeton Research Forum, Princeton, New Jersey
Edmundo Murray, Society for Irish Latin American Studies
Gwenda Young, University College Cork, Ireland

SERIES EDITOR'S PREFACE

The transatlantic relationship has been one of the most dynamic of modern times. Since the great Age of Exploration in the fifteenth and sixteenth centuries, the encounters between the Old World and the New have determined the course of history, culture, and politics for billions of people. The destinies of Europe, Africa, North and South America, and all the islands in between have been intertwined to the extent that none of those areas can be said to exist in isolation. Out of these interconnections comes the concept of the "Atlantic world," which Alan Karras describes in his introductory essay to *Britain and the Americas* in this series: "By looking at the Atlantic world as a single unit, rather than relying upon more traditional national (such as Britain) or regional (such as North or South America) units of analysis, scholars have more nearly been able to re-create the experiences of those who lived in the past." This perspective attempts to redefine and respond to expanding (one might say *globalizing*) pressures and new ways of perceiving interconnections—not only those rooted in history ("the past") but also those that are ongoing. Just one result of this conceptual redefinition has been the emergence of Transatlantic Studies as an area of enquiry in its own right, growing from the soil of separate area studies, whether European, North American, African, Caribbean, or Latin American. Students and scholars working in Transatlantic Studies are embarked on a new course of scholarship that places the transatlantic dynamic at its heart.

In this spirit, the Transatlantic Relations Series is devoted to transcending, or at least challenging, the boundaries of nation/region as well as discipline: we are concerned in this series not only with history but also with culture and politics, race and economics, gender and migration; not only with the distant past but also with this morning. The aim, in a phrase, is to explore the myriad connections and interconnections of the Atlantic world. However, while the Atlantic world concept challenges the isolation of smaller, national perspectives, nations do continue to exist, with boundaries both physical and conceptual. Thus this series acknowledges the intractability of the national and the regional while consistently focusing on the transcending movements—the connections and interconnections—that go beyond the national and the regional. Our mode of operation has been to build an approach to the Atlantic world through attention to the separate vectors between the nations and regions on both sides of the Atlantic. We do this through offering the six titles within the series so far commissioned, devoted, respectively, to Africa, Britain, France, Germany, Iberia, and Ireland in their engagements with the Americas. In each case, the transatlantic exchanges are those of all kinds: cultural, political, and historical, from the moment of first contact to the present day. With that organizing principle in mind, the object is to offer an accessible, precisely focused means of entry into the various portals of the Atlantic world.

Finally, a word about the origins of this series. In 1995, Professor Terry Rodenberg of Central Missouri State University invited scholars and teachers from 18 universities on both sides of the Atlantic to establish an educational and scholarly institution devoted to encouraging a transatlantic perspective. The result was the founding of the Maastricht Center for Transatlantic Studies (MCTS), located in the Dutch city whose name, through its eponymous treaty, resonates with transnational associations. Since its foundation, MCTS has continued to bring together students and scholars from a host of worldwide locations to explore the intricate web of Atlantic connections across all disciplines: it has been a dynamic encounter between cultures and people striving to transcend the limitations of separate area and disciplinary studies. I am pleased to acknowledge the extent to which the Transatlantic Relations Series grows out of the discussions and approaches articulated at MCTS. Therefore, while the separate titles in the series will carry their own dedications, the series as a whole is dedicated with great respect to Terry Rodenberg and the students and scholars at Maastricht.

Will Kaufman
University of Central Lancashire
Maastricht Center for Transatlantic Studies

EDITORS' PREFACE

Defined by the online *Encarta Dictionary* as "a reference work offering comprehensive information on all or specialized areas of knowledge," an encyclopedia strives toward a form of inclusiveness that is ultimately unachievable in real terms. To provide even brief descriptions of *all* of the cultural, political, and historical figures from across the Americas who have had Irish connections would be an impossible task, not least because of the vast number of personalities involved—many of whom are "undocumented"—but also because "Irish-American relations" are currently being re-conceived by scholars of diasporic identities and area studies on both sides of the Atlantic. This work has benefited from the contributions of many individuals working in these and other fields, but in the same way that the process of defining the "Irish-American" experience remains the subject of intense debate and sometimes controversial negotiation, this work is also open-ended insofar as it aims to suggest pathways for further study, conversation, and research, and does not represent a "final" or "conclusive" statement in itself. It goes further than existing accounts of Irish-American relations in terms of its broadening of the scope of inquiry beyond the United States of America to include Canada and Latin American countries such as Argentina and Brazil, but this opening up of the field represents a first step towards a re-description of the multifaceted roles played by the Irish in the western hemisphere. For all of its tentativeness, however, it is a small step that demonstrates the profound influence the Irish have had far beyond the European frame of reference.

The editors wish to thank all of those who contributed to the writing of these volumes—for their patience and goodwill—and the following individuals in particular: David Doyle, Andrew Goodspeed, Benjamin Keatinge, Maureen Mulvihill, Edmundo Murray, and Gwenda Young. Wendy Roseth and Alex Mikaberidze are also to be thanked for their efficient and patient assistance at various stages of the work's development. The editors wish to thank the series editor, Will Kaufman, and all of those behind the scenes at ABC-CLIO who provided essential help along the way.

James P. Byrne, Philip Coleman, Jason King
Boston, Dublin, Concordia
March 2007

TOPIC FINDER

ART AND CULTURE

Allen, Fred

An Tóstal: Ireland
  at Home

Baggot, King

Balfe, Michael William

Ball, Ernest R.

Barry, Philip

Bartholomew, Freddie

Beach, Amy Marcy

Beach, Sylvia

Beckett, Samuel

Bergin, Patrick Connolly

Bord Fáilte Eireann

Brennan, Maeve M.

Brennan, Walter

Brenon, Herbert

Brent, George

Brosnan, Pierce

Brown, Clarence Leon

Bulfin, William

Butler, Jean

Byrne, Donn

Byrne, Gabriel

Cagney, James

Carney, Art

Carolan, Turlough

Carroll, James P.

Chandler, Raymond
  Thornton

Cherish the Ladies

Chieftains, The

Chopin, Kate

Clancy Brothers, the

Coffey, Brian

Cohan, George M.

Coleman, Michael

Colum, Mary

Colum, Padraic

Cowell, Henry Dixon

Crosby, Bing

Crouch, Frederick Nicholls

Curran, Mary Doyle

Cusack, Cyril

Dailey, Dan

Daly, "John" Augustin

Day, Dennis

Day-Lewis, Daniel

Delanty, Greg

Derrane, Joe

Donleavy, J. P.

Donovan, Gerard

Dorsey, Thomas Francis
  "Tommy"

Downey, Morton

Doyle, Roddy

Dunne, Finley Peter

Dunne, Irene Marie

Durcan, Paul

Egan, Desmond

Ellman, Richard David

Farrell, Eileen

Farrow, Mia

Fay, Francis Anthony
  "Frank"

Federal Theatre Project

Fitzgerald, Barry

Fitzgerald, F. Scott

Flaherty, Robert J.

Flanagan, Thomas

Flatley, Michael

Fleming, Thomas J.

Foley, (also Foli) Allan James

Ford, John

Foster, Stephen Collins

Gallagher, Tess

Garland, Judy

Garson, Greer

Gibbons, Cedric

Gilmore, Patrick Sarsfield

Gleason, Jackie

Gleeson, Brendan

Gogarty, Oliver St. John

Gordon, Mary

San Francisco
South Carolina
South Dakota
Tennessee
Texas
Uruguay
Venezuela
Virginia
Washington D.C.

POLITICS
Anglin, Timothy Warren
Arthur, Chester A.
Bennett, William J.
Broderick, David Colberth
Bryan, George
Buchanan, James
Buckley, William F., Jr.
Bulger, William Michael
Burke, Edmund
Carroll, Charles
Clinton, William Jefferson
Cockran, William Bourke
Cooke, John William
Croker, Richard
Curley, James Michael
Davin, Nicholas Flood
De Valera, Eamon
Dongan, Thomas
Farley, James Aloysius
Farrell, Edelmiro Juan
Gore, Robert
Jackson, Andrew
Kelly, "Honest" John
Kennedy Family
Kennedy, John Fitzgerald
Law, Andrew Bonar
Lynch, Elisa (Eliza)
McCarthy, Joseph
McGee, Thomas D'Arcy
Morrison, Bruce
Moynihan, Daniel Patrick

Mulroney, Brian
Murphy, Charles Francis
O'Neill, Jr., Thomas "Tip"
O'Roarke, Julian "Huberto"
Political Parties, Irish
Reagan, Ronald Wilson
Robinson, Mary
Scots-Irish Politics
Smith, Alfred Emmanuel "Al"
Tammany Hall
Tweed, William "Boss"
Wilson, Thomas Woodrow

RACE AND ETHNICITY
Ancient Order of Hibernians
Coghlan, Eduardo Aquilio
Draft Riots
Eire Society of Boston
Ethnic and Race Relations, Irish and African Americans
Ethnic and Race Relations, Irish and French Canadians
Ethnic and Race Relations, Irish and Indigenous Peoples
Ethnic and Race Relations, Irish and Italians
Ethnic and Race Relations, Irish and Latinos
Faction Fighting
Press, the Ethnic Irish
Scots-Irish

RELIGION
Brendan, Saint, "The Navigator"
Carroll, Bishop John
Catholic Church, the

Coughlin, Father Charles Edward
Craig, John
Cusack, Margaret Anna
Dillon, Patrick Joseph
Fahy, Anthony Dominic
Gaughren, Father Matthew
Hayes, Archbishop Patrick Joseph
Hughes, Archbishop John
Ireland, John
Lynch, Archbishop John Joseph
Massacre at Saint Patrick Church, the
Mathew, Father Theobald
Nativism and Anti-Catholicism
O'Gorman, Camila
Orange Order
Presbyterianism
Saint Patrick's Cathedral
Spellman, Archbishop Francis Joseph

SCIENCE AND TECHNOLOGY
Emmet, John Patten
Holland, John Phillip
Maury, Matthew Fontaine

SLAVERY
Abolitionism and Slavery
Douglass, Frederick
Healy, Michael Morris
Mott, Lucretia Coffin
Webb, Richard Davis

SPORTS
Baseball
Baseball Managers, Irish-American
Conn, William David

CHRONOLOGIES OF IRELAND AND THE AMERICAS

IRELAND AND CANADA

ca. 550 Legendary accounts, such as the *Navagatio sancti Brendani Abbatis,* tell of St. Brendan the Navigator reaching Newfoundland.

1622 First documentary record of Irish inhabitants in Newfoundland.

1663 First documentary record of Irish inhabitants in New France.

1789 Future Irish revolutionary Lord Edward Fitzgerald travels through British North America and the United States.

1799 Publication of Irish traveler Isaac Weld's *Travels through the States of North America, and the Provinces of Upper and Lower Canada.*

1800 United Irish uprising in Newfoundland, following failure of 1798 rebellion.

1804 Ireland's "National Poet" Thomas Moore travels to Upper and Lower Canada.

1822 First Orange Parade in York (Toronto).

1823–1825 Assisted emigration schemes led by Peter Robinson settle near Peterborough, Ontario.

1824 First St. Patrick's Day parade in Montreal.

1825–1845 Half million Irish emigrants travel to British North America during years of mass-migration.

1825 Publication of Oliver Goldsmith Jr.'s *The Rising Village.*

1830 Publication of Adam Kidd's *The Huron Chief.*

1830 Ogle Gowan establishes Orange Grand Lodge of British North America.

1832 Quarantine station established at Grosse Ile after outbreak of cholera afflicts Irish emigrants, over 5,000 of whom perished.

1834 Establishment of St. Patrick's Society of Montreal.

1835–1837 Shiner's War in Ottawa Valley, in which Irish lumbermen used their collective power to intimidate their French-Canadian competitors.

1836 Ogle Gowan and his followers in the Orange Order of Canada orchestrate riots to intimidate political opponents during election.

1828–1837 Daniel Tracey and Edmund Bailey O'Callaghan editors of the radical *Irish*

Vindicator and *Vindicator* newspapers in Montreal.

1837–1838 Irish radicals band together with French-Canadian Patriotes to instigate rebellion in Lower Canada in 1837 and in Upper Canada one year later, which other Irish-Canadians help to suppress.

1841 Publication of Standish O'Grady's *The Emigrants.*

1847 More than 100,000 emigrants flee Ireland for British North America at the height of the Famine, most of whom are quarantined at Grosse Ile. At Grosse Ile some 5,000 die and a similar number are reputed to have perished in Montréal, with several hundred more dying in Kingston and Toronto.

1847 Completion of St. Patrick's Church (now Basilica) in Montreal.

1848–1854 Changes in Navigation Act lead to steep decline in number of emigrants embarking for British North American ports.

1849 Ethno-religious violence, commonplace on St. Patrick's Day and July 12, erupt in Saint John, New Brunswick, leaving 12 people dead.

1849 Timothy Warren Anglin emigrates from Clonakilty, Co. Cork, to Saint John, New Brunswick.

1855 Corrigan affair of sectarian violence erupts after murder of Orangeman Hugh Corrigan by Irish Catholic assailants in St. Sylvestre, Quebec.

1857 Thomas D'Arcy McGee leaves the United States for Montreal to publish *The New Era* newspaper, elected to Parliament.

1858 Publication of Thomas D'Arcy McGee's *Canadian Ballads.*

1860 John Joseph Lynch becomes Archbishop of Toronto.

1863 Patrick Boyle establishes the staunchly nationalist *Irish Canadian* that is sympathetic to Fenianism.

1866 Fenian invasion of Canada and Battle of Ridgeway.

1867 Thomas D'Arcy McGee helps to negotiate the British North America Act establishing Canadian Confederation.

1867–1882 There are 22 Orange and Green riots in Toronto.

1868 Assassination of Thomas D'Arcy McGee by Fenian activist Patrick James Whelan, followed by largest public funeral in Canadian history.

1869 Timothy Eaton establishes Eaton's Department Store in Toronto.

1877 Publication of Nicholas Flood Davin's *The Irishman in Canada.*

1880 Massacre of "Black Donnellys" in Biddulph Township, Ontario.

1884 Publication of Isabella Valancy Crawford's *Malcolm's Katie: A Love Story.*

1891 Michael Davitt visits Manitoba, six years after the suppression of Louis Riel's rebellion and execution.

1921 Anglo-Irish Treaty, largely modeled on Canadian Dominion status.

1948 Irish Taoiseach John A. Costello announces the intention to declare the Irish State a republic while on a state visit to Ottawa.

1960 Publication of Brian Moore's novel *The Luck of Ginger Coffey,* winner of the Governor General's Award.

1973 Founding of the Canadian Association for Irish Studies (CAIS).

1975 Establishment of the *Canadian Journal of Irish Studies.*

1977 Publication of Jack Hodgins's *The Invention of the World.*

1983 Publication of James Reaney's dramatic trilogy *The Donnellys,* winner of the Governor General's Award.

1985 Shamrock Summit at which Canadian Prime Minister Brian Mulroney and U.S. President Ronald Reagan sing

"When Irish Eyes Are Smiling" together in Quebec City on St. Patrick's Day.

1986   Establishment of the D'Arcy McGee Chair of Irish Studies at Saint Mary's University, Halifax.

1993   Publication of Jane Urquhart's *Away*, winner of the Trillium Award.

1996   Publication of Margaret Atwood's *Alias Grace*, short listed for the Booker Prize.

1998   Retired Canadian General John de Chastelain appointed to supervise weapons decommissioning in the Belfast Agreement.

2000   Establishment of the Centre for Canadian Irish Studies at Concordia University in Montreal.

2006   Publication of Peter Behren's *The Law of Dreams*, winner of Governor General's Award.

IRELAND AND LATIN AMERICA

ca. 550   Legendary call of St. Brendan of Ardfert and Clonfert (484–580) at Mexico during his American journey.

1477   Columbus visits Galway's St. Nicholas of Myra.

1519–1522   Three Galway sailors follow Ferdinand Magellan in his circumnavigation of the world.

1536   Juan and Tomás Farel (Farrell) are among the first settlers of Buenos Aires in the expedition led by Pedro de Mendoza.

1577   Thomas Field, S. J. (1547–1626) of Limerick arrives in Brazil.

1593   The *Real Colegio de Nobles Irlandeses* opens in Salamanca. Many of the students play religious, military, and administrative roles in colonial Latin America.

1612   Philip and James Purcell establish a plantation on the mouth of the Amazon river, followed by Bernardo O'Brien of Co. Clare.

1651   William Lamport is sentenced by the Mexican Inquisition to be executed in the *Auto da Fé*, or public execution.

1729   Several of the 5,855 slaves in the Caribbean island of Montserrat are owned by Irish families Farrill, Hussey, Lynch, Roach, and others.

1768–1771   An Irish Regiment is established in Mexico by the Spanish government.

1770   First recorded St. Patrick's Day celebration in Latin America in a church built by Lancelot Belfort (1708–1775) at *Kilrue* plantation by the Itapecurú River, Maranhão State, in northern Brazil.

1762   John McNamara and his British 45th regiment attack without success Colonia del Sacramento in the northern bank of the River Plate.

1770   William Farmer (b. 1732) of Youghal, Co. Cork, commands the sloop *Swift* in West Falkland (*Gran Malvina*) waters, but is obliged to evacuate Port Egmont by a Spanish force.

1776   Michael O'Gorman (1749–1819) arrives in the River Plate as the official surgeon in the expedition of the Spanish viceroy Pedro de Ceballos.

1787   Ambrose O'Higgins (1721–1801) of Co. Sligo is made governor of Chile. Later he will be appointed viceroy of Peru.

1806–1807   British forces storm the Spanish viceroyalty of the River Plate. Irish soldiers remain in Argentina and Uruguay and start private migration networks from Westmeath.

1814   William Brown (1777–1857) of Co. Mayo is appointed commander of the Argentine navy.

Peter Campbell (b. 1780), a veteran of the British campaigns in the River Plate, commands the first Uruguayan navy.

John MacKenna (1771–1814), officer in Chile and Peru, dies in a duel in Buenos Aires.

1817 Businessman Thomas Armstrong (1797–1895) of Co. Offaly arrives in Buenos Aires.

1818–1822 John Devereux (1778–1854) recruits soldiers in Ireland to join Simón Bolívar's independence army in South America.

1821 Juan Dumphi O'Donojú (1762–1821), arrives in Mexico as the last Spanish Viceroy.

1823 Stephen Hallet, an Irish-born printer living in Buenos Aires, launches *La Gaceta Mercantil.*

1824 Bernard Kiernan (1780–1863), a surveyor and astronomer of Co. Derry, arrives in Buenos Aires from the United States with other "Irish Yankees."

Francis Burdett O'Connor (1791–1871) is appointed chief of staff of the United Army of Liberation in Peru.

1826 Thomas Wright (1799–1868) of Drogheda founds the nautical school of Ecuador.

John King (1800–1857) of Newport, Co. Mayo, joins the Argentine forces during the war against Brazil.

1827 Col. William Cotter recruits 2,500 Irish men with their families, who arrive in Rio de Janeiro from Cork.

1828 John Thomond O'Brien (1786–1861) is commissioned by the government of Buenos Aires to promote Irish immigration.

1829–1836 Colonies are established in Mexican Texas by Irish *empresarios* John McMullen, James McGloin, James Power, and James Hewetson.

1830 St. Patrick's Day is celebrated with dinner and dancing in Buenos Aires.

John Dillon opens the first brewery in Argentina.

1831 Patrick J. O'Gorman arrives at Buenos Aires as the second chaplain of the Irish.

1833 William Dickson of Dublin, storekeeper in the Falkland Islands, is entrusted with the care of the British flag by Captain Onslow, but is murdered by Antonio Rivera.

Patrick Fleming, a merchant in Buenos Aires, is kidnapped by Ranqueles.

1841 Total Irish population in Buenos Aires is 3,500. At least three-fourths are from Westmeath.

1843 Father Anthony Fahy, the chaplain of the Irish Argentines, arrives in Buenos Aires.

1844 The *William Peile* arrives in Buenos Aires with 114 emigrants from Co. Wexford.

1846 Wexford-born Robert Gore (1810–1854) is appointed as British chargé d'affaires in Montevideo and Buenos Aires.

1847 Camila O'Gorman and Father Uladislao Gutierrez elope from Buenos Aires and are executed the following year.

A Famine Relief Fund is sent by Father Fahy to the Archbishop of Dublin.

September 10–13, more than 50 survivors of the San Patricio Battalion are flogged, branded, and some executed in Mexico by the U.S. military forces.

1848 The Irish Hospital opens in Buenos Aires.

1854 Four hundred Wexford emigrants settle in an Irish Colony in Rio Grande do Sul, Brazil.

Irish laborers arrive from the United States at the construction site of the Panama Railroad.

William Russell Grace (1832–1904) of Co. Laois and his brother Michael establish a merchant house in Callao, Peru.

1855   Eliza Lynch (1835–1886) arrives in Paraguay to join her lover, the dictator Francisco Solano López.

1856   The Sisters of Mercy arrive in Buenos Aires.

1858   Benjamín Vicuña Mackenna launches *La Asamblea Constitucional* paper in Santiago, Chile.

1859   Wool merchant and landowner Thomas Duggan (1827–1913) of Ballymahon, Co. Longford, arrives in Buenos Aires.

1861   Dublin-born brothers Michael G. and Edward T. Mulhall launch the daily *The Buenos Ayres Standard*, the first English-language daily paper in South America.

1863   A subscription is started to support the building of Daniel O'Connell's monument in Dublin.

1864   M. O'Brien, consul of Buenos Aires in Dublin, returns to Argentina.

1865   Wexford-born Thomas J. Hutchinson's *Buenos Aires and Argentine Gleanings* is published in London.

    William Scully (d. 1885) launches *The Anglo-Brazilian Times* in Rio de Janeiro.

1866   Michael Duffy is appointed Major of Carmen de Areco, and John Dowling, Military Commander of the same district in Buenos Aires.

1867   In England and the United States, agents of the Brazilian government actively promote Irish immigration to Santa Catarina.

    Race-meetings gather thousands of *irlandeses* in Luján, Navarro, and Capilla del Señor districts of Buenos Aires.

1869   Patrick Fitzsimons (1802–1872), a teacher of Ennis, Co. Clare, is commissioned by the Argentine President Domingo F. Sarmiento to open the *Colegio Nacional* in Corrientes.

    The National Census returns include 10,709 British subjects residents in Argentina, 8,623 of them bearing Irish surnames, and 5,246 Irish-born.

1870   *Killallen* (Allen's Chapel) opens in Michael Allen's estancia, Castilla.

1873   St. Patrick's Society is founded as the first political undertaking of the Irish in Argentina.

    Stella Maris Chapel opens in Port Stanley, Falkland Islands.

1874   Anarchist physician John "Juan" Creaghe (1841–1920) of Limerick arrives in Buenos Aires from Sheffield.

    Nicholas Lowe (1827–1902) launches the *Daily News*, addressed to Protestant readers, and the *Buenos Ayres News and River Plate Advertiser*.

1875   First issue of *The Southern Cross*, founded by Fr. Patrick J. Dillon.

    Second edition of M. G. and E. T. Mulhall's *Handbook of the River Plate Republics* published in Buenos Aires.

    Father James Foran is the first resident Catholic priest in Falkland Islands.

1876   Santa Lucía chapel opens on Juan Harrington's estancia in San Pedro.

    Michael Mahon (1815–1881) is elected Vice-President of the Home Rule League in Capilla del Señor.

1877   Church of Ireland clergyman Lowther Brandon becomes Colonial Chaplain of the Falkland Islands.

1879   Businessman Eduardo Casey (1847–1906) purchases 1,700 square miles of land from the Government of Santa Fe to start a colony.

1880   The Sisters of Mercy leave Argentina for political reasons. Most of them go to the Order's mission in Mount Gambier, Australia.

1881   A great Land League meeting is held in Salto.

    The Irish Relief Fund is launched by Father Martin Byrne, of the Passionist Order.

1882   Michael Dineen is appointed editor of *The Southern Cross,* succeeding Father Dillon.

1884   William Bulfin (1862–1910), journalist and writer, arrives in Buenos Aires. He contributes to, and later directs and owns, the *Southern Cross* newspaper. Bulfin also launches the first GAA in Latin America.

1886   The Pallotines establish in Argentina.

1888   The Venado Tuerto Polo and Athletic Club is founded.

The *Irish Argentine* newspaper is founded by Father Bernard Feeney (1844–1919) in Azcuénaga, Buenos Aires.

1889   In Uruguay, Eduardo Casey purchases *The River Plate Times* paper.

A branch of the Gaelic League is founded in the Passionist monastery of Capitán Sarmiento.

The "Dresden Affair": 1,774 Irish emigrants deceived by agents Buckley O'Meara and John S. Dillon are embarked in the steamer *City of Dresden* to Buenos Aires. Peter Gartland starts an Irish Colony with 700 of the *Dresden* emigrants.

1890   The Sisters of Mercy are back in Argentina.

1892   Thomas Mason founds Santa Rosa, in La Pampa.

The Lobos Athletic Club is founded in the province of Buenos Aires. Tomás P. Moore is the first captain of the soccer team.

1894   Dublin-born teacher Kathleen Boyle (*née* Jones) (1869–1941) founds the English School of San Martín, in the outskirts of Buenos Aires. It will later be renamed San Patricio.

The Parnell Fund is remitted to Justin MacCarthy for the benefit of the Irish Evicted Tenants.

1895   In the Argentine census 18,617 individuals bear Irish surnames and 5,407 are born in Ireland.

Porteño Athletic Club is founded in Buenos Aires as the first Irish-Argentine soccer institution, with Santiago G. O'Farrell as president.

1896   *Duggan* railway station and town are founded in San Antonio de Areco.

1898   During the Spanish-American War, the head of the Milligan Guards of Arizona, William "Buckey" O'Neill, is killed at San Juan Hill, Cuba.

Gahan railway station and town are founded in Salto.

1899   St. Brigid's school opens in Buenos Aires.

1900   First official hurling match in Argentina, sponsored by the Buenos Aires Hurling Club, presided over by James P. Harte.

William Bulfin's *Tales of the Pampas* published in London by Fisher & Unwin.

1901   St. Patrick's Day is celebrated by 9,000 Irish-Argentine pilgrims in Luján basilica.

1902   Dublin-born William Payne, an evangelist missionary, establishes a mission in Cochabamba, Bolivia.

1904   Paddy McCarthy (1871–1963) of Tipperary is hired by Club Atlético Gimnasia y Esgrima and Boca Juniors of Buenos Aires to train its junior players.

1906   Roger Casement (1864–1916) is appointed British consular official in Brazil. He is sent to the western Amazon to investigate treatment of the local Indian population.

John Nelson (1859–1931) launches the *Hibernian-Argentine Review.*

The entrepreneur Eduardo Casey commits suicide in Buenos Aires.

O'Brien railway station and town are founded in Bragado.

1907   Tomás Mullally founds Realicó, in La Pampa.

1910   John Lalor (1860–1931) establishes a cattle auctioneer business in Buenos Aires.

1911   Padraic MacManus launches *Fianna*, a nationalistic newspaper addressed to Irish Argentines.

1914   Pedro Ricardo Meehan (1890–1972), Gerald I. N. Deane (1886–1962), and other Irish Argentines serve in the British Army in Europe.

1916   During the Easter Rising, Eamon Bulfin (1892–1968) raises the Irish Republic flag over Dublin's General Post Office. His death sentence is pardoned owing to Bulfin's Argentine citizenship.

1919   Thomas Murray's *The Story of the Irish in Argentina* is published in New York by P. J. Kenedy & Sons.

1921   The "Irish Race Congress in South America" is held in Buenos Aires with over 50 delegates. A grant is established for students of Spanish in the National University of Ireland.

Frank W. Egan is the Irish Republic representative in Chile.

After his mission in South Africa, Patrick J. Little is sent to Argentina, Brazil, and Chile as the diplomatic envoy of the Irish Free State.

1922   Hurling championship won by *The Wanderers*, seconded by the *Capilla Boys*.

1923   New wave of Irish immigration to Argentina due to social upheaval in Ireland, including Protestant young professionals and employees from Cork and Dublin.

1924   The Argentine polo team, including Irish Argentines Juan Nelson and

Arturo Kenny, wins a Gold Medal in the Olympic Games in Paris.

1926   The Passionist Sisters found the *Michael Ham Memorial College* for girls.

1930   Juan O'Leary's *El héroe del Paraguay* published in Asunción.

1934   Sean Healy (1894–1982), a chemist from Galway, opens St. Cyran's School of Buenos Aires.

Edificio Kavanagh in Buenos Aires, the tallest building in Latin America at the time, is commissioned by Corina Cavanagh (b. 1910).

1939   Guillermo Furlong, S. J. (1889–1974) is appointed member of the national academy of history.

1942   Carlos Viván "El Irlandesito" (born Miguel Rice Tracy) publishes his tango *Moneda de cobre,* with lyrics by Horacio Sanguinetti.

1944   Edelmiro Juan Farrell (1887–1980) is sworn in as Argentine President after leading a pro-Axe military coup d'état.

1946   Kathleen Nevin's *You'll Never Go Back* published in Boston by Bruce Humphries. The manuscript was completed by her sister Winnie.

1947   An Irish chargé d'affaires, Matthew Murphy, is appointed to Argentina.

1948   Christian Brothers' Cardinal Newman boys school opens in Buenos Aires.

1951   James M. Ussher's *Father Fahy: a Biography of Anthony Dominic Fahy, O. P., Irish Missionary in Argentina (1805–1871)* is published in Buenos Aires.

1953   Juan O'Gorman completes the painting of the Central Library in the campus of Universidad Autónoma de Mexico.

1955   Christian Brothers' Stella Maris school opens in Uruguay.

Lorenzo McGovern is appointed to the Argentine mission in Dublin.

1957   Rodolfo Walsh's *Operación Masacre* published in Buenos Aires.

1958   Edmundo O'Gorman's *La invención de América* published in Mexico.

1964   Michael J. Siejes is appointed first honorary consul of Ireland in Rio de Janeiro. Padraig de Paor is the first non-resident Irish ambassador accredited to Brazil.

Michael Leo Skentelberry appointed first Irish ambassador to Argentina.

The Irish Argentine Miguel Fitzgerald (b. 1926) flies to the Falkland Islands as an act of Argentine sovereignty.

1966   Air Force officer Eduardo F. McLoughlin (b. 1918) is appointed Argentine ambassador to Britain.

John Joseph Scanlan opens St. Brendan's College in Buenos Aires.

1969   Christian Brothers open the school Mundo Mejor in Lima, Peru.

1975   The Irish diplomatic mission is established in Brazil.

1976   The Massacre at St. Patrick: in San Patricio parish church of Buenos Aires, a navy death squad kills five members of the Pallotine community, including Alfie Kelly (parish priest), Alfredo Leaden, Eduardo Dufau, Emilio Barletti and Salvador Barbeito.

1977   Writer and guerrilla fighter Rodolfo Walsh (1927–1977) is killed in a military operation.

An Irish embassy is established in Mexico.

1981   Hilda Sabato and Juan Carlos Korol's *Cómo fue la inmigración irlandesa a la Argentina* published in Buenos Aires.

1982   John Brabazon's memoirs are published in Spanish by Eduardo Coghlan as *Andanzas de un irlandés por el campo porteño.*

During the Falklands War, Irish and Irish-Argentine soldiers fight on both sides of the conflict. Translation is one particularly skilled service rendered by many Irish Argentines. In the European Commission, Ireland supports the removal of economic sanctions on Argentina.

1987   Eduardo A. Coghlan's *Los Irlandeses en Argentina: su Actuación y Descendencia* is published in Buenos Aires.

1992   Peadar Kirby's *Ireland and Latin America: Links and Lessons* is published by Trócaire in Dublin.

1993   Fernando O'Neill's *Anarquistas de acción en Montevideo 1927–1937* is published in Uruguay.

1999   The Associação Brasileira de Estudos Irlandeses at the University of São Paulo publishes the first issue of *ABEI Journal: The Brazilian Journal of Irish Studies.*

2001   Martin Greene, first resident ambassador of Ireland to Brazil arrives in Brasilia.

2002   Two thousand Argentines with Irish ancestry submit a petition to the Irish government demanding Irish nationality based on *ius sanguinis* claims.

2004   John Cribbin O.M.I., of Shanagolden, Co. Limerick, is awarded honorary citizenship of Rio de Janeiro for his 40 years of missionary work in Brazil.

IRA members Niall Connolly, Martin McCauley, and James Monaghan are sentenced to 17 years after an appeal court in Colombia which has found them guilty of training FARC guerrillas.

2006   One-third of the population in Gort, County Galway, is Brazilian-born.

IRELAND AND THE UNITED STATES

ca. 550　Legendary accounts, such as the *Navagatio sancti Brendani Abbatis,* tell of St. Brendan the Navigator reaching inhabited islands and preaching the Gospel to the natives.

1492　William Eris, or Ayers, a native of Galway, is reported to be one of Columbus' sailors. He is among 40 volunteers left behind on Hispaniola, and subsequently killed by the Indians.

1560–1580　English colonization of the New World is precipitated and prepared for by Elizabethan colonization of Ireland.

1600s　Irish emigration to the U.S. is negligible and primarily consists of unmarried, Catholic males. They come as indentured servants, soldiers, sailors, convicts, and rebels.

1621　Daniel Gookin, a Quaker merchant from Cork, heads a party of Irish settlers, who arrive in Newport News, Virginia, on board the *Flying Harte.* His son, Daniel Gookin, the Younger, will become a member of the governor's council of Massachusetts, and Superintendent of Indian affairs.

1630s　Greater religious tolerance in Maryland encourages increased Irish Catholic emigration to this state.

1649–1650　Cromwell's campaign in and subsequent conquest of Ireland dramatically increases the number of Irish Catholics sold into servitude. While these are initially transported as laborers to the West Indies, some eventually make their way to British colonies on the North American mainland.

1682　Thomas Dongan (1634–1715) becomes the first Irish Catholic governor of New York. Dongan convenes the first representative assembly of New York Province on October 14, 1683. The 'Charter of Libertyes and Privileges,' which comes from this assembly (also know as "Dongan's Charter") defines the form of government for the colony and recognizes basic political and personal rights (such as trial by jury and no taxation without representation).

1688　Charles Carroll, founder of one of the most distinguished and prosperous Irish-American families of the colonial era, becomes Attorney General of Maryland. His grandson, Charles Carroll of Carrollton, will be the only Catholic to sign the Declaration of Independence.

1700　Protestant emigration, primarily from the province of Ulster, begins to constitute the majority of Irish immigration to the United States.

1704　Laws discouraging the immigration and importation of Catholics into Maryland, formerly the most tolerant of states, signal the growing anti-Catholicism of the British colonies.

1706　Reverend Francis Makemie (1658–1780), from Ulster, convenes a group of Presbyterian ministers in Philadelphia, and becomes the founder of American Presbyterianism.

1717　Large-scale emigration from Ulster begins in earnest. By 1775 possibly as many as a quarter of a million Ulster-Scots will have left Ireland for the United States. They will eventually become known as Scots-Irish in the United States.

1737　On St. Patrick's Day in Boston, 26 Irishmen found the Charitable Irish Society, the oldest Irish society founded in the United States.

1740–1741　Crop failures in Ireland, caused by one of the most sustained cold periods in modern history, lead to starvation and disease on a scale similar to later famine of 1845–1851. This year becomes known colloquially as the Year of the Slaughter, and one of its subsequent effects is an increase in emigration to the United States.

1770–1775 A decline in the linen trade, compounded by excessive rent increases, sets off a significant wave of Ulster-Scots immigration to the United States.

1776 British troops evacuate Boston on March 17; General Washington makes "St. Patrick" password for his army on this day.

Declaration of Independence is signed by three Irish men and a further five men of Irish heritage.

John Barry (1746–1803), who will later become known as the "Father of the United States Navy," engages and captures the British vessel *Edward* on Arpil 7.

1798 Failed uprising of the Society of United Irishmen in Ireland. This sends a number of political exiles to the United States: Thomas Addis Emmet, William Sampson, and William MacNeven, among others.

1801 Act of Union creates United Kingdom of Great Britain and Ireland. Repeal of this act will become a major goal of Irish and Irish-American nationalism.

1814 Irish Emigrant society is founded in New York City to meet ever increasing numbers of Irish immigrants and aid them in adjusting to the New World.

1815 End of Napoleonic Wars in Europe sends increasing numbers of Irish Catholic immigrants to the United States. Between now and 1845 well over half a million Irish people will immigrate to the United States.

1834 Burning down of Ursuline Convent in Charlestown, Massachusetts, signals a growing anti-Catholic nativism in the United States., brought on by the in-

crease in Irish immigration and the subsequent competition in the job market.

1842 National Repeal Convention inaugurates the Repeal movement as the first major Irish nationalist movement in the United States.

Daniel O'Connell and Father Matthew sign "An Address of the Irish People to Their Countrymen in America" calling on Irish Americans to support the abolition of slavery. Irish Americans reject the call.

1845 A potato blight hits Ireland in September. This is the beginning of The Great Famine, *An Gorta Mhór* (The Great Hunger) as it is colloquially known, which leads to the deaths of as many as 1.5 million Irish people in less than a decade. It further uproots millions more and sends them, fleeing the terror, to the United States.

1848 Failed rebellion by Young Ireland movement, whose leaders had earlier broken with O'Connell's Repeal Association because of their disenchantment with its slow and peaceful strategy. After the failed rebellion a number of its leaders flee to the United States in exile and become major players in Irish-American nationalism and journalism: Thomas D'Arcy McGee, Thomas F. Meagher, John Mitchell, John O'Mahony.

1851 Irish immigration to the United States peaks at 219,232. Between 1846 and 1855 over 1.5 million Irish men and women immigrate to the United States.

1858 Fenian Brotherhood is founded in New York by John O'Mahony, while the Brotherhood (later more popularly know as the Irish Republican Brotherhood) is founded in Dublin by James Stephens (1824–1901).

1861–1865 Nearly 200,000 immigrants and Irish-Americans serve in the American Civil

War, possibly as many as two-thirds of them in the Union forces.

1866   First of three failed Fenian invasions of Canada, in the hopes of engaging British and ultimately persuading the United States to get involved in the "Irish problem."

1867   Failed Fenian Rising in Ireland. This will lead to a reorganization of the movement as Clan na Gael in the United States.

1871   Arrival of John Devoy, Jeremiah O'Donovan Rossa, and a number of other prominent Irish Republican nationalists in New York City.

1880   Irish National Land League of the United States is founded, to support Parnell's Land League in Ireland.

1886   Victor Herbert (1859–1924), a native of Dublin, arrives in New York. He goes on to become one of America's best composers of light opera.

1872   "Honest John" Kelly becomes boss of Tammany Hall in New York. For the next 50 years control of the Tammany machine and, through it, municipal politics in New York City will remain almost exclusively in Irish hands.

1893   Gaelic League founded in Ireland and, subsequently, in the United States. The League seeks to promote the study of Irish and the revival of a distinct national culture.

First appearance of "Mr. Dooley" sketches by Finley Peter Dunne (1867–1936).

1903   Henry Ford (1863–1907), the grandson of John Ford, an emigrant from Co. Cork, establishes the Ford Motor Co.

1916   Irish Race Convention in New York City, out of which come the Friends of Irish Freedom (FOIF), organized in part by John Devoy (1842–1928) and Judge Cohalan (1865–1946).

Easter Rising in Dublin, at which *The Proclamation of the Government of the Irish Republic to the People of Ireland* is read by Pádraig Pearse from the steps of General Post Office (GPO). Britain's execution of the leaders of the rebellion, following their surrender, outrages Irish and Irish-Americans who have until now been indifferent about Irish nationalism.

1919   Eamon de Valera (1882–1975) visits the United States to raise funds and gain recognition for the republic. He ultimately raises about $5 million, but splits from Devoy and Cohalan, and the Friends of Irish Freedom, over a number of issues.

1921   Signing of Anglo-Irish Treaty brings an end to Anglo-Irish War, and establishes the Irish Free State. However, it also allows six heavily Protestant counties in Ulster to remain under British rule, as 'Northern Ireland.'

1922   Outbreak of Civil War between de Valera's Republicans and the Free State Government. When it ends a year later with de Valera's surrender, it will leave many hard-line republicans disenchanted but the majority of Irish and Irish-American people looking to move beyond violence.

1928   Alfred Emmanuel Smith (1873–1944) is nominated by the Democratic Party for the Presidency of the United States. Of Irish origin, Smith is the first Catholic to be nominated by a national party. He will eventually lose to Republican Herbert Hoover, in part because of a recurrence of anti-Catholic bigotry.

1936   Eugene O'Neill (1888–1953), the son of actor James O'Neill, an Irish immigrant from Kilkenny, wins the Nobel Prize for Literature.

1949   The Proclamation of an Irish Republic establishes Ireland as a sovereign republic, but Northern Ireland remains a part of the United Kingdom. The United

States establishes full diplomatic relations with Ireland.

1950   At a Women's Republican Club meeting in Wheeling, West Virginia, Joseph R. McCarthy (1908–1957), a little known senator from Wisconsin, holds up a piece a paper on which he claims are written the names of 205 known communists in the State Department. So begins the anti-communist "crusade" of McCarthyism, which will dominate U.S. political and public culture for the next five years and draw the Irish-American community further into the national spotlight.

1960   John F. Kennedy (1917–1963) is elected President of the United States. He is the first Irish-American Catholic to win the presidency, and his election is seen as proof of the "arrival" of the Irish-American community on the American national stage.

1963   U.S. President John F. Kennedy visits Ireland; later that year he is assassinated while driving through Dallas in his motorcade.

1968   Civil Rights marches by Catholics in Northern Ireland.

        Senator Robert Kennedy, the brother of and possible political successor to John F. Kennedy, is shot and killed in Los Angeles.

1970   Northern Ireland Aid Committee (NORAID) is founded in New York to aid the victims of violence in Northern Ireland. It will later be accused of funding arms shipments to the IRA.

1972   On a Sunday in January, British paratroopers fire upon civil rights marchers in Derry, killing 13. "Bloody Sunday," as it becomes known, causes outrage in Ireland and the United States and leads to an escalation of sectarian violence in Northern Ireland.

1977   Edward Kennedy, "Tip" O'Neill, Senator Daniel P. Moynihan, and Governor

Hugh Carey of New York work with John Hume of the Social Democratic and Labour Party (SDLP) in Northern Ireland to form a coherent position on Northern Ireland Hunger and issue a joint condemnation of the IRA. These four U.S. political figures become known as the "Four Horsemen" of Irish-American politics.

1980s   Illegal Irish immigration to the United States is estimated to be somewhere between 40,000 and 100,000.

1981   Irish republican prisoners in Northern Ireland initiate hunger strikes in an effort to have the British government grant them the status of "political prisoners." In the end, 10 men die of starvation and support for Irish republicanism cause is galvanized in the United States.

        Daily demonstrations are held on the streets of New York City in support of the republican cause, with commemoration services being held in St. Patrick's Cathedral for each of the 10 dead hunger strikers.

1982   Martyred hunger striker Bobby Sands (1954–1982), the first to die in the hunger strike, is elected grand marshal of the St. Patrick's Day Parade.

1984   U.S. President Ronald Reagan (1911–2004) visits Ireland. His unearthing of Irish ancestry works to secure the support of an ever growing number of American Catholic Republican voters.

1994–2005 A series of scandals involving the sexual abuse of children rock the Catholic Church in both Ireland and the United States, severely affecting the Catholic Church's attendance and finances in both countries.

1995   U.S. President William Jefferson Clinton visits Ireland and receives a welcome reminiscent of the one afforded Kennedy on his return.

Riverdance, a theatrical show consisting of Irish dancing, opens in the Point Theatre in Dublin. From an intermission piece during the 1994 European Song Contest, held in Ireland, it goes on to achieve phenomenal success internationally.

1998   Signing of Belfast Agreement on April 10, hereafter known as the "Good Friday" Agreement; it is endorsed by the voters of both Northern Ireland and the Republic of Ireland on May 23. U.S. President Clinton's commitment to the achievement of this agreement plays a large part in its success; it remains a legacy of his administration.

The effects of the "Celtic Tiger"—Ireland's rising economy in the 1990s—result in a change in migration patterns. 21,200 people emigrate from Ireland but over 44,000 people immigrate into the country. Many of these are former emigrants returning from Britain and the United States.

2001   On September 21, 10 days after the September 11 attacks on New York's World Trade Center, the Irish government agrees to provide U.S. aircraft access to Irish airspace and Shannon airport.

2002   President Bush declares March 2002 Irish-American Heritage month and calls on all Americans to observe this month "by learning about and commemorating the contributions of Irish Americans."

2003   U.S. President George W. Bush visits Ireland and receives mixed reception from Irish worried about America's continued involvement in Iraq.

INTRODUCTORY ESSAYS

INTRODUCTION

One of the most important public events in the annual calendar of the Taoiseach or Irish prime minister is the presentation of a bowl of shamrock to the president of the United States on Saint Patrick's Day, March 17. The event symbolizes the special relationship that has existed for many decades between Ireland and the United States, but the fact that the

Irish head of government should leave Ireland and travel across the Atlantic on the day of his own country's national holiday also indicates the importance attached to the Irish-American bond in Irish political life. However, beyond Irish connections with the United States of America— beyond the shamrock bowl, as it were— other points of contact and exchange need to be acknowledged in an attempt to get a sense of Ireland's transatlantic profile. Between Ireland and Canada and Latin American countries such as Argentina, Mexico, Bolivia, and Brazil, important historical, political, and cultural links exist that are rarely acknowledged in considera-

President George W. Bush receives a gift of shamrock from Bertie Ahern, Ireland's prime minister. (AP/Wide World Photos)

tions of the so-called Irish-American nexus. In the three introductory essays that follow, therefore, the stories of Ireland's contacts with Canada, Latin America, and the United States will be summarized as part of this work's broader attempt to describe the ongoing process of exchange between Ireland and the Americas, the complexity of which is suggested by the entries in the main body of the work. These introductory essays indicate the multiplicity of locations out of which the narratives of Ireland's relations with the Americas emerge. The central task of this work, then, is to identify some of those narrative threads in the knowledge that many others remain undocumented: the invisible, the anonymous, those left out or overlooked for one reason or another in the story of any nation's development both inside and outside its borders need to be acknowledged even if they are not explicitly described. The gaps and discontinuities in this work speak to the vastness of the physical task involved in compiling these volumes, but they also represent the many women and men whose stories will be told in a longer, even more substantial account than the one presently offered as a first step toward a revised understanding of the relationships that exist between Ireland and the Americas.

IRELAND AND CANADA

Jason King

On the Celtic cross high above Grosse Ile, Quebec, reads the following inscription:

> Sacred to the memory of thousands of Irish emigrants, who, to preserve the faith, suffered hunger and exile in 1847–48, and stricken with fever, ended here their sorrowful pilgrimage.

The monument, erected by the Ancient Order of Hibernians in America, an expatriate Irish nationalist organization, makes a number of implicit assumptions about the emigrants' social and political affiliations, their ethnic profile, religious orientation, attitudes toward migration, and reasons for leaving Ireland. They are in fact not emigrants at all but exiles, having left their homeland not through their own volition but from economic and political compulsion and under extreme duress. Thus, according to the monument, such "children of the Gael," faced only with "foreign tyrannical laws and an artificial famine" if they remained in Ireland, had no choice but to embark for the United States or British North America. Furthermore, their migration is invested with a religious significance. It is a "pilgrimage," a harrowing journey undertaken by famine-stricken Irish Catholics to preserve their faith, escape from English avarice, and maintain an imperiled Gaelic civilization: their mission is the retention and transplantation of an endangered set of cultural and religious values. For such migrants, then, emigration is a matter of strict necessity— hardly an opportunity for social advancement or the achievement of material prosperity and a better standard of living.

The epic voyage of the Famine emigrants remains firmly lodged in Irish-Canadian popular memory and the literary imagination as the foundational event that brought the Irish to Canada. More than any other topic in Irish-Canadian historiography, the legacy of Grosse Ile continues to generate controversy with respect to how it is interpreted in popular memory and by professional historians and how it should be commemorated by the nation at large. The experiences of the Famine Irish have also become iconic in the Canadian literary imagination. Since 1970, Jack Hodgins's novel *The Invention of the World* (1977), James Reaney's trilogy of plays *The Donnellys* (1983), Jane Urquhart's *Away*

(1993), Margaret Atwood's *Alias Grace* (1996), and Peter Behren's *The Law of Dreams* (2006) have all featured the Famine Irish in their respective texts. Each of them imagines their struggles to represent the crucible upon which was forged such perennial themes in the Canadian psyche as the establishment of communality through adversity, perseverance against seemingly malevolent natural forces, and the quest for ethnic and social harmony through the repudiation of a violent past.

This viewpoint in itself is highly significant, for it pits the creative charge of Irish Canadian historical fiction and drama against the current of professional historical scholarship on the Canadian Irish. The prevailing trend among professional historians of the Irish in Canada, for example, has been to stress the wide disjunction between the traumatic legacy of the Famine migrants enshrined within Irish-Canadian popular culture and the actual, more congenial and verifiable social and economic conditions encountered by the vast majority of nineteenth-century Irish emigrants to British North America upon their arrival. Recent Canadian historical scholarship has thus sought to minimize the impact of the Famine Irish in Canada and to dispel what Houston and Smyth term the romantic and epic aura that surrounds them, because it is seen to inhibit a wider understanding of the social processes of nineteenth-century Irish emigration and Canadian settlement.

There is a general consensus among historians that the great misery of 1847 and the Famine exodus should be considered not as the linchpin but an anomaly in relation to larger trans-Atlantic migration movements. Historians such as Donald Akenson, Bruce Elliott, Cecil Houston, Mark MacGowan, William J. Smyth, Catharine Wilson, and David Wilson have all tended to emphasize the status of the Irish as part of a charter group in the foundation and development of Canadian society, rather than their destitution, recalcitrant nationalist inclinations, or more volatile political activities in the New World. They seek to revise the history of the Irish in nineteenth-century Canada, and stress the agency and relative affluence of the vast majority of Irish migrants upon their arrival in the country. They also insist that most of the Irish who came to Canada during the nineteenth century were of Protestant rather than Catholic or Gaelic descent, were inclined toward rural settlement on their own farmsteads, and experienced no more difficulty adapting to Canadian society than any other ethnic group. Irish-Canadian historical scholarship thus seeks to problematize received images and enduring stereotypes of the Irish in Canada, especially the Famine migrants, as embittered exiles, political outcasts, or vehemently nationalistic refugees. Yet it is only very recently that any historian has even begun to consider Irish Canadian popular culture as a legitimate object of inquiry in its own right, or to account for this wide rift that exists between Irish-Canadian professional historical scholarship and popular memory, with its iconic litany, as Houston and Smyth note, of "the Famine, typhus, cholera, and involuntary exile which have all grown to be the primary image symbolizing Irish emigration."

By the early nineteenth century, the social complexion of British North America was largely determined by emigration from Ireland; the Irish constituted the largest ethnic group in Canada after French Canadians. Approximately one million Irish emigrants traveled to Canada over the course of the nineteenth century, the majority of them in the period before rather than after the Famine. In demographic terms, Irish migrants and their descendants in Canada outnumbered the English, Scottish, and Welsh population combined. In nineteenth-century Ontario, in particular, the concentration of Irish was more considerable than anywhere else in the global Irish diaspora with the exception of New Zealand. Patterns of Irish migration to British North America thus differed profoundly from those to the United States. For if the flood of Famine migrants provided the catalyst for a continuous influx of people into Irish America throughout the rest of the nineteenth and early twentieth centuries, then their arrival in Canada marked the zenith or final crest rather than an initial surge of movement in the flow of mass migration.

Although they peaked during the Famine, patterns of Irish migration to British North America can be traced back to the mid-eighteenth century. Discrete movements from Waterford to Newfoundland and Ulster to Nova Scotia and Prince Edward Island would lay the foundations for subsequent Irish communities that left their imprint on the collective identities of these provinces. By the 1830s, emigrants were traveling to British North America from every part of Ireland, although Ulster migrants would continue to be over-represented. A decade later, in 1847, more than 100,000 emigrants traveled to British North America, 5,000 of whom were buried at the quarantine station at Grosse Ile, their mass graves marking the end of Irish mass migration to Canada. In 1848, the British Passenger Acts were changed to make Canada as expensive a destination to travel to as the United States, after which the outflow of Irish migrants to British North America considerably receded. By the twentieth century, only a tiny proportion of emigrants from Ireland continued to travel to Canada; the vast majority opted either for the United States or Great Britain instead. The Irish community in Canada comprises, of course, not only the migrants themselves but also their generations of descendants: it would be a serious error to extrapolate from the experiences of emigrants alone all of our knowledge about the Canadian Irish. Nevertheless, the huge decline in migration from Ireland to British North America after the Famine has meant that Canadian Irish communities have not been replenished in any meaningful way with substantial numbers of new arrivals from the homeland for well over a century. The question of when the Irish assimilated or integrated into the Canadian social mainstream continues to exercise historians, but there is no doubt that Irish-Canadian identity today is mainly a symbolic form of ethnicity, one that has long been detached from any lived experience in Ireland.

Historians agree that there is a tremendous amount of regional variation in patterns of Irish migration and settlement in Canada, which makes it difficult to generalize about their experiences. Nevertheless, in every part of the fledgling nation Irish communities were deeply interwoven into the Canadian social fabric by the time of Confederation in 1867. For example, Canadian educational and policing institutions—including the iconic Royal Canadian Mounted Police—were directly imported from Irish models; the huge social constituency of Irish unskilled workers provided the impetus for the development of organized labor in Canada. As with Irish institutions, Irish culture also sank deep roots in Victorian British North America. The influence of Irish culture in Newfoundland appears unmistakable even today, although the province's Irish community is the most venerable in Canada. By contrast, the outflow from Ireland to Ontario was considerably later and larger in scope, but the Irish were so thoroughly integrated into the Upper Canadian social structure that they have left relatively little imprint on the region's collective identity. More anomalous is the Irish community in Quebec: mainly Catholic, rather than Protestant, and often inclined to nationalist sympathies, occasionally in alliance with their French Canadian counterparts.

Especially paradoxical is the political behavior of the Irish in Canada. Irish Protestants were more likely than Irish Catholics to identify with the interests of power, habitually defining themselves as British rather than Irish, which allowed them to assimilate more rapidly into the established social order. Symptomatic of this tendency was their transplantation of Orangeism from Ireland to British North America: the Canadian Orange Order was significantly transformed from a narrowly anti-Catholic sectarian organization into a broadly loyalist and Pan-British fraternal association, one that many historians argue was more benign than its Irish progenitor. Orange lodges could be found all across Canada but were most heavily concentrated in Ontario, where they came to function as a virtual organ of local governance. Less conspicuous, outside of Quebec, was the social infrastructure of Irish Catholicism; expressions of anticolonial nationalism were few and far between. Like its American counterpart, the Fenian movement had an underground existence in Canada, but its dedication to the annexation of British North America to the United States limited its possibilities for growth north of the border. Far more common was a compartmentalized outlook on the part of Irish nationalists in Canada that emphasized loyalty to the colony of British North America while desiring independence or some form of political devolution back in Ireland. Thus, Irish Canadian nationalists tended to regard British North America as a model dominion for Ireland to emulate rather than as a symbol of imperial oppression to instigate attacks against.

The diffusion of Irish nationalism in Canada revealed the gradual acculturation of Irish Catholics into the British North American state. Over the course of the nineteenth century, while most of the Protestant and Catholic Irish population in British North America remained loyal to crown and colony, Irish revolutionary nationalism also found many Canadian outlets. In Quebec, in particular, Irish reformist and revolutionary aspirations were projected into the Lower Canadian sphere. Ethnic cooperation with French Canadians to undermine Anglo-Saxon hegemony was often advocated by Irish nationalist leaders. Yet in British North America, any anticipated alliance between the dislocated Irish and French-Canadian discontents to campaign for constitutional reform or foment revolutionary unrest failed fully to materialize. Instead, studies suggest that Irish Canadian political loyalties remained enigmatic, factious, fluctuating, and highly malleable throughout the nineteenth century, although there has been relatively little research on the issue to date. What research has been carried out on the ethnic newspapers of Irish Catholics in British North America indicates that they felt little sense of affinity toward their French Canadian coreligionists. The inculcation of anticolonial sentiment by Irish-Canadian newspapers such as *The Irish Vindicator* and *The Vindicator* did occur to some degree in the 1820s and 1830s; yet their clamor for reform was undermined by a combination of clerical reaction and deepened sectarian divisions both before and after the outbreak of rebellion in 1837. By the 1860s, the diminution of Irish Canadian political radicalism was largely complete, as Canadian Irish communities had by then been absorbed into the hegemonic unifying vision of constitutional nationalism championed by Thomas D'Arcy McGee.

In reality, the vast majority of Irish Catholics in British North America compartmentalized their cultural and political affiliations; they veered between a precarious sense of loyalty to the emergent British Canadian polity, oscillating degrees of sympathy and antipathy toward French Canada, and residual feelings of hostility toward British rule in Ireland that gave rise to some highly convoluted configurations of national identity.

Sporadic outbreaks of sectarian conflict, labor agitations, rural unrest, and factional violence complicated the picture still further, although historians have tended to downplay and underestimate their significance. David Wilson notes that the Shiner's War between rival Irish and French-Canadian lumbermen in the Ottawa Valley in 1835–1837, Orange intimidation of political rivals during the Upper Canadian election in 1836, and the clashes between Irish Protestants and Catholics during the Saint Patrick's Day and Twelfth of July parades in Saint John, New Brunswick, which left twelve people dead, illustrate the types of social, political, and ethno-religious violence that occasionally convulsed Irish communities in British North America, culminating in the assassination of Thomas D'Arcy McGee by a Fenian rival in 1868. Such occurrences were by no means the norm, but neither were they so exceptional as to prove the rule of seamless integration for the Irish into Canadian society without ethnic discord or sectarian strife.

Whatever their proclivities to occasional social discord, the Irish were heavily represented in the expansion of Canadian agriculture, industry, and the resource economy throughout the nineteenth century. They also played a vital role in clearing the wilderness and the settlement process in Upper Canada and points west. Patterns of regulated mobility saw the establishment of Irish settlements in the Canadian wilderness as footholds for future intergenerational chain migration, which leapfrogged ever farther westward. Their superior numbers and relative success in these endeavors prevented the Irish from becoming clustered in any particular geographical or occupational sector, and there is a consensus that they displayed considerable agency in pursuing the economic opportunities that were available to them rather than being buffeted across the continent by sweeping social and economic forces beyond their control.

While Protestant and Catholic emigrants quickly achieved the same social standing and level of affluence as the Canadian population in general, various social and economic indicators suggest that the process took slightly longer for the latter group. Protestants also differed from Catholics in their tendency to settle disproportionately in rural rather than urban areas, whereas approximately one-third of Irish Catholic emigrants resided in Canadian cities. The mainly Catholic Irish in Quebec thus settled disproportionately in Montreal and Quebec City rather than in the countryside, while sizable Irish communities could be found in nineteenth-century Halifax, Saint John, and Toronto. In the late 1840s, tensions broke out in Saint John and Toronto between long-established Protestant Irish communities and the newly arrived Catholic Famine migrants. As noted, highly visible Irish cultural practices such as the annual Saint Patrick's Day Parade and the "Glorious Twelfth" could provide flashpoints for intra-communal violence. More often though Irish collective identities found more peaceful forms of political expression in both rural and urban settings; Thomas D'Arcy McGee was only the most famous of a number of Irish-Canadian politicians. His role as a visionary founder and "Father of Confederation" attests to the place of the Irish in the very establishment rather than on the margins of the Canadian state.

Aside from D'Arcy McGee's literary and political achievements, however, relatively little is known about Irish-Canadian cultural life. Because the scholarship on the Canadian Irish is mainly empirical social history, we have a much better sense of where they came from and where they settled rather than how they saw the world. Irish-Canadian literature provides a partial corrective for this overreliance on quantitative analysis; used sensitively, it can help enable us to imaginatively reconstruct a culturally distinctive Canadian Irish collective outlook and world view. At the heart of this collective outlook was the idea that the Irish in Canada had renounced their ancestral quarrels and become the inhabitants of a peaceable kingdom in which social harmony between all forms of Irish identity prevailed. The quest for this peaceable kingdom provides a consistent refrain in Irish-Canadian literature that remains invisible to the quantitative methods of empirical social history.

The origins of Irish writing in nineteenth-century British North America should be interpreted, then, within the context of this quest for the peaceable kingdom. The cultural nationalist aspirations of the Young Ireland movement were also transmitted by Thomas D'Arcy McGee into a Canadian literary context. As was the case in Ireland, the Canadian literary works of the period tend to be written in verse and often assumed the form of the long poem. Many writers considered the long poem's relatively fluid structure to be the genre most amenable for conveying an idea of Canada's daunting and seemingly unformed wilderness and its precarious state of civilization. In the hands of Irish-Canadian writers, it would also provide a suitable medium for reflecting on the experience of their displacement from Ireland and resettlement within British North America. Thus, the literary endeavors of various Irish authors resident in the Canadas, such as Oliver Goldsmith Jr.'s *The Rising Village* (1825), written in direct response to his uncle and namesake's considerably more famous *The Deserted Village* (1770), Adam Kidd's *The Huron Chief* (1830), (the Canadian) Standish O'Grady's *The Emigrant* (1842), and Isabella Valancy Crawford's *Malcolm's Katie: A Love Story* (1884), would all become incorporated into the annals of early Canadian writing.

Although he was by no means the originator of this literary tradition, D'Arcy McGee consciously sought to cultivate and propagate it in order to facilitate the advancement of a genuinely Canadian national literature. In a wider sense, his program of cultural nationalism was little more than an extension of his involvement in the Young Ireland movement and its romantic attempt "to create and foster public opinion in Ireland," through the development of a national body of verse, into a Canadian literary milieu—but one in which the poetic evocation of "the spirit of the nation" had become imbued with Victorian sentiments of propriety and respectability shorn of any radical political content. Writing in an entirely different vein, the early twentieth-century Quebec-Irish poet Emile Nelligan was inspired by the tradition of French symbolism, and his verse displays only the most tenuous connections with Irish literary themes.

By contrast, the majority of Irish-Canadian writers in the twentieth century have tended to work in prose rather than verse, and their literary endeavors can be schematically subdivided into two distinct forms and periods of composition. In the first half of the twentieth century, Irish-Canadian texts were often written in a biographical mode; were often based on personal, familial, or ancestral experiences of migration from Ireland to Canada; and employed the narrative conventions and generic framework of immigrant memoirs. Never conceived for a mass audience, generally written in an intimate, confessional style, and often understated in tone, these narratives would unconsciously expound upon many of the principal themes of Irish-Canadian literature originally found in the long poem, from the effusive medium of verse to the more private and restricted context of the lives they documented.

Their tendency to transmute various individual and communal experiences of displacement into the form of Irish-Canadian immigrant memoirs reached its apotheosis, however, in Brian Moore's novel *The Luck of Ginger Coffey* (1960). Only very loosely autobiographical in origin; indebted more to the comic vision, modernist narrative techniques, and cuckolded hero of Joyce's *Ulysses* (1922) than his own personal recollection of emigration from Ireland; and preoccupied with the blinkered perceptions, urban misadventures, and irrepressible optimism of its bumbling protagonist, Ginger Coffey, Moore's novel would enjoy considerable critical acclaim as well as popular success to distinguish him from the majority of his predecessors.

Hence, it is only after the creation of *The Luck of Ginger Coffey* that one can speak of the full flowering of a literary tradition based on the experiences of the Irish in Canada, as writers in the latter part of the twentieth century have gravitated away from the form of the immigrant memoir toward the Irish-Canadian historical narrative.

Unlike Moore's text, however, the majority of distinguished works of Irish-Canadian fiction published after *The Luck of Ginger Coffey*, such as Jack Hodgins's *The Invention of the World* (1977), James Reaney's dramatic trilogy *The Donnellys* (1983), Jane Urquhart's *Away* (1993), Margaret Atwood's *Alias Grace* (1996), and Peter Behren's *The Law of Dreams* (2006) have all tended to eschew personal experience or biographical convention and to frame their developing story lines against the backdrop of sweeping nineteenth-century historical surroundings rather than more current narrative settings.

Moreover, like many of the actual nineteenth-century Irish-Canadian literary works created in the form of the long poem, these Irish-Canadian historical novels and plays generally seek to reinforce an ideal of ethnic and social harmony through their various reconstructions of the myth of the Canadian "peaceable kingdom" into a more current narrative framework. Unlike their predecessors, however, what is implicit within their treatment of the historical experience of the Irish in Canada is a gradual realignment of the religious animus of sectarian conflict into the more current fault lines of ethnic friction and class tensions that threaten to undermine the equanimity of the modern, multicultural Canadian state. Their narrative design is premised upon an unfolding conflict between a normative process of social amelioration and the expectation of upward mobility for Irish emigrants in British North America, which becomes disrupted by the recrudescence of communal violence imported by Irish agitators or secret societies from the Old

World to the New. The central conflict that occurs and unfolds in each of these works can be perceived in terms of a form of tension that emerges between the persistence of the ideal of the "peaceable kingdom" and the potential outbreak or recurrence of various types of political violence. Such political violence threatens the stability of Irish communities and places them in deviant relation to the more placid historical development and temperate mores of Canadian society at large.

More to the point, the Irish-Canadian historical novel or play also tends to signal its allegiance to the ideal of the peaceable kingdom by disparaging those antagonists who would attempt to disturb the placidity of Irish settlements in Canada for their own ends. For they portray their respective antagonists not only as agents of discord but as forces of anachrony as well, whose very willingness to countenance violence in the service of any ideal puts them firmly outside the norms of Canadian society. Each of these narratives thus appears inclined toward the propagation of a vision of Canada as a peaceful nation in which internecine ethnic, social, religious, and political conflicts that originated in Ireland or elsewhere, either in the nineteenth century or today, no longer have any place but are consigned to the dustheap of history.

Few writers of Irish origin or descent in nineteenth-century British North America would have considered themselves to be the representatives of a culturally distinctive Irish-Canadian community as such. In the latter half of the twentieth century, on the other hand, Irish-Canadian works of literature have become increasingly regarded as a coherent and distinguished literary corpus in its own right: one whose writers have received numerous accolades and literary prizes following the precedent set by Brian Moore's *The Luck of Ginger Coffey*, which won the Canadian Governor General's Award in 1960. Indeed, since 1970, both of Jack Hodgins' works *The Invention of the World* and *Spit Delaney's Island* have become incorporated into the prestigious New Canadian Library series; James Reaney—like Moore before him—has been awarded the Canadian Governor General's Award no less than three times during his literary career, while *The Donnellys* has become widely regarded as a classic of Canadian theater; Jane Urquhart was corecipient of the Trillium Award for *Away;* and Margaret Atwood's *Alias Grace* was short-listed for the Booker Prize in 1996. Peter Behren's *The Law of Dreams* won the Governor General's award in 2006. Moreover, in addition to these remarkable achievements, the Irish-Canadian community has also generated, in the same short time frame, its own institutions and literary organs for preserving its cultural heritage, including the founding of the Canadian Association for Irish Studies (1973), the *Canadian Journal of Irish Studies* (1975), and, most recently, the establishment of the Centre for Canadian Irish Studies at Concordia University in Montreal (2000).

Yet remarkably, this intensification of Irish-Canadian self-awareness and institutionalization of its cultural heritage have taken place against the backdrop of—or perhaps provide a means of compensation for—the continuing depletion of the Irish-Canadian community itself. As noted, since the mid-nineteenth century, the Irish proportion of the Canadian population has been steadily declining into a demographically insignificant minority. Nevertheless, the seemingly rapid advancement of Irish-Canadian writers into the mainstream of Canadian literature would appear indicative not only of their respective individual achievements but also, on a broader scale, of the historical contribution of the Irish as a charter group in helping to define broader conceptions of Canadian cultural and national identity. In the short term, it would be interesting to consider the way in which this broader and more expansive conception of Canadian identity has laid the groundwork for the development of a literary tradition that is more readily receptive to newcomers and outside voices than has often been the case in Ireland. In the longer term, it may prove fruitful to speculate about the ways in which writers and scholars in Ireland might benefit and learn from the cultural experiences of their Canadian peers, as Ireland continues to undergo rapid demographic change and appears ever more like Canada to be in the process of becoming an increasingly multicultural and plural society.

References

Akenson, Donald. *The Irish Diaspora: A Primer.* Streetsville, Ontario: P. D. Meany, 1993.

Akenson, Donald. *The Irish in Ontario: A Study in Rural History,* 2nd ed. Montreal & Kingston: McGill-Queen's University Press, 1999.

Behrens, Peter. *The Law of Dreams.* Toronto: HarperCollins, 2006.

Elliott, Bruce S. *Irish Migrants in the Canadas: A New Approach.* Kingston: McGill-Queen's University Press, 1988.

Grove-White, Elizabeth, William J. Smyth, Peter M. Toner, Cecil Houston, K. J. James, David A. Wilson, and Michele Holmgren. *The Shamrock and the Maple Leaf: Irish Canadian Documentary Heritage at Library and Archives Canada.* www.collectionscanada.ca/ireland/index-e.html (accessed October 26, 2007).

Hodgins, Jack. *The Invention of the World.* 1977. Reprint, Toronto: New Canadian Library, 1994.

Houston, Cecil, and William J. Smith. *Irish Emigration and Canadian Settlement: Patterns, Links, and Letters.* Toronto: University of Toronto Press, 1990.

James, Kevin, and Jason King, eds. "Irish-Canadian Connections." Special issue, *Canadian Journal of Irish Studies* 31, no. 1 (2005).

McGowan, Mark. *The Waning of the Green: Catholics, The Irish, and Identity in Toronto, 1887–1922.* Montreal: McGill-Queen's University Press, 1999.

McGowan, Mark. *Creating Canadian Historical Memory: The Case of the Famine Migration of 1847.* Canada's Ethnic Groups History Booklets 30. Ottawa: Canadian Historical Association, 2006.

Moore, Brian. *The Luck of Ginger Coffey.* 1960. Reprint, Toronto: New Canadian Library, 1988.

O'Gallagher, Marianna, and Rose Masson Dompierre. *Eyewitness: Grosse Isle 1847.* Sainte-Foy, Quebec: Carraig Books, 1995.

Reaney, James. *The Donnellys: a Trilogy.* Edited by James Noonan. Victoria, British Columbia: Beach Holme Publishing, 1983.

Urquhart, Jane. *Away.* Toronto: McClelland & Stewart, 1993.

Wilson, Catharine Anne. *A New Lease on Life: Landlords, Tenants, and Immigrants in Ireland and Canada.* Montreal: McGill-Queen's University Press, 1994.

Wilson, David A. *The Irish in Canada.* Canada's Ethnic Groups Series. Ottawa: Canadian Historical Association, 1989.

IRELAND AND LATIN AMERICA

Edmundo Murray

INTRODUCTION

Since the mythical visit of Saint Brendan the Navigator to Mexico in the sixth century, through the conviction in December 2004 of three Irishmen accused of training guerrillas in Colombia, the pattern of relations between Ireland and Latin America has been heterogeneous, fragmentary, and erratic. The Irish presence in this part of the world is frequently linked to colonial and postcolonial tensions in Europe and the Americas, which are generally connected to British, French, Portuguese, Spanish, and, more recently, U.S. imperialistic policies and discourses.

Of the forty-odd countries and territories shaping the map of Latin America and the Caribbean, only Argentina and certain Caribbean islands developed recognizable Irish communities that have endured into recent times. Other places in the continent have been visited by Irish missionaries, soldiers, merchants, scientists, teachers, and others who either settled in the region and left their visible or subtle traces, or re-emigrated within the Americas or to other parts of the world (though Brazil, Mexico, and Cuba developed Irish communities that sooner or later disappeared). The number of Irish who emigrated to, or settled temporarily in, Latin America is still a matter of debate among scholars. However, it is significantly lower than that of the immigrants to the English-speaking countries of the United States, Canada, Great Britain, Australia, or New Zealand. Argentina, the country that has attracted the largest quantities of immigrants, received an inflow estimated by some scholars at between 45,000 and 50,000 Irish-born persons. In addition to this, thousands more scattered in the region, especially in Uruguay, Brazil, Venezuela, and Mexico, as a result of military operations, trade, and colonization schemes. It is also important to consider the significant rates of re-emigration within the Americas, especially to the United States, and to Australia, Great Britain, and back to Ireland, as well as from the United States to Argentina in the 1820s, to Cuba where they worked in slave-like conditions in sugar plantations, to Panama where they died among the multinational workforce constructing the Panama railway, and to Brazil where they were recruited in New York for land settlement schemes in the 1860s. Even in the most successful Irish settlement in the region, Argentina, approximately one of every two immigrants re-emigrated to other destinations, and this is an indication of the elevated mobility of the migrants.

The chronicles of the Irish in Latin America often reveal epic qualities, whether from the victim's or from the hero's standpoint. The former expresses an attitude of real or perceived economic exploitation by, and political subordination to, powerful foreign forces, and typically includes the exile mentality by which the British rule in Ireland (or the United States has control over Mexico) led to emigration as the only secure way to ensure survival. The latter—the hero narrative—reveals the position (sometimes perceived as superior) of the Irish with respect to local Latin American ethnic groups. Both perspectives frequently neglect the everyday lives of the immigrants and their families, their settlement patterns, and their relations with other ethnic groups. As Graham Davis argues, "it is tempting in writing on the Irish pioneer settlers to isolate their story and to laud only their achievements. Such an approach distorts the Irish experience by suggesting a privileged contribution to history" (Davis 2002, 238). Furthermore, it neglects the social and economic relations of the Irish and their families with native Amerindians, Hispano-Creoles, Africans, Catalonians, Galicians, Scottish, English, Italians, Germans, French-Basque, and immigrants from other parts of the world, as well as the cultural transfers accomplished among them.

COLONIZED REALMS: IRELAND AND LATIN AMERICA (1500s–1700s)

Details about early links between Ireland and Latin America are derived mainly from mythical sources. Some Mexican historians mention the possibility that Saint Brendan the Navigator of Co. Kerry (ca. 484–580) landed on Mexican shores, and the Aztec deity Quetzalcoatl was identified as a white-skinned and bearded figure who had visited the region and promised to return. Another legend is that Columbus visited Galway on one of his voyages west and prayed there in the church of Saint Nicholas. However, there is historical evidence that Columbus made an earlier visit to Galway in about 1477. The first recorded Irish names in Latin America were the brothers Juan and Tomás Farrel, members of the expedition led by Pedro de Mendoza that arrived in the River Plate in 1536 and founded the city of Buenos Aires.

The early Irish presence in Latin America seems to have been connected with religious, trade, and military relations between traditional families in Ireland and the Catholic establishment in continental Europe. In the last decades of the sixteenth century, many officers and administrators belonging to Old English Catholic families in Ireland withdrew their sons from Oxford and Cambridge colleges and sent them to Catholic universities in Continental Europe. With the Catholic Counter-Reformation at its height, these young members of traditional families were taught the reforming zeal and contributed to a flowering of Catholic spirituality at the popular level and to an anti-Protestant mentality. In Europe the most notable champion of the Counter-Reformation was Philip II of Spain, son of the emperor Charles V, who sought to reestablish Roman Catholicism by force. During the rule of Philip II the first Irish college was opened in 1592 in Salamanca. Spain was at war with England from 1585 to 1604, and the connections of Gaelic and Old English families with Spanish Catholic priests and officers sometimes represented a real threat to England, as when a Spanish force of 4,000 men was established in 1601 at Kinsale in Munster. Unofficial contacts among Ireland, Spain, and Portugal continued thereafter, and thousands of Irish mercenaries (the "Wild Geese") served in French, Spanish, and other foreign armies. Religious, military, and commercial links created an Iberian dimension of the Irish diaspora, which would have direct effects in eighteenth-century and early nineteenth-century connections between Ireland and Latin America.

The first Irish person to leave his mark in Latin America was Thomas Field, S.J. (1547–1626), born in Limerick, who entered the Jesuits in Rome in 1574. Father Field arrived in Brazil in late 1577 and spent three years in Piratininga (today's São Paulo). Then he moved to Paraguay with two other Jesuits, and over the next ten years they established missions among the Guaraní people. Thomas Field, who died in Asunción, is credited with being the first Irish priest to celebrate the Roman Catholic rites in the Americas. Other priests who went to Latin America were born in Spain or Portugal of Irish parents. They were engaged by the Jesuits and the Franciscans because they spoke English and therefore they could work not only to protect the native populations from the Protestant English and Dutch colonizers but could also convert the heretics themselves.

In about 1612 the Irish brothers Philip and James Purcell established a colony in Tauregue, on the mouth of the Amazon River, where English, Dutch, and French settlements were also installed. Huge profits were made by the colonists in tobacco, dyes, and hardwoods. A second group arrived in 1620 led by Bernardo O'Brien of Co. Clare. They built a wood and earth fort on the north bank of the Amazon and named the place Coconut Grove. O'Brien learnt the dialect of the Arruan people, and his colleagues became expert navigators of the maze of tributaries, canals, and islands that form the mouth of the Amazon. Other Irish tradesmen and priests worked in Latin America in the eighteenth century; however, most of the Irish presence in the region from the 1770s onwards was owing to military action.

REBELS IN IRELAND, MERCENARIES IN LATIN AMERICA (1770s–1820s)

The Irish soldiers acting in the region by the end of the eighteenth century and during the wars of independence were members of British, Spanish, Portuguese, and South American armies. From 1768 to 1771 an Irish regiment played a role in the Spanish army that served in Mexico. All its companies were commanded by officers with Irish names, O'Hare, Barry, Fitzpatrick, Quinn, O'Brien, Healy, O'Leary, and Treby (Tracy). Some of them were Irish born, and others were the children of well-known Irish families settled in Spain.

Ambrose O'Higgins (1721–1801) is the supreme example of an Irish emigrant to the Spanish-speaking world who reached the highest ranks in the imperial colonial service.

Born probably in Ballinary, Co. Sligo, O'Higgins was employed as an errand boy by Lady Bective in Dangan Castle, near Summerhill in Meath. An uncle sent him to Cadiz in Spain, from where he traveled to Peru. He first ran a small toy shop in Lima and after studying engineering was involved in improving the Andean roads and building houses for travelers. Recognized by the colonial authorities, O'Higgins was made administrator of the southern frontier of Chile, where he made contact with the Mapuche people. He was appointed governor of Chile in 1787 and set about modernizing the colonial administration. In 1795 Ambrosio O'Higgins was appointed viceroy of Peru, in which office he died in 1801 at the age of eighty.

A tradition of enlisting in the British army developed in Ireland. The enlisting of Irish Protestants began in 1745 and Catholics were permitted to enroll after the Catholic Relief Act of 1793. In the Napoleonic Wars (1796–1815) an estimated 130,000 Irishmen served in the British army, and throughout the nineteenth century a sizable proportion of the British army was Irish, exceeding 40 percent in 1830. Lack of alternative employment opportunities at home (more than any alleged Irish fighting spirit or tradition) contributed to the high levels of Irish enlistment. As recently as in the Falklands/Malvinas War of 1982, the number of Irish names in the rolls of British units was significant.

In November 1762 the Irish-born captain John McNamara and his British 45th regiment attacked Colonia del Sacramento on the northern bank of the River Plate (present-day Uruguay). The colonia was then under Spanish control, and the British intention was to return it to their Portuguese ally. McNamara and most of the crew were killed when the flagship *Lord Clive* blew up, but some waded ashore and were captured and interned in Córdoba, a province in the center of Argentina, and Mendoza in the Andean foothills. When finally released, many of these remained in Argentina. They and some of their descendents were to become involved with the Argentine army of José de San Martín, which gathered in Mendoza in 1816 to invade and liberate Chile.

In 1806 and 1807, Britain made two unsuccessful attempts to displace Spain as the dominant power in the River Plate region. Of the 25,000 men directly involved in both invasions it is likely that a significant number of the officers and rank and file would have been Irish. The first expedition was commanded by William Carr Beresford (b. 1768), of the well-known Irish gentry family. On June 25, 1806, Bereford's troops landed at Quilmes, south of Buenos Aires city. After a skirmish with a force of defenders, Buenos Aires capitulated, and Beresford's men marched into the city to the sound of pipes and drums. The Spanish and Creole forces reacted, and Buenos Aires was recaptured by local regiments. Beresford surrendered in August 1806, but thousands of fighting men were soon dispatched to South America and placed under the command of John Whitelocke. This second British force invaded Montevideo in February 1807 and then attacked, and was repulsed by, Buenos Aires on July 5 of the same year. Some of the Irish soldiers deserted from the British army and settled and prospered in Argentina. After the 1820s they played a role in initiating emigration to Buenos Aires from the Irish midlands.

The other major military involvement of Irish people in Latin America was in the Wars of Independence. As a result of the failed British campaigns in the River Plate, Viscount Castlereagh was of the opinion that the commercial penetration of Spanish America was preferable to its military conquest. This policy came into effect in most parts of Latin America when merchants and their employees from Britain and Ireland invaded the Atlantic and Pacific ports of Latin America. However, the new policy did not prevent British subjects from enlisting in foreign armies. Most Irish saw military action as legionaries in Simón Bolívar's army that liberated Venezuela, Colombia, Ecuador, Peru, and Bolivia.

Recruited in Ireland by John Devereux and other officers, some 2,100 soldiers arrived in Colombia and Venezuela in 1817–1819. The Irish Legion, which received the support of Daniel O'Connell in Ireland, ended in mutinies, epidemics, and a high death toll in Venezuela. Bolívar said he was not surprised at the conduct of the Irish, and he was "pleased to be rid of these mercenaries who would do no killing until they had first been paid for it" (Hasbrouck 1928, 182–183). Devereux himself remained behind in England and Ireland, living sumptuously on the contributions of his dupes, until the return of some of those whom he had cheated exposed him to danger of being arrested or shot, so that he was forced to go to Venezuela many months after his Legion had departed.

Many Irish soldiers took part in the celebrated march across the Andes in 1819 and in the decisive battles of Boyacá (Colombia) and Carabobo (Venezuela). William O'Connor, who came to be known as Francis Burdett O'Connor, served as chief of staff to Antonio José de Sucre (later first president of Bolivia) at the battle of Ayacucho, Peru, in December 1824. In this period Bolívar had a succession of Irish aides-de-camp, of whom the most prestigious was Cork-born Daniel Florence O'Leary, who sustained a serious wound in battle following the Andes march and was decorated with the Order of the Liberator. A recognized hero of the Venezuelan independence, O'Leary settled in Bogotá and held a number of diplomatic appointments for Venezuela and Britain. He died in 1854 in Bogotá and in 1882 his remains were interred in the National Pantheon in Caracas near those of Bolívar.

The South American wars of independence are often regarded as the result of a military strategy developed by the British governing elites and executed by brilliant military and naval commanders. On a pincer movement, Simón Bolívar from the north, José de San Martín from the south, and admirals William Brown and Scottish-born Thomas Cochrane shelling from the Pacific, prevented the arrival of supplies and reinforcements for the Spanish forces and effectively overthrew the Spanish rule in the region. William Brown (1777–1857), founder of the Argentine navy, was born in Foxford, Co. Mayo. He began his naval career as a teenager in merchant ships in the United States, then enlisted in the British navy and was engaged in 1809 in commercial trading in Buenos Aires. Brown got involved when his ship was commandeered by the Spanish during the revolution of 1810. Appointed commander of the local fleet, he broke the Spanish blockade in the River Plate and ended the Spanish threat to the newly independent provinces of the River Plate. Wicklow-born John Thomond O'Brien (1786–1861) arrived in Argentina in 1814 and fought in the siege of Montevideo in that year. He was then appointed aide-de-camp of General San Martín, the liberator of Argentina and Chile, and in this capacity took part in all major actions of the independence struggle in Chile and Peru. Other South American patriots who fought for the new republics were Bernardo O'Higgins (1778–1842), son of Peru's viceroy Ambrose O'Higgins, and regarded as the father of

Chile's independence; Thomas Charles Wright (1799–1868) of Drogheda, founder of the Ecuadorean navy; Peter Campbell (1780–c. 1832) of Tipperary, who organized the first Uruguayan naval force in 1814; George O'Brien, Charles Condell, and Patricio Lynch, naval heroes in Chile; and Diago Nicolau Keating, Diago O'Grady, and Jorge Cowan, who served in Brazilian armies.

ESCRAVOS BRANCOS AND EMPRESARIOS: PRE-FAMINE SETTLEMENTS IN LATIN AMERICA (1820S–1840S)

In 1826, William Cotter, an Irish officer serving in the Brazilian army, was sent to Ireland to recruit a regiment for service against Argentina. He went to Co. Cork where he promised the local people that if they enlisted they would be given a grant of land after five years' service. He left for Rio de Janeiro in 1827 with 2,686 men and their wives and children, but when they arrived they were completely neglected because the war with Argentina was over. The African-Brazilian people taunted them by calling them *escravos brancos,* white slaves. The Irish mutinied, together with a German regiment, and for a few days there was open warfare on the streets of Rio de Janeiro. While most were finally sent home or went to Canada or Argentina, some did stay and were sent to form a colony in the province of Bahia.

A more celebrated military exploit involving Irish troops was that of the San Patricio Battalion made up of deserters from the U.S. army during the Mexican-American war of 1846–1848. Led by John O'Reilly, a deserter from the British army in Canada, hundreds of Irish crossed over to the Mexican side encouraged by Mexican offers of promotion to officer rank and assignment to the artillery unit, as well as offers of land (however, some historians argue that it was drink that lured them). The case shows the fluidity of loyalty and state boundaries at the time. Fighting under a green banner emblazoned with an Irish harp and a shamrock, the Irish won special decorations for their courage in the battle of Buena Vista, but suffered heavy casualties in the fierce battle of Churubusco. Seventy-two were court-martialed and fifty hanged. The bravery of the San Patricio battalion is widely known among Mexicans today, and every September 12 a ceremony in their honor takes place in the San Jacinto plaza in Mexico City. However, they were regarded as traitors in the United States.

Successful Irish settlements were established in Mexican Texas in the period 1829–1836. San Patricio and Refugio colonies on the Gulf coast of Texas owe an important part of their history to the system of land grants allocated under the Mexican colonization law and to the Irish *empresarios* (entrepreneurs): John McMullen, James McGloin, James Power, and James Hewetson. They were men of vision who had perceived themselves as Mexicans through marriage, commercial contacts, and language (as Spanish speakers). During the Texas Revolution of 1835–1836 some of the Irish colonists were loyal to the Mexican government, to whom in law they owed allegiance as Mexican citizens and to whom they were obligated for the land grants bestowed upon them. Furthermore, the Irish colonists who had settled alongside Mexican neighbors acquired from them the skills and know-how of cattle ranching.

Land was the great opportunity that attracted thousands of emigrants from the center and southeast of Ireland to Argentina and Uruguay. This emigration commenced with the Irish soldiers left behind by the 1806–1807 British campaigns in the River Plate, along with the simultaneous settlement of a number of British and Irish merchants in the region. According to the 1822 census, there were 3,500 *ingleses* in the Buenos Aires province. At this time, they made up the majority of foreigners in the city of Buenos Aires. Merchants in Buenos Aires benefited from the policy of *comercio libre* (free trade), which sparked an economic revival in the River Plate area and established businesses to trade for silver from Potosí (Bolivia); maté from the plantations along the river Paraguay; and hides, talon, and jerked-beef from the pampas of Buenos Aires and Uruguay. One of the most influential of the Irish merchants in Buenos Aires was Thomas Armstrong (1797–1875), who came from a well-known Protestant landowning family of the Irish midlands. Together with Father Anthony Fahy (1805–1871), Armstrong was to lead the Irish immigrant community from its early stages in the 1830s until his death. Another influential merchant family in colonial and independent Buenos Aires was the O'Gormans of Ennis, Co. Clare. Members of other prosperous Irish families settled from the end of the eighteenth century in Latin American ports. These families not only wielded considerable economic and political power within Ireland but were also involved in Atlantic trade, with links to North America, Spain and Portugal, the West Indies, South Africa, and later, to Brazil and Argentina. Among these families, a number of Galway and Clare merchants served as agents in commercial houses in the Atlantic coasts and islands. They were Roman Catholics and loyal to the British Crown. Other Irish merchants in Buenos Aires were employed by British firms, like William Mooney and Patrick Bookey from Westmeath, and Patrick Brown and James Pettit from Wexford. They are recognized as the initiators of the early immigration chains from those counties to Argentina and Uruguay.

In the 1820s the majority of foreign merchant ships entering the port of Buenos Aires were English, originating in Liverpool, London, Rio de Janeiro, Gibraltar, and Havana. Much of the loading, unloading, and ferrying was also conducted by British people, and Irish residents in the ports were employed as stevedores. After the signature of the Anglo-Argentine Treaty of Friendship, Navigation and Commerce in 1824, the British presence was further perpetuated, and Argentina followed the first steps to later become an important part of Britain's informal empire. These were ideal circumstances for a massive welcome to *ingleses,* that is, English-speaking immigrants especially from Ireland.

IRISH LANDLORDS IN ARGENTINA AND THEIR WORKERS (1840s–1880s)

The arrival in Buenos Aires of 114 Irish immigrants on board the *William Peile* on June 25, 1844, may be viewed as the beginning of the most important emigration from Ireland to Latin America and, indeed, to any Spanish-speaking country. The *Peile* emigration, though arranged by Irish merchants in Buenos Aires, was not an organized colonization scheme. The successful integration of the immigrants led to the promotion of Latin America at home, with family members, neighbors, and friends in Ireland following them throughout the following decades.

Although the number of immigrants to Argentina is still debated by historians, the latest estimates include 45,000–50,000 immigrants during the 100 years ending in 1929. At least 50 percent of the immigrants did not stay in the country and sooner or later re-emigrated to other destinations, most notably the United States, Australia, or back to Ireland. Arduous working conditions, accidents, and epidemics significantly increased the death rate among those who settled in Argentina, resulting in an Irish-born population of 10,000–15,000, who survived, founded families, and left descendants, forming the nucleus of the Irish-Argentine community. Among the latter group, the success ratio measured in ownership of their means of production was disproportionate compared with other communities of the Irish diaspora, although immigrants in Argentina from other European regions in the same period (especially French-Basque and Catalonian) were equally successful.

Most of the emigrant candidates were the children of tenant farmers in the Irish midlands (Counties Westmeath 43 percent, Longford 15 percent, Offaly 3 percent) and Co. Wexford (16 percent). They were lured by the possibility—often imaginary—of becoming owners of 4,000 acres in Argentina instead of being tenants of 40 acres in Ireland; therefore, they imagined belonging to a fanciful Latin American landed gentry instead of to the Irish farmers' circle. Most of the emigrants in this period were young men in their early twenties, and later young women, from families with Roman Catholic background. Upon arrival they were hired by British, Irish, or Hispano-Creole *estancieros* (ranchers) to work in their holdings, and sometimes to mind their flocks of sheep. Sheep farming and the impressive increase of international wool prices in 1830–1880, together with convenient sharecropping agreements with landowners, allowed a substantial number of the Irish immigrants to establish themselves securely in the countryside and progressively acquire sheep and, finally, land. A few of them, particularly in 1850–1870, managed to acquire large tracts of land from provincial governments in areas gained from Indian control or beyond the frontier. However, the vast majority of the Irish rural settlers were ranch hands, and shepherds on halves or on thirds, and never had access to landownership. Stories circulated in Ireland of poor emigrants who became wealthy landowners in the pampas of Argentina and Uruguay. These stories, frequently exaggerated, were sometimes fueled by those who failed to achieve a successful settlement in Argentina but did not want those at home to know it.

Typically, in the last decades of the nineteenth century, members of the Argentine landowner class with Irish origins perceived themselves as English, and their identity was frequently balanced toward British rather than Irish traditions. At the same time, the middle and lower classes, which were composed of shepherds and ranch hands in the countryside and servants and laborers in the cities, began to be attracted by Irish nationalist appeals from the church and the press. The existence in Buenos Aires of two newspapers owned by Irish-born people, *The Standard* and *The Southern Cross,* may be viewed as a consequence of these differentiated identities connected to diverse social groups.

NATIONALISM IN IRELAND AND IN SOUTH AMERICA (1880s–1930s)

The massive European emigration to Argentina in 1880–1920 was an incentive to attract further emigration from Ireland. However, the failure of a government colonization scheme from Ireland in 1889 known as the Dresden Affair put an end to other official initiatives. Irish immigrants to Argentina in this period usually came from urban areas in Belfast, Cork, Dublin, and Limerick, or from cities in England or the British empire. Except those of the Dresden Affair (who were mostly laborers and servants), the immigrants in this period were professionals, technicians or administrative employees hired by railway companies, banks, or meatpacking plants, and several were from families with a Church of Ireland background. They rapidly integrated into the Anglo-Argentine community, following their social and economic patterns, while some of them actively worked to support Irish nationalism.

At the turn of the nineteenth century, most Irish families were living in the provinces of Buenos Aires, Santa Fe, and Córdoba, as well as in Entre Ríos, Mendoza, and in distant Patagonia and Falklands/Malvinas Islands. The trend to move from the *camp* (sheep-farmers' lingo for countryside) to the cities was led by the wealthiest families, thus imitating the residence patterns of the Argentine landed elite. A majority of the Argentine-born children of Irish immigrants spoke English as their mother tongue and learnt Spanish at school. Those who were bilingual English/Spanish had a linguistic advantage and were often employed by British and later U.S. companies. Their social activities were shared with Irish or British relations, with horseracing and later rugby football, cricket, and hurling being the most popular athletic activities for men, and lawn tennis for women.

After World War I (in which some Irish Argentines fought in British regiments), there was a new peak of emigration from Ireland to Argentina, particularly in the period during and after the Anglo-Irish War of 1919–1921 and the Irish Civil War of 1922–1923. However, the financial crisis of 1929 as well as conflicts and political and social unrest in Europe and later in Latin America were serious barriers to emigration. After 1930 Irish emigration to Argentina virtually came to a halt. Many Irish Argentines did rather well out of World War II. Some thousands of Anglo Argentines (and a few Irish Argentines) joined the British armed forces, vacating jobs with British companies that needed to be filled by bilingual English/Spanish speakers.

Paradoxically, Irish nationalism in Argentina represented a hindrance to new immigrants who did not want to be identified with chaos and turmoil in Ireland, but rather with a perceived notion of British organization and working habits. Furthermore, the newly rich Irish of Argentina, and particularly their Argentine-born sons and daughters, did not want to be considered by the anglophile Argentine elite as belonging to the same circles as their poor relatives in Ireland. A social hiatus arose between the Irish in Argentina and the Irish in Ireland, which gradually weakened the links among members of the same communities—even of the same families—on both sides of the Atlantic. In other countries of the region, British commercial and investment predominance was gradually overtaken by U.S. companies and diplomacy. By the 1920s, most of the families with Irish surnames in Latin America and other countries were considered—and considered themselves—Brazilians, Chileans, Mexican, and other rather than Irish.

SOCIETY AND STATE BUILDING: DIPLOMATIC, RELIGIOUS, AND TRADE LINKS (1930s–2005)

Some Irish diplomats were gaining experience in Latin America before 1930, including Robert Gore in Montevideo and Buenos Aires in the 1850s, Thomas Hutchinson in Rosario in the 1860s, the Irish-Americans Martin MacMahon and Patrick Egan who represented the United States in Paraguay in the 1860s and in Chile in 1889–1893 respectively, and Daniel R. O'Sullivan and the Irish patriot Roger Casement in Brazil in 1906–1911.

The first diplomatic envoy from Ireland to Latin America was Buenos Aires–born Eamon Bulfin, who began working in Argentina in March 1920, after his participation in the Easter Rising and banishment from the British Isles. Bulfin established a contact network in South America and started an Irish Fund. In 1921, two of Ireland's eight diplomats, Bulfin and Laurence Ginnell, were based in Latin America. Patrick J. Little arrived in 1922, being the first representative of the Irish Free State. The establishment of formal diplomatic relations with Latin America had to wait until the end of World War II. In 1947, Matthew Murphy was appointed as chargé d'affaires in Buenos Aires, with Lorenzo McGovern as the first Irish Argentine to be appointed to the Argentine mission in Dublin in 1955. Irish diplomatic missions were established in Brazil and Mexico in 1975 and 1977, respectively, and both countries opened embassies in Dublin in 1991. In other countries, ten honorary consuls of Ireland operate with the supervision of Buenos Aires, Brasilia, Mexico, and New York embassies.

One of the recurring goals of Irish trade missions in Latin America is to foster mutual economic links. However, Ireland is still an almost completely insignificant market for Latin America. Irish exports to Latin America have increased more than 60 percent in 1996–2002. In this period, total Irish exports to Latin America averaged $711 million per annum, though this was only one percent of Ireland's total exports. Mexico, Brazil, Argentina, Chile, and Costa Rica are some of the major Latin American markets for Irish products. Imports from the region remained at less than one half of the exports (*Direction of Trade Statistics Yearbook* 270–271). Some Irish companies have performed well in Latin America. A noteworthy example is Fyffes, an importer of fruit from Jamaica, Belize, Surinam, Honduras, and Ecuador into Europe since the 1920s. Powdered milk is an Irish product frequently exported to Central and South America. Smurfit has subsidiaries manufacturing paperboard and packaging products in Colombia, Venezuela, and Mexico. Guinness Peat Aviation works with Latin American airlines in many countries. Travel and education are other aspects of the exchange, with a steady flow of students going to Ireland to boarding or day schools since the 1870s and, more recently, to study English as a foreign language. Genealogical travel has been exploited sometimes by Argentine and Irish travel agents, and in the 1970s Aer Lingus ran a weekly flight to Buenos Aires and Santiago de Chile. In more recent years Argentina, Brazil, Mexico and the Caribbean islands are increasingly attracting Irish visitors.

Apart from the ever-present pseudo-Irish pubs in many Latin American cities, and the sporadic boom of Celtic music in Argentina and Brazil, very few manifestations of Irish popular culture have had much success in Latin America. The University of São Paulo offers a postgraduate course on Irish literature since 1977. The Associação Brasileira de Estudos Irlandeses has published the *ABEI Journal: the Brazilian Journal of Irish Studies,* edited by professors Munira H. Mutran and Laura P. Z. Izarra, since 1999.

Quite apart from official diplomatic efforts and trade missions in the twentieth century, the most efficient Irish representatives in Latin America have been the religious missionaries. In many parts of Latin America to be Irish means to be a priest or a nun. Likewise, in Ireland a part of people's knowledge of Latin America is derived from notices from these missionaries that were circulated through churches. Furthermore, returning missionaries have had an impact on the Catholic Church in Ireland as they seek to promote the new model of the post–Vatican II social church frequently associated with Latin America. The pioneering work of Father Fahy and other Irish chaplains in nineteenth-century Argentina, Uruguay, and Falkland/Malvinas Islands was followed by religious orders. The Sisters of Mercy and the Passionist and Pallotine fathers served the Irish community and followed the pattern of the Irish missionary movement elsewhere in the nineteenth century—following the Irish diaspora or British colonization. Missionary work with Latin Americans was not established until 1951–1952, when the Columbans opened parishes in Peru and Chile. Furthermore, laypeople were sent to Bogotá in 1953 to establish the Legion of Mary. From Bogotá the work of the Legion extended to other parts of Colombia and then to Venezuela, Ecuador, and almost all countries of Latin America in subsequent years. The Redemptorists were established in Brazil in 1960, the Kiltegans also in Brazil in 1963, the Irish Dominicans in Argentina in 1965, the Holy Ghosts in Brazil in 1967, and the Irish Franciscans in Chile and El Salvador in 1968. The Saint James Society has worked in Peru since 1958. Priests and sisters from Cork were sent to work in Trujillo as an institutional initiative of the diocese of Cork and Ross. One of these Cork missionaries was Father Michael Murphy, who would later become bishop of Cork. The image of the Latin American church exercised a fascination among Irish people. In the early 1980s U.S. policy in El Salvador and Nicaragua occasioned widespread condemnation in Ireland. This culminated in the unprecedented wave of protests that greeted President Ronald Reagan when he visited Ireland in June 1984.

Gradually, in a process that for the Irish in Argentina and other countries in the region may have ended during the Falklands/Malvinas War of 1982, the Irish in Latin American countries began to perceive themselves as Argentines, Brazilians, Uruguayans, or Mexicans with Irish family names, although a few among them held some distinct Irish family traditions. Present-day Latin Americans with Irish background are estimated by some to be between 300,000 and 500,000 persons. Although some may be residents of Mexico and Central America, the northern part of South America, Uruguay, and Brazil, most live in Argentina. A vast majority among them does not speak English as their mother tongue nor do they keep the traditions brought from Ireland by their ancestors. Intercommunity marriage during the twentieth century has allowed most of the families to assert their local Latin American identities.

Nevertheless, perhaps seeking some kind of recognition of their Irish identity, in 2002 a group of about 2,000 Irish Argentines submitted a petition to reside and work in Ireland to the Irish justice minister John O'Donoghue. The petition, which was accompanied by a press campaign targeting Irish politicians and policy-makers, did not obtain a favorable response from the Irish government. However, it demonstrates that the links between Ireland and Latin America, which were lost more than a century ago, can still be reshaped to accommodate the actual needs of Irish-Latin Americans.

Attracting thousands from Latin America to Ireland, the present-day successful Celtic Tiger economy imposes both a public perception of "best place to live" and a government policy of restrictive immigration. However, Argentines who have secured an Irish passport rarely use it to live in Ireland but rather in other European Union countries. The one significant Latin American community in Ireland is a Brazilian one based in counties Galway and Roscommon.

References

Davis, Graham. *Land! Irish Pioneers in Mexican and Revolutionary Texas.* Dallas: Texas A&M University Press, 2002.

Direction of Trade Statistics Yearbook. International Monetary Fund (IMF), 2003.

Hasbrouck, Alfred. *Foreign Legionaries in the Liberation of Spanish South America.* New York: Columbia University, 1928.

Kennedy, Michael. " 'Mr. Blythe, I Think, Hears from Him Occasionally': The Experience of Irish Diplomats in Latin America, 1919–23." In *Irish Foreign Policy 1919–66: From Independence to Internationalism,* edited by Michael Kennedy and J. M. Skelly. Dublin: Four Courts Press, 2000.

Kirby, Peadar. *Ireland and Latin America: Links and Lessons.* Dublin: Trócaire, 1992.

Marshall, Oliver. *English, Irish and Irish-American Pioneer Settlers in Nineteenth-Century Brazil.* Oxford: Centre for Brazilian Studies, 2005.

McGinn, Brian. "The Irish in South America: A Bibliography." Irish Diaspora Net. www.irishdiaspora.net (accessed February 7, 2005).

McKenna, Patrick. "Irish Emigration to Argentina: A Different Model." In *The Irish Diaspora,* edited by Andy Bielenberg. Essex: Pearson Education Ltd., 2000.

Murray, Edmundo. *Becoming "Irlandés": Private Narratives of the Irish Emigration to Argentina, 1844–1912.* Buenos Aires: Literature of Latin America, 2005.

Sabato, Hilda, and Juan Carlos Korol. *Cómo Fue la Inmigración Irlandesa en Argentina.* Buenos Aires: Plus Ultra, 1981.

IRELAND AND THE UNITED STATES OF AMERICA

James P. Byrne

INTRODUCTION

By the turn of the twentieth century, the first- and second-generation Irish population of the United States exceeded that of Ireland by more than half a million people. This reveals many things, but two are of importance here. First, if we extend our understanding of Irish cultural identity to include not just those born in Ireland but also those born of Irish parents, then by 1900 more Irish people lived in the United States than in Ireland. Beyond their numerical significance lies their even more important cultural contribution to modern Irish identity. Second, it tells us that the history of Ireland and the United States is one defined by migration in all its forms: emigration, immigration, and even, in recent times, re-emigration. From mythical beginnings to modern relationship, migration continues to be the thread that interweaves and shapes the destiny of these two nations.

EARLY IRISH IMMIGRATION

The origin of Ireland's first encounter with what would become known as the United States is an event shrouded in myth. Early pre-Christian Irish legends tell of "enchanted Islands to the West"—Tír Na nÓg ("the land of eternal youth") and Hy Brasil (the "island of great desire")—which bespeak of knowledge of a land as yet undiscovered. Legendary accounts of Saint Brendan the Navigator's voyages to inhabited lands in 550, where he preached the Gospel to the natives, have led to speculations as to whether or not Saint Brendan may have reached the New World almost 1,000 years before Christopher Columbus.

With Columbus's "discovery" of America in 1492, comes Ireland's first recorded contact with the New World. According to William D. Griffin, William Eris, or Ayers, a native of

Galway, was one of forty volunteers who remained behind on Hispaniola; they were all later killed by the Indians. By the 1580s, Griffin argues, Ireland had become both a training ground and a staging area for England's empirical ambitions in North America. Elizabethans such as Richard Grenville and Walter Raleigh began adopting the "colonization" techniques of "plantation" practiced in Ireland as a means of establishing an English colony in the New World.

By the seventeenth century, Irish migration to North America had begun in earnest, and between 50,000 and 100,000 Irish emigrants made their way to the American colonies. Most came as soldiers, sailors, convicts, or indentured servants, a consequence not only of the need for cheap labor in the new colonies but also, following Oliver Cromwell's conquest of Ireland in 1649–1650, of the forced indenture of thousands of Irish people. However, Catholic gentry, such as Thomas Dongan and Charles Carroll, also emigrated and left a significant legacy: as governor of New York, Dongan oversaw the drafting of the "Charter of Libertyes," while Carroll's grandson—Charles Carroll III—was the only Catholic to sign the Declaration of Independence.

After the overthrow of King James II in 1689, the concerted Anglicization of the British colonies provoked laws, such as the ones in Maryland in 1704 and again in 1715, which discouraged the entry of Catholics. By the turn of the century, Protestant emigration, primarily from the province of Ulster, had begun to constitute the majority of Irish immigration to the United States. These immigrants were largely Scots-Irish—sometimes called Scotch-Irish, they had first been transplanted from Scotland to Ireland (where they were known as Ulster-Scots)—and Presbyterian, and emigrated in family and congregational groups, rather than individually.

Kevin Kenny records that large-scale emigration from Ulster began in 1717 and that by 1775 possibly as many as 250,000 Ulster-Scots had left Ireland for North America. The Scots-Irish came to America for much the same reasons their ancestors had come to Ireland, in search of land and religious tolerance. However, just as in Ireland, they found both were harder to achieve than they originally expected. Before 1725, they immigrated in significant numbers to New England; however, religious intolerance and the search for land sent them outwards from Boston to the more remote parts of New England and Massachusetts.

Because of its increasing transatlantic trade with Ulster and its religious tolerance, after 1720 Pennsylvania increasingly became the primary destination of Scots-Irish immigrants. Initially settling in significant numbers in the Southeast, they soon began to migrate westward and toward the frontier. In Ireland these Ulster-Scots had formed a Protestant rampart between the Anglican ascendancy and the native Irish; now, as Scots-Irish in America they performed a similar role for the Anglo-American settlers and their American Indian neighbors. In search of land and as a first defense against Indian attack, the Scots-Irish settled the southern backcountry from Pennsylvania to Georgia. By 1790 the numbers of Scots-Irish in the United States were second only to the English, and more than a quarter of them lived in Pennsylvania. While the American Revolution had temporarily affected immigration to the United States, reestablishment of the Atlantic shipping trade in 1783 ensured continued emigration from Ulster on into the early eighteenth century. By the end of the Napoleonic wars in 1815, this resurgence would propel almost 150,000 Irish men, women, and children across the Atlantic to the United States.

The Scots-Irish brought with them not just a religious legacy but also a cultural and political legacy of dissension: part of their significant contribution to the American Revolution. Added to this is the continuing legacy of their descendants: as many as fifteen American presidents, from John Adams to William Jefferson Clinton, have traced their lineage to Irish Protestant ancestors.

BEFORE THE FAMINE

By the 1830s the ethnic and religious makeup of emigration from Ireland to North America had markedly altered: Catholic immigrants had begun to exceed Protestants, and emigration had changed not just in culture but also in scale. Between 1815 and 1845 more than 800,000 Irish people emigrated to North America, which, according to historian Kevin Kenny, "was twice as many as in the preceding two centuries" (45).

In the United States, these new Catholic immigrants were thought to be of significantly lower character than their Scots-Irish predecessors; so much so that previous Irish immigrants now took to calling themselves Scots-Irish. Before the 1830s the Ulster-Scots who immigrated were commonly known as "Irish." It was not until the 1830s that the Ulster-Scots began to appropriate the term "Scots-Irish," and they did so, it seems, to differentiate themselves from the incoming Catholic immigrants. Hence, what was initially simply a difference in religion soon became a difference in ethnic makeup; henceforth, the term "Irish" was applied to the Catholic immigrants from Ireland. This attempt to distance themselves from the more lowly Catholic (and largely southern) Irish immigration also propelled Scots-Irish Americanization by promoting them as an ethnic group who held in common with the Anglo-Americans both a similar culture and a nativist rejection of the "foreign" Irish.

This new emigration had been provoked by the changing nature of nineteenth-century Ireland. Not only was the population increasing dramatically—from 2 million in 1732, it had quadrupled in a little over a century to 8.2 million in 1841—but this over-population, combined with a lack of diversification in the economy, was putting inordinate pressure on the land. Just over half of all rural dwellers in Ireland held less than two acres of land on a tenure basis and under precarious conditions. And yet, too poor, too remote, too fearful, or too unwilling to undertake the transatlantic journey, these rural poor did not constitute the majority of pre-Famine emigration. It seems the majority of pre-Famine emigrants came from the more successful Irish Catholics: the "strong" (30 acres or more) or "middling" (10–30 acres) farmers, the self-employed artisans, or urban shopkeepers and professionals. Compared with the Famine emigration of the following decade (1845–1855) these emigrants were not only economically better off, they were more independent and still perceived emigration as opportunity rather than exile.

And yet they were still sufficiently different from the earlier immigrants to mark them as decidedly "other" to the Anglo-American public. In whatever city they came to live, poverty and disease distinguished these "Irish" immigrants from both their Scots-Irish predecessors and the Anglo-American citizens. In 1834 alone, the Irish constituted half the foreign-born inmates in the almshouses of Philadelphia and New York. They gathered together and lived in ghettoes like the Five Points in New York, where they competed with African Americans for accommodation, employment, and recognition (as American). Irishmen provided an inexpensive and expendable labor force in New York and the industrial cities of the East Coast, in the South and on the canals, while Irish women went into domestic service and the so-called needle trades. They also continued the traditions of faction fighting and secret societies from the Old World. By the 1840s, the Irish were getting involved in labor agitation for better pay and working conditions. All of this only heightened native distrust of and antagonism for the "foreign" Irish.

The downturn in the economy in the 1830s saw an upsurge in nativism and anti-Catholicism directed toward the Irish. Orangemen and Irish Catholics had been clashing in cities like New York and Philadelphia since the 1820s. This escalated in the 1830s, with the burning of the Ursuline Convent in Charlestown, Massachusetts, in 1834, and the publication of *Awful Disclosures* in 1836. In 1844 mounting nativist anger came to a head when native-born workers and Orangemen attacked the Catholic communities in Kensington and Southwark in Philadelphia and burned three churches. These events only strengthened Irish association with Catholicism, which would grow to become the symbolic register of Irish ethnic identity in the following century.

Forced to defend their religion in America, Catholic Irish Americans were also heavily involved in trying to secure the repeal of the Act of Union (1800) in Ireland. The National Repeal Convention, on February 22, 1842, inaugurated the repeal movement as the first major Irish nationalist movement in America. However, its existence was brief and, ironically, it was its hero—Daniel O'Connell—and his emancipatory leanings that perpetuated its downfall. Along with Father Theobald Mathew, in 1842 Daniel O'Connell signed "An Address of the Irish People to Their Countrymen in America," which called on the American Irish to support the abolition of slavery in the United States. Read out at a mass meeting of the Massachusetts Anti-Slavery Society at Fanueil Hall in Boston on January 28, 1842, this address and O'Connell's continued adherence to his antislavery principles ultimately led to the American Irish repudiating O'Connell's cause. As the Irish in America turned inward toward their lives in the United States and away from their nostalgia for a romantic Ireland, an event of unimaginable proportions was about to unfold "at home" that would bring the tragic reality of life in Ireland to their very doorsteps.

THE FAMINE

The Great Famine, or *An Gorta Mhór* (The Great Hunger) as it was colloquially known, hit Ireland in September 1845. In just a decade it ravaged the Irish population; radically altered Irish agrarian, social, and economic practice; and initiated emigration as the social solution to fiscal and national issues. From 1846 to 1855 between 1.1 and 1.5 million men, women, and children died of starvation in Ireland, another 2.1 million Irish people emigrated overseas (more than 1.5 million of them to the United States). Irish immigration peaked at 219,232 in 1851.

It was not just the dramatic increase in numbers from pre-Famine levels that frightened antebellum Americans but, more importantly, the corresponding decline in the physical, economic, and, for them, implicitly moral "character" of these new immigrants. The majority of Famine emigrants came from cottiers (less than 2 acres), small-holding, and middling farmers, and often with only money enough to pay their passage (many benefited from assisted emigration either from former landlords or through remittances from relatives in the United States). After a voyage of anything up to six weeks on board ships colloquially known as "coffin ships" because of their onboard mortality rate, these immigrants arrived in the United States penniless, hungry, diseased, and disheveled. More than 80 percent of them identified themselves to emigration authorities (or were identified) as laborers or servants. A largely rural people with little or no urban skills, they tended to settle in the larger cities. They lived in ethnic ghettoes, such as Seneca Village and the Sixth Ward in New York, which further alienated them from the Anglo-American citizenry of these cities. Still worse, these ethnic enclaves often suffered from the highest rates of crime, disease, and death in the city; the "Bloody Ould Sixth" had the highest death rate in New York City in 1850. As well as falling prey to disease and crime, the Irish also often had the highest levels of poverty and insanity; again in New York, in 1850 they accounted for 60 percent of the population of the almshouses and, in this decade, they made up two-thirds of the foreign-born population of New York City's Bellevue asylum. All of this meant that the Irish Famine immigrants were not just the most impoverished members of American society; they were, at times, regarded both popularly and politically as a race of people unfit for American citizenship.

With the arrival of the Famine immigrants, nativist hostility to the Irish both intensified and became more popular. In 1854, the Native American Party (or the Know-Nothing Party as it was commonly known) went public and carried the elections in Massachusetts and Delaware. It directed its ire against the Irish immigrant's religion: Catholicism. By attacking Catholicism, nativists hoped to prevent the rise of the Catholic Church in the United States while also preventing its primary congregation from getting a foothold in working- and middle-class society. As the influx of Famine immigrants expanded the base of the Catholic Church in the 1840s, nativists attacked Irish Catholics in Philadelphia, Pennsylvania, Richmond, Virginia, and Charleston, South Carolina, but were, ultimately, unable to prevent the rise of the Church or its predominantly Irish congregation. They also attacked the Tammany Hall machine within the Democratic Party, which used Irish immigrants in its system of mass politics, but again though they sought to expose the corruption of democratic government they struggled and failed for many years to effect change. As the Famine immigrants settled into U.S. society, the Catholic Church, the Democratic Party, and Irish nationalism became the three-leafed clover of Irish Americanism.

POST-FAMINE

Immigration to the United States continued into the post-Famine period, as the Irish continued to flee Ireland in the hopes of finding a life, and maybe even making their fortune. The changing rural economy in Ireland—the advance of commercial farming and the introduction of primogeniture—offset by the appeal of high-paying jobs in the United States, the relatively cheap price of passage, and the reduced sailing time (with the introduction of steam ships in the 1850s), sent many young men and women to the United States in the post-Famine period. Post-Famine immigrants were generally young and single, as likely to be women as men, and more than one-quarter of them were Irish speakers (typically from the impoverished areas of Munster and Connaught). Unlike Italian and Eastern European immigrants, only about 10 percent of the Irish emigrants ever returned home. (One of these was Michael MacGowan, who related his experiences in the United States in *The Hard Road to Klondike*). This often led to the performance of the "American wake" in the post-Famine period; this followed the traditional form of the Irish wake, only now the departing son or daughter was there to experience the send-off.

Post-Famine immigrants traveled a path already well-worn, continuing the patterns of Irish immigration and settlement in the United States set by earlier Irish Catholic immigrants. As with the earlier immigrants, they favored the Northeast, Mid-Atlantic, and Midwest and settled predominantly in large urban centers. Only a small number of Catholic Irish lived in the South, but a large number of first- and second-generation Catholic Irish went west in the latter half of the nineteenth century. This migration typically comprised younger men, those more skilled and literate; they favored California and particularly San Francisco. The Irish in the West tended to do much better than those on the East Coast. Also, in the latter half of the nineteenth century, the Catholic Church sponsored resettlement schemes throughout the United States for impoverished and overcrowded Irish communities in the East, but these largely failed.

The Draft Riots (1863) and the Orange and Green Riots (1870 and 1871) sustained and strengthened the popular stereotypical perception of the Irish as violent, drunken, unruly, and unfit for American citizenship. But the Irish were changing and diversifying as a social community as the century progressed, particularly after the Civil War, where their courage and service had won them new-found respect in the eyes of the native public. A new class of Irish was emerging from the ghettoes; these "lace curtain" Irish sought acceptance as middle-class Americans and struggled to disassociate themselves from the working-class, "shanty" Irish mass. They looked for skilled or even professional jobs and moved out of the Irish enclaves and into middle-class American neighborhoods. Also, as a second generation of Irish Americans began to come of age they advanced further into American society and away from the ethnic origins of their parents. This second generation was typically more successful and more American than their forebears.

The Irish also moved away from the more traditional forms of agitation carried over from Ireland—secret societies, faction fighting, rioting—and into the American labor movement. Again both men and women got involved, with Terence V. Powderly standing out as the leader of the Knights of Labor, the largest labor organization in the United States in the late 1870s and 1880s. Still suffering from nativist attack and rhetoric, the Irish themselves were also now heavily involved in similar attacks and charges against newer immigrants. In particular, the Irish dominated the nativist workingmen's movement against the Chinese in California; they organized demonstrations and called for a series of stricter anti-Chinese measures (culminating in the 1882 Chinese Exclusion Act suspending Chinese immigration for ten years). As with the Scots-Irish before them, this gave the Irish the opportunity to demonstrate their fitness for American citizenship by pointing to the presence of a minority immigrant community more alien than themselves. Racial ascendancy had been a fundamental part of American identity ever since the settlers' first encounter with the Native Americans; in learning this, the Irish immigrants were becoming American.

Possibly Irish America's greatest advance in the post-Famine period, and the one that would both indemnify and demonize their social position well into the twentieth century, was their progression toward political agency, achieved through gaining outright control of Tammany Hall. While Tammany involved itself in municipal politics on a local level, the extent of its success in the United States—from San Francisco, to Chicago, to New York—made it a national concern for the reformers who worked to expose and destroy it. New York was the real seat of Tammany municipal power, and with the death of William Tweed in 1871 that power fell into the hands of the Irish. Between "Honest John" Kelly, Richard "Boss" Croker, and "Commissioner" Charles Francis Murphy, the Irish controlled municipal politics in New York City from 1871 to 1924, with only a few brief interruptions. For fifty years the Irish dominated city politics in America by adapting the mass mobilization practices of O'Connellism and what Kevin Kenny calls the "subterranean politics" of Irish tradition. This political power base helped support, promote, and secure Irish America's ascension to the ranks of citizenship.

Also, by the late nineteenth century the triumph of the liberal American Catholic movement (over the more conservative and radical theologies) in promoting a vision of Catholicism that emphasized American secular values such as self-reliance, industry, thrift, and temperance to and in its parishioners helped promote Catholics as American citizens. As these Irish Americans moved toward bourgeois respectability, nationalism—formerly an indication of the community's non-American character—began to respond to and reflect the American conditions and concerns of the first- and second-generation ethnics; for Irish Americans moving into middle-class American society, it became what Kerby Miller calls "a means to ultimate assimilation." However, Republican nationalists, such as John Devoy, Michael Davitt, and Patrick Ford, were still prominent within the movement and continued to direct their attention toward a free Irish republic.

EARLY TWENTIETH CENTURY

By the early twentieth century Irish Americans had left behind their "immigrant" identity and begun to merge into American society. This was certainly helped in part by the arrival in the early part of the twentieth century of "new immigrants," such as the Italians and the Eastern European Jews, whose culture, religion, and lifestyle seemed more alien to the Anglo-American society than that of the Irish. At the same time, the number of Irish immigrating to the United States had significantly decreased, falling to just over 300,000 Irish arrivals between 1901 and 1910. With transatlantic emigration interrupted by World War I, Irish immigration to the United States dipped to under 150,000 in the teens and recovered to just under 250,000 in the twenties. The onslaught of the Great

Depression and then World War II drastically reduced the number of Irish emigrating; in the 1930s the number dropped to as little as 13,167, recovering to just double that in the 1940s, 26,967. The US Immigration Acts of 1921 and 1924 effectively ended mass emigration to the United States as a possible solution to Irish problems, establishing an annual quota of 28,567 for immigrants from the Irish Free State, which was reduced to 17,853 in 1929.

Though immigrant numbers were falling, the number of second-generation Irish Americans was rising. But Irish Americans were not just advancing in generations; they were also advancing socially. By 1900, first- and second-generation Irish Americans had begun to achieve parity with the native-born population in the field of employment. With the arrival of the "new immigrants" the Irish had begun to move out of manual labor and into skilled and blue-collar management jobs; a smaller amount had begun moving into white-collar jobs and professions. As they moved into the second generation, Irish American women, too, were moving out of their traditional employment of domestic service and into areas such as nursing, teaching, secretarial work, and stenography. At this time, the Irish involvement in the American labor movement continued to deepen, and Irish women were also beginning to take a leading role in the movement. One of the foremost labor activists in the U.S. in the early twentieth century was Mary Harris Jones, popularly known as "Mother Jones." A native of Cork, she helped found the Industrial Workers of the World in 1905.

Irish Americans were now spread across the spectrum of American society. Though they still accounted for a disproportionately large number of the indigent population, they were now also producing some of America's best-known writers, dramatists, artists, singers, actors, and directors: F. Scott Fitzgerald, Finley Peter Dunne, James T. Farrell, Eugene O'Neill, Georgia O'Keefe, Chauncey Olcott, James Cagney, John Wayne, John Ford, Walter Huston, and Raoul Walsh, among many others. They made their impact felt in sports as well, particularly in baseball where along with supplying a whole host of players, managers like Ned Hanlon, John McGraw, and Connie Mack became some of the most successful and innovative the game has known.

Catholicism was the fastest-growing religion in the United States in the first half of the twentieth century, thanks in large part to the Irish; by 1915 there were 15 million Catholics in the United States, and this would more than double by 1950. While liberal Catholicism dominated U.S. Catholic thought in the early twentieth century, one of the most famous Catholics of the 1930s was the controversial figure Father Charles Coughlin. His weekly radio sermons against American banking, the Hoover administration, and subsequently President Franklin Roosevelt carried an undercurrent of anti-Semitism and proved very popular, drawing a regular weekly audience of more than 5 million during the Depression. Coughlin's support was strongest among the working to middle-class Irish Americans—those Irish aspiring to become more successful Americans—who Andrew Greeley argues "were probably on the verge of making it when the Great Depression rolled the nation into a decade of economic stagnation" (Greeley 121). By World War II, Coughlin's fascist sympathies had alienated his public, and his archbishop forced him to return to his parish duties.

In politics, Irish Americans continued to dominate on the municipal level through a second generation of "reformed" city machines that incorporated social reforms into their program. Even more powerful than their predecessors, these Irish-led Tammany machines continued to dominate city politics and provide patronage employment for a large number of Irish Americans. However, the birth of the New Deal in the 1930s marked the beginning of the end for these Irish-led political machines. But while Irish representation was declining at the local level, with Alfred Emmanuel Smith's nomination as a presidential candidate in 1928 it was beginning to announce itself at the national level. Al Smith was the first-ever Catholic presidential candidate; unfortunately, due in large part to anti-Catholic bigotry, he won only eight states (losing even in his own state of New York) and was defeated by Republican Herbert Hoover.

Despite this defeat in the United States, by the 1920s Irish Americans had played their part in securing a major Irish achievement: independence. The 1916 Easter Rising in Ireland and the subsequent execution of the Irish "martyrs" by the British helped replace an ailing campaign for constitutional reform with a rejuvenated hard-line republicanism on both sides of the Atlantic. Irish American nationalism had provided much of the impetus for this rebellion; the New York-based organization Clan na Gael, under the leadership of John Devoy and Daniel Cohalan, provided money and support and even helped plan the 1916 insurrection.

POSTWAR IRISH AMERICA

In the postwar era, the history of Irish America is one primarily concerned with the advance and assimilation of Irish Americans already in the United States. After World War II there were just two decades of significant Irish immigration to the United States—the 1950s and the 1980s; immigration would never again reach the numbers or public presence of the late nineteenth century.

This decrease in the influx of new immigrants further loosened ties to an Old World heritage that had been receding with every generation, as the Irish became more and more American. Even the symbolic register of their ethnic identity—Catholicism—had since the end of World War II become a primary marker of their Americanness. During (Irish American) Senator Joseph McCarthy's high-profile crusade against communism in the 1950s Catholicism was established as the antithesis to communism and, as such, became for the Irish Americans the very marker of their American identity. With John F. Kennedy's ascension to the American presidency in 1960, Irish Americans achieved full acceptance as Americans, and Catholicism became the symbol of both their American and ethnic identity. By the time of Kennedy's assassination in Dallas, Texas, on November 22, 1963, Catholicism had become an American religion and the Irish Americans had firmly become American.

By the latter half of the century Irish power in municipal politics had faded. With the exception of Richard J. Daley in Chicago (mayor from 1955 until his death in 1976), the Irish municipal machine had succumbed to factors such as the loosening of ethnic ties and the rise of new immigrant communities. Along with this, their symbiotic relationship with the Democratic Party, which had seen them advance from foreigners to citizens, had also begun to dissolve. No longer synonymous with the Democratic Party, as Irish Americans ascended into middle- and upper-class society their politics became correspondingly more conservative. By 1980 a majority of American Catholics voted Republican, helping to elect Ronald Reagan as president.

As their relationship to Catholicism and the Democratic Party changed, so too did their relationship to nationalism. While Irish Americans continued to contribute to the cause of nationalism in Ireland in the postwar period, the form of that contribution changed significantly as the century progressed. Ireland's neutrality in World War II had upset Irish Americans and led to a decline in interest in Irish affairs; however, the start of the Troubles in Northern Ireland in the late 1960s brought a renewed interest in Irish nationalism in the U.S. The American Congress for Irish Freedom was founded in 1967; the National Association for Irish Justice in 1969; and the most famous of these organizations, the Northern Ireland Aid Committee or NORAID was founded in 1970. Founded to assist the victims of violence in Northern Ireland, including political prisoners and their families, NORAID was repeatedly accused of sending guns to the Irish Republican Army (IRA).

Concerned that violence was not the answer, the "Four Horsemen" of Irish American politics—Edward Kennedy, 'Tip' O'Neill, Daniel Patrick Moynihan, and Hugh Carey— worked closely with the Social Democratic Labour Party's John Hume in the 1970s to find a political approach that would offer an alternative to violence. Though the hunger strikes of the early 1980s briefly escalated Irish American interest in physical-force nationalism and led to a resurgence in support for NORAID, by the mid-1980s (with Sinn Fein's Gerry Adams's recognition that a political campaign could support the republican agenda) interest in both Ireland and the United States had turned toward finding a possible political solution to the troubles in Northern Ireland. This would lead to the declaration of cease-fires by the IRA in the 1990s, which would culminate in the Belfast (or Good Friday) Agreement in May 1998. President Clinton was one of the chief architects in bringing about this agreement and it remains a legacy of his administration, one that he still works to preserve.

By the 1980s, stagnation in the Irish economy would send a new wave of immigrants to the United States. These immigrants generally consisted of two groups: the legal immigrants who availed of the Donnelly and Morrison visas (as well as the normal system) to find jobs and become recognized members of American society, and the illegal immigrants who were effectively economic refugees trying to escape the lack of opportunity in Ireland. Generally, illegal Irish immigrants entered the United States on tourist or student visas and remained in the country to become part of America's undocumented aliens. The level of illegal Irish immigration to the United States in the 1980s is estimated to be somewhere between 40,000 and 100,000.

Better educated and consisting of greater numbers of skilled and professional workers than previous waves, these "new Irish" of the 1980s—legal and illegal—rejuvenated and challenged traditional Irish American identity. One of the traditions the new Irish immigrants broke from was the established pattern of Irish immigrant settlement. Unlike their predecessors, these "new Irish" did not restrict their movement to ethnic Irish neighborhoods; instead, they moved much more widely across both nation and state. While they still immigrated in significant numbers to the major cities of the East, West, and Midwest, they did so it seems not out of a sense of ethnic kinship but rather because these cities provided the best opportunities for the diverse range of employment they were seeking.

With the sundering of old Irish neighborhoods came a significant weakening of ethnic identity among Irish Americans. The new Irish immigrants furthered this dissolution by bringing with them to the United States a modern sense of Irish identity that contradicted the older community's nostalgic sense of a tragic Irish identity conditioned by religion and nationalism. These conflicting views of Ireland would lead to a mixed relationship between the established Irish American community and the new immigrants: while they supported each other on issues such as the Irish Immigration Reform Movement, they clashed on issues such as gay rights, with the new immigrants largely supporting the Irish Lesbian and Gay Organization's petition to march in New York City's Saint Patrick's Day parade. On key issues such as this and the continuing support for the IRA's violent struggle in Northern Ireland, these two groups established their separate and antithetical visions of Irish cultural identity. Having witnessed the dissolution of the "special relationship" between church and state in Ireland and experienced at first hand the deadly consequences of armed resistance in Northern Ireland, the new immigrants had a far looser attachment to Catholicism and nationalism than their Irish American compatriots.

MODERN RELATIONS

The 1990s and the new century have already seen crucial changes in the relationship between Ireland and the United States. One of the most significant changes so far has been the reversal in the traditional pattern of emigration and population loss in Ireland, a consequence of the rising Irish economy in the 1990s (dubbed the "Celtic Tiger"). In 1998, 21,200 people emigrated from Ireland but more than 44,000 people migrated into the country. This is part of a continuing trend. Ireland it seems is becoming a nation of immigrants rather than emigrants, and many of these immigrants are former emigrants returning from Britain and the United States.

Catholicism has also suffered possibly irreparable damage in both Ireland and the United States in the new century. First in Ireland and then in the United States a series of scandals involving pedophiliac priests and the Catholic Church's continued failure to report these criminal acts and their perpetrators have left the Catholic Church reeling not just financially but, more importantly, devotionally, as parishioners begin to question the Church's failure to protect its flock. This controversy has forced the resignations of Brendan Comiskey as bishop of Ferns in Ireland and Bernard Cardinal Law as archbishop of Boston in the United States (for their failure to report incidents to the police) and forced Catholic dioceses in the United States to declare bankruptcy.

In the twenty-first century Ireland has redefined its relationship with the United States. Building on the strong social, political, and economic ties the tradition of emigration has established between the two countries, Ireland has repositioned itself as the gateway to

Europe, and particularly to the lucrative European market for the United States. Rather than exporting its well-educated population to the United States, by the turn of the twenty-first century Ireland was invested in importing major U.S. telecommunications, chemical, and technology companies into Ireland. The Irish government cut taxes on capital, corporate profit, and personal income in the hopes of attracting U.S. companies into Ireland. By 2000 this had resulted in an explosion of economic activity, making Ireland the fastest-growing country in the developed world; with just 1 percent of Europe's population it accounted for 27 percent of U.S. greenfield investment in Europe.

This altered economic relationship—with Ireland playing host to U.S. companies rather than the United States playing host to Irish immigrants—has resulted in a reconsidered and refreshed understanding of Ireland and the Irish in the United States, making the relationship between Irish and American identity much more homeostatic and contemporaneous. While traditional markers such as Catholicism and nationalism may be fading as symbolic registers for Irish identity on both sides of the Atlantic, both Ireland and the United States are now engaged in more comprehensive, considered, and modern understanding of what it means to be Irish, American and Irish American.

References

Adams, William Forbes. *Ireland and Irish Emigration to the New World from 1815 to the Famine.* Baltimore: Genealogical Publishing Co., 1980.

Akenson, D. H. "The Historiography of the Irish in the United States of America." In *The Irish World Wide. History, Heritage, Identity. Vol II. The Irish in New Communities,* edited by Patrick O'Sullivan. Leicester, England: Leicester UniversityPress, 1992: 99–127.

Bayor, Ronald H., and Timothy J. Meagher, eds. *The New York Irish.* Baltimore: Johns Hopkins University Press, 1996.

Blessing, Patrick J. "Irish." In *The Harvard Encyclopedia of American Ethnic Groups,* edited by Stephan Thernstrom. Cambridge: Belknap Press, 1980.

Greeley, Andrew M. *That Most Distressful Nation: The Taming of the American Irish.* Chicago: Quadrangle Books, 1972.

Griffin, William D., ed. *The Irish in America 550–1972: A Chronology & Fact Book.* Dobbs Ferry, New York: Oceana Publications, 1973.

Jones, Maldwyn A. "Scotch-Irish." In *The Harvard Encyclopedia of American Ethnic Groups,* edited by Stephan Thernstrom. Cambridge: Belknap Press, 1980.

Kenny, Kevin. *The American Irish: A History.* New York: Pearson Education, 2000.

MacDonagh, Oliver. "The Irish Famine Emigration to the United States." *Perspectives in American History* 10 (1976): 357–446.

Miller, Kerby. *Emigrants and Exiles: Ireland and the Irish Exodus to North America.* New York: Oxford University Press, 1985.

Shannon, William V. *The American Irish: A Political and Social Portrait.* Amherst: University of Massachusetts Press, 1966.

Walsh, Victor A. "The Great Famine and Its Consequences." *Éire-Ireland* 23, no. 4 (1988): 3–31.

Witte, Carl. *The Irish in America.* New York: Russell & Russell, 1970.

Ireland and the Americas

A

ABOLITIONISM AND SLAVERY

Abolition is the generic name given to a variety of reform efforts dedicated to eliminating slavery immediately and opposed to gradual emancipation or colonization schemes. Although slavery and blacks were quite rare in Ireland, the millions of Irish who emigrated to America in the period before the Civil War could not avoid the issue of slavery given that it was so intertwined with the American political and economic system. Irish Americans, while generally not supporters of slavery, nevertheless had significant problems with abolitionism, which prevented them from ever becoming a force for the peaceful eradication of slavery. In addition, the fierce competition between blacks and Irish for the unskilled jobs at the bottom of the economic ladder brought these two despised groups into continual conflict. Eventually, the Irish played a major role in eliminating slavery through their contributions to the Union cause during the Civil War, even if most Irish saw the war as being fought to preserve the Union and not to end slavery.

Slavery and slaves were rare in Ireland, although there is evidence that slaving ships operated out of ports like Dublin. Despite having failed twice at establishing slaving companies in Ireland (Limerick 1784; Belfast 1786), Irish merchants were very active in supplying slave plantations in the Caribbean. A black population did exist in Ireland, with the largest concentration in Dublin, and although no evidence of public slave markets exists, newspapers did sometimes carry advertisements of slaves for sale and notices of runaway slaves. Ireland also had an active abolitionist community, which paralleled the community in the United States. Its leadership was made up of middle- and upper-class evangelical Protestants, who saw the eradication of slavery as a necessary step toward bringing about God's rule on earth.

In America, Quakers had long opposed slavery, and in the eighteenth century there were more antislavery societies in the South than in the North, but that changed in the early nineteenth century with the increasing profitability of slavery. Organized agitation against slavery really began in 1831 when William Lloyd Garrison started publishing *The Liberator* in Boston. This newspaper soon became the leading organ of American abolitionism. In 1833 the American Anti-Slavery Society was organized in Philadelphia under Garrison's leadership. This national organization was the most militant of all the antislavery organizations. Often seen as fanatics by the general public, the abolitionists were relatively few in number, but they had a significant impact on public discourse because of their profound commitment to the cause of antislavery. Many of the members of abolitionist groups were educated church people of middle-class New England or Quaker heritage, although strong antislavery sentiments could also be found in upstate New York and certain sections of the western states.

The radical abolitionists differed from those of moderate antislavery feelings in that they called for an immediate end to slavery. The most extreme abolitionists denied the validity of any laws that recognized slavery as an institution; thus, they systematically violated the fugitive slave laws by organizing and operating the Underground Railroad, which was used to conceal and transport runaway slaves to Canada. The activities and propaganda of the abolitionists, although discredited in conservative northern quarters and violently opposed in the South, made slavery a national issue.

Few Irish were involved in the antislavery movement and many openly opposed it. The Irish had an antipathy to abolitionism for a number of reasons. For one, locked in intense competition with free blacks and slaves for unskilled jobs, the poor Irish did not look on blacks as fellow sufferers of the free market system; rather, the Irish viewed blacks as having the jobs they needed to survive. Hence, the Irish would often band together to bar blacks from working on the docks and in other labor-intensive occupations. As for slavery, the Irish viewed it as unfair competition that drove down wages. Neither did the Irish have much sympathy for the treatment of slaves, as they saw their own reception in America as being scarcely better. In New Orleans, for example, Irish

immigrants were used in place of slaves to perform the deadly work of filling in the swamps because slaves were seen as valuable property while the Irish were considered expendable.

The antislavery movement, like all the antebellum reform movements, grew out of the evangelical Protestant reform impulse. Although other factors certainly played a part, it can be argued that evangelical Protestantism was the bedrock of the reform movements. A defining attribute of evangelical Protestantism was a strong and virulent anti-Catholicism. When the overwhelmingly Catholic Irish arrived in America in the years 1820–1860, they experienced an extremely negative reception. The attitudes of leaders and members of the reform movements were clearly not meant to be welcoming to the poverty-stricken Irish Catholics who were struggling to make their way in the big cities of the East Coast. Consider, for example, the attitude of the "father" of abolitionism, William Lloyd Garrison. Amazingly progressive for his time, Garrison supported the abolition of slavery, pacifism, and equal rights for free blacks and women and opposed the harsh treatment of Native Americans and Chinese workers. However, as progressive as he was, Garrison was violently anti-Catholic, often making reference to the whore of Babylon and popish plots. He supported the temperance work of Irish priest Father Theobald Mathew only until Mathew refused to speak out against slavery. With Garrison's anti-Catholic prejudice being commonplace in mid-century America, it should not be surprising that Catholics ignored his appeals to oppose slavery.

In addition, the antislavery movement was linked with all the other reform movements, including temperance and women's rights. Taken together, many Catholics viewed the array of proposed reforms as a Protestant attempt to regulate the way they lived, worshipped, and went to school (keeping in mind that the King James Bible and anti-Catholic tracts were used to teach reading in the public schools). A fundamental difference existed between these groups over the meaning of freedom and democracy. For the abolitionists, it meant the freedom to work to improve the lot of your fellow citizens, whether they wanted these improvements or not. For the Irish, it meant freedom to improve your individual circumstances and to live your life the way you saw fit. The Catholic Church's stance on slavery was also a factor in the Irish attitude toward abolition. Although the church spoke out against unjust slavery many times in its history, the presence of slavery in Catholic countries created the impression that the Vatican condoned or even supported the institution. The matter was further muddled by certain nineteenth-century American clergy, including some bishops and theologians, who tried to defend the American slave system. They contended that the long-standing papal condemnations of slavery did not apply to the United States. The slave trade, some argued, had been condemned, but not slavery itself. However, papal teaching condemned both the slave trade and chattel slavery itself. One could argue noncompliance with the teachings of the papal magisterium as a key reason that slavery was not directly opposed by the Catholic Church in the United States.

Another reason may have been the precarious position of the Catholic Church in America before the twentieth century. Catholics were a relatively small and much-despised minority. They were subject to repeated, sometimes violent, attacks by Protestant "nativists." In many ways, the American church was attempting to protect Catholic immigrants in the United States and may not have seen itself as in a position to become the leader in a major social crusade. Regardless, this confusion or complexity surrounding the issue of slavery in America left Irish Catholics less likely to consider opposing slavery as an important teaching of the Catholic Church.

In the political realm, it might be expected that the poor Irish, discriminated against in so many aspects of American society, would be natural supporters of the Republican Party with its slogan of "free soil, free labor and free men." However, the Republican Party and its predecessor, the Whig Party, scorned the immigrant Irish as ignorant and uncivilized and an actual threat to the future of the Republic because of their perceived slavish obedience to Rome. The Democratic Party, however, saw the waves of immigrants as a way to solidify their control over American politics and actively wooed the Irish. They opposed stricter qualifications for citizenship, temperance legislation, and other laws that the Irish saw as being aimed directly at controlling them. Thus, the Democratic Party—a party that did everything possible to avoid the slavery issue altogether—gained the loyalty of Irish Americans for many generations.

In the end, one cannot argue convincingly that the Irish were pro-slavery, but then, neither were they antislavery. Slavery simply was not a high-priority issue for them. What is most amazing about the Irish attitude toward abolition and slavery is not so much the failure of many Irish to join the reform movements, but rather the fact that close to 200,000 of them were willing to enlist, fight, and risk death to save a Union that had done everything possible to make them feel unwelcome and unwanted. In the process of helping to save that Union, they also helped to end slavery.

William B. Rogers

See also: AMERICAN CIVIL WAR; DOUGLASS, Frederick; ETHNIC AND RACE RELATIONS (IRISH AND AFRICAN-AMERICANS); MATHEW, Father Theobald; WEBB, Richard Davis

References
Franklin, John Hope. *From Slavery to Freedom.* New York: Alfred Knopf, 1988.
Mintz, Stephen. *Moralists and Modernizers.* Baltimore: The Johns Hopkins University Press, 1995.
Rogers, William B. *"We Are All Together Now": Frederick Douglass, William Lloyd Garrison, and the Prophetic Tradition.* New York: Garland, 1995.
Walker, Robert. *Reform in America.* Lexington: University of Kentucky Press, 1985.
Walters, Ronald. *American Reformers, 1815–1860.* New York: Hill and Wang, 1978.
Walters, Ronald. *The Antislavery Appeal.* Baltimore: The Johns Hopkins University Press, 1976.

ALABAMA

In the 1900 census, in which there were more than one and a half million people in America whose parents had been born in Ireland, less than two thousand of these people were recorded as living in Alabama. Most of these were concentrated in the counties surrounding the three urban centers of Birmingham, Montgomery, and Mobile. Of these, Mobile had the largest concentration of Irish, as it had long been regarded as a Catholic center. This history dated back to the time of the Civil War when a parish priest, Father Abram Ryan, who was based in Mobile but who had been born in Ireland, was known as the "Poet of the Confederacy" because of the patriotic poems he had penned for the South. The Irish presence

was also visible with Bishop John Quinlan, the second bishop of the diocese of Mobile from 1859 until 1883, who had been born in Cloyne, Co. Cork. After Quinlan's death, he was succeeded by Jeremiah O'Sullivan, who was also born in Co. Cork. Bishop Edward Patrick Allen followed from 1897 to 1926 and Bishop Thomas Toolen from 1927 to 1969, both of whom were of Irish descent. Consequently, for more than a century, priests who were of Irish descent were the leaders of the Catholic Church in Mobile, Alabama.

The Irish were visible not only in the hierarchy of the Catholic Church in Alabama but also in the establishment and administration of some educational institutions. Spring Hill College in Mobile, which was founded in 1830 and was later run by the Jesuits, became closely associated with the Irish. This was as a result of the four presidents of the college: Father David McKinery, S.J. (1883–1887), Father James Lonergan, S.J. (1887–1896), Father Michael S. Moynihan, S.J. (1896–1899) and Father William J. Tyrrell, S.J. (1899–1907). All of these were either born in Ireland or were first-generation Irish-Americans. This tradition has continued up to the present day—numerous other presidents of the college, including the current president, Father Gregory F. Lucey, S.J., have been of Irish descent. Later, with less than 5 percent of Alabama's population declaring themselves to be Catholic, it became necessary for foreign priests, especially Irish ones, to be sent to Alabama. One of the bishops of Alabama, Raymond Boland, was born in Tipperary, trained in Dublin, and sent to Alabama after his ordination.

The Irish in Birmingham were first attracted by the coal and iron mines there but one Dublin-born Irish immigrant,

Frank P. O'Brien, eventually became the mayor of Birmingham and a representative to the state legislature. O'Brien built the city's Opera House and helped establish the first Catholic parish in the city. In 1921, however, the Irish-born pastor of this parish, Father James E. Coyle, was involved in a controversy that attracted national attention and was reported by *The New York Times* as an example of the religious intolerance of the South. A Methodist minister, Edwin R. Stephenson, shot Coyle, who had been named dean of North Alabama in 1913, because he had performed the wedding ceremony of Stephenson's daughter, a Catholic convert, to a black man. The feelings of racial and religious intolerance in the case were not helped when the jury found Stephenson not guilty and he was freed.

An example of the way in which the position of the Irish in Alabama has changed since this case was seen in the 1990 census conducted in the state of Alabama: more than 350,000 people claimed that they were of Irish ancestry. Another instance of the change in the perception of the Irish was seen when the Irish singer Dana, also known as Rosemary Scallon, lived in Birmingham with her family in the 1980s. Having won the Eurovision Song Contest for Ireland in 1970, she moved to Alabama to become a talk show host on the Eternal World Television Network (EWTN). She returned to Ireland in 1997 to become a candidate in the Irish presidency election and was later elected as a member of the European Parliament.

David Doyle

See also: AMERICAN CIVIL WAR; CATHOLIC CHURCH, the

References
Blalock, Kay J. "The Irish Catholic Experience in Birmingham, Alabama." Master's thesis, The University of Alabama, Birmingham, 1989.
Boyle, Charles J. "Alabama." In *The Encyclopedia of the Irish in America*. Notre Dame, IN: University of Notre Dame Press, 1999.
Gleeson, David T. *The Irish in the South, 1815–1877*. Chapel Hill: University of North Carolina Press, 2001.

ALLEN, FRED (1894–1956)

The comedian known as Fred Allen (a show name he came to use personally) was born John Florence Sullivan on May 31, 1894, in Cambridge, Massachusetts. Allen's Irish connections are largely genetic, although late in his life he and his wife, Portland, took—and relished—several vacations there. As a comedian, however, he irritated some culturally sensitive Irish Americans, who took offense at the "Allen's Alley" caricature of an Irishman, Ajax Cassidy. Although the dialectical oddities and logical inconsistencies Cassidy uttered would now be considered unacceptably stereotypical, Allen's

Portrait of ventriloquist Fred Allen with his dummy Jake. (Library of Congress)

work was unusually notable for its refusal to mock people merely for being themselves. Thus, although Ajax Cassidy occasionally bears unfortunate resemblances to the persona of the stage Irishman, it was neither Allen's intention nor his achievement to present the Irish as inherently comic or derisible.

In 1908 Allen's father, a bookbinder, was able to obtain employment for his son in the Boston Public Library. Allen thus spent much of his adolescence there, where he read widely. He became interested in juggling and, after reading several books on the subject, decided to attempt it before an audience. Although he was a competent juggler, he realized that his patter was more original than his juggling; he switched the emphasis of his act to comedy, and began touring as "the world's worst juggler." He attained success as a comedian on the vaudeville circuit, even touring as far as Australia. In a 1922 revue he met his future wife, Portland Hoffa.

Allen's major professional break came in 1932, when he was offered a comedy variety show on the radio. For most of the next twenty years he was employed in radio comedy. The shows kept a basic format, although their titles changed as different sponsors assumed his contracts: *The Linit Bath Club Revue, The Salad Bowl Revue,* and *The Sal Hepatica Revue.* His most extensive associations, however, were with the two shows *Town Hall Tonight* and *The Fred Allen Show.*

In an age when most radio comedy in the United States involved comically mismatched spouses or racial stereotypes, Allen was routinely topical. He read nine newspapers daily, and wrote much of his own material. Widely regarded as the best ad-libber in American comedy at the time

(with the possible exception of Groucho Marx), Allen pioneered comedic styles that are still regarded as risqué: he derided his network, mocked his sponsors' products, harassed guest stars, and questioned the sanity and integrity of anyone who wants public office. He also became involved in the single most popular enduring joke in American radio history, a long-running comic feud with his fellow comedian, Jack Benny. (Benny and Allen were friends off the air). A character and dialect segment of *The Fred Allen Show* (entitled "Allen's Alley") became a widely admired, and widely imitated, comic format.

From approximately 1935–1949 Allen was one of America's premier comedians. Television, however, ate immediately into his appeal, and he felt incapable of integrating his topical style into the new medium. By the middle 1950s Allen had largely retired from radio, and he began writing humorous memoirs. He died suddenly in New York City on March 17, 1956.

Allen's humor is unfortunately dated by the very topicality that initially made it seem so daring. Although some of his remarks retain their power—"Imitation is the sincerest form of television"—jokes about Franklin Roosevelt, the Brooklyn Dodgers, or Amos and Andy are too distant to retain their immediate amusement. Yet Allen knew that his topicality would date his work, calling the comedian's task a "treadmill to oblivion." He felt, however, that it was better to amuse in the present than to attempt to reach a posterity one would never know.

Andrew Goodspeed

See also: MUSIC IN AMERICA, IRISH

References
Allen, Fred. *Much Ado About Me.* Boston: Little, Brown, & Co., 1956.

Allen, Fred. *Treadmill to Oblivion.* Boston: Little, Brown, & Co., 1954.

Dunning, John. *On The Air: The Encyclopedia of Old-Time Radio.* New York: Oxford University Press, 1998.

Taylor, Robert. *Fred Allen: His Life and Wit.* Boston: Little, Brown, & Co., 1989.

AMERICAN CIVIL WAR (1861–1865)

As the most bloody and devastating conflict in America's history, the cost of the Civil War included more than 620,000 dead in a population of 32 million and losses of billions of dollars in resources and destroyed property, in addition to effecting the collapse of the slave economy. The immediate cause of the war was the secession of eleven southern states over their bitter disappointment with the outcome of the 1860 presidential election, in which Abraham Lincoln was elected despite his not even being allowed on the ballot in the southern states. However, scholars today recognize that the underlying cause was the institution of slavery and the key role it played in the widely varying cultures, economies, and worldviews of the different regions. Nearly 200,000 Irish immigrants and Irish Americans fought in the Civil War, and the great preponderance (180,000) supported the Union cause. Despite setbacks such as the New York City Draft Riots, the exploits of certain Irish units, particularly for the North, helped the Irish begin to establish themselves as loyal Americans deserving of full participation in the nation's future. The Civil War ended with Irish heroes as household names and with the Irish further along the path to assimilation into American society.

While Irish immigration had been underway for many decades, the nature of the immigrants began to change significantly in the third and fourth decades of the nineteenth century. About three-fourths of the roughly 5 million Irish immigrants who entered the country after 1820 belonged to the Roman Catholic Church. Most of these Catholic immigrants were impoverished people from rural Ireland. Irish immigration to the United States increased greatly during the 1840s when Ireland suffered through the Great Potato Famine, otherwise known as the Great Hunger (1845–1852), a catastrophic failure of the nation's staple food crop. The famine resulted in disease and starvation that killed at least 1 million people in Ireland and forced another 2 million to flee the country over the period of a decade. After the famine, poor Irish continued to leave the country to find economic opportunities unavailable to them in Ireland.

Throughout the nineteenth century, unskilled and uneducated Irish immigrants settled in large cities on the eastern seaboard of the United States, especially New York City, Philadelphia, and Boston, along with medium-sized cities such as Albany, New York. Although some immigrants went to southern port cities, such as Savannah, Georgia and New Orleans, the great majority ended up in the northern states as these states possessed a much more vibrant economy and a greater demand for unskilled labor. Here Irish Americans often faced discrimination in jobs and housing. Many Americans supported anti-immigrant groups, such as the Know-Nothing political party, which regarded Catholicism as foreign and a danger to American society. They viewed the Irish as barbaric and uncivilized. For the most part, Irish Americans had no choice but to live in squalid conditions surrounded by their countrymen and women and were only able to obtain employment in the least desirable and most dangerous occupations. Irish-American men were usually employed as manual laborers, while Irish-American women often found work as domestic servants.

A prevailing characteristic of the Irish immigrants to be somewhat withdrawn from mainstream American society was evident even in the months leading up to the Civil War. Many Irish Americans were seemingly more interested in events in Ireland than in the political turmoil in the United States. Only six months before the war began at Fort Sumter in Charleston, South Carolina, the colonel of the 69th New York militia, which was composed of Irish Americans, refused to parade his regiment before the Prince of Wales during a state visit to the United States. The regiment refused to march because of the British role in the famine and what Irish Americans saw as the unlawful occupation of their homeland. All talk of court-martialing the

regiment's commander, Colonel Michael Corcoran, or disbanding all Irish regiments, promptly ended with the commencement of hostilities at Fort Sumter in April 1862. The 69th added nearly 800 recruits to its numbers in ten days, and the regiment marched down Broadway on its way to the war on April 23, 1861, a scene famously captured in a well-known Currier and Ives print.

Although ambivalent about the war, most Irish Americans believed the conflict to be centered on the issue of secession and the attempt by Southerners to invalidate the results of a legal election. The country had lawfully elected Abraham Lincoln, and although most Irish were Democrats, they supported the notion that if the losers in a legal election could overturn those results simply because they disagreed with them, then the future of democratic, republican government was doomed. Another important strand of Irish support for the Union

Colonel Michael Corcoran at the Battle of Bull Run, Virginia, on July 21, 1861. (Library of Congress)

AMERICAN CIVIL WAR 49

was the perception that the slaveholding aristocracy in the South was similar to the Protestant, landlord aristocracy in Ireland.

The Irish in the South who remained loyal to their region did so mainly for the same reason as most Southerners, which was that they viewed the northern attempt to enforce the election results and prevent secession as an invasion of their homes. Few Irish were of the slaveholding class, and pro-slavery arguments did not figure in their defense of the South. A prominent exception is John Mitchel, a leading figure in the Young Ireland Rebellion of 1848 (a failed Irish rebellion against the British colonial forces), who argued that slavery was a positive good despite his vehement opposition to the harsh treatment of the Irish by the British, and despite losing two sons fighting for the Confederacy. Catholics and Jews were more accepted in the South than the North, most likely because they were there in much smaller numbers and their common whiteness was more important than any denominational differences from their Protestant neighbors. For example, Supreme Court Justice Roger Taney, author of the Dred Scott decision (which ruled that Dred Scott, a slave who had sued for his freedom, was not a citizen of the U.S. and had no rights to sue in federal court, and hence must remain a slave), was Catholic. Some Southern Irish leaders, like Mitchel, viewed the South as a weak, agrarian underdog trying to free itself from the domineering, ruthless, and capitalistic North, thus attempting to place the South in the role of the Irish in the long struggle against Britain.

The most critical aspect of the Civil War for Irish Americans was the formation and performance of a number of specifically Irish units on both sides, but primarily for the Union. The 69th New York militia performed well during the war's first major battle at Bull Run, and, when subsequently discharged, most reenlisted in the 69th New York Volunteers to serve for a further three years. Colonel Thomas Francis Meagher, the most charismatic of all the 1848 Young Ireland rebels, launched a plan to recruit an entire brigade of Irish soldiers. The idea of an "Irish brigade" had powerful cultural connotations for the Irish, as many exiled Irish had fought for the kings of Europe in the past, particularly against the British. Meagher, his notoriety only enhanced by his brave performance at Bull Run, was able to successfully recruit the brigade and was made its first commander. Subsequently, other Irish brigades were formed in Pennsylvania and Massachusetts, and a total of twelve regiments were deemed to be Irish regiments. A related reason behind this effort to recruit Irish regiments for some Irish-American leaders was that once the Civil War was over, the thousands of Irish combat veterans would be well prepared to liberate Ireland from what they saw as the tyranny of British rule.

These units performed admirably during the war, suffering enormous casualties at such battles as Antietam, Gettysburg, and Spotsylvania Courthouse. Of the 14,000 men in these twelve regiments, more than 3,000 were killed and more than 4,300 were wounded, for total casualties of 53 percent. The 69th New York Volunteers suffered greater casualties than any other New York regiment, and the New York Irish Brigade's loss of 961 men in action was exceeded by only two brigades in the entire Union army. These losses received great attention in the popular press, as did the exploits of the Irish Brigade at the "Bloody Lane" during the battle of Antietam and the "Wheatfield" at

Gettysburg. These accomplishments did much to lessen the anti-Irish and anti-Catholic prejudice rampant during the nineteenth century.

On the other hand, the New York City Draft Riots of July 1863 were widely seen as examples of the worst characteristics of the Irish—violent, lawless, and bigoted. These riots, still the worst in American history, erupted only days after the battle of Gettysburg over the implementation of the new draft law. This law, passed in March 1863, made virtually all men between the ages of 20 and 45 liable for military duty in order to satisfy the ever-growing manpower needs of the Union war effort. Opponents criticized a provision that enabled draftees to obtain exemption from service by supplying a substitute or by paying $300, which made the war appear to be "a rich man's war and a poor man's fight." As the date for enforcing the act approached, dissatisfaction with this provision became widespread among the poor of New York City, especially Irish immigrants.

The city remained quiet on the day the draft came into effect (July 11), but its resumption on the following Monday was marked by the rapid gathering of an unruly crowd, which soon attacked and burned the draft headquarters. The crowds prevented the fire department from reaching the building, and the fire quickly spread. Efforts by the New York City police and small units of soldiers stationed in the city to disperse the rioters provoked them to even greater violence. The mob roamed through New York, destroying property and committing other outrages. These were directed especially against blacks, whom many in the mob considered responsible for the Civil War. Many blacks were lynched, and black

neighborhoods and establishments were attacked. The rioting subsided late Monday night but was resumed with even greater violence on Tuesday, July 14. Rioting continued until July 15, when military detachments reached the city from Gettysburg, Pennsylvania, and West Point, New York. Some of these units were made up of Irish soldiers who had no compunction about opening fire on their fellow immigrants. By Thursday, July 16, the riots had been quelled and calm had been restored to the city. The death toll during the three days of rioting is estimated at more than 1,000; more than fifty large buildings were destroyed by fire and property damage was about $2 million.

Although a setback for the acceptance of the Irish as truly American, the fact that most Americans did not strongly support, and many openly opposed, the draft somewhat mitigated the long-term impact of the riots. In this public relations contest, the bravery of the Irish men fighting and dying on the battlefields all across the nation trumped the negative images of the poor Irish immigrants who instigated the Draft Riots.

In the end, the Civil War provided an opportunity for the Irish to prove their loyalty and worth as full American citizens. As other immigrant groups were to do in future wars, the Irish helped to cement their rights as Americans through the blood of their young men. After the Civil War, Irish Americans made greater progress in moving into the middle classes and in alleviating anti-Irish prejudice. Other factors of course came into play, including the waves of immigrants from countries such as Italy and Poland who seemed even more foreign to Anglo-Saxon Americans than did the Irish, and the fact that the wealth of the Northern states grew by 50 percent during the decade of the 1860s. Still, after the Civil War, it would become more difficult for nativists to make the claim that the Irish did not belong in America or had not earned the status of citizenship. While the hoped-for invasion of Ireland by American Irish veterans never materialized, Irish Americans were the first American ethnic group to become involved in the liberation of their native country. Irish-American financial contributions, personal participation, and political influence, all initiated by the Civil War generation, aided movements to secure Ireland's independence from the United Kingdom. Irish Americans played an important part in creating the Irish Free State in 1921 and the subsequent founding of the Republic of Ireland in 1949.

William B. Rogers

See also: ABOLITIONISM AND SLAVERY; DRAFT RIOTS; EMIGRATION; ETHNIC AND RACE RELATIONS (IRISH AND AFRICAN AMERICANS)

References

Bilby, Joseph G. *The Irish Brigade in the Civil War: The 69th New York and Other Irish Regiments of the Army of the Potomac.* Conshohocken, PA: Combined Publishing, 1998.

Boyle, Frank A. *A Party of Mad Fellows: The Story of the Irish Regiments in the Army of the Potomac.* Dayton, OH: Morningside Press, 1996.

Conyngham, David Power. *The Irish Brigade and Its Campaigns.* New York: Fordham University Press, 1994.

McPherson, James. *Battle Cry of Freedom.* Oxford: Oxford University Press, 1988.

McPherson, James. *For Cause and Comrades: Why Men Fought in the Civil War.* Oxford: Oxford University Press, 1997.

O'Grady, Kelly J. *Clear the Confederate Way: The Irish in the Army of Northern Virginia.* New York: DaCapo Press, 1999.

AMERICAN CONFERENCE FOR IRISH STUDIES

The American Conference for Irish Studies (ACIS) is an American nonprofit organization devoted to discussing and promoting Irish Studies. According to the ACIS bylaws stipulated in its constitution, ACIS "exists to encourage research and writing in Irish Studies by establishing a means of communication between scholars interested in Irish Studies in all disciplines, and to promote Irish Studies as a legitimate and distinct course of studies in American colleges, universities and secondary schools, and to further the development and dissemination of research, teaching and scholarly and critical inquiry in Irish Studies." Striving to support members' interests through annual conferences, scholarships, and book awards, ACIS has been instrumental in creating a climate conducive to and respectful of Irish Studies scholarship in the United States.

Before 1960, those scholars interested in Irish Studies found it difficult to disseminate the information that they had amassed to those most interested in their work, namely other Irish Studies scholars, because a national, American organization dedicated to such an endeavor simply did not exist. Gil Cahill, Emmet Larkin, and Lawrence McCaffrey, Irish Studies scholars frustrated by the situation, sought to fill this void, and, after much help from an academically centered grassroots effort, ACIS was born. From its inception, ACIS (known as the American Committee for Irish Studies from 1960 to 1987), was embraced by both scholars and nonacademics from all disciplines and all walks of life, and it has seen its membership blossom from a few hundred members during its fledgling years to a now thriving international community of more than 1,500.

The executive committee, comprising a president, vice president, secretary, treasurer, regional representatives (Mid-Atlantic, Midwest, New England, Southern, and Western), discipline representatives (arts, Celtic studies, history, Irish language, literature, and social science), and a graduate representative, meets annually at the national conference and is elected on a two-year basis; the vice president succeeds the president, and the previous president remains as an ex-officio member (officially termed the international representative) of the executive committee for a subsequent term.

The annual conferences (national and regional) seek to provide members with a forum in which to discuss and present myriad topics of Irish interest and include scholarly panel discussions, lectures, plays, films, live music, and, traditionally, an end-of-the-conference banquet. Typically, only about a third of the members attend the conferences, but all members are invited and encouraged to attend. Since 1961, the annual national conferences have been held at various universities and colleges in the United States, Ireland, and the United Kingdom, while regional conferences remain contained to their specific regions.

As an organization devoted to promoting intellectual pursuits, ACIS recognizes those worthy individuals who have made or promise to make a significant contribution to the discipline of Irish Studies by annually awarding the Adele Dalsimer Prize for Distinguished Dissertation, the James S. Donnelly, Sr., Prize for Books on History and Social Sciences, the Michael J. Durkan Prize for Books on Language or Culture, the Robert Rhodes Prize for Books on Literature, and the Donald Murphy Prize for Distinguished First Book as well as a postgraduate scholarship in Irish Studies at the University of Limerick in Ireland. ACIS also participates annually in panels and conferences at the Modern Language Association conference and in joint sessions at the American Historical Association.

ACIS has made a name for itself in international circles, particularly Irish ones. Since 1978, the Republic of Ireland's Department of Foreign Affairs has provided distinguished scholars from both the Republic and the North with the means necessary to present their work at the organization's annual conferences. Further, because of another international effort (this time between an Irish university professor named Roger McHugh and his very generous countrymen and women), ACIS was able to reprint a series of seminal essays devoted to Celtic studies, Irish history, and Anglo-Irish literature, known as The Reprint Series. The Massachusetts Institute of Technology and the University of Chicago presses published these selections of essays. But perhaps the most notable international effort involves a relationship between ACIS and the Holy See: ACIS was involved in an international effort to microfilm important Irish and British materials from the Vatican's Propaganda Archives and house them in Chicago's Newberry Library. This was made possible through the initiative of ACIS founder Emmet Larkin with financial assistance from the American Council of Learned Societies and the Newberry Library. In both small and large ways, ACIS has made significant contributions to the promulgation of Irish Studies in the United States. No longer considered simply a beloved hobby for academics with "real subjects to pursue," Irish Studies has become a legitimate and respected course of study in American colleges and universities.

Valerie A. Murrenus

See also: IRISH RESEARCH COLLECTIONS IN THE UNITED STATES

Reference
The American Conference for Irish Studies website. www.acisweb.com/index.php (accessed June 21, 2005).

AMERICAN IRELAND FUND

The American Ireland Fund (AIF) is the United States–based arm of the Ireland Funds, a global network of people of Irish ancestry and friends of Ireland dedicated to raising funds to support programs of peace and reconciliation, arts and culture, education, and community development. The AIF is the largest of ten Ireland Funds worldwide. Headquartered in Boston, the AIF's president and chief executive officer (CEO) is Kingsley Aikens.

The AIF, first named the Ireland Fund, was founded in 1976 as a nonprofit and nonsectarian organization, by Sir Anthony O'Reilly, former president, chairman, and CEO of the H.J. Heinz Company and fellow Pittsburgh businessman Dan Rooney, owner of the Pittsburgh Steelers football team. On St. Patrick's Day in 1987, The Ireland Fund and the American Irish Foundation, founded by Irish President Eamon De Valera and U.S. President John F. Kennedy, merged at a White House ceremony to form the AIF.

As of 2005, the AIF has raised more than $200 million for more than 1,000 projects in Ireland. It is a nonpolitical and nonsectarian fund that assists groups whose initiatives directly serve the people of Ireland, both north and south. Its mission is to provide hope for the people of Ireland, and it stands against violence and supports peace, culture, education, and community development. The organization underwrites cultural festivals, historic preservation, peace initiatives, and integrated schools, and solicits donations in four key giving areas:

- Promoting peace and reconciliation: The Ireland Funds support communities in Northern Ireland working together and toward a shared future. The organization has prioritized programs supporting those affected by the troubles, promoting social inclusion, citizenship, and participation, and encouraging a greater understanding of cultural identity within and between communities.
- Fostering community development: As Ireland experiences extensive economic, social, and cultural changes, the Ireland Funds promote an inclusive and integrated society and ensure the regeneration of marginalized urban and rural communities.
- Advancing education: The Ireland Funds focus on programs supporting access and progression from second to third level, preschool education, lifelong learning, and programs promoting tolerance through education.
- Inspiring arts and culture: The Ireland Funds support excellence and innovation in arts activities. Programs applied in settings of socioeconomic disadvantage and educational and health as well as programs promoting tolerance and reconciliation have been prioritized for assistance.

The fund annually publishes *CON-NECT* magazine, which is distributed to all donors. Anyone with an interest in Ireland and the goals and mission of the AIF is welcome to support the fund's work. Donors may make unrestricted gifts, set up donor-advised funds to accomplish individual or corporate charitable goals in Ireland, contribute to its endowment, include AIF in estate-planning programs, and participate in other giving formats such as sponsorship and advertising. The AIF staff also arranges "fly-ins" to Ireland, allowing donors to visit projects funded by the AIF and see aspects of Ireland not normally available to tourists.

Susan Gedutis Lindsay

See also: DE VALERA, Eamon; KENNEDY, John Fitzgerald

Reference

"Who We Are." Ireland Funds website. www.irlfunds.org/who_we_are/ (accessed May 10, 2005).

"Your Money at Work." Ireland Funds website. www.irlfunds.org/your_money_at_work/ (accessed August 15, 2007).

AMERICAN TEMPERANCE MOVEMENT

The temperance movement is a general term that catalogs a variety of approaches from reduced consumption of liquor to abstinence from all alcohol, and it encompasses a variety of definitions, from moderationists to teetotalers. This range of definitions reflects the internal evolution of the movement. Temperance is seen as part of the nineteenth-century social reform impulse. In reality, the temperance movement touched on many aspects of life in the relatively new American democracy, especially during a century of intense demographic, economic, and social change. Temperance was not a peculiarly American institution and its precepts traveled, particularly to Ireland, where it was one of the most popular reform movements of the nineteenth century. Women had an important role in temperance work. Many female activists found common cause with the temperance movement, including the national Women's Christian Temperance Movement, founded in 1874. Later, some female reformers adopted a more militant stance in the Anti-Saloon League, which was founded in 1893. The temperance movement provided women with the opportunity to articulate and direct personal, political, and social change, and it marked the beginnings of women as a political force. Similarly, African Americans like Frederick Douglass were very vocal on temperance matters. Despite its impact on contemporary American life, historians have neglected serious study of the temperance movement; however, in recent decades, an interest in social history and women's studies has led to a deeper analysis of its role in American life.

Temperance is particularly associated with the period from the mid-nineteenth century to the Volstead Act, ratified in 1919, which was the enforcement arm of the Eighteenth Amendment to the U.S. Constitution. This Act introduced a nation-wide ban on "the manufacture, sale or transportation of intoxicating liquors." Known as "Prohibition," it was the culmination of nearly a century's work by temperance advocates who wished to tackle the problems of alcohol abuse. However, recent analysts offer a variety of interpretations of the motives and results of temperance work.

To challenge the excessive consumption of alcohol, especially liquor, was a condemnation of early American society, as the tavern and church were the principal meeting places of earlier communities and alcohol accompanied every social occasion. This led to a huge consumption of hard liquor and a large incidence of drunkenness. At the turn of the nineteenth century, a physician, Benjamin Rush, wrote "The Effects of Ardent Spirits Upon Man." This essay contained a two-pronged attack on alcohol consumption. Rush used the increasingly scientific approach to medicine and illness to point out the hazards accompanying excessive alcohol consumption. He also cited the moral evils implicit in the overconsumption of liquor, and these scientific and moralistic approaches pervade temperance rhetoric. Initially, temperance societies encouraged people to avoid drunkenness and adopt moderation in their drinking habits. However, this evolved to advocating abstinence from hard liquor, and from the 1830s, a more radical approach was taken advocating total abstinence. As the century progressed the temperance movement grew increasingly vocal and organized in its approach, and moved from targeting individuals within the community to organized and effective political campaigns. This resulted in the Volstead Act and Prohibition.

By its nature, the temperance movement has a wealth of primary resources. Those who sought to promote temperance relied not only on word of mouth, but also on the printed word to publicize anti-liquor propaganda, leaving countless pamphlets, newspaper articles, periodicals, and documents in archives, libraries, and collections around America. However, these resources were imbued with a rhetoric that emphasized the contrasting moral qualities of the temperate and intemperate. This rhetoric also mirrored the social concerns of those who were viewed as truly American and truly respectable. Likewise, temperance inspired much popular temperance literature and drama, though of a sentimental nature. In the past decades, historians and critics have analyzed these primary resources and applied a variety of critical frameworks to the temperance movement; these in turn have yielded new interpretations. Temperance has inspired accounts of the individuals involved, histories of the various groups, and more recently, following on Joseph R. Gusfield's work, the wider context is now scrutinized. He suggests that temperance activity was not merely a response to changes in alcohol consumption but temperance advocates were responding to what they regarded as a threat to their social and economic positions. One of these threats took the form of huge numbers of German and Irish immigrants, who were known to drink heavily. Temperance advocates believed these immigrant groups threatened the established social order and this was justified when the rural agricultural ideal was challenged and increasingly replaced with an urban commercial ideal. Gusfield sees temperance as offering an opportunity to consider how status conflict influenced the development of American society.

Ann Coughlan

See also: DOUGLASS, Frederick; MATHEW, Father Theobald

References

"Temperance and Prohibition Era Propaganda: A Study in Rhetoric." The Brown University Library Digital Collection. http://dl.lib.brown.edu/temperance/rhetoric.htm (accessed October 14, 2005).

Dannenbaum, Jed. "The Crusade against Drink." *Reviews in American History* 9, no. 4 (1981): 497–502.

Gusfield, Joseph R. *Symbolic Crusade: Status Politics and the American Temperance Movement.* Urbana: University of Illinois Press, 1963.

Quinn, John F. *Father Mathew's Crusade: Temperance in Nineteenth-Century Ireland and Irish America*. Amherst: University of Massachusetts Press, 2002.

AMERICAN WAR OF INDEPENDENCE (1775–1781)

Meeting in congress at Philadelphia, Pennsylvania, representatives of the thirteen American colonies declared their independence from the British crown on July 4, 1776. Long-standing disputes over indirect political representation and colonial tax policy had festered for decades, leading ultimately to sufficient—though by no means total—public support for independence. Their declaration, written primarily by the Virginian Thomas Jefferson, is notable for its stirring eloquence in expressing a political philosophy heavily indebted to Enlightenment beliefs about human liberty: "We hold these truths to be self-evident, that all men are created equal, that they are endowed by their Creator with certain inalienable Rights, that among these are Life, Liberty, and the pursuit of Happiness."

British and American troops had already engaged in sporadic battles, most notably the battle of Bunker Hill (on June 17, 1775, near Boston, Massachusetts). Contrary to later romantic notions of Americans unpreparedly stirring to arms, an American army of considerable ability already existed and was commanded by General George Washington, later the first president of the United States. To defeat them, therefore, the British deployed large numbers of their own troops, some already stationed in the colonies, and hired thousands of Hessian mercenaries to accompany fresh troop deployments. They also dispatched numerous Royal Navy ships to the Americas, particularly in attempts to take such harbors as New York. But the distances involved made coordination of the British effort troublesome, and they were hard pressed, on numerous diplomatic fronts, by France. These difficulties prevented the full use of all of Britain's enormous military power against the colonists.

Initial combat actions went against the Americans, and Washington's men were driven south out of New York and into parts of New Jersey. Yet Washington, despite these reverses, understood that the tactical nature of the war favored him. The British were most powerful when they could mass and coordinate their efforts into large, set-piece fighting. Therefore, Washington did not set out to confront the British forces whenever they were near, but instead began a war of attrition and evasion, attacking when possible, then vanishing when the British began to pursue him. Although a somewhat misleading image of Washington retreating into victory has emerged, one of his great tactical strengths was undoubtedly this ability to withdraw aptly when conditions were disadvantageous for his type of fighting. He was also skilled at making unexpected strikes, the most famous of which was his nighttime Christmas attack on Trenton, New Jersey, in 1776.

The year 1777 was marked by several difficult campaigns for New York State and Pennsylvania. Most notably, British troops from Canada, under the command of General John Burgoyne, marched into upper New York State and fought with the colonial armies there. Although the British soldiers fought well, Burgoyne made slow progress and eventually engaged in disastrously misconceived battles against American forces at Saratoga. After this fighting, Burgoyne became convinced that he could not press on, and he surrendered his army on October 17, 1777. This surrender had an electrifying effect: it not only encouraged the rebellious Americans and discouraged the British, but it also led France to seize upon Britain's misfortune by negotiating an alliance with the Americans (February 1778). Spain too joined with France in 1779, seeking to use Britain's present disadvantages to settle long-standing territorial disputes. What had begun as a war against rebellious colonists was now turning, for Britain, into a dangerously international conflict.

Washington's troops, meanwhile, spent the winter of 1777–1778 in Valley Forge, Pennsylvania, in conditions of terrible cold and privation. But they were able to remain a credible army and emerged again to battle British troops. That winter experience is often—although probably with exaggeration—considered the crucible of suffering through which Washington was able to hold his army together; after that, although there were still significant incidents of desertion and insubordination, his army retained its martial ability and ultimate unity.

The British had initially attempted to crush the rebellion by focusing their attention on the northern colonies, where the most significant hotbeds of revolution were to be found—notably Boston and Philadelphia. In late 1778 they began to try to make the southern colonies places of battle. They fought into Savannah, Georgia, at the very end of December 1778, and into Charleston, South Carolina, in 1780, using their significant naval advantage skillfully. They were not idle in the north, however, and continued campaigns there as well.

For the next two years the Americans and the British traded blows, in North Carolina and Virginia particularly, neither being able to destroy the other. Yet as the war progressed, and French assistance began to tell, the British were losing their advantages. They proved unable to draw the American troops into truly decisive battles in which they could crush the revolution permanently. Nor were they able to develop a strategy with which to counteract the American tendency to use the enormous size of the territories to their own advantage. Furthermore, they had difficulty in making their presence hold, even in conquered territories. Although they met with some significant successes on the battlefield, they soon found that they were not truly conquering the lands. Their intention had been to crush and pacify known centers of revolt, then allow support for independence in the rural areas to die of starvation. Yet this strategy was not successful; the American troops proved able to use the rural areas without wholly alienating local support. Britain was winning some battles, but losing the war.

Eventually Britain's Lord Charles Cornwallis was pinned into Yorktown, Virginia, where Washington's men pressed them by land and the powerful French fleet on the Atlantic coast prevented Royal Navy assistance from the seas. On October 19, 1781, Cornwallis surrendered. Although this was not total military defeat for the British war effort, it effectively ended the war. Unable to take the lands by sheer force, and incapable of using the dominating power of the Royal Navy to force coastal resupply and troop movement, they abandoned the effort to suppress American independence. A peace treaty—widely viewed as a skillful triumph of American diplomatic self-interest—was signed in Paris on September 3, 1783.

The Irish played an important role in the American War of Independence—on both sides. Although the sentiment of Irish

Americans endorsing the colonial side was substantial, it must be noted that significant numbers of Irish also fought among the British troops. At a time when many in Ireland did not control their own financial destinies, the British military offered regular employment and the possibility of advancement, both strong inducements to people without numerous other economic options. In Irish-American society, however, there appears to have been strong support for the revolution's goals, and Irish Americans made substantive contributions to its success. Among the most notable Irish-born participants in the American revolution are Richard Montgomery, a general in the American army during the pre-Declaration attack on Quebec in 1775; Charles Thomson, a Philadelphia-based firebrand who subsequently became the secretary of the Continental Congress and helped design the Great Seal of the United States; and Matthew Thornton, who participated in the Continental Congress and signed the Declaration of Independence.

Perhaps the most important element of the American Revolutionary War for Irish-American relations, however, was the example it provided of colonial subjects overthrowing their ties to Britain. Despite being engaged in numerous diplomatic contests with France and Spain, Britain was still widely considered the most powerful force in the world. That a group of colonials could overthrow this power, at least in their own territories, and then defend their independence with arms, appealed strongly to Irish nationalist sentiment. Many Irish also felt a keen sense of approval for the rhetorical expressions of liberty in which the American struggle was expressed. But these hopes for an Irish reenactment of American resistance were illusory, if alluring; in 1800 the Act of Union effectively

General Montgomery and his troops at Crown Point, New York in September 1775, en route to Canada. Despite the capture of Montreal, the subsequent assault on Quebec failed disastrously, leaving Montgomery dead and the invaders obliged to remain in winter quarters.

ended any real possibility, for more than 100 years, of an Irish nation wholly independent of Britain.

Andrew Goodspeed

See also: BARRY, John; BURKE, Edmund; SCOTS-IRISH CULTURE; SCOTS-IRISH AND MILITARY CONFLICT

References

Bailyn, Bernard. *Ideological Origins of the American Revolution*. Cambridge: Belknap,1967.

Doyle, David Noel. *Ireland, Irishmen, and Revolutionary America*. Dublin and Cork: The Mercier Press, 1981.

Hibbert, Christopher. *Redcoats and Rebels*. New York: Avon, 1990.

McDonald, Forrest. *E Pluribus Unum*. Indianapolis: Liberty, 1979.

Middledauf, Robert. *The Glorious Cause*. Rev. ed. New York: Oxford University Press, 2005.

Royster, Charles. *A Revolutionary People at War*. New York: Norton, 1981.

Wood, Gordon S. *The American Revolution*. New York: Modern Library, 2002.

AN TÓSTAL: IRELAND AT HOME (1953–1958)

An Tóstal: Ireland at Home was a nationwide tourism festival and the largest development project undertaken by Ireland's statutory tourist boards during the 1950s. The national festival consisted of both centrally developed spectacles as well as regional events that were planned and executed by local Tóstal councils. Statutory authorities carried out all national and international marketing and publicity.

Juan Trippe, president of Pan-American Airlines, proposed the Tóstal concept in 1951, the same year the British government held the Festival of Britain. Whereas the Festival of Britain was intended to reward the British people for their strength and steadfast determination during World War II and subsequent postwar deprivations, An Tóstal was designed to extend the tourist season while also attracting Irish emigrants, especially from North America, back to Ireland as tourists.

An Tóstal, which means "a gathering," was chosen as the name for the event in an effort to demonstrate the festival's primordial connection to events reportedly from Ireland's ancient past. Likewise, the An Tóstal emblem, created by Dutch designer Guss Melai and featuring an Irish harp and ornamentation inspired by the Book of Kells, was intended to further emphasize the imagined origins of the festival.

The first An Tóstal was held between April 5 and 26, 1953. The scheduling was intended to extend the Irish tourist season, which traditionally runs from late June through August. While a sound idea in theory, the reality was that cold, damp weather dramatically reduced the number of visitors in attendance. In 1955, Tóstal was moved to May; however, there was little corresponding increase in tourist traffic. By 1958, it was clear that An Tóstal had failed to extend the tourist season or attract Irish emigrants back to their homeland, so organizers abandoned the original format, opting instead for a series of events, loosely connected by the name An Tóstal, that would be held from May through October. Ireland was to be rechristened, for marketing purposes, "Ireland of the Festivals."

Despite the failure of An Tóstal itself, the event nevertheless played a defining role for both touristic representation of Irish history and culture as well as the aesthetic reality of Irish landscape. Local Tóstal events were supposed to place "the strongest possible emphasis" on "Gaelic life, history, language, and culture" and were classified under the headings "nationality," "culture," and "constitutional and civic life." Suitable themes included national traditions, language, music, art, drama, folklore, recreation, and leisure, while events ranged from sporting competitions (including fishing, equestrian, hurling, Gaelic football, as well as bicycle, foot, and automotive races) to parades, musical concerts, plays, pageants, and matchmaking festivals. A number of these local events remain a significant element of the contemporary tourist calendar. For example, the Rose of Tralee beauty pageant, Galway Oyster Festival, Dublin Theatre Festival, and Cork Film Festival were all originally held as Tóstal events.

Pageants were a particularly important part of the Tóstal calendar and were used to stress the timeless nature of the event as well to present visitors with a narrative of key moments in Irish history. In 1953, the national pageant was based on the theme "four green fields," which were to symbolize the four historic provinces of Ireland. The event was presented in the Theatre Royal in Dublin. The next year organizers planned a considerably more elaborate pageant that followed the life of Saint Patrick from his arrival in Ireland to his eventual peaceful conversion of the Brehons and Druids at Tara. It was a monumental undertaking, including 500 costumes, 1,300 volunteers, 1,000 pigeons, 24 wolfhounds, and 30 horses, as well as assorted deer and other game that were integrated into the spectacle. As many as 50,000 mostly Irish spectators braved bitterly cold weather to witness the event. In 1955, the Tóstal pageant was less elaborate and was held in the Croke Park Gaelic grounds in Dublin rather than the Boyne Valley.

Beyond stressing Ireland's impressive past, Tóstal organizers also used the festival to demonstrate economic and industrial progress made since independence. Before the 1921 Anglo-Irish Treaty, organizers noted, there was "no systematic establishment of manufacturing industries," yet afterwards hardworking Irish citizens made "considerable progress . . . towards the industrialization of Ireland." Industrial parades and exhibitions such as the "Cork Makes It" display during the 1954 Tóstal further emphasized Irish progress.

Finally, An Tóstal afforded an opportunity to reinvent the Irish countryside as a bright, welcoming, and cozy tourist paradise, a striking contrast to the obvious poverty of derelict buildings and deserted homesteads. From the first, Irish homeowners were urged to plant colorful window boxes, trim hedgerows, and repaint their homes. Initial aesthetic efforts often included window box competitions and town-sponsored decorative campaigns. Cork City, for example, was made up with extensive floral displays and colorful banners. In 1958, Bord Fáilte Eireann took further steps to encourage a redefinition of Irish townscapes by launching the Tidy Towns and Villages Competition— an annual event that rewarded communities that best reflected Ireland as a clean, inviting, and bright country. Although An Tóstal did not survive the 1950s, the Tidy Towns festival was expanded to include cities as well as rural farmsteads, and in 2005 more than 700 towns entered the competition.

An Tóstal ultimately represents the beginning of a new stage of Irish tourism development. While the short-lived event failed to bring Irish emigrants back to Ireland, it nevertheless sparked the creation of a new image of the country.

Eric G. E. Zuelow

See also: BORD FÁILTE EIREANN

References
Conekin, Becky E. *"The Autobiography of a Nation": The 1951 Festival of Britain.*

Manchester, England: Manchester University Press, 2003.

Bord Fáilte. *The Irish Tourist Board Report for the Year Ended March 31 1964*. Dublin: Bord Fáilte Eireann, 1964.

Fógra Fáilte. *An Tóstal: Ireland at Home, 1953; National Programme*. Dublin: Fógra Fáilte, 1953.

Fógra Fáilte. *An Tóstal: Official Souvenir Guide*. Dublin: Fógra Fáilte, 1953.

Furlong, Irene. "Tourism and the Irish State in the 1950s." In *The Lost Decade: Ireland in the 1950s*, edited by Dermot Keogh, Finbarr O'Shea, and Carmel Quinlan, 164–186. Cork: Douglas Village, 2004.

Zuelow, Eric G. E. "The Tourism Nexus: Tourism and National Identity since the Irish Civil War." PhD diss., University of Wisconsin-Madison, 2004.

ANCIENT ORDER OF HIBERNIANS

The Ancient Order of Hibernians (AOH) is one of the oldest Irish organizations in the United States. The AOH has played an important role for Irish Americans culturally, historically, politically, and socially. It was founded in 1836 at the Saint James Church in New York City as a Catholic lay organization for people born in Ireland, and later for people born of Irish descent in the United States. The roots of the AOH stretch back to Ireland where the precursor of the American AOH was founded in 1565 to defend Catholic Ireland against

A member of the Ancient Order of Hibernians plays the bagpipes during the St. Patrick's Day Parade in Clinton, Massachusetts in 2005. (AP/Wide World Photos)

Protestant Britain. The American AOH's motto of "friendship, unity, and Christian charity" was based on that of the original Ancient Order of Hibernians in Ireland. The AOH was brought to New York by Irish immigrants in response to the rise of the Order of the Star Spangled Banner or the Native American Party's (Know-Nothings) bigotry against the Irish. To try and halt the Know-Nothings attacks on both Irish people and church property, the AOH served as guards to defend church property from attack.

Most early AOH activities remain unknown as the society was founded on the basis of secrecy. In addition to defending church property, the organization assisted Irish immigrants financially who came to the United States as members of the Order back in Ireland and provided networks that facilitated employment and upward mobility for their members. The AOH was also instrumental in preserving Irish culture and traditions in America. As the Know-Nothing movement dissipated after the American Civil War, the AOH shifted its focus from defending property to "charitable activities in support of the church's missions, community service, and the promotion of preservation of their Irish cultural heritage in America." (AOH website) Organizations such as the AOH did not hinder assimilation into America, but felt "the development of an ethnic identity expressed through a rich institutional and associational life was the primary means through which the Irish assimilated" (Kenny 148–149). Between 1856 and 1921, more than 3 million Irish immigrated to the United States, increasing membership in the AOH. However, controversy developed over membership in the AOH. In 1884, the AOH debated over whether or not

American-born Irish could be admitted as members. Members of the AOH decided that American-born Irish could be admitted to the order in addition to those who were born in Ireland. This decision ensured that AOH membership would remain strong after the Irish-born members died and their American-born children could carry on the traditions and work of the AOH.

The order is organized at the local, state, and national levels. Divisions make up the local area, while county and state boards oversee the work of the order for that state; all are governed by a national board that is elected every two years. Although the national board provides overall direction for the organization, it is up to each individual state and its divisions to determine what activities that organization will focus on. Each division decides what activities they will pursue among the four goals of the AOH.

The first goal is for Ireland to be united as a thirty-two-county republic. The AOH has played an important role in promoting the Good Friday Agreement of 1998. They began to collaborate with other Irish-American groups such as the Irish American Unity Conference (IAUC). The divisions provided opportunities to learn about the issues in the north so that they can find ways to get involved in the process. Some examples of this are the speakers' forum, which brings in speakers to help divisions understand Irish political issues. Speakers have included Jim Gallagher of the IAUC and the teachers from the Holy Cross School in Belfast.

The second goal is protecting and defending the Catholic faith. During the years that nativism was a force in American politics, the AOH had to address specific nativist threats and defend their churches from attack in cities such as Boston and New York. In other states, such as Ohio, the organization had to address claims about not being loyal Americans. They fought back against such claims by focusing on a campaign to honor Irish Americans who had fought for America's freedom during the Revolutionary War. They also had to contend with defamation—the Irish were often perceived as drunken troublemakers. The AOH has been successful in proving Irish loyalty to America and took on defamation that is still present in today's society. However, there is still work to be done on the defamation front, such as the continued perception of Irish as drunks.

The third goal of the AOH is to preserve and promote Irish culture. Throughout the history of the organization, Hibernians have promoted and preserved Irish culture not only for its own members, but also for the communities in which they live. Irish history, music, literature, step dancing, and historic preservation are brought to the local communities by the divisions to illustrate the importance of preserving and promoting Irish culture so that future Irish Americans may have the chance to learn about their own unique cultural heritage as well. According to the AOH's constitution, the organization "builds upon the past, present, and future of Irish culture in order to foster the ideals and perpetuate the history and traditions of the Irish people [and] to promote Irish culture."

The final goal is for divisions to embrace the AOH's motto of "friendship, unity and Christian charity" by encouraging divisions to help out their local communities. In the beginning, the AOH provided financial assistance to Irish immigrants who were AOH members in good standing from the Irish Order. Local divisions helped immigrants obtain jobs and social services. While Irish immigration to the United States is no longer the major charitable cause of the AOH, divisions now focus on dealing with various Catholic action issues and supporting their local communities in a variety of ways, such as participating in Habitat for Humanity building projects, running Red Cross blood drives, visiting the sick, conducting fund-raising drives for charities, taking up donations for food banks, and becoming involved in other charitable activities within a division's community. National Catholic action initiatives in which local divisions take part are projects such as religious vocations, pro-life, and hunger issues. At times, it can be a struggle for members to become involved in contentious issues such as abortion while others such as hunger are more easily defined and easier to be involved with.

Historically, the AOH helped Irish immigrants to adjust to life in America through employment and housing while keeping the cultural traditions of Ireland alive in the hearts of their members. In the twenty-first century, the organization has helped Irish Americans to go beyond the green beer aspect of their Irish heritage and to use the organization as an eye-opener to the heritage that gives Irish Americans a unique identity. Many aspects of Irish culture, such as music, dance, literature, and history have exposed Americans to the culture of Ireland beyond celebrations of Saint. Patrick's Day. As membership continues to increase and as new divisions form throughout the United States, the link between Ireland and the United States will continue to remain strong not only in the present, but in the future as well.

Nicole Cassidy

See also: CATHOLIC CHURCH, the; NATIVISM AND ANTI-CATHOLICISM; SAINT PATRICK'S DAY PARADES

References

Ancient Order of Hibernians website. http://www.aoh.com (accessed June 30, 2007).

Kenny, Kevin. *The American Irish: A History.* London: Pearson Education Limited, 2000.

ANGLIN, TIMOTHY WARREN (1822–1896)

Timothy Warren Anglin was a journalist, politician, and officeholder in New Brunswick. Born August 31, 1822, he was the son of middle-class Catholic parents, Francis Anglin and Johanna Warren. He received a classical education in his hometown of Clonakilty where he afterwards taught school. After the Great Famine struck Ireland, he left for North America.

On Easter Monday in 1849, Anglin boarded a ship for Saint John, New Brunswick. Shortly after his arrival in Saint John, Anglin founded the *Saint John Weekly Freeman,* through which he sought to defend his fellow Irish Catholics in the city. Like so many other Irish communities of the diaspora, the Irish Catholics of Saint John were seen by 'respectable' citizens as prone to drunkenness and violence. They also faced discrimination on many levels in the British Protestant city of Saint John. Through the columns of the *Freeman,* Anglin not only defended Irish Catholics from attacks by the establishment but also chastised those of his compatriots whom he saw as idle and given to alcohol abuse.

In 1853 Anglin married Margaret O'Regan but she died just two years later, in 1855. He soon became skilled and articulate in his profession as a political journalist, and this led him to seek elected office. Although an earlier attempt to enter municipal politics had failed, he was elected to the New Brunswick House of Assembly in 1861 as an independent for Saint John. While opposed to British domination of Ireland, Anglin viewed with favor the imperial connection for the British North American colonies, as a rampart against aggressive American policies. He was opposed to the project of the confederation of these colonies on the grounds that it was a bad deal for Saint John and New Brunswick.

The anti-confederation arguments Anglin presented in the columns of the *Freeman* helped defeat the government in 1865. He became an executive councillor in the newly elected anti-confederate government. His opponents, the confederates, began to style him as the leader of the disloyal faction of Catholics in the colony. And while neither Anglin nor most of his fellow Irish Catholics in New Brunswick were active Fenians, they did support greater autonomy for Ireland. So when the Fenian menace became serious in the mid-1860s, the confederates seized the opportunity to brand Anglin and New Brunswick's Irish Catholics generally as a band of disloyal, anti-confederate Fenians. Anglin resigned from government before the poorly organized Fenian raid on New Brunswick in April 1866; this appeared to give credence to the confederates and their project of political union.

While Anglin was generally opposed to the specifics of the confederation proposal, he gave the new system a chance and was elected to a seat as an independent in the House of Commons in the first general election in 1867, a seat he would occupy for the next fifteen years. By 1872, Anglin had become a member of the fledgling Liberal Party in Ottawa. In 1874, he was appointed speaker of the House of Commons but continued his journalistic activities for the *Freeman,* which led to accusations of conflict of interest. These latter cost him his seat in 1877, although he was reelected in a by-election in the summer of 1878.

In opposition from 1878 to 1882, Anglin became an outspoken critic of Prime Minister John A. Macdonald's government and a supporter of Home Rule for Ireland. Defeated in the election of 1882, Anglin left the *Freeman* and Saint John in 1883, with his second wife, Ellen MacTavish (whom he had married in 1862) to take up residence in Toronto. After a prolonged period of unemployment interspersed with a few patronage appointments, Anglin finally obtained the position of chief clerk in an Ontario court of law, only to die one year later, in May 1896, from a blood clot to the brain.

Although he was a social conservative who believed religion and morality were the cure for society's ills, Anglin, unlike many of his middle-class contemporaries, was not opposed to trade unions, as long as workers' organizations operated on legal principles. Anglin's major contribution to his adopted country lay in his promotion of the interests of his fellow Irish Catholics, first in New Brunswick, then in Canada generally. While perhaps not the most flamboyant nor the most illustrious of Canada's Irishmen, he was a skillful journalist and a competent and hardworking politician.

Robert J. Grace

See also: NEW BRUNSWICK

References

Baker, William M. "Anglin, Timothy Warren." In *Dictionary of Canadian Biography.* Vol. 12. Toronto: University of Toronto Press, 1990.

Baker, William M. *Timothy Warren Anglin, 1822–96, Irish Catholic Canadian.* Toronto: University of Toronto Press, 1977.

APPALACHIA

Although Appalachia's precise boundaries are subject to debate, all definitions link it to the eastern mountain chain that runs southwest to northeast for some 2,000 miles, from the hills of northern Alabama into Canada. The Appalachian Mountains are the oldest in North America and the highest east of the Mississippi River. Their ridgelines, some of which rise more than 6,000 feet, project a peninsula of northern climate, flora, and fauna deep into the American South. Their terrain made travel in and out of the region difficult and shaped its settlement patterns, creating a land of scattered farms and small towns.

Appalachia has commonly, but mistakenly, been perceived as a homogeneous region. It is far better understood when its diversity is recognized. Subdividing it into northern and southern, or even into northern, central, and southern sections, based on environmental and cultural differences, provides for a more sophisticated appreciation of its complexity.

In the eighteenth and early nineteenth centuries, European immigrants settled Appalachia from New Hampshire to Georgia. A significant number of them came from Ireland, predominantly Ulster, eventually becoming known in America as the Scotch-Irish. Irish pioneers brought folkways that included house plans, livestock practices, Presbyterianism, music, and stories. They also adopted folkways from their new neighbors, including other Europeans, Native Americans, and, especially in southern Appalachia, African Americans, eventually making folkways hard to distinguish from others. This ethnic interaction in antebellum Appalachia created a cultural synthesis that has long been recognized as a valuable repository of American folk life.

While some parts of Appalachia, like Pittsburgh, thrived after the Civil War, southern Appalachia was devastated by it. Its economy lay in ruins, its agriculture was further undermined by midwestern competition, and population growth created intense land hunger. Its resources of coal and timber offered rich opportunities for industrial exploitation, yet most of the profits were exported outside the region. For the first time Appalachia's standard of living plunged far below that of the country in general, beginning a significant migration out of the region that continued to the 1960s.

After the Civil War, a stereotype of Appalachia developed that has dominated perceptions of the region ever since. Created mainly by outsiders—local-color writers, home missionaries, teachers, business investors—it portrayed Appalachia as "a strange land and peculiar people." This "hillbilly" image labeled Appalachian people as poverty-stricken, illiterate, and violent. It besmirches them to the present day.

Appalachia's nadir occurred in the middle of the twentieth century. With its economic difficulties exacerbated by the Great Depression, Appalachia became a national symbol of despair. President Johnson's Great Society program identified it as a key target of the War on Poverty. Special funding from the federal Appalachian Regional Commission and a host of other government and private sources helped Appalachia turn the corner. But homegrown activism, growth in the American economy, steady migration to the Sun Belt, and burgeoning tourism have also helped put Appalachia on an upward path. While it still lags behind many national norms, the future of the region nevertheless now appears promising.

H. Tyler Blethen

See also: COUNTRY AND IRISH MUSIC; SCOTS-IRISH; SCOTS-IRISH PATTERNS OF SETTLEMENT IN THE UNITED STATES

References
Abramson, Rudy, and Jean Haskell, eds. *Encyclopedia of Appalachia.* Knoxville: University of Tennessee Press, 2006.
Batteau, Allen W. *The Invention of Appalachia.* Tucson: University of Arizona Press, 1990.
Drake, Richard B. *A History of Appalachia.* Lexington: University Press of Kentucky, 2001.
Straw, Richard A., and H. Tyler Blethen, eds. *High Mountains Rising: Appalachia in Time and Place.* Urbana: University of Illinois Press, 2004.
Williams, John Alexander. *Appalachia: A History.* Chapel Hill: University of North Carolina Press, 2002.

ARGENTINA

An independent republic since 1816, Argentina only reached relative institutional stability in 1853 after the promulgation of a national constitution. In the second half of the nineteenth century an agricultural revolution was followed by huge demographic expansion, originating in significant immigration inflows from Western and Central Europe, and later from the Middle and Far East and other Latin American countries.

During the nineteenth and part of the twentieth centuries, Argentina was the most important destination for Irish emigrants outside the English-speaking world. It is estimated that between 1830 and 1930 at least 45,000–50,000 Irish-born persons immigrated to Argentina. About half of the immigrants settled in the country and the other half re-immigrated to the United States, Australia, England, and other countries, or went back to Ireland. Today, some authors estimate that 500,000 Argentines have Irish roots, making this the largest community with Irish origins in a Spanish-speaking country. Several Irish Argentines have contributed to the host country with their culture, shaping linguistic, social, and economic characteristics that are unique throughout the Irish Diaspora. (The term "Irish Argentine" was coined by writer William Bulfin in an editorial of the *Southern Cross* of November 10, 1882 to separate the identity of the Irish in Argentina from that of the Anglo Argentines.)

Irish arrivals to Argentina before the nineteenth century were frequently linked to the Spanish colonial administration of the River Plate viceroyalty or to religious missions. Among the religious men, Father Thomas Field, S.J., of Co. Limerick pioneered the Jesuit missions among the Guarani Indians in Paraguay in 1587; Father Pedro José Sullivan, O.F., president of the University of Córdoba, participated in an open meeting of the Buenos Aires city council against the British invaders of 1806; also, naval Sub-lieutenant Jacinto Butler and Corporal Juan Carlos O'Donnell had roles in the defense of Buenos Aires.

A number of officials in the Spanish administration in Buenos Aires had been born in Ireland, many coming from international Irish dynasties such as the O'Reillys in Cuba, the Martins on the Canary Islands, and the O'Higgins and Coughlans in Spain. Some of the Irish administrators who settled in the River Plate before 1810 were Carlos Murphy, Patricio French, Thomas Craig, Admiral William Brown, General John Thomond O'Brien, and brothers Thomas and Dr. Michael O'Gorman.

Trade relations between British commercial houses, which had branches in many points of the North and South Atlantic, and Argentine-based merchants were essential for the development of the new River Plate republics. The exportation of hides and tallow, and later of jerked beef and wool, found markets in Liverpool and London. Conversely, Argentina increased its dependency on manufactured products imported from the British Isles. This increase in trade encouraged Irish-born merchants to settle in Buenos Aires and other cities of the new country. Thomas O'Reilly of Dublin, Thomas O'Gorman, Charles Stuart, Phillip Reilly, Daniel Donoghue of Cork, Robert MacCarthy, and C. O'Donnell were just some of the merchants who settled in Argentina.

The Irish presence increased during the failed British campaigns of 1765 in Colonia del Sacramento, and of 1806 and 1807 in Buenos Aires, after which several Irish-born soldiers remained in the country, among them men by the names of Browne, Nugent, Kenny, Donnelly, Murray, Mahon, Cadogan, and Duff. It is likely that John Murray of Streamstown, Co. Westmeath, who was later employed in an Argentine ranch, initiated the first migration chain from the Irish midlands to Argentina. Other migration sequences, particularly from Co. Wexford, originated in the need for labor of Irish merchants who owned meat-curing plants in Buenos Aires.

Gradually, with the advance over Indian-controlled territories in Buenos Aires and Santa Fe provinces, Irish and Basque immigrants played a key role in sheep farming and in settling new areas in the pampas. Several Irish immigrants worked as shepherds in departments such as Mercedes, Luján, Capilla del Señor, San Pedro, San Andrés de Giles, San Antonio de Areco, Carmen de Areco, and Salto (Buenos Aires province) and by the 1880s in Venado Tuerto (Santa Fe province) and the south of Córdoba. Frequently, they shared the production with landowners or major tenants, and at the term of the agreement received a half or a third of total wool and lamb production without having to invest financial assets. In a time when return on investment of the wool industry was higher than the best financial opportunities in other markets, shepherds often became owners of relatively large flocks of sheep, a fact that allowed some of them to purchase land.

From 1840 to 1880 the possibility of owning land—and the social wish to belong to a class that was conceived like the landed gentry in Ireland—attracted several thousand Irish emigrants to Argentina. Stories (sometimes exaggerated) of young tenant farmers who became owners of huge ranches in the pampas began circulating in Westmeath, Longford, Offaly, Wexford, and, to a lesser extent, Clare, Dublin, and Cork. The earliest settlers, who needed labor to help in their new ranches, did not have great difficulty convincing their brothers, cousins, or neighbors in Ireland to immigrate to Argentina. Female emigration, which was relatively low in the first half of the nineteenth century, began to increase in the 1860s with the prospect of marrying well-established landowners or tenant shepherds with promising futures. Finally, the central role played by Irish chaplains like Father Anthony Fahy and by Irish merchants like Thomas Armstrong provided cohesion to the newly formed community of Irish settlers through the development of an efficient social and economic network. The peak of the traditional emigration from the midlands and Wexford was in the 1860s and 1870s, and it declined after the 1880s. In 1889 a failed emigration scheme, the Dresden Affair, targeting poor emigrants from Dublin, Limerick and Cork cities,

diminished the prestige of Argentina as a valid destination for Irish emigration. Later, in the 1920s a new peak was recorded after the War of Independence in Ireland; the final decline came with the international financial crisis of 1930.

Not all of the Irish immigrants to Argentina worked as ranchers, sheep farmers, shepherds, and ranch hands, and not all of them were Catholics. After 1880, a significant proportion of the immigrants came from urban areas in Ireland and settled in Buenos Aires, Rosario, Bahía Blanca, Córdoba, and other Argentine cities, working as independent professionals or employees in merchant houses, railways, shipping companies, and cold-storage plants, most of them British owned. Many others worked in manual jobs, men as laborers and women as domestic service. Others settled in the sheep farms of Patagonia and the Falklands/Malvinas Islands, or in Chaco and other north-eastern provinces. A relatively high proportion of urban settlers had Church of Ireland background, particularly those who emigrated in the last years of the nineteenth and the first decades of the twentieth century. This group consisted largely of mobile emigrants who looked for opportunities in new countries; when they did not succeed, they went to the United States, Australia, England, or back to Ireland. In general terms, during the first half of the twentieth century the urban settlers with Protestant backgrounds integrated into the Anglo-Argentine community, while the Catholic rural settlers remained relatively isolated in a distinct Irish community for two or sometimes three generations. Ultimately, especially after the Falklands/Malvinas War of 1982, both groups integrated into the larger Argentine society.

Edmundo Murray

See also: ARMSTRONG, Thomas St. George;
BROWN, William; BULFIN, William;
DRESDEN AFFAIR; FAHY, Father
Anthony; FALKLANDS/MALVINAS
ISLANDS; O'BRIEN, John Thomond;
O'GORMAN, Michael; PARAGUAY.

References

Coghlan, Eduardo A. *El Aporte de los Irlandeses a la Formación de la Nación Argentina.* Buenos Aires: Author's Edition, 1982.

McKenna, Patrick. "Irish Emigration to Argentina: A Different Model." In *The Irish Diaspora,* edited by Andy Bielenberg. London: Longman. 2000.

Murray, Edmundo. *Becoming "Irlandés": Private Narratives of the Irish Emigration to Argentina, 1844–1912.* Buenos Aires: Literature of Latin America Press, 2005.

Murray, Thomas. *The Story of the Irish in Argentina.* New York: P. J. Kenedy & Sons, 1919.

Sabato, Hilda, and Juan Carlos Korol. *Cómo Fue la Inmigración Irlandesa en Argentina.* Buenos Aires: Plus Ultra, 1987.

ARKANSAS

The first people of Irish descent in Arkansas were Scots-Irish settlers who formed the most sizable minority in that state. However, it was with the American Civil War that the most prominent Irishman to settle in Arkansas became known. Patrick Ronayne Cleburne was born in 1828 in Co. Cork. He immigrated to America and moved to Helena, Arkansas. In the Civil War he volunteered for the state militia. He fought in the battle of Shiloh and eventually rose to the rank of major-general, making him the highest-ranking Confederate officer of foreign birth. His status within the Confederacy was so great that Jefferson Davis, the president of the Confederacy, later called him "Stonewall of the West." Cleburne later proposed that slaves be enlisted in the Confederate army to provide troops for a rapidly dwindling army. He was killed during the battle of Franklin, Tennessee, in November 1864. He was later buried in his adopted home of Helena, Arkansas.

Although the Irish presence in Arkansas was always small compared with that of other ethnic groups in the state and with their numbers in other states, after the Civil War two governors of Arkansas, who had marked political differences, were both of Irish descent. Harris Flanagin, the last governor of Arkansas during the Civil War, was the first person of Irish ancestry to become the governor of an American state. His grandfather had been born in Ireland and had immigrated to America in 1765. Flanagin had been born in New Jersey and had migrated to Arkansas. He supported secession and served in the Confederate Army during the Civil War. He was inaugurated as state governor in 1862, and he surrendered to the Union Army in Little Rock on May 27, 1865. The man who succeeded him as governor, Isaac Murphy, was born in 1800 in Pennsylvania to a family that had left Ireland in 1740. After settling in Arkansas, he represented voters at the secession convention, where he was the only delegate who opposed secession and later refused to change his vote. Having made contact with the Union Army, he was elected provisional governor and later governor in the Union-controlled parts of Arkansas. Murphy, in 1868, relinquished his position and died in 1882. In spite of the fact that two descendants of Irish immigrants had occupied such high positions at such a crucial time in the state's history, there would never again be such a number of Irish descendants in public life in Arkansas as in those years. Although Arkansas elected another governor of Irish descent, George Washington Donahey in 1908, he failed to win his party's nomination in 1912. Dan Hogan, the son of an

Irish immigrant, became one of the founders of the Arkansas Socialist Party and ran twice for governor on the Socialist ticket.

As in other states, however, there was a preponderance of Irish Americans in religious life in Arkansas. Over 150 years, four of the five Roman Catholic bishops have been either Irish immigrants or second- or third-generation Irish. The first bishop of the Little Rock diocese, Andrew Byrne, was born in Navan, Co. Meath in 1802. In 1844 he was consecrated as the bishop of Little Rock after the diocese was created. Later, he purchased a large amount of land near Fort Smith in the west of Arkansas, where he arranged for 1,000 Irish immigrants to be brought to escape the Great Famine and to bolster the number of Catholics in Arkansas. He died in Helena, Arkansas, in 1862. A few years later, Bishop Edward Mary Fitzgerald, who was born in Limerick City, was appointed as the second bishop of Arkansas in 1866. Earlier, he had become the youngest Catholic bishop in America at the age of thirty-four. In 1888 Fitzgerald opened Saint Vincent's Infirmary, which, under the management of the Sisters of Charity, is the oldest medical institution in the state. The head of the diocese from 1906 to 1946, Bishop John B. Morris, was born in Tennessee of parents who were Irish immigrants, while Bishop Andrew J. McDonald, who was consecrated in 1972, was born in Georgia of two Irish parents.

David Doyle

See also: CLEBURNE, Patrick

References
Donovan, Timothy P., and Willard B. Gatewood Jr., eds. *The Governors of Arkansas: Essays in Political Biography.* Fayetteville: University of Arkansas Press, 1981.
Symonds, Craig L. *Stonewall of the West: Pat Cleburne and the Civil War.* Lawrence: University Press of Kansas, 1997.
Woods, James M. "Arkansas." In *The Encyclopedia of the Irish in America.* Ed. Michael Glazier. Notre Dame, IN: University of Notre Dame Press, 1999.

ARMSTRONG, THOMAS ST. GEORGE (1797–1875)

Thomas St. George Armstrong was a businessman, landowner, and benefactor of the Irish community in Argentina. Born on November 29, 1797, in Garrycastle, Co. Offaly (formerly King's County), he was the son of Colonel Thomas St. George Armstrong and Elizabeth Priaulx. His father was county sheriff and had formerly served as an officer in the King's 8th Regiment of Foot in North America from 1768 to 1785. In 1817, Colonel Armstrong sent his sons Thomas and John to Buenos Aires to run the merchant house Armstrong & Co. In 1826, Thomas Armstrong traveled back to Ireland with John Thomond O'Brien to try to recruit immigrants from Ballymahon, Ballymore, and Mullingar along the Westmeath-Longford border. The Armstrong family were the local landlords and were (and still are) highly respected in that locality. Many of the first Irish immigrants to Argentina were recruited by Armstrong.

Thomas Armstrong was appointed director of the National Bank, the Bank of Buenos Aires Province, and the Bank of the Public Credit. In 1859 he founded the Argentine Insurance Company. He was financial agent of the national government and founding member of the Stranger's Club. In 1863, the government of Buenos Aires province accepted a proposal to build the Southern Railway, signed by Thomas Armstrong, Federico Elortondo, and others. Armstrong was involved in constructing railways to Luján, Central Argentino, and Ensenada and served as their director. He also established rural colonies, particularly in Santa Fe province, where he managed a large *estancia* (ranch).

When Father Anthony Fahy arrived in Argentina, he moved into Thomas Armstrong's house, where he lived rent free for the rest of his life. Although being Protestant and Catholic, respectively, Thomas Armstrong and Father Fahy remained inseparable, lifelong friends. Armstrong had assimilated into the local community in typically Irish merchant fashion. He married Justa Villanueva, the daughter of the *alcalde* (chief officer under Spanish rule) of Buenos Aires of 1807. Being such a powerful business figure and because of his wife's connections, Armstrong was also a very influential if unseen force in the political life of the country. He was the business counselor and close friend of almost every Argentine governmental administration from the directorship of Rodriguez to the presidency of Avellaneda, acting as honest broker between the British and Argentine governments in their commercial affairs for more than forty years. Thomas Armstrong was banker to Father Fahy, and this fact enabled Armstrong to become one of the leading business figures in Buenos Aires. He was a cofounder of the Buenos Aires Stock Exchange and a director of the Provincial Bank, which he made the central bank of Argentina. He was also the director and a substantial investor in the country's major railway company and served on the boards of most of the major stock companies in the city. His connections with the local community were also beyond reproach. Armstrong died on June 1, 1875, in Buenos Aires. A city in Santa Fe was named after him by the government.

Edmundo Murray

See also: FAHY, Father Anthony; O'BRIEN, John Thomond

References

Coghlan, Eduardo A. *Los Irlandeses en la Argentina: Su Actuación y Descendencia.* Buenos Aires: Author's Edition, 1987.

McKenna, Patrick. *Irish Emigration to Argentina: A Different Model.* Cork: Irish Centre for Migration Studies, 2000.

Newton, Jorge. *Diccionario Biográfico del Campo Argentino.* Buenos Aires: Artes Gráficas Bartolomé U. Chiesino SA., 1972.

ARTHUR, CHESTER A. (1829–1886)

Chester Alan Arthur, the twenty-first president of the United States, was the first son of five children born to a Baptist abolitionist Irish immigrant. Born on October 5, 1829, in rural Fairfield, Vermont, he grew up in several parishes in Vermont and New

Chester Arthur, twenty-first president of the United States. (Library of Congress)

York before attending Union College and graduating Phi Beta Kappa. Thereafter, Arthur served as principal of an academy from 1848 to 1851, hiring James Garfield in 1851 to teach penmanship before moving to another principal position in Cohoes, New York. He then began practicing law, taking an active role in the *Lemmon v. New York* case involving two Virginia slaves who sought their freedom.

As far back as 1844 Arthur was a Whig, but he joined the Republicans at their inception and became a protégé of New York state boss Thurlow Weed. Standing six feet tall with a full physique and dark eyes, he had a strict code of personal ethics, contrasting sharply with his connections with the spoils system. Arthur became engineer-in-chief of New York governor Edwin Morgan's military staff, where he was so expert in providing supplies that he was appointed quartermaster general of New York State. Although he demonstrated honesty and ability, he returned to civilian life after Morgan lost in 1862. However, after the Civil War Arthur rose steadily in the Republican ranks, becoming the leading lieutenant of Roscoe Conkling and landing an appointment by President Ulysses S. Grant as collector of the New York Customs House. Here he presided over a large patronage empire that he tolerated and sometimes encouraged to the point where it erupted into a national scandal. Arthur's overstaffing of his workforce with party workers eventually led to his suspension in 1878 and then removal by President Rutherford B. Hayes.

In 1880, in a compromise designed to placate Republican Party divisions over nominating either James G. Blaine or Roscoe Conkling, the convention nominated dark-horse candidate James Garfield as presidential candidate and selected Arthur as his running mate to appease the Stalwarts (a conservative faction who saw themselves as "stalwart" in opposition to Hayes's effort to reconcile with the South). As Conkling's trusted friend, Arthur was expected to tow the Stalwart line in the Garfield administration. However, after only four months in office President Garfield was assassinated, and Arthur's conduct during the assassination crisis won him public sympathy as he distanced himself from machine politics.

Once Arthur assumed the presidency, he ceased to act like the "Gentleman Boss" and was scrupulously on guard against criticism. With a slim majority in Congress he could not accomplish much but surprised everyone by backing reformers, accusing the railroads of price collusion and rate discrimination, and endorsing the regulation of interstate commerce. His administration eschewed both the spoils system (which had made Arthur renowned as head of the New York Customs House) and pork barrel politics (the use of government funds for projects designed to win votes) by appointing both Stalwarts and Half-Breeds (a moderate faction that backed Hayes's lenient treatment of the South and supported moderate civil service reform) and vetoing a pork-laden $18 million harbor and river bill that distanced him from the party faithful. In addition, he vigorously prosecuted the Star Route frauds in the Post Office Department and signed the first federal immigration law, the 1882 Chinese Exclusion Act, and the Pendleton Civil Service Act of 1883.

Known as a fastidious dresser with impeccable manners and a connoisseur of luxuries like Tiffany silver and Havana cigars, Arthur was a widower who cherished his privacy, did not trust the press, had disdain for the masses, and demonstrated apathy toward administrative tasks. Early in his administration he began his working days at 10:00 a.m. but by 1883 his daily meetings began at noon. However, what was viewed as lethargy was in fact the result of Bright's disease, a fatal kidney ailment concealed from the public, press, and politicos. Although Arthur stoically sought renomination in 1884, the party passed him over in favor of James G. Blaine, who lost to Grover Cleveland.

His ideologically rigid notions of economics prevented him from addressing the nation's economic woes while driving Southerners and Westerners to the Democrats, but it is unclear what he was thinking or might have accomplished with a solid majority in Congress, given that he burned his personal papers the day before he died on November 18, 1886. Nevertheless, few men have assumed the office of president with such low expectations and left with such respect.

Mark Connolly

See also: AMERICAN CIVIL WAR; TAMMANY HALL

References

Doenecke, Justus D. *The Presidencies of James Garfield and Chester Arthur.* Lawrence: Regents University Press of Kansas, 1981.

Howe, George F. *Chester A. Arthur.* 1934. Reprint, New York: Unger and Company, 1957.

Reeves, Thomas C. *Gentleman Boss: The Life of Chester Alan Arthur.* New York: Alfred A. Knopf, 1975.

B

BAGGOT, KING (1879–1948)

A popular actor and director in Hollywood during the 1910s and 1920s, King Baggot was born on November 7, 1879, in St. Louis, Missouri. He was the son of William Baggot, who was born in Limerick, Ireland, in 1846, and Harriet King, who was born in Missouri in 1859. King Baggot attended the Christian Brothers College in St Louis and graduated in 1895. After stints working for his uncle in Chicago and playing football for the St. Louis Shamrocks, King Baggot joined an amateur theatrical group. By 1902 he was playing minor roles with professional touring companies; he would remain a traveling actor for the next four years.

Attracted by the growing popularity of moving pictures and the opportunities the emerging industry offered actors, Baggot joined Carl Laemmle's IMP (Independent Moving Pictures) company in 1909 and made his first screen appearance in *The Awakening of Bess*. Over the next two years, he appeared in a number of one- and two-reel films, slowly building a reputation as a solid actor within the industry. His position within the industry, and his growing fan base, was signaled by IMP's decision to cast him in a series of detective films, the first of which, *King, the Detective*, was released in 1911.

Publicity of the time often referred to Baggot's "Celtic temperament," and the public's familiarity with his Irish roots helped contribute to the box office success of one of his most popular films, *Shamus O'Brien*. This 1912 two-reeler was written by the Dublin born writer/director Herbert Brenon and told the story of an Irish patriot fighting for Home Rule in Ireland in 1789. Baggot would work with Brenon on a number of films in the years that followed.

Baggot continued to develop as an actor and often took on dual or multiple roles, appearing in *Dr Jekyll and Mr Hyde* in 1913, and playing ten roles in the 1914 film, *Shadows*. Although Baggot had achieved considerable success with IMP, in 1916 he decided to establish himself as an independent producer. This decision was prompted, in part, by his reluctance to relocate to California with other IMP employees who were now part of the larger Universal film group. Baggot's efforts as an independent producer resulted in only one film, *Absinthe*, a remake of an earlier IMP film that he had made in 1914.

By 1921, Baggot's acting career was on the wane, and he decided to concentrate on establishing himself as a director. Over the next seven years he directed some of cinema's biggest stars, including William Hart

King Baggot (right) and William Hart (left) on the set of Tumbleweeds *in 1925. (United Artists/The Kobal Collection)*

(*Tumbleweeds,* 1925) and Marie Prevost (*Moonlight Follies,* 1921; *Kissed,* 1922). However, the emergence of sound films in 1927, as well as Baggot's worsening alcoholism, hastened the end of his directing career. His last film as a director was released in 1928. He remained on the margins of the industry throughout the 1930s and 1940s, often acting in minor roles for Universal and MGM studios. He died in Hollywood on July 11, 1948.

Gwenda Young

See also: BRENON, Herbert

Reference
Dumaux, Sally A. *King Baggot: A Biography and Filmography of the First King of the Movies.* Jefferson, NC: McFarland, 2002.

BALFE, MICHAEL WILLIAM (1808–1870)

During the nineteenth century there was probably no more popular opera in the United States than Michael Balfe's *The Bohemian Girl*, which premiered in London in November 1843 with phenomenal results. While Dublin-born Balfe wrote twenty-eight operas, his *Bohemian Girl* seemed to have had universal appeal in America, where it is still performed. The opera had its New York premiere at the Park Theatre in November 1844, a year after the London premiere. Unlike a number of his contemporaries, Balfe never visited America, although in the 1850s he had considered a tour with his young daughter,

Portrait of nineteenth-century composer Michael William Balfe. (Library of Congress)

Victoire, who was a well-established opera singer. In 1855 it was announced that Balfe was going to take over New York's Academy of Music at 14th Street as director of the opera. However, this never happened. By that time Balfe's fame as a composer had spread wide and far throughout Europe, where he was in demand, and his operas were being performed in different languages in Paris, Berlin, Vienna, Frankfurt, Stockholm, Prague, Trieste, Verona, Bologna, Madrid, and most capital cities in addition to London and Dublin.

With the success of his *Bohemian Girl* in New York, a number of Balfe's other operas were soon introduced there and along the East Coast of the United States. The ever-popular *Bohemian Girl* was also performed occasionally in an Italian version, *La Zingara,* in selected major American cities. Throughout the nineteenth century the original English version was heard across the country in Sacramento, San Francisco, Denver, Philadelphia, Boston, Providence, Washington, D.C., Baltimore, Richmond, New Orleans, Chicago, Milwaukee, Cleveland, Louisville, and many of the river towns, including Cincinnati and St. Louis. The opera's influence reached far beyond its normal sphere and audience in America because of its beautiful soprano melody, "I dreamt I dwelt in marble halls," and a comparable tenor aria, "Then you'll remember me," which were being sung in the drawing rooms of America by budding young singers in small towns and large cities. Its influence was also seen in other venues. The lush soprano melody was being parodied in a music hall version as "I dreamt I had money to buy a shawl." The opera's title and story also attracted such parodies as *The Bohea-Man's Girl* in the burlesque theatre. The American author Willa Cather was so influenced after seeing a performance as a teenager that it later featured in her writings, as it did in the work of Irish author James Joyce. Some considered the opera, with its memorable melodious tunes and romantic flavor, to be the bridge to what was to become the great American musical, which flourished in later decades. *The Bohemian Girl* was also adapted as a Broadway musical in 1902 with a production that ran for more than 100 nights, while a different adaptation in 1933 had a much shorter run.

In 1936, silent film star Hal Roach produced a Hollywood version of *The Bohemian Girl* featuring Stan Laurel and Oliver Hardy. Some of the main Balfe themes were retained, but with its two featured slapstick comedy artists it was far removed from Balfe's original romantic work. In recent times *The Bohemian Girl* has been performed in Nebraska and in New York both in a college version and at Carnegie Hall in a concert version with a professional cast. Michael Balfe was also a prolific songwriter with more than 250 works to his credit. Many of these became very popular in America, particularly when the great Irish tenor, John McCormack, sang them at his concerts in New York and elsewhere, and on recordings and films in the early decades of the twentieth century. William Balfe died in Ware, outside London, in October 1870.

Basil Walsh

See also: McCORMACK, John; WALLACE, William Vincent

References

Dizikes, John. *Opera in America.* New Haven, CT: Yale University Press, 1993.

Lawrence, Vera Brodsky. *Strong on Music: The New York Music Scene in the Days of George Templeton Strong.* Vols. 2–3. Chicago: University of Chicago Press, 1995.

Maretzek, Max. *Crochets and Quavers or Revaluations of an Opera Manager in America.* New York: S. French, 1855.

Martin, George, *Verdi at the Golden Gate: Opera and San Francisco in the Gold Rush Days.* Los Angeles: University of California Press, 1993.

Preston, Katherine K. *Opera on the Road: Traveling Opera Troupes in the United States, 1825–60.* Urbana: University of Illinois Press, 1993.

BALL, ERNEST R. (1878–1927)

One of the most prolific and successful composers of the commercial Irish songs that flooded American popular music in the early decades of the twentieth century, Ernest Ball was no mere Tin Pan Alley tunesmith. His melodies ran the gamut from the tender sentimentality of "Let the Rest of the World Go By" (1919) to the dramatic masculine sweep of one of his early hits,

"Love Me and the World Is Mine" (1906). He had the knack of turning even the sappiest lyrics into solid popular hits, as he did with an early success, "Will You Love Me in December as You Do in May?" (1905), with words by Jimmy Walker, the future mayor of New York City.

Ball was born in Cleveland, Ohio, on July 21, 1879. His musical talent developed early, and he attended the city's conservatory. He spent most of his career as a staff composer for Witmark & Sons, one of the most successful publishing houses on Tin Pan Alley. This may have been one of the factors that attracted impresario Augustus Pitou to Witmark around 1910. Pitou was looking for lyricists and composers to supply material for his string of Irish musicals built around his new star, Chauncey Olcott. One of Ball's first collaborations with Olcott and Pitou, *The Barrys of Ballymore* (1910), resulted in "Mother Machree," the melody of which demonstrated the composer's ability to showcase Olcott's lyric tenor voice. Tin Pan Alley's motto was that that one good hit deserves two or three more. Thus, Ball's "She's the Daughter of Mother Machree" (1915) and the wartime weeper, "Goodbye Mother Machree" (1918), both written with his frequent lyricist J. K. Brennan.

Although he had success with a wide variety of songs, Ball became famous for his Irish songs, which both mirrored and helped to form the popular image of Irish America, as can be seen from their titles: "The Click of Her Little Brogans" (1906), "It's the Twinkle in Her Eye" (1909), "I Love the Name of Mary" (1910), "Isle O' Dreams" (1911), "With a Twinkle in Her Eye" (1911), "Irish Eyes of Love" (1914), "Ireland is Ireland to Me" (1915), "It is Irish to Me" (1915), "McCarty (What Else

Could You Expect From a Man Named McCarty?)" (1915), "Never Let Yourself Forget That You Are Irish Too" (1915), "Somewhere in Ireland" (1917), "You Brought Ireland Right Over to Me" (1917), and "'Tis an Irish Girl I Love and She's Just Like You" (1919). Most of these were written for Olcott vehicles, often with the star himself listed as a co-lyricist.

While most of these songs have long gathered dust, Ball is credited with three of the most enduring Irish-American popular songs of all time. Along with "Mother Machree," Ball wrote the music for "When Irish Eyes are Smiling" (1912) with Olcott and Geo. Graff, Jr., and "A Little Bit of Heaven, Shure They Call it Ireland" (1914) with J. K. Brennan.

Ball was among a relatively small group of Tin Pan Alley composers who were successful on the vaudeville stage. In the 1920s he performed with his wife, Maude Lambert. At the age of 49 he suffered a fatal heart attack after leaving the stage of a vaudeville house in Santa Ana, California, on May 3, 1927.

William H. A. Williams

See also: MUSIC IN AMERICA, IRISH; OLCOTT, Chauncey

BALTIMORE

The first allusions to Ireland and the Irish in Maryland tend to be notices of runaway indentured servants. Most references to Baltimore Irish refer to their general poverty and visible pauperism. Despite the Catholic origins of the Maryland colony, which was founded by Catholic Cecil Calvert in 1632, the Irish encountered discrimination in Maryland. Although the Act of Toleration granting religious freedom to all Christians passed the Maryland Assembly in 1649, by the early 1700s, royal and Parliamentary acts by the Protestant monarchy of Great Britain disenfranchised and taxed Catholics in all the colonies, including Catholic-founded Maryland.

In fact, aside from a few Catholic elites, the first Irish in the port city of Baltimore were indentured servants. Wealthier Catholics from Ireland chose the countryside estates of western Maryland. Charles Carroll, an Irish Catholic, arrived in Maryland in 1715 and came to own close to 3,000 acres in the Maryland panhandle. A distinct Irish ethnic identity did not emerge during the eighteenth and early nineteenth century, as most servants left the city to farm land in the nearby countryside or assimilated into the larger, "American" culture.

However, there were enough Irish immigrants arriving in Baltimore by the turn of the nineteenth century that the Hibernian Society of Baltimore, an immigrant aid society, was founded in 1803. The Hibernians, led by John Oliver, founded the Hibernian Free School in 1818 to educate recently arrived Irish immigrants. The slow trickle of Irish immigrants into the United States and Baltimore increased to a deluge after the Potato Famine of the late 1840s. Many Irish arrived in Baltimore ports, but they soon left for cities farther west. Of those who stayed, most were laborers who competed with free blacks and urban slaves for bricklaying and railroad-building jobs.

A large percentage of these immigrants settled in the southwestern section of the city near Lemmon and Hollins Streets and went to work for the Baltimore and Ohio (B&O) Railroad. Others settled in outlying towns. With names like Dundalk and Dublin, some Baltimore suburbs reveal their Irish roots. Unlike many East Coast port cities, and despite its Catholic heritage, Baltimore did not become an Irish city in the way Boston or New York did. By 1870, the Irish made up only 6 percent of Baltimore's population, while 14 percent of Philadelphia's population was Irish. Baltimore's German population was a larger group and wielded more influence on the city's business and political life.

In the late nineteenth and early twentieth century, many Irish proved upwardly mobile through the cultivation of skilled trades and joining unions such as the Knights of Labor, and many others found more secure financial and social status with jobs as labor bosses and, later, politicians. After 1900, the stream of Irish immigrants began to fizzle out, except for small waves of immigrants in the 1950s and 1980s. Today little is left of the traditional Irish neighborhoods or way of life aside from a museum dedicated to Irish railroad workers, which today stands at 920 Lemmon Street, and an annual Irish festival.

Chuck McShane

See also: ANCIENT ORDER OF
 HIBERNIANS; KNIGHTS OF LABOR;
 MARYLAND

References

Jones, Maldwyn A. *American Immigration.* Chicago: The University of Chicago Press, 1992.
Olson, Sherry. *Baltimore: The Making of an American City.* Baltimore: The Johns Hopkins University Press, 1997.

BARRY, JOHN (1746–1803)

Born in Co. Wexford in 1746 to John and Catherine Barry, John Barry went to sea at an early age, as an apprentice on a merchant vessel in 1755. Applying himself to the naval profession, Barry immigrated to Philadelphia in 1761, where he became a

Portrait of John Barry, father of the United States Navy. (National Archives)

successful shipbuilder. By the time he was 21, Barry was made captain of a coastal schooner; by age 29, he was master of a transatlantic trader, the 200-ton *Black Prince.*

At the start of the American Revolution, Barry immediately offered his service to the patriots, and he was tasked with protecting American commerce along the mid-Atlantic coast. During these patrols, he became the first captain in the Continental navy to capture a British vessel when the *Lexington* captured the British tender *Edward* on April 7, 1776. By August, Barry had seized two more sloops, *Lady Susan* and *Betsey,* while preventing the capture of valuable caches of gunpowder and other war materiel. In recognition of his talents and contributions, Barry was promoted to captain in October 1776 and given command of the frigate *Effingham,* but a British blockade prevented the vessel from going to sea. Limited to engagements in the lower

Delaware, Barry nonetheless proved his gallantry in several ship actions, harassing British supply and communication lines, confiscating many articles for the use of the Continental Army, and earning the acclaim of George Washington. Shortly thereafter, Barry volunteered for service in the American army, taking part in the battles of Trenton and Princeton. During these engagements, he led an artillery battery composed of volunteer seamen; their main armaments were cannon dragged from the *Effingham.*

Barry returned to Philadelphia and assumed duties as the senior naval officer in February 1777. He took part in the ill-fated Penobscot Expedition of September 1778, where he was forced to run his vessel, the *Raleigh,* aground. A court-martial later acquitted him of any wrongdoing. Subsequent duties included ferrying American diplomats to Europe, combating privateers, and harassing British merchant vessels in the Atlantic. On March 23, 1780, a wounded Barry outmaneuvered and captured two British sloops, *Atalanta* and *Trespass,* in the eastern Atlantic. In 1782, Barry sailed to Havana, where he was responsible for convoying much needed specie to America; on his return voyage, Barry fought the last sea battle of the Revolutionary War when his *Alliance* engaged the British frigate *Sybill* in March 1783.

At the conclusion of hostilities, Barry continued to work in the shipping business, championing the cause of seamen who were excluded from the postwar benefits afforded to soldiers. Active in politics, Barry petitioned Congress on this issue, and lobbied effectively for a new federal system to replace the ineffective Articles of Confederation. In addition, Barry participated in the Pacific trade in the immediate post-Revolution years, trading with China and other parts of Asia as master of the brig *Asia.*

Congress created the United States Navy on March 27, 1794, and Barry accepted his appointment as senior captain on June 4, 1794. He also held a seagoing command, commanding the forty-four-gun frigate *United States,* from which he directed operations in the West Indies during the quasi-war with France. Under his leadership and direction, the fledgling United States Navy provided security for American commercial interests and displayed the emerging power of the United States. He further maintained the security of American commerce in the Caribbean during a period of revolutionary disturbances and increasing piracy, capturing the infamous French privateer *L'Amour de La Patrie* near Martinique on February 3, 1799.

Barry was twice married, but neither union produced children. On October 13, 1767, he married Mary Cleary in Philadelphia; she died in 1774; on July 7, 1777, he married Sarah Austin. The most distinguished Irish American of his day, Barry died on September 13, 1803, while making preparations to lead a naval squadron to the Mediterranean to fight Barbary corsairs. John Barry, the "Father of the United States Navy," was interred with full honors at St. Mary's Church in Philadelphia, and commemorated by statues in his native Wexford, his adopted city of Philadelphia, and the United States Naval Academy in Annapolis.

Tim Lynch

See also: AMERICAN WAR OF
　INDEPENDENCE

Reference

Clark, William Bell. *Gallant John Barry, 1745–1803: The Story of a Naval Hero of Two Wars.* New York: Macmillan, 1938.

BARRY, PHILIP (1896–1949)

Philip Barry was a playwright best known for works such as *Philadelphia Story* (1939), *Holiday* (1926), and *Tomorrow and Tomorrow* (1931), plays that continue to be offered in repertories. His greatest successes came with plays that represented, often through comedy, the ways the upper classes managed their affairs, both financial and emotional. Yet he was not satisfied with reproducing a formula that would guarantee success. He experimented with form and ideas in his work but was often frustrated by the poor reception of some of his more creative and serious dramas, such as *John* (1929) and *Here Come the Clowns* (1937).

An Irish American born in Rochester, New York, Barry was not part of the monied crowd, although his family was far from poor. Barry's father, James Corbett Barry, had come from Ireland as a young boy and, after learning the stonecutting trade as a teen, he became a successful monument builder. James married Mary Agnes Quinn and they had four children. When James died of a ruptured appendix Philip was raised by his mother and his eldest brother, Edmund.

Barry later went to Yale, despite relatively poor high school grades. There he joined the Yale Dramatic Association, and worked for the *Yale Daily News*. His studies were interrupted by World War I, but in 1919, after he returned to Yale, he soon won a Dramat competition with a new one-act play called *Autonomy*. "Meadow's End," a short story he had written while in London during the war, was later published in *Scribner's Magazine* and still later became a play, *In a Garden*. This and *War in Heaven*, a novel based on his play, *Here Come the Clowns*, represent the only prose fiction that Barry published after leaving Yale. Drama was clearly his forte.

His first recognized success was *The Jilts*, later renamed *You and I*, and this allowed him to marry the woman with whom he had fallen in love, Ellen Semple, on July 15, 1922. Barry and his wife had two sons, Philip S. Barry and Jonathan Peter Barry. They divided their time between homes in Manhattan and in Mount Kisco, New York, but they also had a villa in Cannes.

Much of Barry's drama reflects an anxiety about being outside accepted society. He believed wealth brings a kind of grace, as demonstrated in the great wit of his character's dialogue, but he also recognized that wealth brings its own set of problems. Though his more popular plays offer little that is very surprising in our view of the wealthy, some of his other plays explore far more mystical and spiritual issues. *Hotel Universe* (1930), for example, presents a group of people whose smug security and clever repartee is challenged by a man who mysteriously knows all about their secret unhappiness; all of the lives are revealed and then changed. Several of his plays, such as *In a Garden* (1924) and *The Youngest* (1929), are loosely based on his own life, exploring relationships and responsibilities that he himself had experienced in life.

Barry was working on his final play, *The Second Threshold*, when he died of a massive heart attack on December 3, 1949, in his Park Avenue apartment. Using revisions and notes, Robert E. Sherwood completed and produced the play in 1951. Barry was buried in the Catholic cemetery in East Hampton, and on his tombstone is a line from *Hotel Universe*: "All things are turned to a roundness. Wherever there is an end, from it springs the beginning."

Kathleen A. Heininge

References

Barry, Philip, and Elmer Rice. *Cock Robin.* New York: Samuel French, 1927 and 1929.

Gill, Brendan. "The Dark Advantage." In *States of Grace: Eight Plays by Philip Barry,* edited by Brendan Gill. New York and London: Harcourt Brace Jovanovich, 1975.

Hamm, Gerald. "The Drama of Philip Barry." PhD dissertation, University of Pennsylvania, 1948.

Roppolo, Joseph Patrick. *Philip Barry.* New York: Twayne Publishers, 1965.

BARTHOLOMEW, FREDDIE (1924–1992)

According to his obituary published in *The New York Times* on January 24, 1992, Freddie Bartholomew was born Frederick Llewellyn March in Dublin on March 28, 1924, and brought up in London. Estranged from his parents, he was reared by his grandparents and his aunt, Millicent Bartholomew, whose name he later adopted. He began appearing in London theater in 1930, and his first film, *Fascination,* was released the same year. In 1934 he caught the attention of eminent American film director George Cukor, who was on a casting visit to Britain. Cukor was impressed by Bartholomew and believed him perfect for the title role in his production of *David Copperfield.* Although Louis B. Mayer favored the established child actor Jackie Cooper for the role, Cukor and his producer, David O. Selznick, persuaded Mayer to cast Bartholomew instead. His sensitive portrayal of the eponymous character won him widespread acclaim and, as a result, Selznick focused his attention on making him a star.

Bartholomew's gentility lent him a certain otherworldly quality, which determined the roles that he was given. In 1935 Selznick cast him as Anna's son in *Anna Karenina,* costarring him with Greta Garbo, who was then MGM's most illustrious star. Following a loan out to Twentieth Century for *Professional Soldier* (1936), Selznick gave him the title role in his prestigious production of *Little Lord Fauntleroy,* based on Frances Hodgson Burnett's 1886 novel. During the next two years Bartholomew was usually showcased in roles that emphasized his refinement and sensitivity, although he was cast against type as a spoilt brat in *Captains Courageous,* which also starred Spencer Tracy. In 1938 he played the lead in a film adaptation of Robert Louis Stevenson's *Kidnapped* and played his first teenage role opposite Judy Garland in *Listen Darling.* By the late 1930s, Bartholomew was one of the highest-paid child stars in America—second only to Shirley Temple—but his unstable family background resurfaced in 1937 when his mother initiated a legal challenge against his guardian aunt over his substantial earnings. The legal wrangling that ensued considerably reduced the fortune he had made at MGM.

As so often happens with child actors, as Bartholomew grew up his popularity began to decline. Although he still acted in such major films as *The Spirit of Culver, The Swiss Family Robinson,* and *Tom Brown's Schooldays,* he found himself eclipsed by other child stars such as Judy Garland and Mickey Rooney, both of whom were deemed more "American" by wartime audiences. His decline is evidenced by his fourth billing in 1942's *A Yank At Eton.* Having served in the U.S. Air Force, he returned to Hollywood but could only find roles in minor films, such as *Sepia Cinderella* (1947) and *St. Benny the Dip* (1951). Like many Hollywood actors in the postwar period, he branched into television in 1949, initially hosting a movie show, before becoming a director of television shows (mostly soap operas) and commercials in the 1950s. He followed his advertising career from television to New York, where he became a successful executive. Often bitter about the way in which Hollywood had used and discarded him, Bartholomew died of emphysema on January 23, 1992 in Sarasota, Florida. He was survived by his third wife, Elizabeth.

Gwenda Young

See also: GARLAND, Judy

References

Katz, Ephraim. *The Film Encyclopedia.* New York: Perigee Books, 1979.

Shipman, David. *The Great Movie Stars: The Golden Years.* New York: Da Capo, 1986.

BASEBALL

Considered the great American pastime, baseball owes much to the influence of immigrant populations, particularly the Irish, for its development in the United States. Irish-American baseball players innovated the way the game was played and managed, how leagues were run, and how equipment was developed. Indeed, the popular view during the late nineteenth century was that the Irish were born to the game, in a manner similar to how African Americans dominated professional basketball a century later. Though Irish-American baseball players competed at the major league level in the 1870s, it was in the 1880s and 1890s that they emerged as the game's biggest stars. Sources differ on the percentage of major leaguers who were of Irish descent during the 1880s, but it was at least 33 percent and possibly more than 40 percent; nearly forty players were born in Ireland. The St. Louis Browns of the American Association (AA) were a largely Irish-American team, yet enjoyed strong support among the city's German-American population. The rosters of nearly all major and local minor league teams contained several Irish surnames, with players born in northeastern cities such as Boston, Philadelphia, and towns throughout New England helping encourage young Irish boys in strongly immigrant towns become fans and players.

As the game evolved into a professional sport in the latter three decades of the century, Irish Americans became star players and even national celebrities. Moreover, many of the rough stereotypical attributes often ascribed to Irish Americans were manifested in many stars of the day and perpetuated the negative image. Reports of Irish ballplayers' drunken, unruly behavior made it difficult for teams to book rooms at the best hotels. The Irish influence from the early years of professional baseball can still be seen in the song "Take Me Out To The Ballgame," which features an Irish woman who roots for the home team, and Earnest Thayer's poem "Casey At The Bat," in which the Mudville Nine, including "Flynn" and "Jimmy Blake" lose when "Mighty Casey" strikes out.

In the 1887 season, when eleven players achieved batting averages of .400 or better, St. Louis's James "Tip" O'Neill led the AA with a .435 average. That season, averages were high partly because walks were recorded as hits as well as at bats (neither of which is true today), yet his achievements in 1887 were phenomenal, as he led the league in hits, doubles, triples, home runs, runs scored, slugging average, and batting average. His nickname arose from his skill at fouling off pitches to get a pitcher to walk him, and O'Neill's fame led many adoring Irish-American fans to name their sons after him.

During the National League's (NL) first two seasons (1876–1877), James Devlin pitched every inning of his team's games. Also in 1877, Terry Larkin and Irish-born Tommy Bond pitched every inning of their teams' games. Devlin never played major league baseball after 1877, however, after allegedly losing games for gamblers.

Frequently called baseball's first superstar, Michael "King" Kelly was one of the first $10,000 players. Baseball fans (then known as "cranks") often cheered "Slide, Kelly, slide!" when he ran the bases, which was then turned into a song. An Irish Catholic, Kelly attracted Irish fans to the game, which had seen several English-descended stars in its pre-NL days. Enshrined in baseball's Hall of Fame, Kelly also innovated the game's rules, sometimes by taking advantage of their lack of detail. Though four umpires working a game are the norm today, there were rarely more than two in Kelly's era. When an umpire's attention was elsewhere, Kelly was known to cut across the infield while running the bases. Kelly also receives credit for pioneering the injury decoy before stealing a base. When rules were changed to allow substitutions during the game, initially players were allowed to announce themselves. Sitting on the bench late in a game, Kelly reportedly once caught a foul ball when he announced himself while the ball was in flight.

Born in Cork, Tony Mullane played for thirteen seasons, during which he won 285 games, ending his career in 1894. Baseball's most notable ambidextrous pitcher, Mullane pitched without a glove, won more than thirty games for five consecutive seasons (1882–1887; he was declared ineligible for the 1885 season), and

topped twenty wins another three times. Mullane's good looks and popularity with female fans led to the institution of "ladies' day" on Mondays when he pitched. A prime example of the labor battles during the period of baseball history, Mullane held out from playing in 1892 and was held in breach of contract in 1885. Arguably baseball's best Irish-born player, Mullane is not in the Hall of Fame. Had he played in 1885, during his run of thirty-win seasons, he likely would have topped 300 for his career—a milestone that virtually guarantees entry into the Hall of Fame. Mullane also had a reputation as an irascible teammate and a gambler. He also revealed his racism when he admitted his racially motivated dislike of baseball's first African-American major league ballplayer, Moses "Fleet" Walker, his catcher. Mullane purposely crossed Walker's signals, and the catcher went through the season not knowing what the pitcher would throw.

Jimmy Collins revolutionized play at third base because he was unfamiliar with the traditions of the game, which had maintained that the shortstop fielded all grounders on the left side of the infield, leaving teams susceptible to bunts. An outfielder when he joined Louisville of the NL in 1895, Collins was moved to third and fielded the bunts barehanded. Soon all third basemen copied Collins. Sold to the Boston NL club, Collins became a fan favorite. When Collins signed with the new American League (AL) team in Boston in 1901, many NL fans changed their allegiance, following Collins. Collins also led Boston to victory in the first World Series in 1903.

Though more than 100 players had hit 300 home runs by the end of the 2004 season, a century earlier the record stood at

136, held by Roger Connor for nearly twenty-five years. In an era when some teams did not hit ten home runs all season, Connor hit more than ten seven times. Elected to the Hall of Fame in 1976, Connor also hit 233 triples, which remain among the most ever hit by one player.

Credited with the NL's first official hit, "Orator" Jim O'Rourke played for several championship teams during a career that touched four decades. The New York Giants manager, John McGraw, brought him out of retirement to catch a major league game when he was fifty-two years old.

Short in stature, five-foot-seven-inch Hugh Duffy reached great heights, achieving a .440 batting average in 1894, which has never been matched. That season he also accomplished baseball's first Triple Crown, leading the league in home runs, runs batted in, and batting average. Playing beside fellow Hall of Famer Tommy McCarthy in the Boston Beaneaters outfield, Duffy was one of the "Heavenly Twins" that led the team to championships. During the 1890s, Duffy played the most games, hit the most home runs, and drove in the most runs of all major leaguers. McCarthy's Hall of Fame credentials have more to do with his defensive abilities and innovation of outfield play than his offense, yet he has been credited with perfecting, if not inventing, the hit-and-run play, in which a runner goes into motion off first base as the pitch is delivered, in order to reach third base on a hit. Defensively McCarthy was known for freezing runners in the base paths, trapping the ball and getting either a force-out or a double play; offensively, as a runner, he passed signals to batters.

Two of baseball's greatest managers, and the winners of the most games in their leagues, were Irish Americans. John McGraw

Portrait of Hugh Duffy (1866–1954), Hall of Fame outfielder around the turn of the century for a number of National League baseball teams. This photograph was taken in 1899, when Duffy was captain of the Boston Braves. (Corbis)

stood at the center of the creation of the AL, though he is best known today as the Hall of Fame manager of the New York Giants of the NL. As a third baseman playing with the Baltimore Orioles in the NL, McGraw is among those credited with developing the suicide squeeze play, where a runner on third base scores on a batter's bunt. During thirty-one years as the Giants' manager, McGraw's teams won ten pennants, three World Series, and 2,840 victories—second only to Connie Mack. Before joining the Giants, however, McGraw was best known as one of the notorious Baltimore Orioles, whose aggressive, innovative play in the 1890s became legendary. McGraw spurned a chance to manage the Cincinnati Reds, accepting an offer from Byron "Ban" Johnson's new AL, to manage a resurrected Orioles franchise. In developing the league, McGraw and Mack, who took over the Philadelphia Athletics franchise, and other managers helped sell players on the idea of jumping to the new league. Within two seasons, however, McGraw learned of Johnson's intentions to move the Baltimore team to New York (where they would later be known as the Yankees), along with rumors of his being frozen out of the move. McGraw helped maneuver his own departure from the Baltimore club, becoming manager of the Giants and obtaining several of the star players from Baltimore, including pitcher "Iron" Joe McGinnity.

Born Cornelius McGillicuddy, Connie Mack ran the Philadelphia Athletics for half a century, winning (and losing) more games than any other manager. Mack also owned the club, touting a famous "$100,000 infield" of players. Later, he ran the team into financial ruin, trading away many of his early stars. His A's teams won or appeared in the World Series in five of the first twelve series. After losing the 1914 World Series, Mack sold many of his stars and saw his clubs languish at or near the bottom of the AL for the next decade, not winning a league championship again until 1929. The A's won the World Series that year and in 1930, losing the World Series in 1931. Mack never appeared in another World Series.

In the 1890s, the notorious Orioles were managed by Ned Hanlon, whose team of mainly Irish Americans innovated through aggressive play, creating the "Baltimore chop," in which batters perfected a high bouncing hit leaving fielders to wait for the ball to land while the runner reached first base, and encouraging his

players to refine or develop stratagems such as the hit-and-run and the suicide squeeze.

Ed Delahanty's star shone bright enough to earn him entry to the Hall of Fame in 1945. The oldest of five brothers who played major league baseball, "Big Ed" died in 1903, falling over Niagara Falls under mysterious circumstances. Whether he was robbed and pushed or fell due to intoxication remains a mystery more than a century later. Delahanty's career included a four–home run game (1896), two six-hit games, and the batting average title in 1899. Delahanty has received credit for ordering the first intentional walk, in which four pitches are purposely thrown outside the strike zone to advance the batter to first base. N.Y. Giant Tom O'Brien's lone claim to baseball fame is that he received that intentional pass, which led to a double play.

Roger Bresnahan has been erroneously credited with inventing the face mask, which was in use in the minor leagues long before Bresnahan played, though he often faced ridicule for using it when he played. He is likely to have developed shin guards, however, which evolved from the guards used in cricket, and was among the first to use batting helmets more than a half century before they became common. Known as "Duke of Tralee," Bresnahan was proud of his Irish heritage and known to slip into a brogue when the moment struck him; he was born and raised in Toledo, Ohio.

Though baseball's rosters became more diverse in the early decades of the twentieth century, Irish Americans continued to succeed and hold places of power within the game. John K. Tener served as NL president from 1914 to 1918. Born in Ireland, Tener's major league pitching career did not amount to much; two seasons on Chicago's NL team and one season in the ill-fated Player's League (PL) franchise in Pittsburgh. Tener, who worked as an accountant in the off-season, became involved in the creation of baseball's first attempt at a union, the Brotherhood of Professional Players, which led to the PL. In addition to pitching for Pittsburgh, Tener served as league secretary. The league folded, and his baseball career ended. His experience, however, led to a political career, including a term in Congress in 1908 and a four-year term as governor of Pennsylvania. While in Congress, he started an annual Congressional baseball game between Republicans and Democrats on Capitol Hill. Tener's tenure as NL president occurred amid the emergence of the Federal League, which challenged the other two leagues by signing away star players. Tener helped drive the new league out of business.

Joe Cronin achieved success at nearly every level of the game. A star player in the 1920s, player-manager in the 1930s (including leading the Washington Senators to their last AL championship in 1933), a manager in the 1940s, general manager in the 1940s and 1950s, and AL president during the 1950s and 1960s, Cronin was voted into the Hall of Fame in 1956. He oversaw two expansions of the AL, from eight teams to ten in 1961 and then two more teams in 1969. He objected to the players' labor movement toward economic fairness within its system and fired two umpires in 1969 for incompetence, though they claimed it was because they tried to form an umpires' union.

Cronin's tenure was over by the mid-1970s, when baseball's era of owners controlling player movement came to an end. Dave McNally was among the first players to be declared a free agent when the term of his contract expired, bringing about an end to the reserve clause, which had been a contentious part of baseball since the days of "King" Kelly.

Matthew Sinclair

See also: BASEBALL MANAGERS, IRISH-AMERICAN; HANLON, Ned; MACK, Connie; McCARTHY, Joseph Vincent; McGRAW, John

References

Alexander, Charles C. *Our Game: An American Baseball History*. New York: Henry Holt & Co., 1991.

Ginsburg, Daniel E. *The Fix Is In: A History of Baseball Gambling and Game-Fixing Scandals*. Jefferson, NC: McFarland & Co., 1995.

Helyar, John. *Lords of the Realm*. New York: Villard Books, 1994.

Levine, Peter, ed. *Baseball History*. Westport, CT: Meckler Books, 1989.

Seymour, Harold. *Baseball: The People's Game*. Oxford: Oxford University Press, 1990.

Solomon, Burt. *Where They Ain't: The Fabled Life and Untimely Death of the Original Baltimore Orioles, the Team That Gave Birth To Modern Baseball*. New York: Free Press, 1999.

Sowell, Mike. *The Mysterious Death of Hall of Famer Big Ed Delahanty*. New York: Macmillan, 1992

Wolff, Rick, et al. *The Baseball Encyclopedia*. New York: Macmillan, 1993.

BASEBALL MANAGERS, IRISH-AMERICAN

Though Irish Americans were professional baseball's first star players, their influence was keenly felt emanating from the dugouts. From Ned Hanlon in the 1890s to his former players John McGraw and Connie Mack in the first half of the twentieth century, Irish Americans have been among the most successful and innovative managers the game has known.

Stemming from Hanlon, today's successful managers can be traced through

McGraw and Miller Huggins like a family tree. For example, 1950s New York Yankees dynasty leader Casey Stengel played for McGraw, but he was also influenced by managers Bill Dahlen and Wilbert Robinson, who both played for Hanlon. Huggins, who played for Hanlon's Joe Kelley, mentored Leo Durocher, whose influence upon Bill Rigney and Earl Weaver is still felt in the Major Leagues. Through Stengel, Hanlon's "great-grandsons" and "great-great-grandsons" include Billy Martin and Lou Piniella. Even successful managers of the 1990s, such as Joe Torre and Tony LaRussa, can trace their managerial influences back to Hanlon.

Best known for leading the Baltimore Orioles in the 1890s, Hanlon led his teams to five National League (NL) pennants from 1894 to 1901, and saw several of his players become successful managers. He directly assisted in the managerial development of McGraw, Hughie Jennings, Wilbert Robinson, and dozens of other successful managers. A Hanlon club was aggressive, bunting, running, and hitting to spots by design. While he may not have invented the plays, his teams perfected the hit-and-run and the sacrifice bunt; the Baltimore chop, where a batter purposely bounces the ball high enough so he can reach first base before a play is made, was developed by his Orioles. By 1910, most managers in both the American League (AL) and NL were men who had played for Hanlon during the 1890s.

Taking what they learned from Hanlon, Mack and McGraw are largely responsible for the manager's role as we know it today. McGraw expanded upon Hanlon's aggressive style of "baseball as she is played," pressuring his opponents into making mistakes and exhibiting personal discipline (at least on the field), physical conditioning, speed, and aggressiveness. To McGraw, the manager had absolute authority, and that led to success. His Giants won the second modern World Series in 1905. In his twenty-nine years with the Giants, his teams won three World Series and ten NL pennants and were either first or second twenty-one times. John McGraw retired early in the 1932 season due to ill health. He managed the NL the next year in the inaugural All Star Game, against Connie Mack, who was still managing the Philadelphia Athletics.

The antithesis of McGraw, Mack managed for more than fifty years with a grandfatherly calm and an analytical style for assessing talent and positioning players, which earned his players' respect. Mack is best known for his longevity and for wearing street clothes (which precluded him by rule from entering the field), a throwback to the nineteenth century, but his Philadelphia Athletics won five World Series and four other AL championships during his half-century tenure. Mack owned the team and, during the nation's economic doldrums, sold off star players he'd scouted and developed to manage the team's finances. The "Tall Tactician" may have outlasted his managerial effectiveness, as his teams never finished higher than fourth place during his final seventeen years. Mack, who caught for Hanlon's Pittsburgh club in the 1880s, led the A's for the team's first fifty years. Neither his record 3,731 wins nor his 3,948 losses will likely ever be matched. He has nearly 1,000 more victories than McGraw, who is second overall.

While McGraw's descendants can still be traced to current managers, Mack's lineage has virtually died out. One of Mack's most notable successors was Joe McCarthy, the first manager to take teams from the NL and the AL to the World Series. His Chicago Cubs lost the 1929 series to Mack's A's. "Marse Joe" joined the Yankees in 1931, taking them to a series victory in 1932 before three consecutive second-place finishes. His teams then won four consecutive World Series championships and six in eight years. McCarthy's legacy as an innovator is not as well publicized as that of his predecessors, but he has been credited with making distinct the line between starting pitchers and relievers. Only McGraw disciple Casey Stengel equaled McCarthy's seven championships. McCarthy's .614 winning percentage (2,126–1,335 record) is the highest among all managers of at least 1,000 games. However, few of McCarthy's players went on to become successful managers themselves.

Matthew Sinclair

See also: BASEBALL; HANLON, Ned; MACK, Connie; McCARTHY, Joe McGRAW, John

References

Alexander, Charles C. *Our Game: An American Baseball History.* New York: Henry Holt and Co., 1991.

James, Bill. *Bill James' Guide to Baseball Managers.* New York: Scribner, 1997.

Koppett, Leonard. *The Man in the Dugout.* New York: Random House, 1994.

Wolff, Rick, et al. *The Baseball Encyclopedia.* New York: Macmillan, 1993.

BAXTER, JOSÉ LUIS "JOE" (1940–1973)

José Luis "Joe" Baxter was born on May 24, 1940, at El Moro stud farm in Marcos Paz (Buenos Aires province of Argentina), the son of Joseph Baxter (1888–1952) and his wife María Luisa, née Denaro (1910–1996); they also had a daughter, Mary, born in 1947. A professional racehorse trainer,

Joseph Baxter was born in London and immigrated to Argentina, probably with his Irish-born father Joseph Baxter, who found employment as a cattle rancher in Buenos Aires. The family had an Anglo-Irish protestant background.

Joe Baxter learned English as his first language, and was a skilled horse rider at an early age. He was sent to elementary school in the English School of Córdoba, where he used to receive visits from his family every two weeks. At ten, Baxter had an accident in the school and broke his elbow. For this reason, he would not be able to move his right arm correctly. One of those physical types inclined to be rather corpulent, Joe was nicknamed *el Gordo*.

When Joe Baxter's father Joseph died in 1952 the family relocated to Buenos Aires and lived in the district of Villa Urquiza (Alvarez Thomas Avenue). Mrs. Baxter had to work as a children's nurse to supplement the family's income. Joe was sent to another English School in Lomas de Zamora, where he received a tuition grant and assisted younger pupils. Baxter was a good student and became a keen reader of adventure novels, history, and poetry. At fifteen, Baxter entered Instituto Martínez school of Buenos Aires, which was a mediocre secondary school. Joe had plenty of time to hang around the political debate meetings at Café Paulista together with pupils of Salvador and San Agustín Catholic schools. He was fascinated by their nationalist discourse and became an enthusiastic pro-Nazi and anti-Semitic activist. He rejected the Argentine bourgeois ideology that supported the fall of Juan Manuel de Rosas in 1852, and was against the conventional political practises.

After the Soviet occupation of Hungary in November 1956, Baxter joined the

Nationalist Union of Secondary Students (UNES), a high-school student branch of the right-wing Catholic organization Tacuara, led by Alberto Ezcurra Uriburu (1937–1993). Joe Baxter was an enthusiastic supporter of the weekly nationalist paper *Azul y Blanco*. Two years later, he was appointed Tacuara's secretary-general. At the same time, he was studying in the School of Law and, thanks to his English skills, was working as international operator in the state-owned telephone company. His political activities, on top of the frequent meetings, included violent raids against the URSS consulate, synagogues, and other Jewish institutions. In spite of the fact that Tacuara was inspired by Catholic priests and modeled after Primo de Rivera's Falange in Spain, Joe Baxter was distrustful of any religious ideology. He described himself as a nationalist and anti-imperialist. An admirer of the poet Ezra Pound, in 1959 Baxter published the poem "Nüremberg" in the publication *Tacuara*. He supported a strong militarization of the movement. After the demonstrations during President Dwight Eisenhower's visit to Argentina in February 1962, Joe Baxter was imprisoned, together with other nationalist activists. In prison he met Guillermo Patricio Kelly (1922–2005), with whom he disagreed ideologically, and José Luis Nell (1941–1974), who would be his companion in later years.

When the Cuban president Osvaldo Dorticós visited Argentina in 1962, Joe Baxter was captivated with Castro's revolution and its anti-imperialist challenge to the United States. Owing to the creation by Father Julio Menvielle of Guardia Restauradora—a Catholic segment within Tacuara—the organization split and Baxter and others set up Tacuara Revolutionary Nationalist Movement (MNRT). Thus began Joe Baxter's metamorphosis from fascism to Marxism, a transformation that would be shared by several members of his generation. In his view, the Peronist labor structure was necessary to attain the national revolution. As an illustration of his ambiguous and complex ideological development, when policemen raided his house in Villa Urquiza, they were bewildered by portraits of Hitler, Mussolini, and Castro decorating his bedroom.

By 1963 Joe Baxter was a full-time political activist. He admired Algeria's nationalist revolution and rejected anti-Semitism. At the same time, his group received arms from Peronist army officers and was planning radical operations to finance their activities, which included among others a planned invasion of the Falkland/Malvinas Islands. Although he did not play a direct role (but was implicitly concerned) in the raid on the bank labor union's hospital Policlínico Bancario on August 29, 1963—the first urban guerrilla operation in Argentina—Joe Baxter was responsible for laundering part of the booty in Brazil in 1964.

That year was the start of Baxter's international career. From Brazil he traveled to Madrid and met Juan Domingo Perón at his house. Perón introduced him to Héctor Villalón, a businessman with good connections in Cuba, China, and Egypt. Baxter then moved to Algeria and Egypt and worked with several revolutionaries. To avoid the Argentine authorities, he settled for some time in Uruguay and transformed the Tupamaros revolutionary group into an urban guerrilla organization. In 1965, he received training in northern Vietnam. During a sudden attack he ignored the withdrawal order and fired on the enemy, being rewarded for this action. Baxter also traveled to China to receive military and ideological training.

In 1966 Joe Baxter entered Argentina clandestinely, and the following year went to Cuba thanks to his connection with the Tupamaros organization. In Havana he married Ruth Arrieta, daughter of a Bolivian nationalist officer. Joe Baxter was in Paris during the Fourth International of 1968, where he represented the Trotskyist groups. In these circumstances Baxter met Rubén P. Bonnet, Luis Pujals, and Mario R. Santucho, who would be founding members of the Peoples Revolutionary Army (ERP), a Trotskyist terrorist organization in Argentina. After the hijacking of Fiat Argentina's chief executive Oberdan Sallustro that year, Baxter broke with ERP and created other radical groups like Leninist Trend and Red Fraction. By the early 1970s he was living in Chile with his wife and daughter Mariana, who was born in 1968 in Cuba.

Political activist and revolutionary Joe Baxter died on July 11, 1973, when the Boeing 707 of Varig Airlines, en route to Rio de Janeiro, crashed while attempting an emergency landing near Paris Orly airport, killing 123 passengers. He was traveling on a false passport and carried with him $40,000, presumably to support the fighting of the Sandinista National Liberation Front (FSLN) of Nicaragua. Joe Baxter was buried beside his father and mother at the British cemetery of Chacarita in Buenos Aires. The stone that marks his grave carries the inscription *El no quiso nada para sí* (he wanted nothing for himself).

Edmundo Murray

See also: ARGENTINA;
FALKLAND/MALVINAS ISLANDS

References

Bardini, Roberto, *Tacuara: la Pólvora y la Sangre.* Mexico: Océano, 2002).

Bardini, Roberto, *A 30 Años de la Muerte de Joe Baxter. Una Rosa Roja en un Casquillo de Obús Chino Disparado en Viet Nam. Entrevista a Alberto Pérez Iriarte.* www.rodelu.net (accessed October 2, 2005).

García, Karina. "Tacuara y el Asalto al Policlínico Bancario." *Todo es Historia* (Buenos Aires) 373 (August 1998).

Gutman, Daniel, *Tacuara: Historia de la Primera Guerrilla Urbana Aargentina.* Buenos Aires: Vergara, 2003.

Kremer, Arnold, *Hombres y Mujeres del PRT-ERP: La Pasión militante.* Buenos Aires: Contrapunto, 1990.

Navarro Gerassi, Marisa, *Los Nacionalistas.* Buenos Aires: Alvarez, 1968.

BEACH, AMY MARCY (1867–1944)

Amy Marcy Cheney was the first significant American woman composer. Born in Henniker, New Hampshire, on September 5, 1867, she moved with her family to Chelsea, Massachusetts, in 1874 and to Boston in 1875. Beach displayed a remarkable musical talent from an early age, first appearing in public when she was seven years old. In 1883 she made her debut as a pianist in Boston. In 1885, she married Dr. Henry Harris Aubrey Beach. Soon after, on her husband's advice, she changed to composition, but she received little formal training. Amy Beach toured in Europe from 1911 to 1914, finally settling in Hillsborough, New Hampshire in 1916. She was an energetic promoter of her own works and of other female American composers, becoming the cofounder and first president of the Society of American Women Composers in 1925.

Amy Beach mainly wrote art songs and piano music, but it was with her *Mass in E flat* op. 5 (1890) and *Gaelic Symphony* op. 32

(1897) that she won acceptance and international success. In seeking an American style in art music she occasionally referred to Irish traditional music, which she considered the most traditional music in America. In works like the *Gaelic Symphony* and piano pieces like *The Fair Hills of Eire* op. 91 (1922) and the *Suite for two Pianos Founded upon Old Irish Melodies* op. 104 (1924) she used a number of Irish traditional melodies as thematic material, thereby expressing her conviction that American folk music was mainly derived from the Irish, a belief gained without any direct family connection to Ireland.

Axel Klein

See also: MUSIC IN AMERICA, IRISH

References
Block, Adrienne Fried. *Amy Beach, Passionate Victorian: An American Composer's Life and Work.* New York: Oxford University Press, 1998.
Jenkins, Walter S. *The Remarkable Mrs. Beach: American Composer.* Warren, MI: Harmonie Park Press, 1994.

BEACH, SYLVIA (1887–1962)

The daughter of a Presbyterian minister, Sylvia Beach (she was born Nancy, but preferred to be called Sylvia) spent much of her youth in Bridgeton, New Jersey. Youthful illness and impatience with tedious study left her erratically educated, despite her undoubted intellectual gifts. In 1902 she accompanied her father when he assumed a three-year mission to Paris, and this period of residence instilled in her a lifelong passion for France and French culture.

A natural bohemianism of temperament led her to return to Paris in 1916, after working as a nurse during World War I. In November 1919 she decided to open a bookshop and lending library. Located on the Rue de l'Odeon, Shakespeare and Company soon became the focus of Anglophonic literary life in Paris. Regular visitors included Ezra Pound, Ernest Hemingway, F. Scott Fitzgerald, and most importantly, James Joyce.

Despite the financial difficulties of her endeavor, Beach was able to keep the bookstore open until the Nazi occupation of Paris. She hid the store's contents during the war, but decided against reopening it in the postwar years. Beach spent the remainder of her life in active retirement, occasionally taking part in public celebrations of her literary friends. She died in Paris in 1962. Her memoirs, *Shakespeare and Company,* contain engaging and intimate portraits of numerous great writers who frequented her shop; the somewhat uncritical portraits conform to her conviction that artists' personal idiosyncrasies should not misbalance a proper recognition of their achievements.

Sylvia Beach was probably James Joyce's most important American benefactor. She befriended him, encouraged him, frequently advanced him needed money, and generously demonstrated her unstinting belief in the value and significance of his work. When Joyce despaired of *Ulysses* ever being published, she offered to publish it herself, under the Shakespeare & Co. colophon. This offer, as well as her extraordinary patience in permitting Joyce time for rewriting and revision, ensured that he was able to publish his work substantially as he wished it to appear. Beach also published his 1927 verse collection, *Pomes Penyeach,* and a series of essays in defense of his draft chapters that became *Finnegans Wake, Our Exagmination Round his Factification for Incamination of Work in Progress* (1929).

Although Joyce's incessant personal demands and borrowing of money caused friction between them, he remained grateful to Beach for her kindness and assistance, and she always regarded him as the most important writer of his era.

Andrew Goodspeed

See also: JOYCE, James Augustine Aloysius

References

Beach, Sylvia. *Shakespeare and Company.* New York: Harcourt & Brace, 1959.

Ellmann, Richard. *James Joyce.* Rev. ed. Oxford: Oxford University Press, 1982.

Fitch, Noel Riley. *Sylvia Beach and the Lost Generation.* New York: W. W. Norton, 1983.

Hemingway, Ernest. *A Moveable Feast.* New York: Scribners, 1964.

Monnier, Adrienne. *The Very Rich Hours of Adrienne Monnier.* New York: Scribners, 1976.

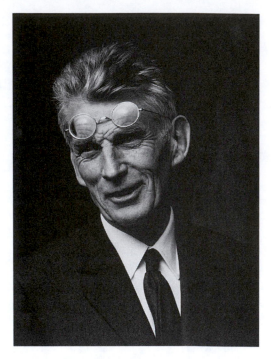

Portrait of Irish writer, Samuel Beckett. (Corbis)

BECKETT, SAMUEL (1906–1989)

Samuel Beckett achieved worldwide fame in 1953 with his play *Waiting for Godot.* He was awarded the Nobel Prize for Literature in 1969 and was a hugely influential figure in twentieth-century drama. Also a major novelist, Beckett's trilogy of novels, *Molloy, Malone Dies,* and *The Unnamable,* is his most notable achievement in prose. Born in Ireland into an affluent, Protestant family, he was educated at Trinity College Dublin where he studied modern languages. A brilliant linguist, he would write many of his major works in French and had excellent Italian and German as well as adequate Spanish and Latin. After his graduation in 1927, he went to live in Paris for the first time, where he met Joyce and other writers and artists in the prewar avant-garde. He returned to Dublin in 1930 and took up a lecturing position in French at Trinity College Dublin. Academic life and the provincial philistinism of Dublin in the 1930s exasperated Beckett, and he resigned his position a year later. In poor health, he spent 1934–1935 in London undergoing psychoanalysis with W. R. Bion (1897–1979) at the Tavistock Clinic, and he also wrote his first novel, *Murphy.* After a year spent in Germany pursuing his deep interest in the visual arts, Beckett moved permanently to Paris in 1937. He would stay in France even during the war years (when he narrowly evaded arrest for his involvement in the French resistance), and it was in France that he gained recognition in the postwar years.

Beckett was very much a European writer, involved as he was in the international trends of modernism. His work owes as much to continental writers as to those in the Anglo-American tradition, although he was not especially familiar with the literature of the Americas. He would only visit the United States once, in 1964, when he stayed for nearly a month in New York to work on his film project. Beckett had written his *Film* at the suggestion of his American publisher Barney Rosset who, with Alan Schneider (a long-standing friend of Beckett and director of his plays in America) had lured the reclusive author across the Atlantic for the filming. With Alan Schneider directing and Buster Keaton as the main protagonist, they shot Beckett's *Film* in the sweltering heat of New York in July. Beckett was actively involved on the set, enjoying this foray into a new medium. According to one of Beckett's biographers, Deirdre Bair, "Beckett was terrified of the city at first" (Bair, 572) but he soon found things to enjoy in Greenwich Village, visiting, for example, Cherry Lane Theatre, where many of his plays had first been performed in the United States under Alan Schneider's direction. He was also able to see old friends, such as American novelist Kay Boyle and Irish poet and publisher George Reavey. However, Beckett's overall impression of New York was negative and on leaving he confessed to his host, Barney Rosset, "This is somehow not the right country for me . . . the people are too strange" (cited in Knowlson, 525).

It is ironic, therefore, that much of the critical exegesis of Beckett's work has come from America. Important Beckett critics such as Stanley Gontarski and Ruby Cohn were part of the first wave of Beckett criticism, and many Beckett manuscripts have found their way to American universities, with major holdings at the Harry Ransom Research Center, Austin, Texas, and at Dartmouth College. Much important Beckett criticism continues to come from the United States.

Beckett's only link with the Latin American world came entirely by chance in 1949. He had applied to UNESCO (the United Nations Educational, Scientific, and Cultural Organization) for translation work to supplement his meager post-war income and was commissioned to translate an anthology of Mexican poetry edited by Octavio Paz. This was not published until 1958, by which time Beckett's reputation (and financial security) had been made. Beckett regarded these particular translations as perfunctory and amounting to little more than hack work even though he was, as is universally recognized, a masterful translator of his own and other people's work.

Benjamin Keatinge

See also: BOYLE, Kathleen; COFFEY, Brian; THEATER AND DRAMA, IRISH AMERICAN

References
Bair, Deirdre. *Samuel Beckett: A Biography*. London: Jonathan Cape, 1978.
Beckett, Samuel. *The Complete Dramatic Works*. London: Faber and Faber, 1986.
Beckett, Samuel. *Three Novels: Molloy, Malone Dies, The Unnamable*. London: John Calder, 1959.
Harmon, Maurice, ed. *No Author Better Served: The Correspondence of Samuel Beckett and Alan Schneider*. Cambridge, MA; London: Harvard University Press, 1998.
Knowlson, James. *Damned to Fame: The Life of Samuel Beckett*. London: Bloomsbury, 1996.

BELIZE

Belize, which was formerly British Honduras, a colony on the Caribbean coast of Central America, is geographically a part of Central America, although administratively it is usually regarded as a Caribbean country. The area that now forms Belize had been popular with British pirates from the early seventeenth century as its coastline was protected by reefs. By the 1670s, many pirates had moved into logging, and a sizable timber industry developed, especially of logwood, which was used for a dye important for the European wool industry. With a population that was British by heritage and/or sympathy, it was not long before a British administrator was appointed, under the control of the governor of Jamaica. The defeat of a Spanish fleet in 1798 off St. George's Caye ensured that the region would become British, which was confirmed in 1862 when the colony of British Honduras was formally established.

Some of the colonial officials serving in British Honduras were Irish. Indeed, the superintendent from 1787 until 1790 was Edward Marcus Despard (1751–1803), born in Queen's County, Ireland, the youngest of six brothers, all except one of whom joined the British Army. Despard was posted to Jamaica, where he left the 50th Regiment to work as an engineer under Captain (later Admiral) Horatio Nelson. He was initially put in charge of the offshore islands, before he was appointed to run British Honduras. After his return to London he was involved in a conspiracy to kill the king of England, and seize the Tower of London and the Bank of England. Despite a character reference by Nelson at his trial, Despard was sentenced to death and executed.

In 1862, taking advantage of the American Civil War and the United States being unable to enforce the Monroe Doctrine, the colony of British Honduras was officially proclaimed. Irish-born Spaniard Juan Galindo had campaigned against British sovereignty some 25 years earlier, but his arguments had not been followed up by the Spanish. With British Honduras

as a colony, the superintendent for the previous five years, Frederick Seymour (1820–1869), became the first governor. Seymour, born in Belfast, was the fourth and youngest son of Henry Augustus Seymour and Margaret (née Williams)— Henry being the illegitimate son of the second Marquis of Hertford. Frederick Seymour had been assistant colonial secretary of Van Diemen's Land (Tasmania), and when his position was abolished, he became magistrate of Antigua in 1848 and president of Nevis five years later, and finally was appointed to British Honduras and was superintendent and then lieutenant governor of the Bay Islands. He remained as lieutenant-governor until 1864.

The lieutenant governor of British Honduras from 1870 until 1874, William Cairns (1828–1888), was also born in Belfast. On his return to the British Isles, William Cairns retired to Jersey. Another Irishman, Sir Cornelius Alfred Moloney (1848–1913), was the governor of British Honduras from 1891 until 1897.

In addition to Despard, Seymour, Cairns, and Moloney, there were other Irish who served in the British administration or army in British Honduras, such as Dublin-born Luke Smythe O'Connor (1806–1873), who was involved in fighting the Yucatan Indians in British Honduras in 1848. In 1905 the pathologist Rupert (later Sir Rupert) Boyce (1863–1911), born in Carlow, visited the colony to study yellow fever; and in 1934 Alan Pinn (1871–1958), born in Dublin, was appointed to overhaul the colony's finances. Others were involved in logging mahogany, forming the "settler class" of British Honduras. In the early twentieth century the growing of chicle for chewing gum also became important. In 1865, two groups of Americans, a few of whom were of Irish descent, also settled in British Honduras. From Louisiana and Mississippi, the groups formed two Confederate settlements in British Honduras after leaving America at the end of the Civil War. The first group had returned to America by 1870, but the second colony continued until 1925.

In 1954, British Honduras was given a new constitution, and self-government came ten years later. With independence delayed many times on account of neighboring Guatemala's claim on Belize, Sir John Rennie (1914–1981) was sent to the region in 1964 to try to resolve problems; in the early 1970s Rennie was to become involved in events in Northern Ireland. In 1972 the colony changed its name to Belize—the name of the major city. Belize was granted independence in 1981, and its capital was established at Belmopan, an inland town—Belize City having been devastated by a hurricane in 1961. Ireland has always recognised Belize's sovereignty and Irish diplomatic representation in Belize is handled by the Irish Embassy to the United Nations, at New York.

Justin Corfield

See also: AMERICAN CIVIL WAR;
    HONDURAS

Reference

Moberg, Mark. *Myths of Ethnicity and Nation: Immigration, Work, and Identity in the Belize Banana Industry.* Knoxville: University of Tennessee Press, 1997.

BENNETT, WILLIAM J. (1943–)

Born July 3, 1943, William John Bennett spent his early childhood in Brooklyn, New York. Although a native of Brooklyn, Bennett did his preparatory studies in Washington, D.C., where he attended Gonzaga College High School. After his studies there, he pursued his undergraduate degree at Williams College, going on to receive a PhD in political philosophy from the University of Texas. He also obtained a degree in law from Harvard Law School.

In 1976, Bennett attracted national recognition when he assumed his post as executive director of the National Humanities Center, a private research think tank located in North Carolina. Working with the center until 1981, Bennett was able to make many connections in Washington and was soon called upon to work there.

In 1981, President Ronald Reagan appointed Bennett to lead the National Endowment for the Humanities, a post that he kept until 1985. Once again, he was called upon by President Reagan, this time to become secretary of education. Utilizing the powers of his post, Bennett put forward a platform firmly based on his conservative views, emphasizing school vouchers, curriculum reform, religion in education, and the removal of affirmative action policies. Being an overwhelmingly strong supporter of classical education, Bennett disliked education's move toward multiculturalism, preferring a system of education based on Western culture, politics, and literature.

Bennett believed standards were not effectively enforced on all levels of education. For example, he strongly criticized colleges and universities for failing to enforce alcohol and drinking laws on their campus and among their student bodies. On the primary and secondary levels of education, he criticized many schools for low standards.

Bennett believed certain parts of the educational system caused the continuance of low standards and underachievement. He was in favor of regular competency testing for all teachers, allowing those who did not graduate from schools of education to teach if they were particularly experienced in a certain specialty, instating a performance-based pay scale, increased educator accountability, an end to tenure, and improved nationwide standardized tests to evaluate children's performance.

Bennett, however, was unable to avoid controversy for long. President George H. W. Bush appointed him to become the nation's first "drug czar" as director of the Office of National Drug Control Policy. Having established himself as one of the nation's most well-known moral crusaders, Bennett's selection was not a surprise to many on Capitol Hill, and he was confirmed in a 97 to 2 vote by the Senate. From the post, Bennett conducted the nation's war on drugs, but soon after decided to leave the position in 1990.

Drawing upon his many experiences in Washington, D.C., and his long career with the Republic Party, Bennett became a conservative writer and public speaker after leaving government office. Through his work, he has continued his moral crusade, attacking what he perceives as the lack of virtue in American society, particularly among the nation's youth. He has continued his efforts to improve the nation's public and private schools, basing his plans on what he calls the most important "Three C's: Choice, Content, and Character." He has also written and edited more than ten books, including *The Book of Virtues, The Children's Book of Virtues*, and *The Death of Outrage: Bill Clinton and the Assault on American Ideals,* which was briefly number one on *The New York Times*' best-seller list.

In 2003, Bennett revealed that he was an extremely high-stakes gambler who had lost millions of dollars in Las Vegas and Atlantic City. This was clearly a contradiction with his public moral crusader image, and Bennett's status as a conservative virtue and moral defender began to crumble, and he was no longer as highly sought after on the lecture circuit.

Most recently, Bennett has given most of his attention to his daily radio show and a project known as Americans for Victory Over Terrorism. Bennett is also a director of Empower America and a distinguished fellow at the Heritage Foundation. He works alongside former Democratic Senator Sam Nunn as a cochair of the National Commission on Civic Renewal. He continues his work in the war on drugs with the Partnership for a Drug-Free America, collaborating with former New York Governor Mario Cuomo. Bennett and his wife, Elayne, have two sons, John and Joseph.

Arthur Holst

See also: REAGAN, Ronald Wilson

References
"Bio—William Bennett." The Heritage Foundation Online. www.heritage.org/About/Staff/WilliamBennett.cfm (accessed December 10, 2005).
"GOP Moralist Bennett Gives Up Gambling." May 5, 2003. CNN Online. www.cnn.com/2003/ALLPOLITICS/05/05/bennett.gambling/ (accessed December 10, 2005).
"William Bennett." Empower America Online. www.empoweramerica.org/stories/storyReader$120 (accessed December 10, 2005).

BERGIN, PATRICK CONNOLLY (1951–)

Probably best known for his role as Julia Roberts's terrorizing husband in the 1991 film *Sleeping with the Enemy,* Patrick Bergin is an actor who is adept at tackling a diversity of roles. Born on February 4, 1951, in Dublin, he is the son of Paddy Bergin, who was a trade union organizer and Labour Party senator in the Irish Seanad. Patrick and his three brothers, Sean, Pearse, and Emmet (also an actor), grew up in Co. Carlow and in the Dublin suburb of Drimnagh. He appeared in some school productions in Drimnagh and went to London at the age of seventeen to do a BA degree in London, after which he taught disadvantaged children. After some training at the Royal Academy of Dramatic Art, he made his debut in an adaptation of Harold Pinter's *The Birthday Party*. He also acted in a National Film and Television School short film, *No Man's Land*. His debut in feature films was in the Dublin crime film, *The Courier* (1988), in which he acted alongside Gabriel Byrne; he followed it with another Irish thriller, *Taffin* (1988), in which he had a small role opposite Pierce Brosnan.

Soon after, Bergin secured television parts in the highly popular series *The Real Charlotte*, based on Somerville and Ross's novel, and the Australian miniseries, *Act of Betrayal* (1988) in which he played an Irish Republican Army (IRA) informer. His acting in the latter caught the eye of the renowned film director, Bob Rafelson, who cast him as Sir Richard Burton in *Mountains of the Moon* (1991). His performance as the Victorian explorer won him critical praise and led to his casting in several Hollywood films, of which *Sleeping with the Enemy* (1991) was the most high profile.

Despite the success of *Sleeping with the Enemy*, and the publicity that it earned for Bergin, the films that followed failed to elevate Bergin to A-list status in Hollywood. He played the title role in *Robin Hood*, produced in 1991, but the film was overshadowed by the release of the Kevin Costner

big-budget vehicle, *Robin Hood: Prince of Thieves*, the same year. Many of the projects he took on were made-for-television films or art-house films such as *Map of the Human Heart* (1993).

Bergin has appeared in many Irish films, or in American films with Irish themes. He had a role as an IRA man in the Hollywood blockbuster *Patriot Games* (1992), alongside fellow Irishman Richard Harris; and played a garda detective in *When the Sky Falls* (2000), the first of two American films based on the life of the murdered Irish journalist, Veronica Guerin (played by American actress Joan Allen). He also took a role in the 1996 film, *Angela Mooney*, directed by Tommy McArdle with a predominantly Irish cast, and played Saint Patrick in an American television film, *The Legend of St. Patrick* (2000). Another Irish-themed film, *The Boys from County Clare*, directed by British director John Irvin, followed in 2003.

More recently, Bergin has ventured into writing and directing with his adaptation of three plays by William Butler Yeats, *Some Other Place* (2000). One of the segments, *Calvary*, was directed by his wife, Paula Fraser, with Bergin playing the role of Christ. He has also dabbled in music, releasing a song, "The Knacker," about a legendary member of the Travelling community. The dubiously titled song was received with outrage by Pavee Point, the official representative body of the Travelling community in Ireland.

One of Bergin's latest projects was a stage production of a Ulick O'Connor play, *A Trinity of Two*, in which he played Edward Carson, the Dublin-born lawyer who led the defense case in the libel trial brought by Oscar Wilde in 1895. The production teamed him up with Fermanagh-born actor

Adrian Dunbar, and in 2006 they announced plans to costar in a film about the life of Scottish-born Irish patriot and union leader James Connolly. Patrick Bergin is married to Paula Fraser and they have a daughter, Tatiana (born 1996).

Gwenda Young

See also: BROSNAN, Pierce; BYRNE, Gabriel; IRISH REPUBLICAN ARMY; YEATS, William Butler

References
O'Connor, Aine. *Leading Hollywood.* Dublin: Wolfhound Press, 1996.
O'Donoghue, Donal. "Man in Black." *RTÉ Guide,* March 1, 2000, 10.
Regan, Colin. "Patrick Bergin's Boston Showcase." *The Irish Voice,* April 18, 2001, 32.
Sheehy, Ted. "Bergin Brassed Off." *Film Ireland,* August/September 2000, 26–28.

BOLAND, EAVAN (1944–)

Eavan Boland was born in Dublin to Frederick Boland, the first Irish diplomat to Britain and the United Nations, and Frances Kelly, a renowned post-expressionist painter. The Boland family lived in Ireland until 1950, when they moved to London. In 1956 Eavann's father became the first permanent Irish representative to the United Nations, and the family moved to New York, where Eavan first came into close contact with American culture. Boland returned to Dublin for her studies and after her graduation in 1962 she published a pamphlet entitled *23 Poems.* She received her BA in English and Latin from Trinity College Dublin in 1966. Three years later she married the novelist Kevin Casey and moved to the neighborhood of Dundrum, where she continued to write while raising their daughters Sarah Margaret and Eavan Francis.

Boland started lecturing at Trinity College Dublin and University College Dublin when she was 23 years old, but in 1967, when her first book, *New Territory,* came out, she felt more suited for writing poetry than developing an academic career. In this period, she met the poets Patrick Kavanagh, Michael Longley, and Brendan Kennelly, and she worked as a columnist for RTÉ and *The Irish Times,* where she often took a firm stand on gender issues. During this period she also read and learned from American female models, especially Elizabeth Bishop, Denise Levertov, Adrienne Rich, and Sylvia Plath. *The War Horse* (1975) shows her reflection on the violence affecting Irish history and her attempt to create her own poetic voice.

The Boland family moved to the United States in 1979, where the poet attended the International Writing Program at Iowa University. Boland was also a cofounder of Arlen House, the feminist publishing company that published *In Her Own Image* (1980) and *Night Feed* (1982). In these collections Boland uses Rich's poetry, in particular, as sustenance for her efforts to transform the Irish male poetic tradition, although their trajectories evolve in different ways. Plath's *Ariel* provided Boland with a style characterized by short lines grouped in tercets and other useful aesthetic models for her poetics. Her next volumes were published by Carcanet in the United Kingdom and Ireland and W. W. Norton in the United States. *The Journey* (1987) marks the entrance to her more mature work. She has collected her poetry in three different volumes throughout her career: *Selected Poems* (1989), *Outside History: Selected Poems 1980-1990* (1990), and *An Origin Like Water: Collected Poems 1967–87* (1996).

In the 1990s, Boland was invited to lecture at a number of universities in the

United States, including Bowdoin College, the University of Houston, the University of Utah, Washington University in St. Louis, where she was Hurst Professor, and the University of California at Santa Barbara, where she was Regent's Lecturer. *In a Time of Violence* (1994) investigates the issues of womanhood in relation to tradition. Boland has also written *Object Lessons: The Life of the Woman and the Poet in Our Time* (1995), in which she explains her poetical stance in depth. In 1996, the Stanford English department offered her a post where she would teach for a quarter of the academic year in their creative writing program. The following year she succeeded her friend, the poet Denise Levertov, in the post full-time as director of the program. Boland is currently the Melvin and Bill Lane Professor for Director of the Creative Writing Program and the Bella Mabury and Eloise Mabury Knapp Professor in the Humanities at Stanford. She divides her time between Dublin and Palo Alto, California.

In 1997, Boland received the Irish Literature Prize, and in recent years her poetry has become part of the syllabus studied by high school students in Ireland. She has published *The Lost Land* (1998), *Code* (2001), and *Against Love Poetry* (2003). Her latest volume of poetry is *Domestic Violence* (2007). She received the Lannan Foundation Award for Poetry in 2004 and an American Ireland Fund Literary Award. That Boland is completely involved both in Irish and American literary culture is evident through her membership on the boards of the Irish Arts Council and the Irish Academy of Letters as well as the advisory board of the International Writers Center at Washington University.

Cristina María Gámez-Fernández

See also: GRENNAN, Eamon; HEANEY, Seamus; MONTAGUE, John; MULDOON, Paul

References

Allen-Randolph, Jody. "An Interview with Eavan Boland." *Irish University Review* 23 (1993): 117–130.

Fogarty, Anne. "'The Influence of Absences': Eavan Boland and the Silenced History of Irish Women's Poetry." *Colby Quarterly* 35, no. 4 (1999): 256–274.

Gelpi, Albert. "'Hazard and Death': The Poetry of Eavan Boland." *Colby Quarterly* 35, no. 4 (1999): 210–228.

Grennan, Eamon. "American Relations." In *Irish Poetry since Kavanagh*, edited by Theo Dorgan, 95–105. Dublin: Four Courts Press, 1996.

BONNEY, WILLIAM "BILLY THE KID" (CA. 1860–1881)

The infamous Irish-American outlaw, born Henry McCarty or possibly William Henry Bonney, "Billy the Kid" also used the pseudonym of Kid Antrim. Very little is known about his birth and early childhood, and it has yet to be established whether he was born in Co. Limerick, Ireland, or in New York City, around 1860. His mother was an Irish immigrant named Catherine McCarty. His father, also an Irish immigrant, was named either William Bonney or Patrick Henry McCarty. Billy's father died around 1865. Catherine then took Billy and his brother Joseph to Indiana, where she married Civil War veteran William H. Antrim in 1873. Because Catherine married Antrim in a Presbyterian church, she and her sons may have converted from Roman Catholicism to Protestantism at some point, but this is not certain.

From Indiana the family moved to Silver City, New Mexico. Catherine died when Billy was 14, and after her death

Infamous Irish-American outlaw William H. Bonney (aka Billy the Kid). (Library of Congress)

William Antrim left his stepsons and moved to Arizona. Billy began to work waiting tables and washing dishes in a hotel. First jailed at the age of fifteen for petty theft, he soon escaped and fled to southeastern Arizona, where he worked as a ranch hand and sheepherder. In 1877, Billy became a civilian teamster at Camp Grant Army Post. Later that year, he committed his first murder, shooting another camp worker, Francis Cahill (who according to some contemporary accounts had bullied Billy without provocation), during a fight. Whether Billy shot Cahill deliberately or his gun went off accidentally during their struggle is unclear. Jailed for "unjustifiable homicide," Billy escaped and fled to New Mexico, where he eventually became involved in the Lincoln County War, a bitter dispute between cattle owners and a powerful group of local merchants over U.S. government beef contracts.

After rivals murdered his employer, a local tycoon named John Tunstall, Billy decided to avenge Tunstall's death. He joined a group of former Tunstall employees who called themselves the Regulators. The Regulators soon caught two men, who were promised their lives if they returned to town for a trial. Billy and another Regulator, however, killed both prisoners, as well as a member of the Regulators who tried to stop them. Billy escaped punishment and eventually gathered a small band of misfits around him. They began a life of cattle rustling and petty crime. When the new governor of Lincoln County offered a general amnesty for those involved in the Lincoln County War, Billy agreed to give evidence against others in return for a pardon. On March 17, 1879, he surrendered and was confined to the vicinity of Lincoln. After a few weeks, however, he broke parole and rejoined his former gang. A new sheriff in Lincoln County, Pat Garrett, determined to stop Billy's career. After several failed attempts, Garrett, who knew Billy casually, caught up with him at a small ranch called Stinking Springs shortly before Christmas 1880, and, after a brief gunfight, brought him as a prisoner to Fort Sumner, New Mexico. Billy was later transferred to jail in Santa Fe, New Mexico. By the spring of 1881, Billy had become nationally infamous as Billy the Kid. Readers across the country followed his story as the Kid was tried in the southern New Mexico town of Mesilla, found guilty of a murder that he insisted he had not committed, and sentenced to hang. On April 22, 1881, Billy was taken to Lincoln to await execution. Six days later he overpowered his guards, killing them both, and escaped. On July 13, 1881, Garrett heard reports that Billy was hiding out on a ranch in Fort Sumner, New Mexico. When Billy showed up at the ranch house later that night, Garrett shot him dead. Billy was buried in Fort Sumner.

The Kid's exploits and death quickly became an indelible part of American legend. The first book about Billy the Kid, Thomas F. Daggett's *Billy Le Roy: The Colorado Bandit,* appeared in 1881 shortly after Billy's death. Between 1881 and 1882, seven more pulp fiction novels were published with some version of Billy the Kid as the lead character. Most depicted him as a cold-blooded killer who had committed as many murders as he had years, hence the persistent and most likely exaggerated claim that he had slain "21 men in his 21 years." Irish writer Fintan O'Toole contends that "[I]n the hands of the best-selling dime novelist Emerson Hough, Pat Garrett was Anglo-Saxon civilization and Billy the Kid was the wildness of the inferior races" (O'Toole 1991). Sheriff Garrett produced his own memoir in 1882. Entitled *Billy, the Kid: The Noted Desperado of the Southwest,* Garrett's account is most responsible for the enduring myths of Billy the Kid, repeating stories that the author knew to be untrue and inventing others. Billy the Kid remains a popular enigma. A study conducted in the early 1950s found that at least 437 books, major magazine articles, movies, plays, and songs had been produced about the Kid since his death, and many more have appeared since that time.

Danielle Maze

References

O'Toole, Fintan. "The Many Stories of Billy the Kid." *The New Yorker,* December 1999: 61–70.

Walker, Dale L. *Legends and Lies: Great Mysteries of the American West.* New York: Tom Doherty Associates, 1997.

BORD FÁILTE EIREANN (1955–2003)

Bord Fáilte Eireann (BFE), the Republic of Ireland's most successful semi-state tourism organization, was created in 1955. From its inception, the board handled tourism development, marketing, and hospitality training, although the latter function was devolved to a new organization, CERT, the State Tourism Training Agency, in 1963.

Bord Fáilte was the product of an extended period of debate and discussion concerning how best to approach tourism development in southern Ireland. The first post-independence tourism dialogue began in 1923–1924 with the formation of a series of private tourism development organizations composed mainly of men representing business and tourism interests. In June 1924, these groups merged into a single organization, the Irish Tourist Association (ITA). Although the ITA was primarily a publicity body, it served as a pro-tourism lobby that pressured the Free State government, which faced tight spending restrictions, to invest heavily in tourism. Rather than provide state support, however, the 1925 and 1931 Tourism Traffic Acts encouraged county councils to fund ITA promotional efforts.

The Irish government opted to support tourism more directly in 1939 by creating the Irish Tourist Board (ITB), a statutory tourism organization that was authorized to acquire land, conduct hotel inspections, set hotel standards, define "special tourist areas," operate hotel training programs, provide development grants, and engage in publicity operations. Shortly after its creation, the ITB undertook a variety of development projects that were designed both to prepare Ireland for a predicted postwar tourism boom and to create jobs during the "Emergency" (the Irish government's term for its position during World War II). At the same time, the board drew harsh criticism from many observers who rejected the government's desire to support tourism development. As attacks grew more strident, the ITB was increasingly paralyzed and board efforts stalled. The inaction ended when the Economic Cooperation Administration demanded that Ireland either overhaul the country's tourism development effort or face termination of Marshall Plan aid.

In 1952, the government proposed the creation of two new statutory tourism bodies to replace the ITB. The first of these, An Bord Fáilte, was responsible for tourism development, including road signage, creation of tourist festivals, management of tourist sites, hotel ratings, and so forth. A second board, Fógra Fáilte, would handle all tourism publicity efforts, including publishing guidebooks and administering overseas marketing campaigns.

The two-board structure quickly proved untenable and was formally replaced in 1955 by Bord Fáilte Eireann (BFE). BFE was responsible for all tourism development efforts, including publicity and development. Like its statutory predecessors, BFE was required to submit an annual report of its activities and accounts to the government. Day-to-day tourism operations were handled entirely by the board while larger tourism initiatives required state approval.

Initially, BFE focused primarily on projects started during the two-board period. For example, production of publications such as the travel magazine *Ireland of the Welcomes* and the guidebook *Ireland Guide* continued under the new board. Likewise, the single largest tourism development project of the 1950s, a nationwide tourism festival called "An Tóstal: Ireland at Home," first held in 1953, demanded much of the new board's attention until the event was finally dropped in 1959. The new board also undertook an assortment of limited development efforts such as installing informational signage at various ancient sites and constructing car parks at tourism centers such as Glendalough, Mellifont Abbey, and Newgrange.

An Tóstal, the board's primary concern during the 1950s, drew together local committees responsible for organizing pageants, competitions, and displays while the central tourist board coordinated the scheduling and promotion of the various events. Although the festival largely failed to accomplish either of its stated aims—to either extend the tourist season (it was held in the early spring) or attract Irish Americans back to Ireland for a visit—it spawned numerous long-lasting events, including the Rose of Tralee, Wexford Opera Festival, Cork Film Festival, and Dublin Theatre Festival. Following the demise of An Tóstal, government grants administered by BFE kept these events alive. An Tóstal also generated the Tidy Towns and Villages Competition, which pitted Irish communities and even rural homesteads against one another in an effort to create the cleanest, prettiest, and most Irish community or farm possible. The pastel-painted towns of tourist postcards are largely the result of this event.

By the late 1950s, tourism was widely acknowledged as one of Ireland's most important industries. In 1958, tourism earnings reached £34.6 million and the industry was still growing; in 1960, earnings hit £42.4 million and topped £49 million in 1963. This upward trend prompted the government to include tourism in its Programmes for Economic Expansion beginning in 1958, making tourism a cornerstone of the government's effort to revitalize the Irish economy. This added pressure led Bord Fáilte to revisit the administration of tourism yet again. Unlike previous reforms, however, the new concern was localized effectiveness, not the tourism board itself. In 1964, eight Regional Tourism Organisations (RTOs) were created to promote greater communication between the Bord Fáilte central office in Dublin and various regional development groups.

In 1963, the government assigned Bord Fáilte a role in reviewing planning petitions under the 1963 Local Government (Planning and Development Act). Although tourism officials were long concerned with landscape aesthetics and environmental impact, the new role gave the tourist board an official role in approving building projects—a role that, in turn, prompted BFE to gradually shape itself into an environmental lobby, repeatedly pointing out that Irish tourism was dependent on an attractive environment.

During the 1990s, and partly because of the board's long-standing development and promotional effort, Ireland experienced a massive increase in tourism revenue. From 1994, tourism income increased by as much as 18 percent a year versus the international average of 4.5 percent growth during the same period.

During the early 2000s, the Irish government became convinced that a new tourism arrangement was required to ensure continued success. In 2000, it incorporated an all-Ireland tourism marketing company, Tourism Ireland Ltd., to handle publicity for both Northern Ireland and the Republic, largely usurping Bord Fáilte's former publicity role. Increased North/South cooperation on publicity demanded a similar expansion of cross-border development efforts, while at the same time the sheer number of tourists now visiting the island posed a threat to Ireland's reputation as an untouched tourism mecca—a challenge that seemed to demand a whole new approach to tourism policy.

To meet these challenges, and to facilitate cooperation with the recently established Tourism Ireland Ltd., the Irish government proposed the formation of a new tourism authority. The National Tourism Development Authority Act of 2003 created a new tourist board, Fáilte Ireland. This new body merged CERT and Bord Fáilte and is responsible for tourism training as well as strategic and practical development initiatives.

Eric G. E. Zuelow

See also: AN TÓSTAL: IRELAND AT HOME

References

Bord Fáilte. *Bord Fáilte Report and Financial Statements 2000.* Dublin: Bord Fáilte, 2000.

Deegan, James, and Donal A. Dineen. *Tourism Policy and Performance: The Irish Experience.* London: International Thompson Business Press, 1997.

Fáilte Ireland: The National Tourism Development Authority. November 2005. Fáilte Ireland website. www.failteireland.ie/ (accessed November 9, 2005).

Zuelow, Eric G. E. "The Tourism Nexus: Tourism and National Identity since the Irish Civil War." PhD dissertation, University of Wisconsin-Madison, 2004.

BOSTON

Often described as the "capital of Irish America," Boston, Massachusetts is a major center for Irish immigrants and Irish Americans in the United States. While actual numbers are smaller than in New York and other larger cities, people of Irish birth or descent make up 29 percent of greater Boston's population—by far the largest national group in the area—compared with 12 percent in metropolitan New York. As such, despite entrenched memories of nativist discrimination, Irish immigrants and their descendants have played a large role in shaping Boston's social, political, and cultural identity.

Given its roots as the Puritan "city upon the hill," Boston received few Irish immigrants before the mid-nineteenth century. Those who did come in the eighteenth and early nineteenth centuries were mostly Presbyterian indentured servants and craftspeople from Ulster, who either quickly moved on to the frontier or assimilated into the native population. The Great Famine of the 1840s brought large numbers of Catholic Irish for the first time—increasing their population from 4,000 in 1820 to 117,000 in 1850. While nearly half arrived directly from Ireland, countless more traveled down from the quays at Quebec. By 1860, 26 percent of Boston's population was Irish, in contrast to Germans and African Americans, who made up less than one percent each.

Largely unskilled, Irish immigrants had few options in finding employment. For the most part, men became manual laborers, while women found work as domestic servants or in the nearby Lowell and Lawrence textile mills. Bostonians were initially sympathetic toward the starving immigrants, but their increasing numbers soon provoked anti-Catholic and anti-Irish hostility. This hostility sometimes turned into violence, such as in 1834 when nativist mobs burnt an Ursuline convent in nearby Charlestown. Work advertisements often stated "No Irish Need Apply," while political parties like the Know-Nothings gained strength, winning statewide elections in 1854. These memories persisted in Irish minds, contributing to a separatist mentality long after they achieved success.

To help them settle into city life, the Irish established various cultural, charitable, and religious institutions. For example, the *Pilot,* a newspaper founded in 1829 and edited by well-known Irishmen such as John Boyle O'Reilly, offered a "missing friends" column and kept immigrants informed of news from Ireland. The Charitable Irish Society, founded in 1737, served the dual purpose of charitable organization and social club. The most important institution was the Catholic Church. The diocese's Irish-American bishops created a network of parishes, schools, hospitals, and orphanages designed to help immigrants maintain their religious identity while assimilating to American life.

By the late 1800s, many Irish had become more economically mobile, moving out of North End slums to such "streetcar suburbs" as South Boston and Dorchester. This mobility was aided by Irish dominance of public education; by the first decade of the twentieth century 25 percent of the teachers were Irish and 75 percent of all Irish children attended public schools. Yet while many became teachers, lawyers, and priests, the community was still heavily concentrated in unskilled labor well into the 1960s.

Because of the difficulty of penetrating the rigid Yankee social hierarchy, politics became one of the few ways for the Irish to advance. From Hugh O'Brien (1885–1888) to Raymond L. Flynn (1984–1993), the Irish dominated city government and slowly began to infiltrate the cultural establishment. Politicians like John "Honey Fitz" Fitzgerald and James Michael Curley practiced ward-based politics, playing on ethnic and racial tensions and constructing widespread patronage networks. This local success was duplicated on the national level in 1963 with the election of President John F. Kennedy—a symbol to Irish Americans everywhere that they had finally achieved acceptance. Following in his footsteps were his brother, Senator Edward Kennedy, and Thomas P. "Tip" O'Neill (speaker of the House of Representatives from 1977 to 1987). Both worked not only for social, economic, and educational improvements in America but also for peace in Northern Ireland after the outbreak of the Troubles.

While Boston's Irish-born population decreased during the twentieth century—from 71,441 in 1890 to 57,011 in 1920—the American-born generations have maintained a strong regional Irish identity, strengthened through local events like the "Southie" Saint Patrick's Day parade. In addition, such organizations as the Irish Cultural Centre and Boston College's Irish Studies Program, both founded in the 1990s, work to foster greater connections with Ireland. At the beginning of the twenty-first century, Boston continues to be a popular destination for Irish immigrants, businesspeople, and students, and remains a center of Irish culture in America.

Meaghan Dwyer

See also: GREAT FAMINE, THE; KENNEDY, John F.; O'NEILL, Thomas P.; O'REILLY, John Boyle

References

Connolly, James. *The Triumph of Ethnic Progressivism: Urban Political Culture in Boston, 1900–1925.* Cambridge, MA: Harvard University Press, 1998.

O'Connor, Thomas. *The Boston Irish: A Political History.* Boston: Northeastern University Press, 1995.

Ryan, Denis P. *Beyond the Ballot Box: A Social History of the Boston Irish.* Amherst: University of Massachusetts Press, 1983.

BOURKE, JOHN GREGORY (1846–1896)

John Gregory Bourke, an Army officer and ethnologist who used his writings to advocate for Native Americans, was born in Philadelphia on June 23, 1846, to booksellers Edward Joseph Bourke and Anna Morton Bourke. Both parents were Irish immigrants and Roman Catholic. On August 12, 1862, following his father's death and in a rush of excitement about the Civil War, Bourke lied about his age to join the 15th Pennsylvania Volunteer Cavalry. At the 1862 Battle of Stones River, he earned the Medal of Honor for rallying his fellow cavalrymen and leading a charge after all of their officers had been killed. He subsequently saw action at Chickamauga and Chattanooga before joining Sherman's March through Georgia. Mustered out of the cavalry in July 1865, Bourke entered West Point. He graduated eleventh out of thirty-nine in June 1869.

Posted to the 3rd Cavalry at Camp Grant in the Arizona Territory in 1870, Bourke found himself in the heart of Apache country and in the middle of the Indian Wars. Like many other soldiers, he initially saw nothing wrong with matching the Native Americans brutality for brutality. When a visitor nearly fainted after seeing two Indian ears and a scalp displayed on Bourke's wall, the young soldier began to reconsider his views. However, he remained firm in his commitment to subdue the Indians and make the Far West safe for Anglo-American settlement.

To divert his attention from warfare and the monotony of garrison life, Bourke began studying the history and culture of all the people of the West, including the Native Americans. In honor of his interest in Indian life, the Apaches nicknamed Bourke *naltsus-bichidin* or Paper Medicine Man. His opinions on the settlement of the West were far more critical than those of the other scholars of his era, such as Frederick Jackson Turner. Bourke saw a heritage of epic heroism but also of greed and the scandalous treatment of native culture. He was a staunch advocate of the Indians' rights in an age when they had few friends or defenders. Bourke's published writings on Indian life and culture brought him international acclaim, but his open and vocal concern for the Indians eventually crippled his military career.

In 1871, Bourke became aide-de-camp to Brigadier General George Crook. He would remain in this position for the next fourteen years, serving in every major Indian campaign in Arizona and on the Northern Plains. A tall man with a heavy mustache, Bourke had a reputation as a raconteur. His memoir, *On the Border with Crook,* has since become a military history classic. In 1885, Bourke received command of Camp Rice (later Fort Hancock), Texas. In March 1886, he transferred to Washington, D.C. so that he could continue his ethnological studies. Bourke never advanced past the rank of captain. In 1891, he commanded Fort Ringgold in Texas, but complaints about his abusive treatment of private citizens during border troubles with Mexico led to

his recall. Bourke finished his career at Fort Ethan Allen in Vermont. He died June 8, 1896, and is buried at Arlington National Cemetary.

Caryn E. Neumann

See also: AMERICAN CIVIL WAR

References

Porter, Joseph C. *Paper Medicine Man: John Gregory Bourke and His American West.* Norman: University of Oklahoma Press, 1986.

Robinson, Claude M., III, ed. *The Diaries of John Gregory Bourke.* Denton: University of North Texas Press, 2003.

BOYLE, KATHLEEN (1869–1941)

Kathleen Boyle was an educator and founder of the St. Patrick's School in San Martín, a suburb of Buenos Aires. Born Kathleen Milton Jones in Dublin on October 18, 1869, she was the daughter of Francis P. Jones and Elizabeth Dowling. She was sent to England to study literature at the University of Cambridge. Her father died in 1886, and the family immigrated to Rio de Janeiro, where Kathleen taught English, music and arts in the Colegio Americano Brasileiro. A yellow fever outbreak forced them to travel to Argentina. Their cousins John and Robert Hallahan, sons of the Rev. John Hallahan of Castletown, Berehaven (Co. Cork), were physicians in the British Hospital of Buenos Aires, and in 1891 received Kathleen's mother and her four children in Buenos Aires.

Kathleen resumed her teaching profession in 1894 when she founded the English Schoool of San Martín, which was later renamed St. Patrick's School. In 1899, she married Andrew T. S. Boyle (a former major in the British Army) at St. John's Pro-Cathedral, the Anglican church of

Portrait of award-winning writer, educator, and political activist Kathleen Boyle. (Library of Congress)

Buenos Aires. She later converted to Catholicism, and they both remarried and re-baptized their children.

Unlike other Irish schools, from the beginning St. Patrick's School was open to students of any origin or religion and was a laboratory to test the latest educational techniques. Boyle implemented new methods to teach English as a foreign language and, according to the examination results, there was a significant improvement of the students' knowledge and enthusiasm. Her motivation schemes, including awards to the best students, prompted the children to work harder. When the number of students grew and she was not able to teach all of them personally, she hired qualified teachers who had graduated from prestigious Argentine schools.

During Boyle's lifetime, Argentina was a country whose population was growing dramatically. Its postcolonial bourgeois structure was challenged by massive inflows of new immigrants from disparate cultures in Europe and the Middle East. On August 4, 1932, the *Standard,* the newspaper edited by Michael G. Mulhall, published a letter sent by Katheen Boyle but signed "Miss Justice." In it she argued against the perspective of some readers who thought women should give up their jobs in favor of men to relieve unemployment. In her letter Boyle focused on gender imbalance in the contemporary Argentinean workplace and a proposed 10 percent cut on salaries, she argued, should be applied only to those with higher incomes, not to low-paid workers with large families. She ended with an appeal to wealthy men to sacrifice half of their salaries and see that those working under them earn a living salary.

Kathleen Boyle died in October 1941. A street in the San Martín district Villa Piaggio was named after her, and a bronze bust was placed in Nueve de Julio and Mitre streets, and later moved to the cemetery. Her life challenges the traditional historical narrative of the Irish in Argentina, which frequently depicts Roman Catholic male emigrants from rural townlands in the Irish midlands or Wexford who settled in the countryside of Buenos Aires or other provinces to work in sheep farming.

Edmundo Murray

See also: MULHALL, Michael George

References
Coughlan, Eduardo A. *Los Irlandeses en la Argentina: Su Actuación y Descendencia.* Buenos Aires: Author's Edition, 1987.
Roger, María José. "The Children of the Diaspora: Irish Schools and Educators in Argentina, 1850–1950." www.irishargentine.org (accessed March 12, 2004).

BRAZIL

The first Irish settler in Brazil was a missionary, Thomas Field, S.J. (1547–1626), born in Limerick, who entered the Jesuits in Rome in 1574. Father Field arrived in Brazil in late 1577 and spent three years in Piratininga (today's São Paulo). Then he moved to Paraguay with two other Jesuits, and over the next ten years they established missions among the Guaraní people. Thomas Field, who died in Asunción, is credited with being the first priest to celebrate the Roman Catholic rites in the Americas.

In about 1612 the Irish brothers Philip and James Purcell established a colony in Tauregue, on the mouth of the Amazon River, where English, Dutch, and French settlements were also installed. Huge profits were made by the colonists in tobacco, dyes, and hardwoods. A second group arrived in 1620 led by Bernardo O'Brien of Co. Clare. They built a wood and earthen fort on the north bank of the Amazon and named the place Coconut Grove. O'Brien learned the dialect of the Arruan people, and his colleagues became expert navigators of the maze of tributaries, canals, and islands that form the mouth of the Amazon. The first recorded Saint Patrick's Day celebration was on March 17, 1770, at a church built in honor of the saint by Lancelot Belfort (1708–1775) on his estate known as Kilrue by the Itapecurú River, in the state of Maranhão, in northern Brazil.

Several Irish soldiers served in Brazilian armies, including Diago Nicolau Keating, Diago O'Grady, and Jorge Cowan. Another Irish military man, William Cotter, was sent to Ireland in 1826 to recruit a regiment for service against Argentina. Cotter went to Co. Cork where he promised the local people that if they enlisted they would be given a grant of land after five years' service.

He left for Rio de Janeiro in 1827 with 2,400 men and their women and children, but they were completely neglected when they arrived. The Irish mutinied, together with a German regiment, and for a few days there was open warfare on the streets of Rio de Janeiro. While most were finally sent home or went to Canada or Argentina, some did stay and were sent to form a colony in the province of Bahia.

In the 1850s the Brazilian government was anxious to raise agricultural production and to increase the population of its southern provinces, in particular with northern Europeans. After German and Swiss governments imposed restrictions on emigration to Brazil as the consequence of the poor conditions that many of these countries' citizens had experienced there, Brazil turned its attention to other possible immigration sources. Father T. Donovan, an Irish Catholic priest, led up to 400 from Co. Wexford's barony of Forth to Monte Bonito, near Pelotas in the then province of Rio Grande do Sul. The Irish colony rapidly collapsed, and most of the survivors made their way to Argentina or Uruguay, complaining of the lack of preparations for the reception, lack of agricultural tools, poor land, scarce water, and inadequacy of the local diet.

Further colonization schemes in Brazil were also failures. In 1867, the Brazilian government sent Quintino Bocayuva, a Brazilian newspaper editor and future republican leader, to New York to recruit immigrants. His mission was to sign up former Confederates, but to help fill ships he also dispatched several hundred poverty-stricken Irish. Most of these were sent to Colônia Príncipe Dom Pedro, near present-day Brusque in the province of Santa Catarina. Father Joseph Lazenby, an Irish

Jesuit living in the provincial capital, made his way to Príncipe Dom Pedro and declared that it would develop into an Irish Catholic colony. Lazenby soon entered into contact with Father George Montgomery, an Irish Catholic priest in the English "Black Country" town of Wednesbury, who arranged in 1868 for some 300 of his parishioners to be sent to Brazil. Montgomery held that the Irish had no future in England and saw in Brazil an opportunity to create Irish Catholic communities. He firmly believed that thousands more Irish living in England would soon be joining the first emigrants. But within just two years the new Irish colony failed. It was located far from any possible markets, and its land was subject to flooding. Many of the immigrants died, and the survivors soon moved to other parts of Brazil, Argentina, or the United States or returned to England.

Irish immigration to Brazil was also the main objective of the *Anglo-Brazilian Times* newspaper, published weekly by William Scully in Rio de Janeiro between 1865 and 1884. Scully was also the founder of the Sociedade Internacional de Imigraçao in 1866, which represented his material support to the Brazilian government.

A number of Irish diplomats served British interests in Brazil. Daniel Robert O'Sullivan (1865–1921), a medical doctor, army officer, and diplomat whose career was largely spent in East Africa and Brazil, served as British consul or consul-general in Bahia (1907), São Paulo (1910), and Rio de Janeiro (1907–1908, 1913–1915, 1919–1921). The Irish patriot Roger Casement (1864–1916) was a British consular official in Brazil in 1906–1911. In 1906 Casement was appointed consul in Santos, and in 1908 he became the consul in Pará (Belém). He was promoted to consul-general in Rio de Janeiro in 1909, a position he retained until 1913. In 1910 the Foreign Office directed Casement to occupy a commission of enquiry sent to the rubber-bearing Putumayo region of the western Amazon (an area straddling the Peruvian-Colombian frontier) to investigate treatment of the local Indian population by the Peruvian Amazon Company. He was knighted in 1911 for this and for similar work in Africa. During World War I, Casement sided with Germany as a tactic to achieve Irish independence, and in 1916 he was hanged by the British for treason. To damage his reputation, the British publicized the existence of Casement's diaries, which included numerous graphic and coded accounts of his homosexual activities in Brazil and elsewhere.

In 1964 Michael J. Siejes was appointed as the first honorary consul of Ireland in Rio de Janeiro, and later Padraig de Paor as nonresident Irish ambassador accredited to Brazil. In September 1975, an Irish trade mission led by Robin Bury visited São Paulo and Rio de Janeiro. The Irish diplomatic mission was established in Brazil in 1975, and Brazil opened its embassy in Dublin in 1991. The first resident ambassador of Ireland to Brazil, Martin Greene, arrived in Brasilia in December 2001. In Latin America, Brazil is the second trading partner of Ireland after Mexico, with an average of $154 million in exports and $80 million in imports per annum in 1996–2002 (International Monetary Fund, *Direction of Trade Statistics, Yearbook 2003*). In 1999, Kerry do Brasil was the first major Irish company with a $20 million investment in a production plant in Três Corações.

There are also a significant number of missionary works of religious orders in

Brazil. The Redemptorists were established in Brazil in 1960, the Kiltegans in 1963, and the Holy Ghost Fathers in 1967. In 2004, John Cribbin, O.M.I., of Shanagolden, Co. Limerick, was awarded honorary citizenship of Rio de Janeiro for his work since 1962. Among the academic initiatives in the region, since 1999, the Associação Brasileira de Estudos Irlandeses at the University of São Paulo has published the *ABEI Journal: The Brazilian Journal of Irish Studies*, edited by Munira H. Mutran and Laura P. Z. Izarra. University of São Paulo has offered a postgraduate course on Irish literature since 1977. By the end of 2000, it was estimated that 925 Irish citizens were living in Brazil, 64 percent of them in São Paulo, Rio de Janeiro, and Bahia.

Edmundo Murray

See also: CASEMENT, Roger; COTTER, William; SCULLY, William J.

References

International Monetary Fund, *Direction of Trade Statistics*, Yearbook 2003.
Marshall, Oliver. *English, Irish and Irish-American Pioneer Settlers in Nineteenth-Century Brazil.* Oxford: Centre for Brazilian Studies, 2005.
Marshall, Oliver. *Brazil in British and Irish Archives.* Oxford: Centre for Brazilian Studies, 2002.
O'Neill, Peter. "Links Between Brazil and Ireland." www.gogobrazil.com (accessed March 27, 2005).
Platt, D. C. M. "British Agricultural Colonization in Latin America." *Inter-American Economic Affairs* 28, no. 3 (Winter 1964): 3–38.

BRENDAN, SAINT, "THE NAVIGATOR" (CA. 484–CA. 577)

Very little is known about the historical Saint Brendan. He was born in Kerry toward the end of the fifth century CE, and entered the church ca. 512, rising to become abbot of Clonfert in Co. Galway. He may have had a reputation as a traveler in his lifetime, as it is very likely that he visited Iona sometime after 563 and may also have made a journey to Wales. He was a powerful and influential figure in the early Irish church, and many religious houses claim him as a founder.

Legendary versions of the saint's life, however, are much more detailed and fantastic. Two principal sources exist: the *Vita sancti Brendani*, probably composed in the eighth or ninth century, and the *Navagatio sancti Brendani Abbatis,* perhaps composed a little later, but certainly in existence by 900. Matters are complicated by the interpolation of the *Navagatio* in all but two surviving copies of the *Vita*. Whereas the *Vita* includes numerous biographical details and accounts of other voyages, the *Navagatio* is the story of a single voyage, in which generations of enthusiasts have tried to discern the lineaments of a transatlantic crossing.

The *Navagatio* is heavily influenced by folklore, particularly of the Irish *immram* type (literally "rowing around" or voyage tales). All the surviving *immrama* tell the story of a sea voyage punctuated by visits to amazing legendary islands. This is also the structure of the *Navagatio,* which may have been influenced by the seventh-century *Voyage of Bran* and in turn itself influenced the most well-known *immram,* the *Voyage of Mael Duin.* The Brendan legend was immensely popular in the Middle Ages, and versions exist in many European vernaculars, the most famous of which is perhaps Benedeit's Anglo-Norman verse account. Versions in the Irish language, however, are late and often corrupt.

Scholars and interested amateurs have long speculated on the question of whether

Brendan reached the New World. Geoffrey Ashe, in his 1962 book *Land to the West*, links phenomena described in the *Navagatio* to locations along a conjectured transatlantic route. In 1976–1977 Tim Severin proved that it was possible for a leather boat to withstand an Atlantic crossing, captaining the small crew of the *Brendan*, a specially constructed seagoing curragh, from Kerry to Newfoundland. Severin offers a fascinating account of the journey in *The Brendan Voyage* (1978), claiming that his experiences aboard the small craft gave him access to a medieval worldview that made sense of many of the fantastical episodes in the *Navagatio*. Such claims, like Ashe's geographical and climatological parallels, are by their nature unprovable. While it is possible that sixth-century Irish monks had the nautical technology and expertise to undertake long, even transatlantic voyages, there is no reliable evidence that the abbot of Clonfert ever did so.

Kit Fryatt

References

Ashe, Geoffrey. *Land to the West*. London: Collins, 1962.
Benedeit. *The Anglo-Norman 'Voyage of St Brendan'*, ed. Ian Short and Brian Merrilees. Manchester: Manchester University Press, 1979.
Burgess, Glyn S., and Clara Strijbosch. *The Legend of St Brendan: A Critical Reference*. Dublin: Royal Irish Academy, 2000.
Severin, Tim. *The Brendan Voyage*. London: Hutchinson, 1978.
Webb, J. F., ed. and trans. *Lives of the Saints*. Baltimore: Penguin Books, 1965.

BRENNAN, MAEVE M. (1917–1993)

A novelist, short-story writer, and journalist, Maeve Brennan was born in Dublin on January 6, 1917, the second daughter of Una (née Bolger) and Robert Brennan. Both her parents were active in Irish nationalism at the beginning of the century; Robert Brennan was imprisoned for his part in the Easter Rising at the time of Maeve's birth. During the Anglo-Irish War, Robert Brennan worked as director of publicity for Sinn Féin, making him and his family a target for the Black and Tans. In the Civil War he took an anti-Treaty position, spending most of the war on the run. His daughter's short story "The Day We Got Our Own Back," recalls a raid on their home by agents of the Free State. After the upheavals of the Civil War the Brennans led a comfortable, middle-class life in suburban South Dublin, recorded in a number of autobiographical stories, including "The Morning After the Big Fire," "The Lie," and "The Clever One." After a troubled period at a boarding school in Kildare (see her story "The Devil in Us"), Maeve completed her secondary education at Louise Gavan Duffy's progressive, Irish-speaking Scoil Bhríghde. In 1933 Robert Brennan was appointed Secretary of the Irish Legation in Washington, D.C., and his family joined him in the United States the following year.

Maeve attended college in Washington and in 1942 moved to New York, working first for *Harper's Bazaar* and later joining *The New Yorker* as a staff writer in 1949. Her father and mother had returned to Ireland in 1947, but Maeve never lived in her home country again. However, most of her stories and her novella *The Visitor*, are set in Ireland and painstakingly recall local color and idiom. At *The New Yorker*, Brennan wrote book reviews and fashion pieces and contributed to the celebrated "Talk of the Town" column, under the pseudonym "The Long-Winded Lady." The Long-Winded Lady's style is both a parody and celebration of the inconsequential, overemphatic idiom of a privileged lady of leisure, a "forthright spendthrift as far as italics go." Beneath this chatty persona the Long-Winded Lady exhibited, as Ben Yagoda notes, "a quality of observation, a connection to the city streets, a nonfacetious humour, a personality and an ineffable sadness." At this time, Brennan was also publishing short stories, including her only work set in America, the "Herbert's Retreat" stories, which deal with an affluent close-knit community of writers and artists in upstate New York. These stories are slighter than her Irish-based work and have received less critical approbation. In 1954 she married St. Clair McKelway and moved to the neighborhood on which she had based Herbert's Retreat, Sneden's Landing. The marriage was troubled: McKelway was an alcoholic, and the couple lived beyond their means, and more than once had to be bailed out of debt by the editor of *The New Yorker*. They separated in 1959 and subsequently divorced.

Brennan's divorce from McKelway began a period of increased instability in her life in which she rented or borrowed houses and apartments, or lived as "a traveller in residence" in a series of hotels. Toward the end of the 1960s she began to show the first signs of the mental illness that would trouble the last two decades of her life. In 1968 she published a collection of her Talk of the Town pieces, followed in 1969 by *In and Out of Never-Never Land*. In 1972 *The New Yorker* published her masterpiece, "The Springs of Affection," an extended short story about the Bagot family of Wexford, who appear in a number of her other stories. "The Springs of Affection" is a brilliant exercise in free indirect style, comparable to James Joyce's "The Dead" in its evocation of a particular Irish milieu and idiolect. Her last work of fiction to appear in the *New Yorker*, "Family Walls," was published in 1973. In 1974 another collection, *Christmas Eve*, was published, and the following year her work was anthologized alongside such writers as Edith Wharton and Alice Munro. By this time, however, Brennan was suffering seriously from mental illness. She spent periods in hospital and recovered with the aid of medication, but increasingly relapsed during the later 1970s. Though she had occasional periods of lucidity, as evidenced by her last Long-Winded Lady piece, which appeared in 1981, she was also frequently homeless and disengaged from mainstream society. She died at the Lawrence Nursing Home in Arverne, New York on November 1, 1993. Since her death, her work has undergone something of a critical revival, with the publication of *The Springs of Affection: Stories of Dublin* in 1997, and the revised edition of *The Long-Winded Lady* in 1998. Her novella, *The Visitor*, was posthumously published in 2000, and a biography by Angela Bourke, *Maeve Brennan: Homesick at the New Yorker*, appeared in 2004.

Kit Fryatt

See also: JOYCE, James Augustine Aloysius

References

Bourke, Angela. *Maeve Brennan: Homesick at the New Yorker* Washington, DC: Counterpoint, 2004.

Brennan, Maeve. *The Long-Winded Lady*, Boston: Houghton Mifflin, 1998.

Brennan, Maeve. *The Rose Garden: Short Stories*, Washington, DC: Counterpoint, 2000.

Brennan, Maeve. *The Springs of Affection: Stories of Dublin*, Boston: Houghton Mifflin, 1997.

Brennan, Maeve. *The Visitor*, Dublin, Ireland: New Island, 2001.

Yagoda, Ben. *About Town: The New Yorker and the World it Made*, New York: Scribner, 2000.

BRENNAN, WALTER (1894–1972)

Walter Andrew Brennan was the definitive character actor in American cinema of the 1930s, 1940s, and 1950s. Born on July 25, 1894 in Swampscott, Massachusetts, his parents, William John Brennan and Margaret Elizabeth Flanagan Brennan, were of Irish background. Brennan attended college in Cambridge, Massachusetts, where he studied engineering. During his time at college he became interested in acting and began to appear in roles in local vaudeville; he also took on jobs as a lumberjack and as a bank clerk. In 1917 he enlisted in the army. After his demobilization, he settled in Los Angeles, where he began to speculate in real estate. However, the lure of acting continued, and from 1923 on he was securing extra roles in films. By 1927 he was featured as a supporting actor in a variety of films, including many westerns and comedies, including *Tearin' Into Trouble* and *The Ridin' Rowdy* (both 1927), *Silks and Saddles* (1928), and *The Long Trail* (1929). Even in the early years of his career Brennan was a much favored character actor for directors such as Richard Thorpe, who gave him his earliest featured role in *Tearin' Into Trouble* and who went on to direct him in six further films.

Brennan's popularity among directors continued in the 1930s, the decade that established him as a well-loved and popular character actor. Top directors such as William Wyler and George Stevens cast him in supporting roles in prestigious films and quite often Brennan's natural, humorous performances stole the scenes in which he appeared. Even in this early stage of his career, Brennan was establishing the persona of the ornery sidekick or cantankerous antagonist that would serve him well for four decades in films and television. He often played Irish-American roles in such films as *The Shannons of Broadway* and *The Cohens and Kellys in Atlantic City* (both 1929) as well as *She's Dangerous* and *Wild and Woolly* (both 1937), but Brennan was never confined to Irish roles: more often than not, he was cast as crotchety Americans.

Brennan's outstanding character roles were in films directed by William Wyler and Howard Hawks. Both directors worked with him on one of his most memorable films, *Barbary Coast,* in 1935. Made for the independent producer, Sam Goldwyn, the film started shooting under the direction of William Wyler. Wyler had worked with Brennan on *A House Divided* in 1931 and cast him in an important role as Old Atrocity in *Barbary Coast.* Wyler was replaced by Hawks during the shoot, and Hawks later admitted he wasn't sure about Brennan's performance. Hawks's reservations were allayed when he saw how warmly audiences and critics responded to Brennan's perfectly pitched comic playing. The director worked with him again on *Come and Get It* in 1936 (this time it was Hawks who was replaced by Wyler during shooting!), which won Brennan his first Academy Award for supporting actor. Both Wyler and Hawks proved to be lucky charms for Brennan: he would win a third Academy Award (having won a second statue in 1938 for *Kentucky*) for his performance as Judge Roy Bean in Wyler's *The Westerner* (1940), while Hawks cast him in a key role in the first Humphrey Bogart/Lauren Bacall vehicle, *To Have and Have Not* (1944), and as an ornery toothless sidekick to John Wayne in *Red River* (1948) and *Rio Bravo* (1959). In a later interview with Joseph McBride, Hawks observed that

Brennan had an "amazing quality, to be able to play anything and do it right." Brennan remained one of a handful of outstanding character actors throughout the 1940s and 1950s and continued to work with prestigious directors such as John Ford (the 1946 *My Darling Clementine* in which he played a rare villainous role) and Frank Capra (in 1941's *Meet John Doe*).

In the 1950s, Brennan branched out into television and won a new audience with his role in the long-running television series, *The Real McCoys* (1957). He also had some success as a singer, releasing several records, the most memorable of which was 1962's *Old Rivers*. Despite his prolific acting career, Brennan found time to be a successful businessman, and he owned several businesses and a ranch in Oregon. His close association with westerns throughout his career earned him a place in the Western Performers Hall of Fame at the National Cowboy & Western Heritage Museum in Oklahoma in 1970. For the remaining two decades of his life Brennan continued to appear in many films and on television, demonstrating his versatility in the broad range of character roles he played. He worked right up until his death from emphysema on September 21, 1974.

Brennan was married to Ruth Wells (1897–1997) from 1920 until his death and is survived by her and their children.

Gwenda Young

See also: FORD, John; WAYNE, John

References

Carzo, Eileen Daney. "Walter Brennan." *The Encyclopedia of the Irish in America*. Ed. Michael Glazier. Notre Dame, IN: University of Notre Dame Press, 1999.

Katz, Ephraim. *The Film Encyclopedia*. New York: Perigee Books, 1979

McBride, Joseph. *Hawks on Hawks*. New York: Faber and Faber, 1996.

BRENNAN, WILLIAM J., JR. (1906–1997)

Born in Newark, New Jersey, on April 25, 1906, William Joseph Brennan, Jr., was the second of eight children born to Irish immigrants William Brennan and Agnes McDermott. Arriving from Co. Roscommon, Ireland, in 1893, William Brennan, Sr., had initially worked as a New Jersey laborer before rising to a position of labor leadership, and finally, commissioner of public safety for the city of Newark from 1917 to 1930.

William J. Brennan, Jr., received his bachelor's in economics from the University of Pennsylvania in 1928 and went on to obtain his law degree from Harvard in 1931. Before his graduation from law school, Brennan would marry Marjorie Leonard, with whom he would go on to have three children. Upon completion of his studies, Brennan, largely influenced by his father's experiences, practiced labor law in a private New Jersey practice. In 1942, Brennan entered the Army, where he served as Army Judge Advocate General until 1946. Upon his return to civilian life Brennan was appointed to a position on the Superior Court of New Jersey in 1949, followed by an appointment to the New Jersey Supreme Court in 1951.

In 1956, President Dwight Eisenhower appointed William J. Brennan, Jr., to the Supreme Court of the United States. Although Eisenhower was a Republican, he appointed Brennan, a Catholic Democrat, upon the guidance of his advisers, who believed Brennan's religious and political affiliations would help sway the voters of the northeastern United States in an upcoming presidential election. However, Brennan's appointment to the Supreme Court would become a decision that Eisenhower would reportedly come to regret as Brennan enforcement to warn suspects of their right to a lawyer, and to the consequences of a confession. The Warren Court was also responsible for establishing a woman's right to choose an abortion in *Roe v. Wade* (1972). Brennan was also an outspoken critic of capital punishment, dissenting in each case that passed before him while on the bench.

By the late 1970s, Brennan's voice was increasingly becoming one of dissent as the makeup of the Court underwent changes with more conservative appointments. Brennan finally retired from the Supreme Court of the United States on July 20, 1990, after handing down 1,360 opinions over the course of almost 34 years. His decisions on desegregation, criminal rights, welfare rights, and women's rights helped to redefine constitutional law and the face of America. Brennan died on July 24, 1997, and is buried in Arlington National Cemetery in Virginia. His second wife, Mary Fowler, survived him.

Teresa Iacobelli

Portrait of U.S. Supreme Court Justice William Brennan, Jr. (Library of Congress)

proved to be one of the most liberal justices the Supreme Court had ever known.

Brennan was a staunch supporter of individual liberties and one biographer referred to him as "the architect of much of the revolution in constitutional law that took place in the 1960s and 1970s." Brennan was as a key member of what came to be known as the Warren Court, headed by Chief Justice Earl Warren. With a five-person liberal majority during the 1960s, the Warren Court redefined individual rights with important decisions on free speech, affirmative action, and school prayer. Brennan was a key voice in establishing the rights of all of society's members, including welfare recipients and criminals. A 1966 decision in *Miranda v. Arizona* resulted in the creation of the Miranda rights, which established the right of the accused to due process and required members of law

References
Hopkins, W. Wat. *Mr. Justice Brennan and Freedom of Expression.* New York: Praeger, 1991.
Tribe, Laurence. "Common Sense and Uncommon Wisdom: A Tribute to Justice Brennan." *Harvard Law Review* 1 (1990). www.law.harvard.edu/alumni/bulletin/backissues/fall97/brennan.html (accessed July 15, 2005).
Wermiel, Stephen J. 'William Joseph Brennan, Jr'. *The Supreme Court Justices: A Biograhphical Dictionary*, ed. Melvin I. Urofsky. New York: Garland Publishing Inc., 1994.

BRENON, HERBERT (1880–1958)

Alexander Herbert Reginald St. John Brenon was born on January 13, 1880, in Kingstown (now Dun Laoghaire), Co.

Portrait of theater and film director Herbert Brenon.
(Library of Congress)

Dublin. His family came from an Anglo-Irish background and both his parents, Edward and Frances, were involved in literary circles as writers and editors. In 1882 the family left Ireland and settled in London, where Herbert attended St. Paul's school. By 1896 the family had moved to America, and within a year, Herbert had found employment in the office of Joseph Vion, a vaudeville booking agent based in New York. By the 1897–1898 season he was taking on small roles in vaudeville shows and serving as an assistant stage manager for touring shows. In 1904 he married a fellow actor, Helen Oberg, and their only child, Cyril Herbert Brenon, was born in 1906.

In 1908 the Brenons bought a theater in Johnstown, Pennsylvania, which they operated successfully as a movie theater. This peripheral involvement, and success,

in the film industry inspired him to switch from exhibition to production, and in 1910 he signed with the IMP Company as a scenario writer. Among his earliest credits as a writer was an early version of *The Scarlet Letter*, directed by George Loane Tucker. In 1912 Brenon received his first directing credit on a film called *All For Her*; this was soon followed by a version of *Camille* starring Gertrude Shipman. Reviews of the latter film praised Brenon's handling of his star and the film's fine pictorial qualities.

During the five years that he spent with IMP Brenon directed more than forty films, including two adaptations from Dion Boucicault, *The Long Strike* (1912) and *Kathleen Mavoureen* (1913); critically acclaimed versions of *Dr Jekyll and Mr Hyde* and *Ivanhoe*, starring King Baggot; and the box office smash, *Neptune's Daughter*, starring Olympic swimmer Annette Kellerman. His prolific output as a director during these years attracted the attention of other studios and stars, and after a short stint as an independent, Brenon signed a contract with Fox studios in 1915. At Fox Brenon directed a number of famous stars, most notably Theda Bara, the original screen vamp, and he reunited with Kellerman to direct a sequel to *Neptune's Daughter* called *A Daughter of the Gods*. Following an argument over credit for *A Daughter of the Gods*, Brenon left Fox and signed with Lewis Selznick. They set up the Herbert Brenon Film Corporation and produced one of Brenon's most famous and controversial films, *War Brides*, starring Alla Nazimova. The film was not a commerical success upon its initial release, possibly because of the unpopularity of its pacifist tone.

In 1918 Brenon took American citizenship but returned to Europe to direct a propaganda film, *The Invasion of Britain*, which was shelved as World War I ended. By 1920 he was back in America, directing Norma Talmadge in *The Passion Flower* (1921), Pola Negri in *The Spanish Dancer* (1923), and Betty Compson in *The Woman with Four Faces* (1923). Brenon's greatest success came in 1924 with his production of *Peter Pan,* still regarded by many critics as the best adaptation of J. M. Barrie's play. The rights to the play had been bought by Famous-Players/Paramount back in 1918, but it was Brenon, along with screenwriter Willis Goldbeck and star Betty Bronson, who finally got the film made. The film was lavishly promoted, critically acclaimed, and commercially successful.

Brenon's output over the next four years tapped into the zeitgeist of the Jazz Age with flapper films (*Dancing Mothers* in 1926, which starred the "It Girl," Clara Bow); gung-ho adventures (*Beau Geste* in 1926); and the first screen adaptation of F. Scott Fitzgerald's *The Great Gatsby* (1926, starring Lois Wilson and Warner Baxter). After his departure from Paramount in 1927, Brenon joined United Artists where he directed *Sorrell and Son,* which won him a best director nomination in the first Academy Awards list. Brenon was critical of the introduction of sound in film, believing it "violated the pantomimic art," and his reluctance to move into the talking pictures era may account for the decline in the numbers of films that he directed after 1927. Brenon's reputation for temperament in his dealings with studios may also have had an impact on his career. By 1934 his Hollywood career was over, and he left America to work for a number of British studios. Although he had some moderate success in Britain, Brenon directed his last film, *The Flying Squad,* in 1940. He retired to Los Angeles where he lived with his wife,

Helen Oberg, until his death on June 21, 1958.

Gwenda Young

See also: BAGGOT, King

References

Gillett, John. "Herbert Brenon." In *Cinema: A Critical Dictionary,* edited by Richard Roud. Vol. 2, ed. New York: Secker & Warburg, 1978: 141.

Lodge, Jack. "The Career of Herbert Brenon." *Griffithiana* 57, no. 8 (1996): 5–133.

BRENT, GEORGE (CA. 1899–1979)

Some confusion exists over the exact birth date of George Brendan Nolan (George Brent). Some sources list it as March 15, 1899 (www.imdb.com), while others list it as March 15, 1904 (Katz 1979). However, there is no doubt that he was born in Shannonbridge, Co. Offaly, the son of a British Army officer. According to his own account, his interest in acting was sparked by some experience working as a child actor at the Abbey Theatre in Dublin. During the Irish War of Independence (1919–1921), he became involved in the Irish Republican Army, serving as a messenger boy for a unit headed by Michael Collins. He left Ireland, possibly under threat of imprisonment or execution from British forces, and traveled to Canada, where he continued his acting career in stock companies. By 1925 he was in the United States, touring with a production of *Abie's Irish Rose,* and for the next two years he built up considerable experience as an actor in companies in Colorado, Rhode Island, Florida, and Massachusetts. In 1927 he appeared on Broadway, alongside Clark Gable (then an up-and-coming theater actor), in *Love, Honor, and Betray.*

In 1930 Brent moved to Hollywood and shortly afterwards he was cast in his first film, *Under Suspicion.* This debut was followed by a number of appearances in minor films produced by Fox and Universal. In 1932 Brent was signed to a contract with Warner Brothers, and over the next decade his output was prolific. Initially cast in a variety of roles, which included a farmer (*The Purchase Price,* 1932), a sculptor (*So Big,* 1932), a police inspector (*Miss Pinkerton,* 1932) and a doctor (*Luxury Liner,* 1933), he found his niche as a romantic leading man opposite such major stars as Ruth Chatterton, with whom he starred in four films between 1932 and 1933. Their on-screen partnership led to a relationship that resulted in a brief marriage. Warner Brothers regarded Brent as ideal leading-man material: handsome and suave, he served as a useful romantic partner for the headstrong heroines of many Warner Brothers films. His most famous roles, in *Jezebel, The Old Maid, In this Our Life, The Great Lie,* and *Dark Victory,* saw him star opposite Bette Davis, Warner Brothers studio's preeminent female star of the 1930s.

Throughout the 1930s and 1940s, Brent continued to take roles opposite strong actresses such as Greta Garbo, Bette Davis, Mary Astor, and Barbara Stanwyck, and invariably suffered the typecasting that was common within the Hollywood studio system. In an effort to break free from the limited roles he was assigned, he took the role of a psychopathic killer in Robert Siodmak's atmospheric noir melodrama, *The Spiral Staircase* (1946). Although the film remains a classic of its genre, Brent's performance perhaps shows the limits of his acting abilities.

Brent worked steadily throughout the 1940s but found that roles began to fall off as he grew older and audience tastes changed in the 1950s. He retired in 1956, announcing his intention to run a horse-breeding ranch. Although he made occasional guest appearances on such television shows as *Rawhide* and *Studio 57* in the 1950s and 1960s, it wasn't until 1978 that he returned to films. Coaxed back to Hollywood by director Irving Rapper, with whom he had worked on *The Gay Sisters* in 1942, he appeared as Judge Gesell in the 1978 film *Born Again.* It was to be his final film role.

Married five times, George Brent died on May 26, 1979. He was survived by his children, Barry and Suzanne.

Gwenda Young

See also: IRISH REPUBLICAN ARMY

References
"George Brent." Internet Movie Database website. http://www.imdb.com/name/nm0107575/ (accessed June 30, 2007).
Katz, Ephraim. *The Film Encyclopedia.* New York: Perigee Books, 1979.
Vinson, James. *International Dictionary of Films and Filmmakers: Actors and Actresses.* Chicago: St. James Press, 1986.

BRODERICK, DAVID COLBRETH (1820–1859)

Born in Washington, D.C., where his Irish immigrant father was working as a stonecutter on the U.S. Capitol building, Broderick moved to New York City with his parents when he was three. He attended free common schools until becoming an apprentice stonecutter. He later became a stonemason and a saloonkeeper.

As a young man Broderick joined the Democratic Party's Tammany Society, which was gaining power as Irish immigrants fleeing the Potato Famine flowed into the City. Broderick ran for Congress in New York in 1846 but lost. He headed and a decade-long split of the California Democratic Party between Gwin's Chivalry and Broderick's Northern factions.

However, Broderick's supporters won more seats than Gwin's in California's 1854 elections, and he succeeded in having the California legislature not reelect Gwin as U.S. senator after his term expired in March 1855. California's other senator, Democrat John Weller, served alone for two years until his own term expired in March 1857. The 1857 California legislature elected Broderick to its six-year U.S. Senate seat, but could not decide whom to choose for the remaining four-year term of Gwin's former seat. Broderick's supporters finally agreed to Gwin's reelection, but only after Gwin agreed that Broderick would control federal appointments in California.

After they were sworn in as U.S. Senators, Gwin effectively double-crossed Broderick by taking control of federal patronage in California despite their agreement. Newly elected President James Buchanan liked Gwin and disliked the outspoken Broderick. In addition, Buchanan and most other Democrats held views closer to Gwin's. Illinois Senator Stephen Douglas, who supported Broderick, was one of the few Democratic senators with views close to his.

By 1859, Broderick's use of his sharp tongue to speak out against Buchanan and Gwin had angered Chief Justice David Terry of the California Supreme Court, a slavery sympathizer and friend of Gwin's. Terry verbally attacked Broderick at an 1859 Democratic state convention, and when Broderick responded in kind, Terry demanded satisfaction. After Broderick refused, Terry resigned from the court and demanded a retraction, effectively requiring a duel once Broderick, inevitably, refused to

Portrait of U.S. Senator David Colbreth Broderick. (Library of Congress)

West for Gold Rush California after the March 1849 inauguration of President Zachary Taylor, a Whig, temporarily ended Tammany's federal patronage power.

After arriving in San Francisco, Broderick worked as a smelter and seller of gold and silver and introduced Tammany's ward system of political organization. He was elected to California's new state senate in 1850, and became president of the state senate in 1851. Once the California legislature enacted a fugitive slave law in 1852, Broderick, who strongly opposed slavery, worked statewide to build up opposition to U.S. Senator William Gwin, the strongest force in California's Democratic Party, and an outspoken propent of slavery. The result was Broderick's exclusion from the 1852 convention that selected California delegates for the Democratic National Convention, retract anything. The two met at Lake Merced, outside San Francisco's city limits, on September 13, 1859, with approximately seventy spectators present. Broderick's pistol went off prematurely, firing into the ground before he aimed. Terry then took careful aim and shot Broderick in the chest. He died three days later, the first sitting U.S. senator to be killed in a duel.

Broderick continued to be a political force, even in death. The split between Chivalry and Northern Democrats continued to divide California's Democratic Party, and Abraham Lincoln's California victory in the 1860 presidential election was attributed to Broderick supporters who voted for the antislavery Republican. Gwin's public career soon ended. He did not seek reelection, and his senate term expired in March 1861. He was twice arrested for disloyalty during the Civil War.

Terry himself met a violent end. A U.S. Marshal serving as U.S. Supreme Court Justice Stephen Field's bodyguard shot and killed Terry in 1889, after Terry, then 66, assaulted Field, a former Northern Democrat and a friend of Broderick's, in a central California railway station.

Steven B. Jacobson

See also: SAN FRANCISCO; TAMMANY HALL

References
Davis, Winfield J. *History of Political Conventions in California: 1849–1892*. Sacramento: California State Library, 1893.
Hargis, Donald E. "The Issues in the Broderick-Gwin Debates of 1859." *California Historical Society Quarterly* 32 (1953): 313–325.
Lynch, Jeremiah C. *Senator of the Fifties: David C. Broderick of California*. New York: Beck & Taylor, 1911.
Quinn, Arthur. *Rivals: William Gwin, David Broderick, and the Birth of California*. Lincoln: University of Nebraska Press, 1997.
Rolle, Andrew F. *California: A History*. 2nd ed. New York: Thomas Y. Crowell, 1969.
Williams, David A. *David C. Broderick: A Political Portrait*. San Marino, CA: Huntington Library, 1969.

BROPHY, JOHN (1883–1963)

Labor organizer John Brophy was born in St. Helens, Lancashire, England, to Irish immigrants; his father's family was originally from Dublin. Brophy's father worked as a miner before joining the British Army and serving in Ireland, Egypt, and South Africa. When he was discharged he married Mary Dagnall, whose family had come to England from Dundalk, Co. Louth. Together they had eleven children, five of whom survived until adulthood; John was the eldest. When he was nine years old, John emigrated with his family to America, where they eventually settled in Pennsylvania. For the next few years his family moved to different mining communities across Pennsylvania to earn a living. At the age of twelve John began working as his father's helper in the mines in Urey, Pennsylvania. Within two years he had joined the United Mine Workers (UMW). After contracting typhoid fever, he was elected to the post of secretary of a UMW local in 1904, and later he was elected checkweighman at the Greenwich mine, a position that ensured that all the miners were paid the correct amount of money. In 1916, after having held a number of posts in the UMW, he was elected president of District 2, a position that covered all of the mines in central Pennsylvania.

In 1918 he married Anita Anstead, and they had two children together. During this time he met John L. Lewis, the future UMW president and founder of the Congress of Industrial Organizations (CIO).

Brophy's relationship with Lewis and their mutual rivalry would color much of his later career in the union. Lewis was elected president of the UMW in 1920, but six years later Brophy ran against him for the presidency. Brophy ran on a "Save the Union" slate and called for the nationalization of the coal industry, a demand that Lewis rejected. Brophy lost the election, although he probably would have won if the election had been truly democratic. Brophy was forced to leave the union in 1928, and Lewis accused him of dual unionism on the basis of the Communist Party's support for his candidacy. After being driven from the UMW Brophy worked as a salesman for the Columbia Conserve Company. During this time he also studied economics and philosophy.

In 1933, with the New Deal and the National Industrial Recovery Act, Lewis brought Brophy back into the UMW to help increase the membership. In 1938, Lewis appointed Brophy as one of the directors of the CIO, which was formed by a number of groups that had been expelled from the American Federation of Labor (AFL). However, Lewis was fearful of Brophy's status and overlooked him for the position of secretary of the CIO. In 1940 Brophy suffered a heart attack, and the following year Lewis left the CIO after he opposed Franklin Roosevelt's candidacy for president. That same year, President Roosevelt appointed Brophy to be a member of the Fair Employment Practices Commission. During World War II Brophy served as the labor representative on the National War Labor Board and the Wage Stabilization Board. Lewis's successor, Philip Murray, appointed him as the director of Industrial Union Councils, and in that position he oversaw the expulsion of Communist-led unions from the CIO. He also served as the CIO representative to international labor organizations such as the World Federation of Trade Unions and the International Confederation of Free Trade Unions. Brophy continued to work for the CIO after it merged with the AFL in 1955. He was a religious man and he viewed *Rerum Novarum,* the papal encyclical of Pope Leo XIII that supported the right of workers to form unions, as a key document. Later he would advocate an industrial relations model based on the model set forth by Pope Pius XI in his 1931 encyclical *Quadrogesimo Anno.* He retired in 1961, and two years later he died in Falls Church, Virginia.

David Doyle

See also: PENNSYLVANIA

References
Brophy, John. *A Miner's Life: An Autobiography.* Edited and Supplemented by John O. P. Hall. Madison: University of Wisconsin Press, 1964.
O'Donnell, L. A. "John Brophy." *The Encyclopedia of the Irish in America.* Notre Dame: University of Notre Dame Press, 1999.

BROSNAN, PIERCE (1953–)

Possibly Ireland's most commercially successful actor, Pierce Brendan Brosnan was born in Drogheda, Co. Louth on May 16, 1953, the only child of Thomas Brosnan (born 1915, Tralee, Co. Kerry) and May Brosnan (née Smith, born in 1932 in Navan, Co. Meath). He was brought up in Navan, Co. Meath, and lived with a succession of relatives after the breakdown of his parents' marriage and his mother's departure to London to train as a nurse. He was educated in Scoil Mhuire, Navan, and in interviews he has been critical of the frequent corporal punishment meted out to students there in the 1950s.

In 1964 he moved to London to be reunited with his mother and her new husband, Bill Carmichael. He continued his education at Elliott Secondary School, where he was a mediocre student. After leaving school in 1969 he found work as a trainee commercial artist in a photographic studio and became involved in the Oval House Theatre. The Oval House had a reputation for mounting unusual, slightly avant-garde productions that included street theater. Among the productions that Brosnan appeared in were *Pucka Ri* and *A Feast of Fools,* both staged very much in the spirit of the counterculture so prominent at the time. In 1973 he enrolled in the Drama Centre, Camden, a school whose alumni included such leading stage actors as Simon Callow, Geraldine James, and Frances de la Tour. The centre was renowned for its tough teaching methods and a method approach to acting modeled on the theories of Konstantin Stanislavsky. Brosnan served his apprenticeship in an assortment of roles in the centre's productions. Upon graduation in 1976 he became an assistant stage manager at the Theatre Royal in York and continued acting in plays (e.g., *Wait Until Dark; The Red Devil Battery Sign*) and pantomimes (*The Wizard of Oz*). He also appeared in regional theater in Westcliff and, more importantly, in Glasgow's Citizens' Theatre in a revival of Noel Coward's *Semi-Monde*. In the 1970s the Citizens' Theatre was regarded as one of the most vibrant and innovative theaters in the United Kingdom, and Brosnan appeared in four productions there: he followed the Coward play with productions of *No Orchids for Miss Blandish,* based on the detective novel by James Hadley Chase; *The Painter's Palace of Pleasure,* which was based on three Jacobean tragedies; and *The Maid's Tragedy.* Each production attracted critical and public attention and proved that Brosnan was not afraid to take on challenging and controversial roles.

In 1978 he met Cassandra Harris (née Gleeson), an Australian model and actress; the couple married in 1980 and Brosnan became adoptive father to her two children from a previous relationship. Cassandra proved to be a formative influence on the development of his career, and she also provided him with his first link to the James Bond franchise—in 1982 she appeared as a Bond girl in *For Your Eyes Only.* In 1979 Brosnan won a small role in a West End production of *Filumena,* directed by Italian maestro Franco Zeffirelli. The play was a commercial and critical success, and soon after he made his debut on television in *Murphy's Stroke,* a story about four Irish builders' adventures in the British horseracing world. Other screen roles followed, including a brief appearance as an Irish Republican Army hit man in a seminal British thriller of the 1980s, John Mackenzie's *The Long Good Friday* (1980), and a supporting role in *The Mirror Crack'd* (1980), which featured an all-star cast that included Elizabeth Taylor.

Brosnan's work on *Murphy's Stroke* attracted the attention of American television producers, and he was cast in a high profile miniseries, *The Manions of America* (1981), about the experiences of an Irish family of immigrants in America. Described by reviewers as an Irish-American *Roots,* the miniseries was panned by critics but proved popular with U.S audiences. It was an important break into the American market for Brosnan, and his profile continued to rise with his casting in a long-running television show, *Remington Steele* (1982–1986; 1987). The series was a popular hit in America, and although it never taxed Brosnan's acting abilities, it did demonstrate his comedic skills.

After *Remington Steele* was axed in 1986, rumors circulated that Brosnan might be in line for one of the most coveted roles in cinema: that of James Bond. Bond producer Cubby Broccoli clearly believed Brosnan had the necessary charisma, looks, and talent to take over from Roger Moore, and in late 1986 Brosnan was offered the part. However, the role that he was intent on securing was taken from him by the producers of *Remington Steele*: Brosnan had signed a seven-year contract with them in 1982, and even though the series had been canceled in 1986, producers decided to enforce the final year of his contract and make more episodes of the series to sell to another television network. Bitterly disillusioned by the loss of the Bond role, Brosnan honored his *Remington Steele* contract and appeared in six more episodes. Brosnan's loss was Timothy Dalton's gain, albeit temporarily.

In spite of his disappointment at losing the Bond role, Brosnan's film career progressed steadily in the late 1980s. He appeared in a number of big-budget films, including *Nomads* (1986) and *The Fourth Protocol* (1987), and reestablished his links with Ireland in 1987 by starring in a rather mediocre thriller, *Taffin,* with Ray McAnally. More interesting was his appearance in *Mister Johnson,* shot in Nigeria by acclaimed Australian director Bruce Beresford and adapted from Joyce Cary's novel. The film, while not a box office hit, received positive reviews. Yet Brosnan's career choices were not always wise: he followed *Mister Johnson* with a trite, conventional thriller,

Live Wire, which won him few plaudits with critics.

In 1987 Brosnan returned to television, appearing in a miniseries, *Noble House,* and as Phileas Fogg in a new version of Jules Verne's *Around the World in 80 Days.* Just as his career seemed to be advancing at a steady pace, Brosnan received the shocking news that his wife, Cassandra, had been diagnosed with ovarian cancer. The Brosnan marriage was an unusual entity in Hollywood: it was a solid and happy partnership that had given Pierce a birth son, Sean, and two adopted children. Despite successive bouts of treatment, Cassandra died of ovarian cancer in 1991, and her death left him devastated. In interviews after her death he expressed his grief at the loss of his soul mate, and it seemed that his only remedy was to immerse himself in work.

The films in which Brosnan appeared after his wife's death were significant box office successes and again demonstrated his versatility: *The Lawnmower Man* (1997) featured him in an eccentric scientist role, while his performance in *Mrs Doubtfire* (1993) confirmed his talent for comedy. Following an appearance in Warren Beatty's forgettable *Love Affair* (1994), a remake of the 1957 classic *An Affair to Remember,* Cubby Broccoli approached him again for the Bond role. Broccoli was not happy with the current Bond, Timothy Dalton, and was reluctant to make a third Bond film with him; in turn, Dalton was also anxious to move on from the Bond role. Brosnan may not have been the producer's first choice for the role: there were rumors that the role had been offered to Mel Gibson, Liam Neeson, Harrison Ford, and Hugh Grant. Nevertheless, Brosnan was offered and accepted the role, and his first appearance as Bond was 1995's *Goldeneye*, a film received by fans and reviewers as a return to form for the Bond franchise. Many commentators praised Brosnan as the "best Bond since Connery," and he made a convincing action hero and romantic lead. While being cast as Bond undoubtedly established him as an A-list star, it had its disadvantages, too: Brosnan had always attempted to produce a varied body of work, and his experiences on *Remington* Steele alerted him to the pitfalls of typecasting. As a way of proving his star status and his versatility, he continued to take roles outside Bond, appearing in *The Mirror Has Two Faces* (1997), *Dante's Peak* (1997), and in a comic role in Tim Burton's science fiction spoof, *Mars Attacks!* (1997).

Although Brosnan was now a full-time resident of the United States, he maintained connections with Ireland and referred more and more to his Irish birth and childhood in interviews. In 1997 he returned to Ireland to make a film financed by his own production company, Irish Dreamtime. Shot on location in Co. Wicklow, *The Nephew* featured Brosnan in an Irish role alongside Donal McCann. The film's release was delayed until 1998, and it was received with mixed reviews.

Another Bond outing, *Tomorrow Never Dies*, was released in 1998, but a bigger hit was his slick remake of the Steve McQueen film, *The Thomas Crown Affair* (1999), costarring Rene Russo and acclaimed for its style and sophistication. Having acted as suave Englishmen in the Bond films and *The Thomas Crown Affair*, Brosnan played another Englishman, albeit one in disguise, in Richard Attenborough's *Grey Owl*. The film told the true story of an Englishman who masqueraded as a Native American in the 1930s, becoming a celebrity and a symbol of early conservationism. (Brosnan's interest in conservation and ecological issues was further evident in his narration of a documentary on dolphins in 2000.) Although *Grey Owl* garnered critical praise, the film was given only a limited release in both Europe and America, much to the disappointment of both its director and star.

Brosnan scored another box office hit with a third Bond film, *The World is Not Enough* (1999), and critical acclaim in John Boorman's clever thriller, *The Tailor of Panama* (2001), in which he played an amoral English spy. More sympathetic was his role in *Evelyn,* shot in Dublin in 2002 and financed by his production company. Brosnan played Desmond Doyle, a Dublin father who fought the Irish state and the Catholic Church to have his children restored to him after his wife's desertion. The film was a personal affair for Brosnan, evoking as it did his own fractured family background and his experience of the repressive society of Ireland in the 1950s.

Brosnan's most recent (and possibly last) outing as Bond was in 2002's *Die Another Day,* directed by New Zealander Lee Tamahori. Since leaving the Bond role he has broadened his range still further by playing a fast-talking lawyer in the romantic comedy *Laws of Attraction* (2004), an aging thief in *After the Sunset* (2004), and an assassin in *The Matador* (2005).

Brosnan has been the recipient of awards for his charitable and humanitarian work; has received an honorary Order of the British Empire from the Queen; an Honorary Doctorate from University College Cork (2004); and was made a Free Man of Navan in 1999. In 2001 he married his long-time partner, Keely Shaye Smith, and they have two children, Dylan (b. 1997) and Paris (b. 2001). His first marriage to

Cassandra Harris resulted in one birth son, Sean (b. 1983) and two adopted children, Charlotte (b. 1971) and Christopher (b. 1973).

Gwenda Young

See also: BERGIN, Patrick Connolly

References

Caughie, John, and Kevin Rockett. *The Companion to British and Irish Cinema.* London: British Film Institute, 1996.

Membery, York. *Pierce Brosnan: The Biography.* London: Virgin Books, 2002.

BROWN, ALEXANDER (1764–1834)

Born in Ballymena, Co. Antrim, Ireland, Alexander Brown was raised by his parents, William Brown and Margaretta Davison. His work in the linen trade began at an early age, and he married in 1783. In 1800 Brown migrated to America, settling in the expanding port city of Baltimore (as had his brother, Stewart, earlier) with his wife, Grace, and their eldest son, William. There Alexander established the Irish Linen Warehouse. While his earliest business activities are best described as those of a general linen merchant, the enterprising and hardworking Brown was soon involved in other aspects of transatlantic trade, including the export of cotton, wheat, flour, and tobacco. Increasingly, too, he looked to financial services, such as insurance and, eventually, the opening of letters of credit. Especially important was the expanding American cotton industry, and by 1803 Brown was shipping raw cotton (secured through agents in Savannah and other American towns) to markets in England. In 1810 he arranged to have a sailing vessel,

the *Armata,* built in New York. That was also the year William (his eldest son, who had been a business partner since 1805) went to England to set up a branch office in Liverpool. While mercantile transactions continued to form the backbone of Brown's daily business activities, he also began to tap into the foreign exchange market. Brown's financial capital grew with his business activities. The firm's capital stood at over one quarter of a million dollars by 1814. By the beginning of the 1820s it had surpassed $1 million. By the end of the 1820s all of Brown's four sons (William, George, John A., and James) were at the head of branch offices, giving Alexander Brown & Sons a solid presence not only in Baltimore and Liverpool but also in the growing cities of Philadelphia and New York. By the time Brown posed for his portrait by Sarah Peale in the early 1830s, his firm had become the second largest foreign exchange dealer in America, second only to the Second Bank of the United States. At the time of Alexander Brown's death, in the spring of 1834, the Irish Linen Warehouse he had begun in the winter of 1800 was worth some $4.5 million, and Brown Brothers & Co. was situated to become the most significant merchant banking firm in the United States.

Mark G. Spencer

See also: IRISH LINEN IN NORTH AMERICA

References

Brown, John Crosby. *A Hundred Years of Merchant Banking.* 1909. Reprint, New York: Arno Press, 1978.

Kent, Frank R. *The Story of Alexander Brown & Sons.* Baltimore, 1925.

Kouwenhoven, John A. *Partners in Banking: An Historical Portrait of a Great Private Bank, Brown Brothers Harriman & Co. 1818–1968.* Garden City, NY: Doubleday & Company, 1968.

Perkins, Edwin J. *Financing Anglo-American Trade: The House of Brown, 1800–1880*. Cambridge, MA: Harvard University Press, 1975.

Perkins, Edwin J. "Alexander Brown." In *American National Biography,* edited by John A. Garraty and Mark C. Carnes. New York: Oxford University Press, 1999.

BROWN, CLARENCE LEON (1890–1987)

Clarence Leon Brown was born on May 10, 1890, in Clinton, Massachusetts, the son of Larkin Brown, a loom maker (born in Pennsylvania in 1866) and Catherine Brown (née Gaw, born in Greyabbey, Co. Down, in 1865). The Browns settled in Knoxville, Tennessee, where Clarence attended high school, graduating in 1905. Something of a child prodigy, Clarence enrolled in the University of Tennessee at the age of fifteen and graduated with a double major in electrical and mechanical engineering in 1910. During the next five years, Brown worked for the Stevens Duryea Company and established his own dealership, the Brown Motor Car Company, in Alabama. By 1915 he had grown restless with the automobile trade and, prompted by a developing fascination with the films that he saw in his leisure time, he traveled to the East Coast, then the center of the movie industry, to seek out opportunities in the film industry.

Shortly after his arrival in New Jersey he became an assistant, then editor and codirector, to the great French director, Maurice Tourneur. Tourneur was an exacting employer, famous for meting out harsh treatment to his actors and crews, but Brown flourished under his tutelage and was soon promoted. In 1920 Brown directed his first feature film, a melodrama called *The Great Redeemer,* which received critical praise and attracted the interest of several producers and studios. Brown left Tourneur's company in 1923, but he would always credit the French director as his greatest influence. The rich pictorial style that can be seen in Tourneur's films is also present in many of Brown's films in both the silent and sound eras.

Brown quickly built up a reputation as a solid craftsman who could direct films in a variety of genres and who had a particular talent for eliciting strong performances from female stars, such as Laura LaPlante in *Butterfly* (1924) and *Smoldering Fires* (1925), Louise Dresser in *The Goose Woman* and *The Eagle* (both 1925), and Pauline Frederick in *Smoldering Fires* (1925). Brown's versatility and flair landed him contracts with Universal (1923–1924), United Artists (1925–1926), and Metro-Goldwyn-Mayer (1926–1952). During his time at United Artists he helped revive the careers of Rudolph Valentino (with *The Eagle*), Louise Dresser, and Pauline Frederick, while his long career at MGM saw him working with both established and emerging stars.

Profiles and assessments of Brown usually refer to him as Greta Garbo's favorite director, and indeed no other director worked as frequently with the Swedish actress as Brown. He directed her first American hit, *Flesh and the Devil,* as well as her first sound film, *Anna Christie,* and he was the first American director to realize Garbo's full star potential. Brown was also influential in guiding the career of other stars, including Joan Crawford, whom he directed, credited and uncredited, in six films. Brown's sensitive handling of actresses typed him as a "woman's director," but he proved equally adept at directing male stars, such as Clark Gable, James Stewart, and Walter Huston, and child actors, such as Elizabeth Taylor (*National Velvet*), Gene Reynolds (*Of Human Hearts*), and Mickey Rooney (in four films). However, his greatest success with a child actor came in 1946 when he directed twelve-year-old Claude Jarman Jr., whom he had discovered in a Nashville school, in an Academy Award–winning performance in *The Yearling*.

Most of Brown's career was spent working for MGM, and he was a close friend of Louis B. Mayer, MGM's head of production. Brown's commercial success and his reliability and versatility as a director enabled him to make more personal films such as *Of Human Hearts*, a sentimental paean to American values, and *Intruder in the Dust*, a stark meditation on the South and on race relations that many critics regard as his greatest film. Brown's last film, *The Plymouth Adventure*, was produced in 1952, and he retired from the film industry shortly after its release. For the next thirty-five years he concentrated on managing his real estate investments and developing a relationship with the University of Tennessee that resulted in the naming of a theater in his honor.

Brown died on August 17, 1987, and was survived by his fourth wife, Marian Brown (née Spies).

Gwenda Young

See also: HUSTON, Walter

References

Brownlow, Kevin. *The Parade's Gone By.* New York: A. P. Knopf, 1968.

Estrin, Allen. *The Hollywood Professionals.* Vol. 6, *Capra, Cukor, Brown.* Stamford, CT: A. S. Barnes, 1979.

BROWN, WILLIAM (1777–1857)

William Brown was one of the most important Irish military commanders in the Argentine War of Independence from Spain and the war against Brazil, and he was the founder of the Argentine navy. Born in Foxford, Co. Mayo, on June 22, 1777, he went with his father to settle in Pennsylvania in 1786 (though some historians argue that he was an illegitimate son of William Gannon and Mrs. Brown from Sligo). Brown began his naval career as a cabin boy in merchant ships, and he was pressed into service by the British navy in 1796. During the Napoleonic Wars he was imprisoned by the French and sent to Lorient. On being transferred to Metz he succeeded in escaping, disguised in a French officer's uniform. Brown was recaptured, however, and then imprisoned in the fortress of Verdun. From there, in 1809, he escaped in the company of a British colonel named Clutchwell and eventually reached Germany, from where he traveled to England. That year he married Eliza Chitty in Kent.

Later in 1809 William Brown was engaged in commercial business with the River Plate, chiefly trading arms and munitions on both sides of the river. Brown got involved in the War of Independence when he arrived in the Buenos Aires port during the revolution of 1810 to find it blockaded by Spanish ships. When his ship was commandeered by the Spanish, Brown organized an expedition that captured one of the blockading ships and brought it in triumph into port. Brown went back to England and returned to Buenos Aires definitively in 1812 with his wife and two children. Offered the command of a small fleet by the

Argentine authorities, he defeated the Spanish in Martín García and broke their blockade of Montevideo in March 1814, allowing its capture by the patriot army and effectively ending the Spanish threat to the newly independent state.

In 1815 the government of Buenos Aires sent Brown and his fleet to the Pacific. In 1816 he led the forces that during three weeks stormed the Peruvian port of Callao, a Spanish stronghold in South America. Brown then went on to capture the fort of Punta de las Piedras at the mouth of Guayaquil Bay in southern Ecuador. Before finding his way back to Buenos Aires, Brown was captured by the Spanish in Ecuador, and then his ship and cargo were seized by the British in Barbados, and he had to fight his case in a British court to obtain the return of his property. On return, he faced a government investigation into his exploits and was retired from active service in 1819. However, Brown was recalled to service upon the outbreak of war with Brazil in 1825–1828, during which he achieved a number of major victories in Montevideo, Pozos, Juncal, Quilmes and again in Martín García. In 1828 Brown was appointed governor of Buenos Aires. Later, in 1841, he led the successful campaign against Giuseppe Garibaldi and Admiral John H. Coe. In 1847 Brown visited his native Foxford accompanied by his daughter. On his death on March 4, 1857, in Buenos Aires, William Brown was given a public funeral and buried with full honors in Recoleta cemetery.

Edmundo Murray

See also: ARGENTINA; BRAZIL

References

De Courcy Ireland, John. *The Admiral from Mayo: A Life of Almirante William Brown from Foxford*. Dublin: Eamonn de Burca, 1995.

Ratto, Héctor R. *Historia del Almirante Brown*. Buenos Aires: Instituto de Publicaciones Navales, 1985.

Read, Jan. *The New Conquistadors*. London: Evans Brothers, 1980.

BRYAN, GEORGE (1731–1791)

George Bryan was a Philadelphia merchant and politician and a leading defender of the radical Pennsylvania constitution of 1776. Bryan was born in Dublin, the oldest son of Samuel and Sarah Dennis Bryan. In 1752, Bryan moved to Philadelphia, where his father helped establish him in the firm of Wallace and Bryan. The partnership dissolved in 1755. Bryan was heavily engaged in the transatlantic and intercolonial trades, and by 1760 he owned six vessels. He was in the top fifth of Philadelphia's merchants, but suffered financial reverses, leading to his bankruptcy in 1771.

Bryan was an active Presbyterian throughout his adult life, and he helped heal the rift between the New Light and Old Light Presbyterian churches in 1758. His religious activism led him into politics. In 1764 Bryan and Thomas Willing ran on the Presbyterian ticket for Philadelphia's two seats in the Pennsylvania Assembly, defeating the Quaker ticket of Benjamin Franklin and Joseph Galloway. In November 1764 Bryan was appointed a judge of the Philadelphia courts, a position he held until the outbreak of the American Revolution.

Bryan was active in the resistance movement. He represented Pennsylvania in the Stamp Act Congress in 1765, and joined in the non-importation movements in 1765 and 1767. In 1768 he collaborated with John Dickinson and Francis Alison on a series of essays under the pseudonym Centinel, attacking plans to establish an Anglican bishop in the colonies. Financial problems drove him out of politics in the early 1770s, but by 1776 he recovered enough to resume his career as a leader in Philadelphia and Pennsylvania politics.

One historian has called Bryan the "high priest" of Pennsylvania's radicals. His most prominent role was as an officeholder under and defender of the 1776 state constitution. It was the most radical of all the state constitutions, placing almost all of the power in a unicameral assembly, with a limited executive power in the Supreme Executive Council. Bryan was elected to the council in February 1777, becoming vice president in March. Between Thomas Willing's death in May and Joseph Reed's election in December, Bryan acted as president. Bryan was elected to the assembly in 1779, and with Reed dominated the Constitutionalist Party until 1782, when Reed began to side with the Republicans, who opposed the constitution.

While on the executive council, Bryan defended the constitution against an attack by Benjamin Rush. In 1777, Bryan, writing as Whitlocke, cheered Pennsylvania and rejected some of the main tenets of American political thought, including the need for an independent executive and a legislative upper house. Bryan argued that such balances were necessary only in a monarchy. The constitution made the people as a whole the executive power, and he believed a governor with a veto would act as a tyrant. Similarly, an upper house would mark the introduction of aristocratic privilege.

As a member of the assembly, Bryan introduced a bill for the abolition of slavery. In 1780, Pennsylvania became the first state to approve such a measure. Also in that year, Reed appointed Bryan to the Pennsylvania Supreme Court, where he served until his death in 1791. In 1784, Bryan was elected to the Council of Censors, a body consisting of two representatives from each county, which met every seven years to consider changes in the constitution. Later that year, the council issued a report that argued against changing the constitution. Bryan opposed the ratification of the United States Constitution in 1787, and he suffered a final defeat with the ratification of a new Pennsylvania constitution in 1790. In addition to his political offices, Bryan sat on the Board of Trustees of the University of Pennsylvania.

Robert W. Smith

See also: PENNSYLVANIA

References

Brunhouse, Robert. *The Counter-Revolution in Pennsylvania 1776–1790.* Harrisburg: Pennsylvania Historical and Museum Commission, 1942.

Foster, Joseph S. *In Pursuit of Equal Liberty: George Bryan and the Revolution in Pennsylvania.* University Park: Pennsylvania State University Press, 1994.

Konkle, Burton Alva. *George Bryan and the Constitution of Pennsylvania, 1731–1791.* Philadelphia: W. J. Campbell, 1922.

BUCHANAN, JAMES (1791–1868)

James Buchanan was the fifteenth president of the United States. During his presidency, between 1857 and 1861, the United States was facing a crisis that was to divide public opinion and lead to the Civil War. At the time of his death, the country was reunited, although the bitter legacy of the war took longer to fade.

Buchanan was born in 1791 to a wealthy Pennsylvania family. He was one of eleven children. His parents, James Buchanan and Elizabeth Speer, were Presbyterian immigrants from Ireland. James Sr. was born in Donegal in 1761 and had moved to Deroran near Omagh in Co. Tyrone. He arrived in the United States in 1783 and initially worked as a store-keeper, but eventually amassed a consider-able fortune. Buchanan's family was part of a wave of Protestant immigrants from the north of Ireland who settled in America in the late eighteenth century. Like many other Ulster Scots, they had migrated to Ulster from Scotland in the seventeenth century. The Buchanans had probably left Dumbarton in Scotland in the 1670s and settled in Co. Donegal.

Before becoming president, James Buchanan had a long and distinguished po-litical career. He had trained as a lawyer and had a successful practice, but in 1814 he was elected to the Pennsylvanian legisla-ture. In total, he served five terms in the House of Representatives and more than a decade in the Senate, from 1834 to 1845. Between 1832 and 1834 he was American Minister to Russia. President James K. Polk appointed Buchanan as Secretary of State in 1845, and the next few years were ones of diplomatic tension, dominated by the Oregon dispute and the conflict with Mexico. In 1848 Buchanan found himself at odds with the British government over their treatment of the Young Irelanders, who had led a small rebellion in Tipperary in July. During his meetings with British officials, he admitted that he had attended meetings of their supporters in New York and that he sympathized with their desire to achieve political independence. In the same year he also attempted unsuccessfully to be selected as the presidential candidate for the Democrat Party. From 1853 to 1856 Buchanan served as minister to Great Britain under President Franklin Pierce. Being out of the country was to his advan-tage as it meant that he remained untainted by the bitter struggles emerging over the slave question.

In March 1857 Buchanan became president of the United States. He served only one term, and did not seek reelection in 1860. As president Buchanan attempted to find a constitutional solution to the quandary caused by slavery, but he failed to recognize how deep the rift had become be-tween the North and the South. It was left to his successor, Abraham Lincoln, to find a solution to the impasse. During the war, Buchanan supported the federal govern-ment. His critics, however, vilified him and accused Buchanan of not having done enough to avert a civil war. Consequently, he became a scapegoat for the country's problems. In retirement, he wrote a defence of his actions, entitled *Mr Buchanan's Administration on the Eve of Rebellion* (1866).

Buchanan died in Pennsylvania in June 1868. He was the only president who never married. He had, however, been engaged as a young man but his fiancée's family re-garded him as unsuitable. A few days after the relationship ended, his former fiancée died, possibly having committed suicide.

Christine Kinealy

See also: ABOLITIONISM AND SLAVERY; AMERICAN CIVIL WAR

References
Auchampaugh, Philip G. *James Buchanan and His Cabinet on the Eve of Succession.* Boston: Canner Press, 1965.
Klein, Philip S. *President James Buchanan. A Biography.* University Park: Pennsylvania State University Press, 1962.
Smith, Elbert B. *The Presidency of James Buchanan.* Lawrence: University Press of Kansas, 1975.

BUCKLEY, WILLIAM F., JR. (1925–)

William F. Buckley, Jr., was born on November 24, 1925, in New York City, the sixth of ten children. Though he was of Irish ancestry, Buckley insisted—as his father had—that he was not "Irish American" but simply "American." Buckley's childhood was one of privilege; his early years were divided between Europe, where the family lived from 1929 through 1933, and Sharon, Connecticut, where the family's 47-acre estate was located. Buckley's father, William F. Buckley, Sr., had amassed considerable wealth in the oil business and was able to provide his children with private governesses, music teachers, rhetoric coaches, and language tutors. He ensured that his children lived a life far removed from the experiences of the stereotypical Irish Catholic immigrant to America.

Bill Buckley graduated from Millbrook, a small Protestant preparatory school in New York, in June 1943. A year later he was inducted into the Army, where he qualified for Officer Candidate School. After he was honorably discharged from the Army, Buckley entered Yale University in September 1946. As a student at Yale, Buckley was a member of the debate team and chairman of the *Yale Daily News*. He was also inducted into the secret senior honor society, Skull and Bones. After graduating from Yale, Buckley wrote his first book, *God and Man at Yale* (1951), in which he rejects the laissez-faire theory of education and charges certain faculty members with fostering atheism and socialism. His first book launched him on a successful writing career, both as a political commentator and as a spy novelist. Buckley would go on to publish more than forty books.

During 1952–1953, Buckley spent nine months working for the Central Intelligence Agency in Mexico City. Ostensibly there to set up an import-export business, Buckley was put in charge of gathering information on the Mexican student movement. When he and his wife, Pat, returned to the United States, Buckley began work on his second book, *McCarthy and His Enemies* (1954), a lengthy defense of the controversial senator Joseph McCarthy. In 1955 Buckley launched the *National Review*, a journal of conservative thought and opinion. He served as editor until the early 1990s, after which time he continued to contribute articles. Buckley also began writing a very successful syndicated newspaper column in 1962; his column is now carried in more than 300 newspapers.

In 1965 Buckley ran unsuccessfully for mayor of New York City. While Buckley's campaign did not land him the mayoralty, he did manage to garner 13.4 percent of the vote—a record for a conservative candidate in New York. Moreover, the campaign itself helped propel Buckley to celebrity status as he began to appear on national television with increasing regularity. Impressed by Buckley's wit and talent during the mayoral debates, WOR-TV in New York City agreed to syndicate a new television show, *Firing Line*, which would feature Buckley debating prominent political opponents. The show was a huge success, winning an Emmy in 1968. Buckley continued to host *Firing Line* until 2000. In 1991, William F. Buckley received the Presidential Medal of Freedom from President George W. Bush in recognition of all that Buckley has contributed to the intellectual foundation of the American conservative movement.

Kathleen Ruppert

See also: WASHINGTON, D.C.

References

Buckley, William F. *Miles Gone By: A Literary Autobiography*. Washington, DC: Regnery Publishing, 2004.

Judis, John B. *William F. Buckley, Jr.: Patron Saint of the Conservatives*. New York: Simon and Schuster, 1988.

BULFIN, EAMON (1892–1968)

Eamon Bulfin was an Argentine-born patriot of the Irish Easter Rising of 1916, and a son of the writer William Bulfin (1864–1910) and Anne O'Rourke. Eamon was sent to Ireland to study at St. Enda's in Rathfarnham, the bilingual school established by Padraic Pearse in 1908. In the School Roll of 1908–1909 Bulfin was one of the three pupils in Division I of First Class, together with Denis Gwyn and Frank Connolly. He was also the football captain and vice-captain of the students' office. At eighteen he entered University College Dublin, where Pearse taught. In August 1909 Eamon Bulfin adhered to the Fianna Éireann, the Irish Republican youth movement founded by Countess Markievicz as a male youth organization for what would in 1914 become the Irish Volunteers. In 1912 Bulfin followed Con Colbert and others to form a special Fianna circle of the Irish Republican Brotherhood. By the end of 1915, Eamon Bulfin had become heavily influenced by Catholic nationalism and by Pearse's idea that a personal blood sacrifice was necessary to gain Irish independence. He also became involved in organizing the Easter Rising.

The rising began before noon on Easter Monday, April 24, 1916, when 1,200 members of the Irish Volunteers and the Irish Citizen Army seized a number of strategic points in Dublin. Eamon Bulfin was charged with hoisting two Irish tricolor flags on the top of the General Post Office building, the rebels' headquarters, at the same time Pearse was reading the proclamation of the Irish Republic's provisional government. When the leaders faced certain defeat, they accepted unconditional surrender and were condemned to death by the British. Bulfin saved his life thanks to his Argentine passport (the Argentine ambassador in London interceded). Under the provisions of the Aliens Restriction Act of 1914, Bulfin was deported from the United Kingdom on March 21, 1916.

Bulfin arrived in Buenos Aires, and the Argentine authorities convicted him of deserting from the military service. Finally freed in 1919, Bulfin was appointed by Eamon de Valera as the first representative of the Ireland Republic to the Argentine Government. Among the aims of his mission were to inaugurate direct trade between Ireland and the Argentine Republic, to influence Irish opinion in Argentina, and to bring it into line with the Irish demand for a republic. In this position, Bulfin established a contact network with government officials and Irish-Argentine leaders, launched the Irish Fund to collect funds for the republican struggle, and negotiated shipments of ammunitions from Argentina to the Irish Republican Army/Irish Volunteers.

In 1922 Bulfin went back to Ireland and lived in Derrinlough, Birr, Co. Offaly. In 1920 he had been appointed chairman of the first Co. Offaly republican council (elected in absence, when he was in Argentina). He died in Ireland in 1968. His sister Catalina (1901–1976), also born in Argentina, was secretary to Austin Stack (a famuous Irish revolutionary and early Sinn Féin member of the Dáil) and married Seán MacBride (a prominent Irish international

politician and winner of the Nobel Peace
Prize in 1974).

Edmundo Murray

See also: BULFIN, William

References
Coghlan, Eduardo A. *Los Irlandeses en la
    Argentina: Su Actuación Descendencia.*
    Buenos Aires: Author's Edition, 1987.
Kennedy, Michael. "'Mr Blythe, I Think,
    Hears from him Occasionally': The
    Experiences of Irish Diplomats in Latin
    America, 1919–23." In *Irish Foreign Policy
    1919–1966: From Independence to
    Internationalism,* edited by Michael
    Kennedy and J. M. Skelly. Dublin: Four
    Courts Press, 2000, pp. 44–60.

BULFIN, WILLIAM (1863–1910)

William Bulfin, the Irish writer, journalist,
and founder of the Buenos Aires Branch of
the Gaelic League, was born at Derrinlough
near Birr, King's County (Co. Offaly) in
1863. He immigrated to Argentina in 1884
where he lived for more than twenty-two
years. The fourth of ten children of William
Bulfin and Margaret Grogan, William Bulfin
went to the national school at Cloghan,
where it is believed he was taught by
Seamus MacDonagh, father of Thomas,
the 1916 Easter Rising leader. Bulfin was
educated at the Classical Academy in Birr;
he then went to Cuba College, the Royal
Free School at Banagher founded by King
Charles I and under the Catholic headmas-
tership of Dr. King Joyce. When the Presentation Brothers opened a School in
Birr, many of the Catholic pupils were sent
to them but Bulfin was later sent back to
Banagher. He finished his education at
Galway Grammar School.

In 1884 or 1885, Bulfin and his next
eldest brother, Peter, immigrated to
Argentina. Their uncle, the Passionate

priest Father Vincent Grogan, arranged
through his friend Father Victor Carolan
in Salto Argentino, for William to get a
position. He worked first as a gaucho, a
mounted herdsman, on the pampas, and
then as camp worker and *capataz* for John
Dowling, a Longford man, at his *Estancia
Ranchos* near Carmen de Areco (a province
of Buenos Aires), where he met and fell in
love with Annie O'Rourke, the governess of
Dowling's children, who had come from
Ballacura, Ballymore, Co. Westmeath. They
became engaged in 1887, were married
in 1891, and had five children: Eamon
(1892–1968), who joined the Irish Republican Brotherhood and was active in the
lead up to the 1916 rising (he was one of
the first to enter the General Post Office
and raised one of the two flags to fly over
it for Easter week); Mary (1894–1930);
Ana (1897–1923); Eibhlínn (1899–1984);
and Catalina (1901–1976), who took the
Republican side in the Civil War, acting as
dispatch carrier, and later worked with Seán
MacBride, whom she married in 1926.

In 1888, Bulfin started writing under
the pen name of Bullfinch for the *Irish
Argentine* and later for the New York *Daily
News, The United Irishman,* and *The Southern
Cross,* adopting the nom de plume Che
Buono. In 1889, Bulfin moved to Buenos
Aires to find Mr. Mariño who "promised
him a situation in Buenos Aires in case *The
Irish Argentine* went badly with him" (letter
to Annie, February 23, 1889). After some
vicissitudes he worked for H. C. Thompson,
a furniture maker and retailer, and supported his family teaching English and
doing translations. In 1892 he got a full-
time job on *The Southern Cross,* and became
its editor and owner from 1896 until 1906,
when he fell seriously ill with rheumatic
fever.

Bulfin's episodic series of gaucho stories and sketches of rural and urban life illuminate the social history of the period of Argentine modernization. In a realistic style, he described the Irish settlers in Argentina between the 1880s and the 1900s, emphasizing the survival of their culture and character, the solidarity of the Irish community, and the hospitality and formal courtesy of the gaucho brotherhood. At the same time, he demonstrated how exile modified the Irish temperament in a series of paradoxical transformations that included practices of resistance, reproaches of assimilation, and the necessity of self-discrimination. Bulfin also reproduced "Irish-Porteño slang," a comic mixture of English, Gaelic, and Spanish. In London, T. S. Fisher Unwin published *Tales of the Pampas* (1900), Bulfin's collection of camp stories, in its Overseas Library Series. The collection was reprinted in Buenos Aires in 1997 by Literature of Latin America.

Bulfin supported the Buenos Aires branch of the Gaelic League to aid the language movement in Ireland and to promote its national aspirations and traditions. He believed cultural nationalism could unite an immigrant community and support the development of an independent Irish state. He raised money periodically for the Oireachtas Fund in Dublin, and *The Southern Cross* did the Gaelic League printing free of charge. *An Claidheamh Soluis* acknowledged this support and identified *The Southern Cross* as the South American frontier of the Irish Ireland movement. Bulfin helped introduce the game of hurling to Argentina and promoted it enthusiastically in the newspaper. He advocated for the Irish Orphanage and recorded the controversy over the administration of the Irish Catholic Association property in *The Southern Cross*.

In 1902 Bulfin returned to Ireland, where he met the Irish Irelanders at An Stad (The Stop), Cathal MacGarvey's tobacco shop, a gathering place for nationalists. He admired Thomas Davis (Irish writer and chief organizer of the Young Ireland movement) and was a great friend of Arthur Griffith (founder and first leader of Sinn Féin) and Seamus MacManus (a noted Donegal writer). It is likely that Griffith introduced Bulfin to Maud Gonne and through her he became acquainted with W. B. Yeats and Dr. Douglas Hyde. Bulfin bicycled around the country and wrote his impressions in sketches that were published serially in *The Southern Cross,* the *United Irishman,* and in the New York *Daily News* before they appeared in book form as *Rambles in Eirinn* (1907). *Rambles* was written from an emigrant's point of view for other exiles to keep alive the collective memories of home and to reassure them that they were remembered at home. He criticized the British government's policy that failed to promote sound economic development, and he rejected the materialism of Dublin and Belfast; he complained about Anglicization, lack of religious devotion, education, land policy, and emigration.

About 1905 Bulfin moved his family back to Derrinlough. He traveled back and forth between Ireland and Argentina with some stops in New York to raise money for the Gaelic League and, in 1909, to save Griffith's paper *Sinn Féin,* which was in serious debt (it appeared for the last time on January 23, 1910). In 1906 Bulfin received the Cross "Pro Ecclesia et Pontífice" from Pope Pius X for his service to the poor, orphans, immigrants, and Chaco Indians. When Bulfin was in Ireland, he was reknowned for his spirited lectures to various branches of the Gaelic League and to schools and for promoting the cause of a National University. He was known as Che Buono, Señor Bulfin, and "the Argentine

Republic Man." He handled many requests for information about trade between the two countries: the sale of Argentinean wood to Robert Johnston in the north of Mahogany and the registration of the Irish Industrial Association's Irish Trade Mark to sell linen in the country. Among Bulfin's writings, which fall into several categories, are sketches; short stories; lectures on the national language movement, heraldry, the conditions of Ireland, Irish heritage, and general education; essays on Buenos Aires, the Latin American Church, and Argentinean patriots; reviews of Irish books; and two unpublished novels, *A Man of the Pampas. A Story of Camp Life in The Argentine Republic* (1901) and *Rose of the Eskar.*

Maureen Murphy and Laura Izarra

See also: ARGENTINA; BULFIN, Eamon; HURLING IN ARGENTINA; IRISH-ARGENTINE PRESS; IRISH LINEN IN NORTH AMERICA

References

Delaney, Juan José. "The Language and Literature of the Irish in Argentina." *ABEI Journal* 2 (2000): 131–143.

Izarra, Laura. "The Irish Diaspora in Argentina." *British Association for Irish Studies Newsletter* 32 (October 2002): 5–9.

Murphy, Maureen. "The Cultural Nationalism of William Bulfin." In *John Quinn: Selected Irish Writers from His Library*, edited by Janis and Richard Londraville, 45–69. West Cornwall, CT: Locust Hill Press, 2001.

Winder, Jeanne Bulfin. "Bulfin: A Derrinlough Family." In *English and Drumcullen: a Parish in Firceall*, edited by Brian Pey. Fivealley, Birr: Firceall Heritage Group, 2003, pp. 305–323.

BULGER, JAMES "WHITEY" (1929–)

James "Whitey" Bulger was born to a large Irish-American Catholic family in the Old Harbor projects of South Boston. His younger brother, William, would later become president of the Massachusetts Senate for seventeen years. Bulger had early run-ins with the police as a teenager before joining the United States Air Force. After his discharge he took part in a series of bank robberies in Indiana for which he was arrested and sentenced to a twenty-year prison term. During his incarceration at a federal penitentiary, Bulger was accused of conspiring to escape and was transferred to Alcatraz Prison to serve the remainder of his sentence. Upon his release Bulger returned to South Boston, where he worked for a bookmaker before transferring his loyalties to the predominantly Irish Summer Hill Gang of Somerville, Massachusetts.

Bulger's criminal career reached new heights after 1975 when he began a partnership with another product of the Old Harbor projects, John Connolly, who also happened to be an agent in the Federal Bureau of Investigation (FBI). Remaining mindful of the long-standing strictures against informers among the South Boston Irish, Bulger provided Connolly with information that brought successful prosecutions against Boston's Italian mob. Connolly soon enjoyed great success in the FBI, but Bulger's cooperation came at a price: he skillfully used the FBI to target other Irish gangsters in South Boston, and then secured special protection through his connection with the increasingly influential Connolly. Bulger and his associate, Steve "The Rifleman" Flemmi, rose to the top of the organized crime scene in Boston through a tightly organized, ruthless syndicate that even used information from Connolly to murder potential informants. Bulger's subterranean connections soon stretched far beyond South Boston, with the murder of a Tulsa businessman and a foiled transatlantic gunrunning operation with the Irish Republican Army.

Bulger was as ruthless as he was resourceful, and he supplemented his image as a benevolent gangster in South Boston with a brutal willingness to dispatch even the most peripheral bystanders. Bulger kept his operation out of the public eye by playing off the bonds of ethnic loyalty among the marginalized residents of South Boston's housing projects. He had a deep disdain for the ostentatious ways of his predecessors, he abstained from smoking and drinking, and he continued to reside with his mother in the Old Harbor projects, all of which helped him to cultivate the image of a loyal son of Southie. Continuing to manipulate Connolly and his supervisor, Jack Morris, Bulger maintained absolute discipline throughout his South Boston operation.

This balancing act finally ended in the early 1990s when Connolly retired and other law-enforcement agencies and the Boston federal prosecutor's office set their sights on Bulger. Flemmi was arrested in 1995 on racketeering charges, but Bulger escaped. In 1999 a federal judge indicted Connolly on five counts, one of which stemmed from allegations that the FBI agent's warning had allowed Bulger to narrowly avert capture by the police after 1995. Whitey Bulger's continued flight also brought down his brother: in 2003 William Bulger resigned his position as chancellor of the University of Massachusetts system after disclosing that he had talked with his fugitive brother. Meanwhile, in South Boston, the disclosure of Bulger's career as an informant prompted a backlash against the former crime boss, which was presented with particular poignancy in Michael MacDonald's memoir, *All Souls: A Family Story from Southie*. Whitey Bulger's legend has continued to grow

as more accounts of his ruthless operations continue to surface, but Bulger has managed to evade apprehension despite being placed on the FBI's Top 10 Most Wanted List.

Matthew J. O'Brien

See also: BULGER, William; MacDONALD, Michael

References

Bulger, William. *While the Music Lasts: My Life in Politics.* Boston: Houghton Mifflin, 1996.

Lehr, Dick, and Gerard O'Neill. *Black Mass: The Irish Mob, the F.B.I., and a Devil's Deal.* New York: Public Affairs, 2000.

MacDonald, Michael Patrick. *All Souls: A Family Story from Southie.* New York: Random House, 1999.

BULGER, WILLIAM MICHAEL (1934–)

William Michael Bulger, born February 2, 1934, in Boston, Massachusetts, the second son of James and Jean (McCarthy) Bulger, has been a lawyer, politician, and college president. He is also the younger brother of one of Boston's most notorious gangsters, James "Whitey" Bulger, a connection that has overshadowed his otherwise very successful career, for Billy Bulger represents the Irish-American rags-to-riches story. With his brother, Billy grew up in the Old Harbor Housing Projects, in South Boston, a heavily Irish section of Boston, Massachusetts, the son of Irish-Catholic working parents. He graduated from Boston College (BA) and its law school (JD), then served in the Massachusetts House of Representatives (1961–1970), and in the Massachusetts Senate, first as a member (1971–1996), then for nine terms as its very powerful president (1978–1996). In 1996, Bulger left the political arena to become president of the University of

Massachusetts. He married Mary Foley in 1960; they had nine children.

While working his way through law school, Bulger was elected to the Massachusetts House of Representatives in 1960. He sponsored legislation to curb child abuse and to provide solar energy incentives and worked to create the Boston Housing Court and the Government Land Bank Commission, establish marine sanctuaries off the Massachusetts coast, and create a Massachusetts Water Resources Authority principally to assist in the Boston Harbor cleanup effort. He has also been chairman of the board of the State Legislative Leaders Foundation and was a former editor of the Boston College Law Annual Survey of Massachusetts Law.

Bulger has been described as sharp-witted, devout, and loyal to his old neighborhood, a classical scholar, who follows traditional social and cultural values, and politically savvy; he has suffered few losses during his political career. In his public positions, he has been a firm foe of abortion and busing and an advocate of education vouchers. In June 2003, Thomas Reilly, the state attorney general, accused Bulger of choosing loyalty to his brother over duty to the public trust, charges that followed Bulger during his entire political career. Reilly wanted Bulger to resign from the University of Massachusetts (which Bulger eventually did) as did new Republican governor Mitt Romney, who proposed eliminating Bulger's office. Bulger responded with what for him was a standard reply: He had told his brother, currently on the FBI's ten-most-wanted list, to give up crime. To further undercut Billy Bulger, in April 2003, his younger brother, Jackie, pleaded guilty to perjury and obstruction of justice after he lied to a grand jury about a Florida safe-deposit box Whitey had used.

Billy Bulger has not been indicted or faced any criminal charges as a result of his brothers' criminal activities, but he has been questioned about them. In 1990, Billy's role in a real estate deal in the Boston business district was investigated by the Massachusetts attorney general's office. In 2001, he testified, with immunity, before a federal grand jury that was interested in any possible contacts he had with brother Whitey. On June 19, 2003, the full committee of the U.S. House Government Reform Committee continued its hearings on the misuse of informants by the FBI. Bulger reasserted that he did not know where his brother was hiding as a fugitive, denied that he used his political office to get back at Whitey's enemies, or that he benefited in any way from his relationship with Whitey.

Martin J. Manning

See also: BULGER, James "Whitey"

References

Bulger, William M. *While the Music Lasts: My Life in Politics.* Boston: Houghton Mifflin, 1996.

Carr, Howie. *The Brothers Bulger: How They Terrorized and Corrupted Boston for a Quarter Century.* New York: Warner Books, 2006.

Lehr, Dick, and Gerard O'Neill. *Black Mass: The True Story of an Unholy Alliance Between the FBI and the Irish Mob.* New York: Perennial, 2001.

U.S. Congress, House Committee on Government Reform. *The Next Step in the Investigation of the Use of Informants by the Department of Justice: The Testimony of William Bulger,* hearing, 108th Congress, first Session. Washington, DC: Government Printing Office, 2003.

BURKE, EDMUND (1729–1792)

Edmund Burke was a major figure in eighteenth-century British politics and is also known to posterity as a philosopher

Portrait of Irish statesman and author Edmund Burke, who served for many years in the British House of Commons as a member of the Whig Party. (Library of Congress)

and political thinker. His most famous work, *Reflections on the Revolution in France* (1790), was a contemporary condemnation of revolutionary France, and it remains a key text in ongoing debates about the events of 1789. A conservative thinker, Burke defended aristocracy, privilege, and tradition with such eloquence that his works have become foundational texts in political theory. Always preferring the tried and tested mechanisms of the State against speculative and idealistic innovations, Burke gave a rational defense of pragmatic and incremental change in the body politic.

Paradoxically, Burke was vocal in his opposition to corruption and abuse of power, notably in his condemnation of colonial exploitation in India, embodied by the East India Company and Warren Hastings, against whom he drew up impeachment charges in 1786. His opposition to the Penal Laws in Ireland and his conciliatory speeches at the onset of the American Revolution show how his sense of justice and equity extended to a variety of causes.

Born in Dublin in 1729, Burke was early on exposed to the religious and civil divisions in Ireland during the Ascendancy period. His mother may have been a Catholic, and Burke, in his subsequent political career, was regarded with suspicion by opponents for his supposedly Catholic origins and sympathies. Certainly, he forcefully condemned the exclusion of Catholics from civil freedoms in Ireland, pointing to the absurdity and injustice of "a law directed against the mass of a nation" (*Tract on the Popery Laws*, 1765). By emphasizing the magnitude of these "unjust, impolitic and inefficacious" exclusions, Burke successfully demonstrated the moral enormity of religious persecution in Ireland, its unprecedented scale and pernicious effects.

Burke studied at Trinity College Dublin before embarking on a political career in England through the patronage of Whig magnate Lord Rockingham. Entering Parliament in 1765 and acting as Rockingham's private secretary, Burke's brilliant oratory and forensic intelligence made him a formidable parliamentarian. However, his manifest abilities were not fully compensated by the rewards of office, and his career as a practical politician was less distinguished than his abilities would suggest. Preferring opposition to power, his crusading intellect worked best in holding successive administrations to account.

Foremost amongst his concerns were the worsening relations between Britain and America in the 1760s and 1770s. Based on his paternalistic view of colonialism, Burke urged conciliatory policies on the part of Britain toward her empire. In his celebrated *Speech on American Taxation* (1774) he identified the likely outcome of

Lord North's policies toward America as secession, and he urged a return to the moderation of the Rockingham administration. His advice went unheeded, however, leading to a breakdown of trust in America and to the American Declaration of Independence in 1776.

Burke's contribution to the debates of his day was immense. The analytical rigor of his prose illuminated knotty, practical problems with general insights and general principles that are of enduring value. The prophet of conservative Europe was also a spokesman against injustice and iniquity. His principled stands on Ireland and America can be seen as continuous with, rather than contradictory to, his views on the French Revolution. His "great melody," as William Butler Yeats termed it, continues to be heard today.

Benjamin Keatinge

See also: AMERICAN WAR OF INDEPENDENCE; YEATS, William Butler

References

Burke, Edmund. *The Portable Edmund Burke*, edited by Isaac Kramnick. London: Penguin, 1999.

Burke, Edmund. *Reflections on the Revolution in France*, edited by Conor Cruise-O'Brien. London: Penguin, 1968.

Crowe, Ian, ed. *Edmund Burke: His Life and Legacy*. Dublin: Four Courts Press, 1997.

Gibbons, Luke. *Edmund Burke and Ireland: Aesthetics, Politics and the Colonial Sublime*. Cambridge: Cambridge University Press, 2003.

O'Brien, Conor Cruise. *The Great Melody: A Thematic Biography of Edmund Burke*. London: Sinclair-Stevenson, 1992.

BUTLER, JEAN (1971–)

Best known for her role in *Riverdance*, Jean Butler was born in Minneola, New York. Her mother, originally from Co. Mayo, enrolled her in Irish dance classes at age four under the tutelage of renowned teacher Donald Golden. Though trained in ballet and tap, she specialized in Irish dancing, and she won consecutive regional, national, and world championships. Her first large-scale performance was with her dancing teacher and Mick Moloney's band, Greenfields of America, and later with the well-known Irish traditional group Cherish the Ladies. At 17, Butler debuted at Carnegie Hall with the Chieftains on Saint Patrick's Day, and for several years after toured extensively with the band in America, Canada, Europe, and Japan. During this time, she and dancing partner Colin Dunne received a standing ovation for their interpretation of the Chieftains' "Cotton-Eyed Joe." Butler can be seen on the video *The Chieftains: Live From Belfast,* with Roger Daltrey and Nanci Griffith. Her taps are heard on the Chieftains' "The Long Black Veil" with Mick Jagger and the Rolling Stones. Butler has also performed with the Pogues at Brixton Academy. She later rejoined Colin Dunne in the critically acclaimed show *Dancing on Dangerous Ground.*

While studying drama at the University of Birmingham, Butler received an invitation to perform at the 1994 Eurovision Song Contest with Michael Flatley. The resulting piece, entitled *Riverdance*, caused a sensation in Europe, and producer Moya Doherty extended it into a full-scale show. Butler starred in and choreographed *Riverdance—The Show,* which toured the world in acclaimed sellout performances.

Butler's television credits include several appearances on *The Late Late Show,* with David Letterman and Jay Leno. In the United Kingdom, Butler has performed for the royal family on several occasions, most notably the Royal Variety Show. She also appeared in the Kennedy Honors in 1996, in her last public engagement for *Riverdance*. She made her acting debut in the film *The Brylcreem Boys*, alongside Gabriel Byrne, Bill Campbell, John Gordon Sinclair, and Angus McFadden.

Butler has collaborated with Donal Lunny, recording on his latest album *Coolfin* and performing with the Japanese Kodo Drummers to a sellout audience at Dublin's Royal Dublin Society. In April 1999, her contributions to the dancing world were honored with the prestigious Irish Post Award for "outstanding contribution to Irish Dance." Since marrying in 2001, Butler has been involved in several different creative mediums, including film, television, and journalism. In 2004, she appeared in three different films: as Christopher Eccleston's wife in *The Revengers Tragedy*, starring Eddie Izzard and Derek Jacobi; as Sean Champion's girlfriend in the quirky Irish independent film *Goldfish Memory*; and as one half of a dysfunctional marriage in *Old Friends*, written and directed by John Breen (*Alone It Stands*). Butler also writes a monthly column for *The Dubliner* magazine. Butler was the artist in residence for the Irish World Music Centre at the University of Limerick 2003–2005, where she completed her master's degree in contemporary dance.

Susan Gedutis Lindsay

See also: BYRNE, Gabriel; CHIEFTAINS, The; FLATLEY, Michael; MOLONEY, Mick

Reference

Jean Butler. "Biography." www.jeanbutler.com (accessed May 5, 2005).

BYRNE, DONN (1889–1928)

Brian Oswald Donn-Byrne was born on November 20, 1889, in New York City. After a few months the Byrne family returned home to Camlough, near Newry, South Armagh. Byrne, known in his teens as Brian O'Beirne, grew up speaking Irish and English. While studying romance languages and Irish literature at University College on a scholarship, Byrne came to the attention of Douglas Hyde. Hyde, the author of *Songs of Raftery*, a translation of the work of the balladeer Anthony Raftery (1784–1835), made a strong impression on Byrne. As a student Byrne helped found a literary journal, the *National Student*. He also won prizes for boxing, which he would later romanticize in his short story "Irish," in *Changeling and Other Stories* (1923).

After graduating in 1910, Byrne went to France and Germany, intending to earn a doctorate, but then went instead to New York in 1911, hoping to become a poet. There he married Dorothea Cadogan, a fellow student from Dublin. He worked as a dictionary editor, supplementing his income by writing verse, book reviews, and literary journalism. Byrne first tasted success when, writing for the first time under the name "Donn Byrne," he submitted a story, "Battle," to *Smart Set*, in February 1914, and was paid the considerable sum of $50. His first novel, *The Stranger's Banquet*, was published in 1919. Reception both for this novel and his next, *Foolish Matrons* (1920), was mixed, although each brought him $10,000 for film rights. His third novel, *Messer Marco Polo* (1921), which retold the life of Marco Polo through the mouth of a ninety-year-old Irish balladeer named Malachai Campbell of the Long Glen, established his reputation in England and the United States. Among Byrne's sources for the novel was a folk tale, "Turus Marc O'Polo," which he had heard as a boy.

As the world, and particularly Ireland, changed, the tone of Byrne's writing moved from tragic-heroic to ironic. Yet Byrne rarely commented directly on the changes. In *Hangman's House* (1926), a tale of fox hunting and horse racing, Byrne's idea of Ireland is rooted in the past. Against the landscape of what he sees in *Hangman's House* as the horrors of modern-day Ireland, Byrne sees himself as "the last traditional Irish novelist," following on from Goldsmith and Sterne. This self-image informs Byrne's novel *Blind Raftery and His Wife, Hilaria* (1924), in which Raftery is resurrected as an icon for modern Ireland.

Byrne sold his Connecticut house in 1922 and moved his family to England, but the proceeds from the sale went to creditors. After 1922 he traveled through Europe and the United States, his itinerant and extravagant lifestyle reflecting his inability to settle into the 1920s. On May 31, 1928, in a letter to Lady Barker, Byrne claimed to have suffered "a complete breakdown." Planning to rest, he bought Coolmain Castle in Cork and moved in on Friday, June 15, 1928. The following Monday, his car plunged over a bridge into Coutmacsherry Bay, West Cork. He was thirty-eight.

Byrne's tendency to romanticize Irish culture while dismissing contemporary issues came at the expense of lasting critical success. Now his work is rarely included in anthologies and, excepting a recent reappraisal by Ron Ebest, receives little attention from critics. But Byrne's contemporaries viewed his work in a more positive light. Both his novel *Field of Honor*, received as one of the best novels of the year, and his unintentionally amusing "travel guide" *Ireland: The Rock Whence I was Hewn*, were brought out in 1929. The flurry of posthumous publications continued with several novels and short story collections and a collection of *Poems* published in 1934.

Tara Stubbs

References

Bannister, Henry S., *Donn Byrne: A Descriptive Bibliography, 1912–1935.* New York: Garland, 1982.
Byrne, Donn. *Blind Raftery and His Wife, Hilaria.* New York: Century, 1924.
Byrne, Donn. *Changeling and Other Stories.* New York: Century, 1923.
Byrne, Donn. *Field of Honor.* New York: Century, 1929.
Byrne, Donn. *Hangman's House.* New York: Century, 1926.
Byrne, Donn. *Ireland: The Rock Whence I was Hewn.* London: Low, Marston, 1929.
Byrne, Donn. *Messer Marco Polo.* New York: Century, 1921.
Byrne, Donn. *Poems.* London: Low, Marston, 1934.
Ebest, Ron. "Donn Byrne: Bard of Armagh." In *New Perspectives on the Irish Diaspora,* edited by Charles Fanning, 266–280. Carbondale: Southern Illinois University, 2000.
Macauley, Thurston. *Donn Byrne: Bard of Armagh.* New York: Century, 1929.

BYRNE, GABRIEL (1950–)

Born in Dublin in 1950, Gabriel Byrne grew up in a comfortable working-class Irish Catholic family, his father having a steady job working for the Guinness brewery. The Catholic influence was quite strong on Byrne in his early years: besides receiving his primary and secondary education from nuns and priests, he briefly considered the priesthood himself, departing Ireland at age 12 to become a Catholic novitiate in Birmingham, England. Byrne remained there for only four years, dismissed, as he himself recalls, for "smoking in the graveyard." Abandoning his ambitions to become a priest, he returned to Dublin. Over the next several years he held a wide assortment of jobs, including plumber's apprentice, insurance clerk, and even morgue attendant at St. James Hospital in Dublin.

In 1969 Byrne entered University College Dublin as an undergraduate and began to explore a range of artistic pursuits. Chief among these were short-story writing and working as an editor for the literary magazine, *The Bridge,* which Byrne himself founded. *The Bridge* would go on to publish the work of a variety of now famous Irish authors and intellectuals, including Ulick O'Connor, John B. Keane, Mary Lavin, and Richard Kearney. It was also during this time that Byrne began to develop a passion for the theater and acting, which he added to his lifelong love for cinema. He was particularly drawn to the international fare of the Gate theatre in Dublin, and to the great actors who had performed there, including Mícheál MacLiammóir, Orson Welles, and James Mason. After acting in several amateur productions, Byrne had his professional debut in a production of Henrik Ibsen's *Rosmersholm* at Dublin's Focus Theatre.

Byrne's acting career quickly accelerated, and he soon gave up a teaching position he had recently acquired to dedicate himself to acting full time. He quickly became affiliated with the Project Arts Centre, run by the future film director Jim Sheridan and his brother Peter. At that time the Project was already well on its way to becoming one of the most important avant-garde theatres in Dublin. At the Project Byrne not only formed a lifelong partnership with Jim Sheridan, but he also met many of the actors and directors who would become the most well-known of their generation, including Garreth Keogh, Liam Neeson, Susan Slott, Neil Jordan, and

Alan Stanford. Throughout the 1970s Byrne appeared in numerous Project productions. He also took various roles on RTÉ, Ireland's public television station, appearing in the long-running Irish serial *The Riordans* and subsequently in *Bracken.* It was also at this time that Byrne landed his first role in a feature film, playing Uther Pendragon, King Arthur's father, in John Boorman's epic film *Excalibur* (1981).

The lack of a dynamic indigenous film industry forced Byrne to leave Ireland. In 1982, he relocated to London. He appeared there in various professional productions at venues such as the Royal Court before moving almost exclusively into film acting. During his four years in London he appeared in a variety of films, including *Reflections* (1983), *Defense of the Realm* (1985), and *Gothic* (1986). On the set of the film *Siesta* (1987), he met his future wife, the American actress Ellen Barkin, whom he would follow back to New York to settle there in the late 1980s. New York captivated Byrne, who felt "instantly at home and paradoxically alienated" walking its streets. Residing in New York, Byrne began to commute between Ireland and Los Angeles as his career continued to improve, purchasing the cottage White O'Morn, which had served as John Wayne's ancestral home in John Ford's *The Quiet Man* (1952), as his own summer home in western Ireland.

The 1990s saw Byrne become an international film star, appearing in a sizable number of works too numerous to summarize here. Among the highlights are *Miller's Crossing* (1990), *Little Women* (1994), and the Oscar award–winning *The Usual Suspects* (1995). He also became an avid producer, using revenues from his own acting work to fund a series of Irish-themed films, including two collaborations with his long-time friend, director Jim Sheridan. Byrne served as executive producer for Sheridan's *In the Name of the Father* (1993), which was nominated for seven Academy Awards, as well as associate producer for *Into the West* (1992), which Sheridan wrote. Both movies deal with darker sides of the Irish experience: *In the Name of the Father* stars Daniel Day-Lewis as Gerry Conlon, accused and wrongly imprisoned for fifteen years as one of the Guildford Four, the group charged with the 1975 IRA bombing campaign in London. *Into the West*, in which Byrne also starred, explores the day-to day racism that the Irish Traveler (gypsy) community faces as Ireland's critically and culturally ignored underclass.

Splitting his time between Ireland and the United States, Gabriel Byrne still remains a distinctly Irish presence in Hollywood, while at the same time remaining deeply involved in the cultural politics of his home country.

Michael P. Jaros

See also: DAY-LEWIS, Daniel; FORD, John; JORDAN, Neil; NEESON, Liam; SHERIDAN, Jim

References

Byrne, Gabriel. *Pictures in My Head.* Boulder, CO: Roberts Rinehart Publishers, 1995.
Naughton, John. "Byrne, Baby, Byrne." *Premiere,* June 1994, 86–90.
Rockett, Kevin. *Irish Filmography: Fiction Films 1896–1996.* Dublin: Red Mountain Media, 1988.
Sheehy, Ted. "Devil, actor, priest." *Film Ireland,* February 2000, 18–19.

CAGNEY, JAMES (1899–1986)

James Francis Cagney was one of the most recognized movie gangsters and popular culture icons of the twentieth century. Cagney was born on July 14, 1899, the son of an Irish-Norwegian mother and an alcoholic Irish father. After his father's death, his strong-willed mother moved the family uptown to the Bronx. Growing up in a working-class, heavily Jewish neighborhood provided him with the notable gestures, speech mannerisms, and staccato delivery that he would later use in films—as well as an ability to speak Yiddish. Red-haired and muscular, the five-foot-eight-inch Cagney was a scrappy street fighter, yet he somehow managed to escape the trap of alcoholism and crime into which so many of his neighborhood fell.

After a series of odd jobs, Cagney began working as a vaudeville dancer on the New York circuit. Here he met his wife of 64 years, Frances "Bill" Vernon. His move to Hollywood came in 1930, with the offer of a small role in the film version of *Sinner's Holiday,* in which he was performing on Broadway with Joan Blondell. Following this, he received a contract with Warner Brothers Studios, which assigned him supporting roles in several low-budget gangster films, a genre that had been gaining in popularity since the start of the Depression. Like other contract actors at the studio, Cagney was kept working at a frenetic pace, making thirty-six films in the next decade alone. He finally received a chance to play a leading role in his fourth film, *Public Enemy* (1931).

Cagney's portrayal of the fearless but charismatic machine-gunning gangster Tom Powers made him a star. His quick delivery and humorous asides, as well as the famous scene in which he smashes a grapefruit in Mae Clarke's face, sealed his on-screen persona as the fast-talking, womanizing gangster with the Irish smile. He perfected the character in the next few years in films like *Smart Money* (1931), *Angels With Dirty Faces* (1938), and *The Roaring Twenties* (1939). Critics have argued that Cagney created a new icon that resonated with the masses. As thoroughly American as the cowboy, yet set firmly in the ethnic neighborhoods of the city, the movie gangster as represented by Cagney became the new urban antihero, just right for the mood of the Depression. While violent, Cagney's gangsters were not one-dimensional villains, but ordinary guys whom society had failed. They took matters into their own hands and shaped their own destinies, rather than waiting patiently for good things to come

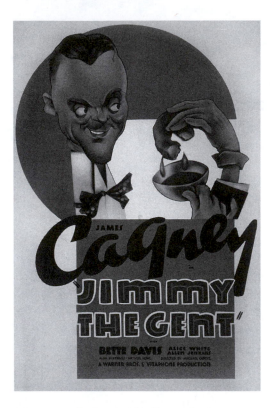

Movie poster for the 1934 film Jimmy the Gent, *starring Jimmy Cagney and Bette Davis. (Library of Congress)*

to them. Their unhappy, often violent endings represented the bitterness of a working class tired of the rough times.

Gangsters were just one of many Irish characters present in the movies during the 1930s. In *Angels With Dirty Faces,* for example, Cagney's gangster was paired with another Irish-American stock character of the period—the neighborhood priest, played by Pat O'Brien. Arguably Cagney's best depiction of the gangster antihero and his best Irish-American role of the thirties is Rocky Sullivan, a criminal idolized by the neighborhood boys to the dismay of his childhood friend turned priest, Father Connolly. When Rocky is captured and sentenced to the electric chair, Connolly tries to convince Rocky to turn "yellow" in an attempt to lessen his mythos with the

boys and teach them that crime does not pay. Cagney's Oscar-nominated performance won the film critical acclaim and lasting success, but Spencer Tracy won the Academy Award that year for his portrayal of Father Flanagan in *Boys Town.* Ironically, Cagney's association with gangster roles caused him not only to lose the Flanagan role to Tracy but also the lead in *Knute Rockne, All-American* to Pat O'Brien in 1940. While gangster films brought Cagney great financial and critical success, they also led to typecasting, as his on-screen persona and friendships with other actors in Hollywood's "Irish Mafia" gave him a reputation as a carouser and heavy drinker. Off-screen, however, Cagney was a devoted family man content to stay at his ranch in upstate New York and his farm on Martha's Vineyard.

Wearying of the gangster theme and the ill treatment studios gave actors, Cagney left Warners to set up his own production company with his brother in the mid-thirties, but he had to return when they lost money on films. Cagney did play other roles during this period, including a hoofer in *Footlight Parade* (1933), a federal agent in *G-Men* (1935), and a soldier to O'Brien's Father Duffy in *The Fighting 69th* (1940). However, the role that really changed his image, finally allowing him to break free of the gangster typecasting, was that of George M. Cohan in *Yankee Doodle Dandy* (1942). While mainly a wartime vehicle to raise morale, the film also demonstrates the acceptance that Irish Americans had won by this period; respected as loyal Americans, they nevertheless maintained an ethnic identity. In many ways, Cagney was a logical choice to play Cohan: he resembled him in build and stature, his background as a dancer allowed him to completely capture Cohan's distinctive stiff-legged style, and as one reviewer noted, "Irish Jimmy Cagney" was as "typically American" as Cohan himself. Cagney's portrayal of the flag-waving Irish-American showman won him his only Oscar, and helped dispel rumors of his Communist leanings—accusations derived from his support of Roosevelt's New Deal and the Popular Front in the Spanish Civil War.

In 1942, Cagney became president of the Screen Actors Guild (SAG), of which he was a founding member. Warner Brothers had long considered Cagney a troublemaker because of his SAG involvement, his attempts to break out of his contract, and his lobbying for more money. He left Warner Brothers again in 1943, returning in 1949 for the commercially successful gangster film, *White Heat,* in which he uttered just one of his more memorable lines, "Top o' the world, Ma!" Cagney broadened his range as an actor in the 1950s in such films as *Love Me or Leave Me* (1955), which earned him another Oscar nomination, *Mr. Roberts* (1955), *A Man of a Thousand Faces* (1957), and *Shake Hands With the Devil* (1959).

By the 1960s, Cagney was losing his enthusiasm for the business. He retired after starring in Billy Wilder's *One, Two, Three* (1961), dividing his time between upstate New York and Martha's Vineyard. In 1974, Cagney became the first actor honored with the American Film Institute's prestigious Lifetime Achievement Award. He returned to acting in 1981 to star in an adaptation of E. L. Doctorow's *Ragtime.* His last performance was with Art Carney in the television movie *Terrible Joe Moran* in 1984. Long troubled by diabetes, Cagney died on March 30, 1986, after a heart attack.

Meaghan Dwyer

See also: O' BRIEN, Pat; COHAN, George M.

References

Cagney, James. *Cagney by Cagney.* Garden City, NY: Doubleday, 1976.

Curran, Joseph M. *Hibernian Green on the Silver Screen: The Irish and American Movies.* New York: Greenwood Press, 1989.

James, C. L. R. *American Civilization.* Cambridge, MA: Blackwell Publishers, 1993.

Warren, Doug. *James Cagney, the Authorized Biography.* New York: St. Martin's Press, 1983.

CAMPBELL, PETER (1780–Ca.1832)

Born in Ireland in 1780, Peter Campbell enlisted in the 71st Highland Regiment that sailed in July 1805, with other divisions, for the Cape of Good Hope, and in 1806 invaded Buenos Aires under William Carr Beresford. After the British campaigns failed and the regiment withdrew, Campbell was one of the soldiers who managed to remain in the River Plate region. He joined the patriot ranks as a guerrilla leader, harassing Spanish forces both on land and on the Paraná River. He had a notorious dexterity in the gaucho form of dueling, wielding a long knife in one hand and wrapping a poncho around the other arm as a protective measure. Campbell carried two riding pistols, a sabre, and a large knife in a leather sheath, for his personal protection, and was assisted by a Tipperary-born gaucho.

Campbell rose to prominence as a superb guerrilla fighter, serving under José Artigas, the *caudillo* of a region including today's Argentine provinces of Entre Ríos and Corrientes, and much of Uruguay, and who is regarded as one of Uruguay's founding fathers. Campbell played a prominent role in the affairs of Corrientes province, and for a period after 1819 acted as its deputy governor. He made a notable contribution to the tactics used by the local military forces, first against the Spaniards during the War of Independence, and later against Buenos Aires in the civil wars that followed Argentine sovereignty.

Peter Campbell was responsible for establishing a regiment of mounted Tape Indians, who were feared as both a cavalry and an infantry force because their tactics were so difficult to counter. Armed with rifles with long bayonets attached, his Indian force was trained to charge the enemy on horseback at great speed and to dismount and open fire with their rifles. Campbell's military prowess and organizational ability were not confined to terra firma. In 1814 he began building up a squadron of river vessels to support Artigas on the Paraná. In 1818 Peter Campbell was responsible for the second squadron of the Uruguayan naval forces, based on Goya and Esquina. He became naval commander-in-chief of the region and the scourge of the Paraguayan dictator Francia's river fleet. On August 21, 1818, Artigas appointed Campbell as the first naval commander of the patriot fleet. For this reason, the Irishman is acknowledged as the founder of the Uruguayan navy. In September 1818 Peter Campbell managed to seize two vessels carrying arms for the Paraguayan army. In January-March 1819, together with the land forces of governor López, Campbell besieged the town of Capilla del Rosario. On March 10, 1919, the Uruguayan army won the battle of Barrancas against the army of Buenos Aires. Advancing over the Argentine city, the combined federalist forces defeated the *porteños* at Cepeda (February 1, 1820) and San Nicolás (February 13, 1820).

However, in the last naval battle against Monteverde on July 30, 1820, Artigas was defeated by Ramírez, a rival warlord from Entre Ríos province. Campbell, who initially escaped, was captured and banished in shackles to Paraguay. Dictator Francia, instead of putting his former foe to death, spared Campbell's life, possibly out of respect for his adversary's courage and military prowess. Peter Campbell was allowed to settle in the Paraguayan town of Neembucú, where he returned to his old trade of tanner. There is disagreement over the location and date of his death, which occurred in or about 1832. After his burial place in Villa del Pilar was discovered in 1961, his remains were handed over to Uruguay for reinterment in Montevideo on May 18, 1961, as befitted the founder of that country's navy.

Edmundo Murray

See also: URUGUAY

Reference
Pyne, Peter. *The Invasions of Buenos Aires, 1806–1807: The Irish Dimension*. Research Paper 20. Liverpool: University of Liverpool, Institute of Latin American Studies, 1996.

CANALS AND THE IRISH INVOLVEMENT

A crucial factor in the commercial and industrial development of the United States was the construction of canals, artificially created waterways that were connected to natural bodies of water to transport goods and people; and the involvement of immigrant Irish labor was integral to the digging of those canals. These waterways had a profound effect on the exploration and modernization of the eastern part of the North American continent, especially in the early 1800s. The construction and usage of canals were important parts of the North American economy (which included both

Canada and the United States) in the nineteenth century, although much of the construction came during a burst of activity from 1817 to 1850.

The history of canal construction in the eastern Americas can be traced back to William Penn, who in 1676 signed a document authorizing surveyors to examine the possibility of constructing a canal that could handle vessels of 100 tons from the Delaware River, on the western side of New Jersey, to New York Bay, on the eastern side, as a way to facilitate the movement of goods from New York City to Philadelphia. No construction was undertaken, however, and no written report has been found. Canal, lockage, and river improvement projects were begun in the 1780s, but there were only 100 miles of canals in the United States by 1816.

That changed with the construction of the Erie Canal, which is 340 miles long (originally 363) and crosses central New York State from Albany on the Hudson River in the east to Buffalo on Lake Erie and the Niagara River in the west. Construction on the Erie Canal lasted from 1817 to 1825, and once the Erie started being used, there was an outbreak of what some called "canal fever"—that is, a frenzy of canal construction brought on by visions of high profits and low freight rates. As a result, there were about 1,300 miles of canals in the United States by 1830, 3,325 miles by 1840, and 4,254 by 1860; this is referred to as the canal era. At the same time, the Welland and Rideau canals were dug in Canada, with distances of 27 and 120 miles, respectively. Engineering as a profession in North America traces its roots largely to the construction of canals, and the Erie Canal was a source of technical know-how for most canal building. In addition, the Erie Canal is credited with giving an enormous boost to the economy of all of New York State and helping open the American Midwest to exploration. A major use of canals in the New York-New Jersey-Pennsylvania area was for shipping coal from mining areas to consumer markets, so that canals provided a huge boost to the prosperity associated with coal.

The first canal workers, in both the United States and Canada, tended to be native-born Americans who went to canal work from farms on a casual or seasonal basis (mostly farm laborers but sometimes even farm owners). Thus, areas where farms were not doing well could see some surpluses of available laborers, but the presence of a canal project could also cause shortages on farms during planting or harvesting time. As time passed, the majority of canal workers came to be immigrants from Europe, for most of whom canal work was just a passing stage in their work career, although some Canadians worked on canals in the United States. Canal work lent itself to the system of working for a while and returning home periodically with money.

In the late eighteenth and very early nineteenth centuries indentured servants sometimes worked on canals. They were required to work a number of years in return for passage and provisions during the time of indenture (at one point $12 steerage and $15 provision fee). The practice was never significant in New England, however, and was more important in the South and parts of the Mid-Atlantic states. Indenture as a practice on canals was already dying out by the end of the eighteenth century, although there were isolated cases in the 1820s. Most of the indentured servants were Irish, a few were English and German; newspaper advertisements for runaways, when giving ethnicity, always specified Irish. Runaways who were caught had their eyebrows shaved and a cross shaved in their scalp.

Irish involvement in the construction of canals in North America may even be said to have begun in Ireland, with the construction of Dublin's Grand Canal and the Royal Canal in the eighteenth century. In 1816, a group of American engineers who were working on plans for the Erie Canal made a fact-finding trip to England, and word spread about work opportunities in the United States. The following year, Canvass White, an engineer from New York State, went back to England and recruited a workforce of experienced Irish workers. By 1818, it was reported that of a canal workforce of about 4,000 on the Erie Canal, about one-quarter (1,000) were foreign born, and most of those were Irish. Thousands of Irish people moved into Albany in 1824, many of them involved in canal work.

There is no reliable information on exactly how many canal workers were Irish, just as there is no reliable information about how many had already been living in the United States and how many had just arrived, or where they came from either in America or Ireland. This is because much canal construction in the United States was handled by contractors who agreed to build sections of each canal. These contractors were notorious for not keeping records; in fact, some were accused of absconding without paying their workers. For the most part, the employees were unable to read or write; and, even if they could, they had no time for record keeping.

The nature of canal work remained largely the same throughout the entire canal-building period, powered by humans and beasts using traditional tools. The workday extended from before sunrise until after sunset, every day, weather permitting, with two-hour dinner breaks. Most workers lived in all-male barracks or family shanties on the work site or in nearby towns; accommodations were meant to be temporary and were limited in comfort. The shantytowns were the setting for much drinking, criminal activity, and violence and were looked down on by permanent residents, who avoided them as much as possible. Canal workers were thus set off from society by the kind of work they did as well as their ethnic background; so that they became further stigmatized even in the minds of other potential workers; canal work came to be seen as the lowest of the low labor, done only by Irishmen and slaves. In fact, many slave owners would not allow their slaves to perform canal work because it was too dangerous. Irish laborers became so numerous in canal construction that it was said that to build a canal four things were needed: a pick, a shovel, a wheelbarrow, and an Irishman.

The workforce primarily consisted of unmarried males, although some were married. Women could often work as cooks, cleaners, and laundresses, and were often paid by the same contractors who paid the diggers. For married women, the income, although less than what the men received, could help a family make ends meet.

The question arises as to why so many Irish people took part in constructing America's canals. For one thing, no skills were needed, and most of the Irish coming to America in the nineteenth century were unskilled. Also, there appears to have been a kinship network of communication about canal work opportunities; for example, one group of workers on the Susquehanna

Canal in Pennsylvania knew each other from the same place in Ireland. Similar networks have been discerned on the Miami Canal in Ohio as well as on the Blackstone Canal in Massachusetts and Rhode Island, where canal workers arrived after gaining experience in Britain and on the Erie Canal. It is also possible that taverns served as recruiting grounds. In addition, Irish immigrants found out about available work from agencies set up to help them, including the Irish Emigrant Association (founded 1825; its successor, was the Irish Emigrant Society, 1841) and the Union Emigrant Society (formed 1829) in New York. A publication, the New York *Truth Teller,* which addressed an immigrant audience, became an active promoter of public works employment. The *Truth Teller* directed readers to specific projects, providing detailed information on how these places could be reached, how much money they might pay, and where a Catholic priest would be available. It is also believed that Irish grocers, who also sold liquor, allowed their countrymen to run up bills and then bargained with contractors to supply laborers from among these debtors. Traditionally, it has been assumed that the Irish arrived as peasants, that is, people who had experience with the land but not with commercial relations and wage labor, but some scholars dispute that, noting that workers on the Rideau Canal in 1829 came mostly from Ulster and Leinster, the two most commercial parts of Ireland, as opposed to coming from the agrarian south and west. In 1832, laborers could earn $12 to $16 a month and board. For many in Ireland, this was considered a handsome sum.

Wages were not always a certainty, however. For instance, in 1804 Irish laborers on the Chesapeake and Delaware Canal who were disgruntled about not receiving wages, took their anger out by picking a fight with jockeys, gamblers, and residents of Elkton, Maryland, during a fair at a racetrack. This happened at a time of financial difficulties for the canal contractors that resulted in problems paying canal workers. In 1826 ground was broken for the Shubenacadie Canal, a 70-mile waterway that bisects Nova Scotia. Work ceased when the construction company ran out of money, but it was resumed in 1853. The money problems that caused the construction stoppage also led to a protest by Irish workers. After they had not been paid for a while, they were angered to learn that the Scottish masons (who could be considered skilled) had received a pay-and-hours adjustment that was denied to the Irish laborers.

Despite difficulties, canal building continued. In 1830 ground was broken for the Delaware and Raritan Canal, which would cut across New Jersey on approximately the route William Penn had envisioned. Canvass White, the engineer who had traveled to England, was appointed chief engineer. The Delaware and Raritan Canal had a main canal 44 miles long in a northwesterly/southeasterly diagonal, linking New Brunswick to Trenton. To ensure a flow of water into the canal, a feeder canal 22 miles long was built to bring in water from the Delaware River. One of White's associates was a man named Ashbel Lynch, who was put in charge of the feeder canal.

The workforce on the Delaware and Raritan Canal has been estimated at between 3,000 and 5,000 workers, most of whom were Irish. As with other canals, it is impossible to ascertain any precise numbers because of a lack of records. Although most workers on the Delaware and Raritan did a lot of digging, they also built stone walls in certain sections, so that they came to be seen as having a skill above simple wielding of a pick or shovel.

In 1832 there was another kind of canal fever at the Delaware and Raritan Canal—an outbreak of cholera, which some historians believe came from the Erie Canal and others from the West Indies. The outbreak spread rapidly, abetted by a lack of ordinary sanitary precaution in the squalid shantytowns, and spread to surrounding areas, including Princeton, New Jersey. An isolation hospital was set up in the Princeton municipal hall, and this, along with Ashbel Lynch's work to improve sanitary conditions on the canal sites, helped bring the disease under control by 1833.

Once again, it is impossible to know with any certainty how many laborers died from this outbreak of sickness. Few workers had family ties in the United States, and canal contractors made no attempt to notify relatives in Ireland about the death of a loved one. The dead were buried in unmarked graves, usually in hastily conducted funerals. In 1970, more than 50 graves with crude headstones were reported on Bull's Island, a small island in the Delaware River; these graves are believed to be those of canal fever victims; but there is no knowing if each grave held one body or more.

What may serve as an indication of how many died is an advertisement that appeared in the *Truth Teller* on May 4, 1833, calling for 2,000 laborers, who would receive free transportation to the work site. The figure of 2,000 may not be a reliable indicator of the actual number of employees needed, however, because historically canal contractors would inflate the number of worker vacancies in order to get a large applicant pool and thus depress wages.

The Erie Canal continues to be used and is an important waterway in the northeastern United States, although it has been rerouted slightly. In 1933 the Delaware and Raritan Canal was abandoned because it was no longer serving a useful commercial purpose; this was the fate of most canals in the United States and Canada. Many canals were simply supplanted by railroads, which could move in a more direct line and were not subject to vagaries of the weather; many canals were useless in the winter because they froze over. Canals would be built after the canal era, but they were large ship-navigation systems that could compete with railroads, such as the St. Lawrence Seaway, and not towpath canals, such as the Delaware and Raritan. In 1973 the Delaware and Raritan Canal was named to the National Register of Historic places, and in 1974 it was made a state park. Today there are memorial tablets along the Delaware and Raritan, erected by the Ancient Order of Hibernians. These tablets commemorate the part played by Irish labor in the construction of the Delaware and Raritan.

Donald McNamara

See also: PENNSYLVANIA

References

Barth, Linda J. *The Delaware and Raritan Canal.* Charleston, SC: Arcadia, 2002.

Latta, Peter M. "Cabins and Protest on the Shubenacadie Canal." *Canal History and Technology Proceedings* 25 (March 1996): 9–22.

Miller, Kerby A. *Emigrants and Exiles: Ireland and the Irish Exodus to North America.* Oxford: Oxford University Press, 1985.

Potter, George. *To the Golden Door: The Story of the Irish in Ireland and America.* Westport, CT: Greenwood Press, 1960.

Tobin, Catherine. "Irish Labor on American Canals." *Canal History and Technology Proceedings* 9 (March 1990): 163–186.

Way, Peter. *Common Labour: Workers and the Digging of the North American Canals, 1780–1860*. Cambridge: Cambridge University Press, 1993.

CARNEY, ANDREW (1794–1864)

An entrepreneur and philanthropist, Andrew Carney was one of Boston's most famous Irish-American Catholics. Born in Co. Cavan in Northern Ireland, he immigrated to Boston in 1816 where he became a successful clothing manufacturer. He and his partner, Jacob Sleeper, a Methodist from Maine, earned their fortunes in the firm Carney & Sleeper Clothiers by manufacturing military uniforms in the 1830s. Carney was an organizer of the Montgomery Guards, an Irish-American company in the Massachusetts militia in 1837. Despite widespread nativism and anti-Catholicism, by the 1850s Carney increased his fortune with prudent investments in Boston real estate. He was a founder of the First National Bank of Boston and the John Hancock Insurance Company.

Carney devoted much of his time and money to Catholic charities. He purchased a Unitarian church in the Irish Fort Hill neighborhood as St. Vincent's Church. He was a major supporter of Father Theobold Mathew's temperance crusade in 1850, and purchased the land in the South End on which the new Cathedral of the Holy Cross was built in 1860. Carney also supported the Jesuit priests who built the magnificent Church of the Immaculate Conception in Boston's South End. With his close friend Bishop John B. Fitzpatrick, Carney's home on Ann Street in Boston was a center of Irish-American community activities.

Carney was also a founder of the St. Vincent Home for Girls (1858), and he established the Carney Hospital in South Boston (1863), the first Catholic hospital in New England. During the Civil War, Carney was also a benefactor of Bishop John J. Williams's orphanage, the Home for Destitute Catholic Children (1864), and the House of the Angel Guardian (1855) for homeless boys in Boston's North End. With Bishop Fitzpatrick and the Reverend John McElroy, S. J., Carney founded Boston College (1863) and was its chief benefactor as early as 1858 when ground was broken in the South End of the city. His role in founding the college was remembered in the Boston College centennial year when a new campus building was named in his honor in 1963. Carney, the state's leading Catholic philanthropist, died in Boston on April 4, 1864, and was buried at Forest Hills Cemetery.

Peter C. Holloran

See also: AMERICAN TEMPERANCE MOVEMENT; BOSTON; MATHEW, Father Theobald

References
Donovan, Charles F., David R. Dunigan, and Paul A. Fitzgerald. *History of Boston College: From the Beginnings to 1990*. Boston: University Press of Boston College, 1990.
Holloran, Peter C. *Boston's Wayward Children: Social Services for Homeless Children, 1820 to 1920*. Boston: Northeastern University Press, 1994.
O'Connore, Thomas H. *Fitzpatrick's Boston, 1846–1866: John Bernard Fitzpatrick, Third Bishop of Boston*. Boston: Northeastern University Press, 1984.

CARNEY, ART (1918–2003)

Born Arthur William Matthew Carney in Mount Vernon, New York, Art Carney was the youngest of six sons born to Edward Michael and Helen (Farrell) Carney, who were both of Irish descent. In 1936 Art graduated from the A. B. Davis High

School, where he had gained a reputation for impersonations and had won a talent contest. He never attended acting school but, after a period spent working in a jewelry store, his brother, who worked for the MCA agency, got him a job working with the Horace Heidt Orchestra. Carney spent three years on the road with the Heidt Orchestra, performing impersonations and novelty songs. In 1941 he appeared in the Heidt film *Pot o' Gold.* He tried to make a career in stand-up comedy and provided one of the voices on *Gangbusters,* a popular radio series in the 1930s. In 1940 he married Jean Myers, and they had three children together. During World War II he was sent to France as an infantryman, where he was wounded in the right leg by shrapnel during the Battle of Normandy. This led to his spending nine months recovering in the hospital. As a result of this injury he walked with a limp for the rest of his life as one leg was shorter than the other.

In the late 1940s Carney appeared on Henry Morgan's radio show, and he provided the voice of Red Lantern on the radio show *Land of the Lost.* He also became a regular on Morey Amsterdam's television show, in which he played a waiter. He worked with Jackie Gleason in his series *Cavalcade of Stars,* and from this emerged the role for which he is remembered most fondly, that of Ed Norton in *The Honeymooners,* one of the most popular television series of its time. Carney played the dim-witted sewer worker Norton opposite Gleason, who played his neighbor Ralph Kramden, the bus driver who always had a get-rich-quick scheme. The pair's onscreen chemistry was summed up in Norton's cry, "Hey, there, Ralphie Boy!" Set in an apartment building in Brooklyn,

the show offered a comic look at urban working class life and ran for 39 episodes on CBS from 1955 until the following year. It was frequently shown again in later years. After *The Honeymooners,* Carney played opposite Siobhan McKenna in *The Rope Dancers* on Broadway, and he appeared in the television versions of *Harvey* and *Our Town.* In 1960 he appeared on Broadway in *Take Her, She's Mine,* and in 1965 he starred as Felix Unger opposite Walter Matthau in the Broadway production of Neil Simon's play *The Odd Couple.* However, he was forced to drop out of the show after he suffered a nervous breakdown as a result of which he became addicted to alcohol, amphetamines, and barbiturates. At this time his marriage to Jean Myers ended and they divorced. He recovered in a Connecticut sanatorium when his old friend Jackie Gleason helped him by casting him in new episodes of *The Honeymooners.*

In 1966 he married Barbara Isaacs. He was nominated for Broadway's 1969 Tony Award as Best Actor (Dramatic) for his performance in Brian Friel's *Lovers.* For his first leading role in a film, in *Harry and Tonto,* he beat Jack Nicholson, Al Pacino, Dustin Hoffman, and Albert Finney to win the Academy Award for Best Actor in 1974. In 1977 he divorced Barbara Isaacs, and three years later he remarried Jean Myers, with whom he remained until his death. He was nominated for seven Emmy awards throughout his career. He won six times, five times for his work with Gleason and once for supporting James Cagney in *Terrible Joe Moran.* In 1985 he teamed up with Gleason again for the television movie *Izzy and Moe,* in which they played two prohibition agents. He was awarded a star on the Hollywood Walk of Fame at 6627

Hollywood Boulevard. Carney died five days after his 85th birthday on November 9, 2003, in Chester, Conneticut.

David Doyle

See also: CAGNEY, James; GLEASON, John Herbert

References

Harrell, Joy. "Art Carney." *The Encyclopedia of the Irish in America.* Ed. Michael Glazier. Notre Dame, IN: University of Notre Dame Press, 1999.

Smith, Ronald L. *Who's Who in Comedy.* New York: Facts on File, 1992.

Starr, Michael Seth. *Art Carney: A Biography.* New York: Applause Theatre & Cinema Books, 2002.

CAROLAN, TURLOCH (1670–1738)

With more than 200 harp tunes attributed to him, Turloch Carolan is the best known Irish composer in the world. Born at Nobber, Co. Meath, Carolan was four when his parents moved to Co. Roscommon, where his father was employed by the Mac Dermott Roe family. Mrs. Mac Dermott Roe evidently saw some promise in the boy and had him educated along with her own children. When Carolan was blinded by smallpox at the age of eighteen, Mrs. Mac Dermott Roe apprenticed him to a harper. Three years later, the young man embarked on his career as an itinerant musician, playing in the houses of the aristocracy. According to one story, because Carolan had learned the harp too late in life to become a virtuoso performer, he was advised to specialize in writing songs dedicated to his upper-class patrons. Many of his airs, therefore, were created as settings for dedicatory songs, all of which were in Gaelic.

Carolan's travels took him to Dublin, where he encountered the popular Italian baroque music of the day. He was particularly taken with the music of Corelli and may have met violinist and composer Francesco Geminiani, who had settled in the city. Being blind, Carolan could not study, much less master, the theories and complex structures of baroque music. However, he became a kind of "fusion" artist, blending the tradition of Irish harp music and the melodic figures of the baroque with the popular dance tunes and rhythms of Irish traditional music.

Carolan's compositions were published throughout the eighteenth century. Some of his pieces were still in the repertory of the aging harpers assembled for the Belfast Harp Festival of 1792, where Edward Bunting noted and later published some of them in his various collections. When Chicago police superintendent Francis O'Neill published *The Music of Ireland* in 1903, he included 76 tunes that he attributed (sometimes inaccurately) to Carolan. Nevertheless, Carolan's music was little known outside of the intimate circles of Irish music enthusiasts in Ireland and the United States. Then in 1958, Donal O'Sullivan published his biography of Carolan, along with 200 tunes. A few years later Irish composer Seán Ó Riada and his folk band Ceoltóirí Chualann began performing and recording Carolan's music. Later, The Chieftains also included Carolan pieces in their recordings and concerts. Other traditional groups followed suit, and by the end of the twentieth century, Carolan favorites such as "Planxty Irwin," "Sheebeg, Sheemore," "George Brabazon," "A Fine Toast to Hewlett," "Lord Inchiquin," and "Morgan Magan" had become part of the standard repertory for many Irish bands. Carolan's music has become particularly popular in America, where many consider it emblematic of Celtic or even New Age music.

William H. A. Williams

See also: CHIEFTAINS, The

Reference

O'Sullivan, Donal. *Carolan: The Life Times and Music of an Irish Harper.* Cork: Ossian, 2001.

CARROLL, CHARLES (1737–1832)

Charles Carroll of Carrollton was the only Catholic signer of the Declaration of Independence. Born on September 19, 1737, he was the son of Charles Carroll of Annapolis and Elizabeth Brooke. The Carroll family was descended from the O'Carroll's of King's County, Ireland. The first Charles Carroll came to Maryland in 1688 and briefly served as attorney general. In 1748, Carroll's father sent him to college at his alma mater, St. Omer in France. He spent the next seventeen years abroad, living in London after finishing his studies in France. He always intended to return to Maryland and had to dissuade his father from migrating to a colony on the Arkansas River. Carroll returned to Maryland in February 1765. Although trained in the law, he did not practice, and lived as a country squire. As a Catholic, Carroll was barred from the political life of the province.

Carroll entered public debate as a newspaper essayist in 1773. Three years before, Governor Robert Eden had issued a proclamation fixing fees charged by provincial officers and the clergy at a level higher than that approved by the assembly. Daniel Dulany, Jr., defended the move under the pseudonym Antilon. Carroll responded with a dialogue between First Citizen and Second Citizen in the February 4, 1773, *Maryland Gazette.* First Citizen, an Eden opponent, won the argument. Carroll abandoned the dialogue format and attacked the Eden administration as First Citizen. The articles established Carroll's patriot credentials. In May 1774 he was appointed to the Annapolis Committee of Correspondence. It was his first political office. He was not elected to the first Continental Congress but accompanied the Maryland delegation as a private citizen.

In February 1776, Congress chose Carroll, Benjamin Franklin, and Samuel Chase for a diplomatic mission designed to induce Canada to join the rebellion. Carroll's fluency in French, his impeccable patriot credentials, and his religion all worked in his favor. Congress also asked Carroll to prevail upon his cousin John Carroll, the future bishop of Baltimore, to accompany the mission. Lack of money and troops from Congress and lack of interest from the people of Quebec doomed the mission. On June 11, 1776, Carroll and Chase reported the failure of the mission to Congress.

On July 4 the Maryland legislature elected Carroll as a delegate to the Continental Congress. He arrived at Philadelphia on July 18, in time to vote for the embossment of the Declaration of Independence the next day. He signed the document on August 2. Soon after, Carroll left to attend the convention that drafted the Maryland Declaration of Rights and constitution. The constitution took effect in February 1777, and Carroll took office as a senator. He established himself as a conservative revolutionary, vehemently opposing a legal tender bill supported by Samuel Chase. Carroll returned to Congress in May 1777 and served until June 1778. He was on the board of war and was part of the investigation of conditions at Valley Forge. He was frequently mentioned for higher posts, such as minister to France or president of Congress.

Carroll was elected to represent Maryland at the Constitutional Convention but did not attend. He supported ratification and became a Federalist of the Hamiltonian variety. He served as a U.S. senator from 1789 to 1792, while serving concurrently as a Maryland state senator. Carroll resigned from the United States Senate when Maryland outlawed dual office-holding. He remained a state senator until 1800. Carroll spent the rest of his life tending to his estates and promoting internal improvements. He served on the boards of the Potomac Company, which became the Chesapeake and Ohio Canal Company in 1823, and the Baltimore and Ohio Railroad. Carroll died on November 14, 1832.

Robert W. Smith

See also: CARROLL, Bishop John; MARYLAND

References

Gurn, Joseph. *Charles Carroll of Carrollton.* New York: P. J. Kenedy & Sons, 1932.
Hanley, Thomas O'Brien. *Revolutionary Statesman: Charles Carroll and the War.* Chicago: Loyola University Press, 1983.
Smith, Ellen Hart. *Charles Carroll of Carrollton.* Cambridge, MA: Harvard University Press, 1942.

CARROLL, JAMES P. (1943–)

Born in Chicago in 1943, James Carroll spent most of his formative years in Washington, D.C. where his father worked as an Air Force general and the director of the Defense Intelligence Agency. Typical of a son of a man in the military, Carroll spent

some time abroad during his youth, which gave him a more worldly perspective despite his youth. Strong academically, he was educated at Washington's Priory School and at an American high school in Wiesbaden, Germany, where his father was stationed.

Carroll attended Georgetown University before he decided to move on and attend St. Paul's College, also known as the Paulist Fathers' seminary, where he received his bachelor's and master's degrees. After completing his education, Carroll was ordained to the priesthood in 1969, beginning his work within the church as the Catholic chaplain at Boston University from 1969 to 1974. While at Boston University, he was able to connect with many influential journalists, writers, and intellectuals, who helped to foster his own love of writing. He benefited from his time there by taking the opportunity to study poetry with George Starbuck. Making use of what he learned, Carroll published a book of poems as well as books dealing with religious subject matter. Additionally, in 1972 he began working as a columnist for the *National Catholic Report.* He worked with the Reporter until 1975 and received nationwide recognition when he was named best columnist by the Catholic Press Association.

Not only was he a successful journalist, but Carroll soon also received praise for his writings on religion and politics, earning him the first Thomas Merton Award from Pittsburgh's Thomas Merton Center in 1972. In light of growing success and his desire to more actively pursue his writing, he left the priesthood in 1974.

Soon after, he became a playwright and was in residence at the Berkshire Theater Festival. His plays have been staged not only at the Berkshire Theater Festival but also at Boston's Next Move Theater. Not simply satisfied with theater, Carroll published his first novel, *Madonna Red,* in 1976. He went on to publish a string of successful novels, and his works include *Mortal Friends* (1978), *Prince of Peace* (1984), *Memorial Bridge* (1991), and *The City Below* (1994).

In 1997, Carroll achieved one of his greatest successes with the publication of *An American Requiem: God, My Father, and the War That Came Between Us.* It is the story about the effect of the Vietnam War on his family that is not only autobiographical but also able to speak about the experiences of an entire generation. Originally an ROTC (Reserve Officer Training Corps) student at Georgetown, Carroll quickly changed his perspective on the war and decided to join the priesthood and become active in the protest movement, even though he was fearful of his father's response. In recognition of his gripping work, Carroll was awarded the National Book Award.

Carroll has maintained his antiwar stance and his love of writing and journalism. He has written for a number of different publications, most often *The New Yorker.* Additionally, he writes a weekly editorial piece for the *Boston Globe* newspaper. Most recently, he has strongly condemned President George W. Bush's war on terror not only in his weekly columns but also in his latest book publication, *Crusade: Chronicles of an Unjust War.* Made up of his thoughts on the war on terror and some of his weekly columns from the *Boston Globe,* the book protests Bush's conduct while offering Carroll's beliefs on what America was meant to be. Currently, Carroll and his wife, novelist Alexandra Marshall, live in Boston with their two children.

Arthur Holst

See also: CATHOLIC CHURCH, the

References
Carroll, James. *An American Requiem: God, My Father, and the War That Came Between Us.* New York: Mariner Books, 2001.
"Crusade: Chronicles of an Unjust War." Written Voices Radio Online. www.writtenvoices.com/titlepage.asp?ISBN=0805077030 (accessed December 10, 2005).
"James Carroll: Author/Illustrator Bio." www.houghtonmifflinbooks.com/catalog/authordetail.cfm?authorID=1380 (accessed December 10, 2005).

CARROLL, BISHOP JOHN (1736–1815)

John Carroll, the first Roman Catholic bishop in the United States, was born in Upper Marlboro, Maryland, on January 8, 1736, the son of Daniel Carroll and Eleanor Darnell. His grandfather was Keane O'Carroll, the oldest brother of Charles Carroll the attorney general. In 1748, Carroll and his cousin, another Charles Carroll, embarked for their studies at St. Omer in France. He began studies to enter the Jesuit order in 1753. He then studied at the English College at Liege and was ordained on February 14, 1761. Carroll spent the next decade teaching and touring Europe. His career came to a halt with the suppression of the Society of Jesus in 1773, and he returned to Maryland the next year, serving as priest to local Catholics.

In 1776 Carroll accompanied his cousin Charles Carroll, Samuel Chase, and Benjamin Franklin on a diplomatic mission to Canada. The group arrived at Montreal on April 29, 1776. Carroll's assignment was to administer the sacraments to pro-American Quebecois who had been refused by pro-British priests. It was soon clear that the mission was doomed. Franklin was ill and left Canada on May 11. Carroll volunteered to accompany him back to

Philadelphia. While the mission did not bring Canada into the union, it forged a friendship between John Carroll and Franklin that furthered Carroll's career. Before independence, Catholics in the British colonies fell under the jurisdiction of the vicar apostolic of London. In 1783, Carroll and other former Jesuits in Maryland drew up plans for the structure of the American church and petitioned the pope for the authority to implement those plans. At the same time, Vatican diplomats in Paris approached Benjamin Franklin about the proper method of organizing the Catholic Church in the United States. Franklin replied that neither he nor the Continental Congress had any authority over religious matters but added that he would recommend Carroll for any appointment the pope might make. In June 1784 the pope appointed Carroll "head of the missions of the provinces of the new Republic of the United States of North America," under the supervision of the Congregation of the Propaganda Fide. The same year, Carroll wrote his *Address to the Roman Catholics of the United States of America,* rebutting former Catholic priest Charles Henry Wharton's charge that Catholicism was incompatible with liberty.

Carroll had great difficulties handling such a geographically large and ethnically diverse church province. German Catholics in Philadelphia demanded a separate church, for instance. And a schism led by Andrew Nugent in New York convinced Carroll that the American church needed the greater authority of a bishop. On May 11, 1789, twenty-six priests met at White Marsh, Maryland, and voted 24–2 to elect Carroll bishop. On November 6, 1789, the pope named Carroll bishop of Baltimore. Carroll held his only synod November 7–10, 1791, ensuring uniformity of the Mass and clerical dress. Carroll founded Catholic seminaries and colleges, including Georgetown College in Washington, D.C. He also invited in various religious orders, such as the English Carmelites, the Sisters of the Visitation and the Sisters of Charity, the last led by Elizabeth Ann Seton. On July 6, 1806, Carroll laid the cornerstone for a new cathedral in Baltimore.

Even as bishop, Carroll had a difficult task in administering a diocese scattered all over the United States. In June 1802 he formulated a plan to divide the United States into several suffragen dioceses, to be established in Boston, New York, Philadelphia, and Bardstown, Kentucky. The pope approved the plan on April 8, 1808, making Baltimore the metropolitan see, elevating it to the status of archdiocese. Carroll was appointed the first archbishop. Of the new sees, only New York had a bishop not recommended by Carroll. The leading historian of the Archdiocese of Baltimore portrays Carroll as the architect of the "Maryland tradition" of relative administrative autonomy from Rome and lay trustee control of church property, which he saw as most compatible with American life. He died on December 3, 1815.

Robert W. Smith

See also: CARROLL, Charles; CATHOLIC CHURCH, the; MARYLAND

References
Guilday, Peter. *The Life and Times of John Carroll.* Westminster, MD: The Newman Press, 1954.
Melville, Annabelle M. *John Carroll of Baltimore: Founder of the American Catholic Hierarchy.* New York: Charles Scribner's Sons, 1955.
Spalding, Thomas W. *The Premier See: A History of the Archdiocese of Baltimore, 1789–1994.* Baltimore: The Johns Hopkins University Press, 1995.

CASEMENT, ROGER DAVID (1864–1916)

An Irish revolutionary executed following his failed attempt to import arms from Germany, Roger Casement spent his early life serving the British Foreign Office in various places in Africa, Portugal, and South America. In that role he protected British subjects, formulated minor consular reforms, and furthered British interests, including the promotion of Irish trade. In Brazil, he was consul in Santos (1906–1907) and Belém do Pará (1908) and consul-general in Rio de Janeiro (1909). Among his famous antislavery reports are those about the atrocities committed in connection with the harvesting of wild rubber in Leopold II's Congo Free State and in the Putumayo region. These cases were the subjects of Parliamentary Blue Books in 1904 and 1912, respectively. He also wrote about labor and health issues in building the Madeira-Mamoré Railway to develop the Amazonian Basin. When on leave, he always returned to England or Ireland, where he studied Irish, comparing it to the Tupi-Guarani language. Though a declared Protestant, he was involved with the nationalist movement and the Gaelic League. In 1914, he traveled to the United States seeking financial and political support for the Irish cause. Casement was one of the sixteen Irish revolutionary leaders tried, convicted, and executed after the Easter Rising. A controversy about the authenticity of his "Black" diaries with accounts of Casement's supposed homosexuality, which circulated shortly before execution to blacken his reputation in the 1916 trial, is still being debated.

Casement's life was marked by the ambiguities of a divided Ireland. Born on September 1, 1864, in Kingstown, later

Portrait of Irish revolutionary Roger Casement. (Library of Congress)

renamed its original Dun Laoghaire by the Irish Free State Government, he was the youngest of four children of a Protestant father, Roger Casement, and a Roman Catholic mother Anne Jephson. Brought up and educated a Protestant, Casement was baptized secretly by his mother when he was four and finally became a Roman Catholic a day before his execution. At the age of nine, he went to live with his uncle John Casement at Magherintemple in northern Co. Antrim. He was sent to the boarding Church of Ireland Diocesan School at Ballymena. He spent his holidays at his family home in Ulster or in Liverpool, where he stayed with his mother's sister and her husband, Edward Bannister, who looked after the West African interests of a Liverpool trading company. Later Bannister preceded Casement in two West African appointments.

In 1883 Casement was ship's purser on the SS *Bonny*, which traded with West Africa. In 1884, he went out to Africa as an employee of the African International Association. In 1887, he joined the expedition of Henry Shelton Sanford, a rich American diplomat, to survey the Congo region for the development of African means of communication. He left the Sanford expedition when he realized its aims were commercial rather than the welfare of the Africans. Then he directed the construction of the Congo Railway from Matadi to Stanley Pool until the Belgian government actively intervened in the work. In 1892 he became a member of the British staff of the Survey Department of the Oil Rivers Protectorate, which later became Nigeria.

In 1895 he took his first consular posting at Lorenzo Marques in Portuguese East Africa. He went on to serve the British government in Portuguese West Africa, South Africa, the Congo State, Portugal and Brazil. In all his posts, Casement insisted on representing Great Britain and Ireland; he advocated the provision of Irish manufactured goods to help Ireland's overseas trade. According to Maud Gonne, Casement defended Ireland's control of its own commerce and turned Cork and other privileged ports into centers of transatlantic trade.

While in Santos, Casement considered possible openings for Irish ham and bacon dealers. His main complaint was that all goods coming from Great Britain and Ireland (with the exception of Guinness because of its famous brand name) were all labeled in Brazilian Customs as "Ingleze," thus making it impossible to take Ireland into account for statistical report. He promoted trade on both sides and was particularly concerned with a wide range of Brazilian products seen in the context of world markets. He did not restrict his interest to rubber, cocoa, and Brazil nuts but gave emphasis to timber, which was a latent source of wealth. At Pará, he reported on health statistics and basic food problems recommending the use of banana flour as a wheat substitute for baking. Though he supported the development of a tourist industry, he also denounced the ways commerce and international trade were destroying the native way of life. During his trips, he kept journals and diaries, which contain contradictory descriptions of the Brazilian people, geographical and sociological accounts, and the history of the district of his consulate.

Casement was knighted in 1911 for his investigations of the mistreatment of Barbadian British subjects and local rubber tappers by the British Peruvian Amazon Company under the command of Julio Cesar Araña in the Putumayo region of the western Amazon. In 1913, he resigned from the Consular Service. Though he was a British national hero, he soon became sympathetic toward the nationalist cause of the Irish Volunteers. When World War I broke out, he was fund-raising in the United States. He sought German help and arms to support the Easter Rising but the British Intelligence captured him off the Kerry coast. Stripped of his knighthood, he was executed for high treason against the British Crown on August 3, 1916.

Laura Izarra

See also: BRAZIL.

References

Inglis, Brian. *Roger Casement*. London: Coronet Books, 1973.

Mitchell, Angus, ed. *The Amazon Journal of Roger Casement*. London: Anaconda Editions, 1997.

Sawyer, Roger. *Casement. The Flawed Hero.* London: Routledge & Kegan Paul, 1984.

Sawyer, Roger, ed. *Roger Casement's Diaries. 1910: The Black & the White.* London: Pimlico, 1997.

Singleton-Gates, Peter, and Maurice Girodias, eds. *The Black Diaries. An Account of Roger Casement's Life and Times with a Collection of his Diaries and Public Writings.* New York: Grove Press, 1959.

CASEY, EDUARDO (1847–1906)

An Irish-Argentine businessman and landowner, Eduardo Casey was founder of Venado Tuerto in Santa Fe province. He was born on April 20, 1847 in Lobos, Buenos Aires, the son of Lawrence Casey (1803–1876) of Co. Westmeath, and Mary O'Neill (1806–1910) of Co. Wicklow. His father had been the first rancher to pay one million pesos for a league of land in an auction in Buenos Aires. Eduardo Casey followed his father into farm work. To improve the breeding of his ranch's horses he founded a stud farm; in 1878, at the age of thirty, he owned a farming agent company. Casey was the first exporter of bovine cattle on the hoof to England, shipping 500 head on the *Nestorian* of Allan Lines company. He was one of the founders of La Blanca cold-storage plant, and served as a member of the board of the Western Railway Company and the Buenos Aires Provincial Bank.

Casey's best business achievement was the purchase, in 1881, of seventy-two leagues of land (130,000 hectares) in Venado Tuerto, southern Santa Fe province, together with William R. Gilmour. These lands had been recently taken from Indian control and were considered very productive by the Argentine public. In 1881,

Casey also acquired 100 leagues of land in Curumalal, Coronel Suárez, south of Buenos Aires province. Two years later, this land was fenced and settled with 40,000 cows, 50,000 sheep, and 10,000 horses.

As a member of the Sociedad de Elevadores y Depósitos de Granos del Riachuelo, and in partnership with Thomas Duggan, Casey made investments in Uruguay, a strategy that weakened his financial position. In 1890, the crisis of Uruguay seriously affected the company. Casey lost all his assets, and his private properties were put on auction. After this, he went to London to obtain funding and recover economically. When he returned to Buenos Aires with £100,000 fresh from loans, he repaid in its entirety the debt incurred with small investors who had deposited in his firm.

In many ways Casey was the typical pioneer of 1880s Argentina. He was involved in the turbulence of business and financial speculation. He reached the top, and he experienced the madness of accumulating a colossal wealth and losing it in seconds during the economic crash of the 1890s. He was one of the founders of the Buenos Aires Jockey Club, together with Carlos Pellegrini and others. He built the Central Market in Avellaneda, the Customs House, the port, and Reus quarter in Montevideo, Uruguay. When his friends were visiting his ranch Curumalal, in Buenos Aires, Casey used to arrange for a railway convoy for guests and victuals. He was a handsome man, a very good dancer and singer, and a skilled impersonator. Casey met with Buffalo Bill, who asked him for gaucho horse-breakers for his circus; ten *gauchos* (among them, Gorosito of Melincué) were selected by Casey and sent to England. When he was declared bankrupt, however, all his properties were auctioned, including his personal furniture. His brother Santiago bought them anonymously and gave them back to him. By the end of his life, Casey was on his own, his wife having abandoned him in 1902. By 1906 he was promoting new projects but nobody wanted to hear about them. He wanted to build inexpensive houses for poor workers who were living in city tenements, like the Reus quarter of Montevideo.

For sixteen years, Casey tried unsuccessfully to recover his financial losses. On June 16, 1906, he died on the railway tracks near the Central Market of Buenos Aires. He was fifty-eight years old, broken, and rejected by the society that owed so much to his contributions. Historians frequently do not mention the fact that he committed suicide. His remains were buried in Venado Tuerto, together with those of his wife and two children.

Edmundo Murray

See also: ARGENTINA; DUGGAN, Thomas

References

Landaburu, Roberto. *Irlandeses: Eduardo Casey, Vida y Obra.* Venado Tuerto: Fondo Editor Mutual de Venado Tuerto, 1995.

Wallace, José Brendan. "Eduardo Casey: Perfil de un Adelantado." www.irlandeses.com.ar (accessed January 13, 2005).

CATHOLIC CHURCH, THE

The Catholic Church is the largest body of organized Christian worship in the world. According to Catholic doctrine, the Church was both foretold and formulated (Matthew 16:18–19) by Jesus himself: "Thou art Peter, and upon this rock I will build my church; and the gates of hell shall not prevail against it. And I will give unto thee the keys of the kingdom of heaven."

The Catholic Church regards this proclamation as establishing the basic structure of the formal Church itself, as well as proclaiming the authority of the papacy, under the direction of the first Pope, Peter.

The history of the Catholic Church is enormously complex and is, in many ways, the touchstone of postclassical European culture. Although the early Christian churches were objects of severe repression, the adoption of Christianity by the Roman Emperor Constantine led slowly to a predominantly Christian Europe. The 1,000-year rise (300–1300) of the Catholic Church eventually placed it at the center of European power. In the eras before and during the Italian Renaissance the Church directly influenced extraordinary artistic accomplishments (for example, Dante's *Divine Comedy* and Michelangelo's paintings in the Sistine Chapel), yet it also presided over frightfully severe repressions of unorthodoxy (as in the Spanish Inquisition, or in the specific suppressions of Galileo and Bruno). The Church has since lost much of its direct political power through a succession of theological and political disputes, the most notable of which are the schism (1054) between Western and Eastern Christianity, the development of Protestantism, the rise of nation states, and the general spread of rights-based Enlightenment political philosophy. The Church has had mixed results in attempting to use its political power in the modern world; the Church has been severely criticized for not adequately opposing the Nazi genocide of European Jewry, but it has also been widely praised for its prominent role in confronting totalitarian Communist regimes in Central and Eastern Europe. The Church remains highly influential in political and social disputes, despite now possessing almost no coercive power beyond moral example.

Although the temporal center of the Church is the sovereign state of Vatican City (entirely surrounded by Rome, Italy), and the Pope is accorded all honors appropriate to a head of state, the Catholic Church is today primarily a body of worship. The Church is worldwide in extent, and the word "Catholic" itself refers to the "universal" nature of the Church and to the universality of its message of salvation. The Catholic Church is hierarchical in structure, with spiritual guidance ultimately deriving from the proclamations of the pope; yet the vast majority of the Church's spiritual ministries are undertaken by local Catholic leaders in their home communities.

Tradition holds that it was the fifth-century missionary Saint Patrick who brought Christianity to Ireland. This is a sentimental simplification, as Ireland had substantial trade and travel contacts with Britain and northern France before the fifth century. (The man considered Ireland's first bishop is a figure named Palladius, who was ordered to Ireland by Pope Celestine in 431.) Despite not being the first missionary, Patrick is undoubtedly the figure with whom the conversion of Ireland to Christianity is associated. He remains a figure of unusual public affection and continues to hold a position of veneration and admiration perhaps unique among national patron saints.

In the centuries after Patrick's mission the Irish became determinedly devoted to the Church. Belying the notion of Ireland as distant, wild, and outlandish, research indicates that early Irish worshippers practiced Christianity with serious intent and built significant structures as centers of faith, such as the monastery at Clonmacnoise. Works of Irish devotion from this period remain admired for the beauty of their worshipful elaboration; most notable of these is the world-famous Book of Kells (an intricately decorated gospel now displayed in Trinity College Dublin). What is unclear is the degree of direct association between Roman and Irish Churches before the high middle ages. Indications suggest that the early Irish Church may have had several idiosyncratic peculiarities, which may have arisen simply through distance and isolation, but which may indicate more serious theological disagreement. (Of these, perhaps the heavy reliance of the Irish on monasticism is most prominent.)

The political role of the Catholic Church in Ireland erupted with unforeseeable gravity as a consequence of the rise of English Protestantism. Ireland's continuing adherence to Catholicism aligned the Irish with the Catholic continental powers (notably, the then-strongest Catholic power, Spain), leaving Protestant England feeling extremely vulnerable to a multinational Catholic attack. The Papal bull *Regnans in Excelsis* (1570) absolved English Catholics of their allegiance to Queen Elizabeth I, thereby marking them all as potential traitors or fifth columnists. With such antagonisms in the air, England watched overwhelmingly Catholic Ireland with a greater than usual suspicion. The wreck of the Spanish Armada (1588) largely ended the direct threat of Catholic invasion and the overthrow of English Protestantism, but feelings of suspicion and vulnerability lingered. Cromwell's conquest (1649–1650) led to a decade of particularly intense suppression of Catholicism in Ireland, as well as to several centuries of diminished status for Irish Catholics. The post-Cromwellian period also brought increased Protestant settlement to Ireland. Although located throughout the island, the greatest portion of the Protestant settlement was in the northern territories. The social distinctions of power and wealth that often arose from conflicting national and religious allegiances laid the foundation for centuries of struggle, misery, and internecine conflict.

During the eighteenth and nineteenth centuries, the Catholic Church continued to provide both spiritual teaching and public education throughout Ireland. Sometimes this was necessarily covert, as in the famous "hedge schools," (clandestine schools which sprung up in response to the Penal law which outlawed education for Catholics in Ireland) although as direct religious repression diminished the Catholics became more open in their activities. Because being Catholic was itself a cause of diminished social opportunity, during the period of the Penal Laws, Catholicism came to be increasingly associated with movements of political and social resistance. Most notable of these social protest organizations was perhaps the Catholic Association (1824–1825), which, by collecting small sums from a huge number of Catholics ("the Catholic Rent"), hoped to provide relief for their oppressed or disadvantaged correligionists. Although the Catholic Church itself was reluctant to embrace direct political subversion, many Catholic nationalists used the uniting bond of Catholicism for political purposes. Daniel O'Connell, for one, was exceptionally skilled at conflating appeals to Catholics and nationalists. Though frequently artificial, such conflations evoked significant popular enthusiasm. Particularly in the nineteenth and early twentieth centuries, many believed English power and Irish subordinacy divided a native, Catholic Ireland from a transplanted, inauthentic Protestantism. That this conception was a labored simplification has not mitigated the hatreds it unleashed.

The division of Ireland (1921) left the Catholic Church in a position of extraordinary influence in the southern part of the island (today's Republic of Ireland). There the Church was not only the religious home of the vast majority of the citizenry; it also wielded a social, educational, and censorial power on the civil government almost unprecedented elsewhere in the modern Catholic world. In Northern Ireland, however, the association of Catholicism with Irish independence movements further antagonized already painful social and cultural divisions. The period of the 1970s and 1980s saw staggering outbursts of religious and national hatreds known, with despairing brevity, as "The Troubles." Subsequent negotiation has ameliorated those conflicts, without fully removing the abhorrent possibility of resumed violence. In the Republic of Ireland, however, religious circumstances were also changing. From the foundation of the independent nation until the 1980s, the Catholic Church was undoubtedly the most powerful nongovernmental agency in the Republic. But in the late 1980s and throughout the 1990s a general sense of cultural strangulation, combined with shocking revelations of abuse, intolerance, and concealment by religious authorities, caused an unprecedented abandonment of the Catholic Church. The transformation was significant; although the Republic of Ireland remains a notably Catholic country, with a high level of Catholic social influence, the Irish are now united more by cultural and historical associations than by shared religious outlook or identity.

In contrast to the extraordinary influence of the Catholic Church in Ireland, Catholicism has always been a distinctly minority religion in the United States. Although many of the initial explorers and settlers to the American continent were Catholic—particularly the Spanish, who built missions throughout Central and South America, as well as in what would become the states of New Mexico, Texas, and California—subsequent British, Scandinavian, and Germanic settlements tended to bring Protestantism instead of Catholicism. The solidification of British control over the eastern North American territories, followed by the near-complete Protestantism of the founding fathers of the American Revolution, fixed the ascendancy of Protestantism in the United States. Indeed, it was primarily the vast migrations of Irish and Italians in the nineteenth and twentieth centuries that brought substantial numbers of Catholics into the United States. Although there can be no doubt that Catholicism has flourished in North America, there can be equally little doubt that it has never had the social or religious predominance there that it held in Ireland.

Irish-American Catholics have been uncommonly successful at simultaneously maintaining their cultural, ethnic, and religious identities while integrating into the larger body of the American populace. This has not been a painless process: Irish Catholics particularly were detested by the aggressive Know-Nothing movement of the nineteenth century. It is also true that, despite such important Irish-American Catholic leaders as John Carroll (first bishop of Baltimore) and John Connolly (influential early bishop of New York), the most notable Irish-American Catholic leader was the notorious Father Charles Coughlin, whose popular radio broadcasts of the 1930s helped him spread a noxious blend of anti-Semitism and crankish economic theory. Yet the distinguishing feature of Irish-American Catholicism has long been the ease with which those three identities—Irish by ethnicity, American by citizenship, and Catholic by religious affiliation—cohere.

The Irish remain among the most prominent American Catholics, and many Catholic institutions in the United States are distinctly Irish. The most notable cathedral in the United States, and perhaps the most famous in all North America, is Saint Patrick's Cathedral in New York City. One of the foremost universities in North America is the University of Notre Dame, an institution that has long attracted Irish Americans, and which names its sports teams "The Fighting Irish." The first Catholic president of the United States, John F. Kennedy, was of Irish descent; his brother Robert Kennedy was both attorney general of the United States and a senator for New York, and his brother Edward has enjoyed a long and distinguished career as a senator for Massachusetts. Although the influence of Catholicism has never been as strong in the United States as it was in Ireland, the Church would have had a much lesser role in American cultural life without the continuing adherence of Irish-Catholic immigrants and of their descendants.

Andrew Goodspeed

See also: CARROLL, John; COUGHLIN, Father Charles; KENNEDY, John F.; NATIVISM AND ANTI-CATHOLICISM; NOTRE DAME UNIVERSITY; O'CONNELL, Daniel; SAINT PATRICK'S CATHEDRAL

References

Bokenkotter, Thomas. *A Concise History of the Catholic Church.* New York: Doubleday, 2004.

Corish, Patrick. *The Irish Catholic Experience.* Dublin: Gill & MacMillan, 1985.

McAvoy, Thomas. *The United States of America: The Irish Clergyman.* Dublin: Gill and MacMillan, 1970.

McCaffrey, Lawrence. *The Irish Catholic Diaspora in America.* Washington, DC: The Catholic University of America Press, 1997.

Mooney, Canice. *The Church in Gaelic Ireland: Thirteenth through Fifteenth Centuries.* Dublin: Gill and MacMillan, 1969.

CHANDLER, RAYMOND THORNTON (1888–1959)

In the second half of the twentieth century, Raymond Chandler achieved world renown as a writer of detective fiction. He invented a new genre of crime writing that became known as the "hard-boiled" school. Along with Dashiell Hammett and Ross Macdonald, Chandler was the main exponent of this mold-breaking outgrowth of the traditional detective novel.

Chandler created a character named Philip Marlowe who has become the archetype of the private detective. Marlowe's gruff vernacular and hard-bitten exploits epitomize Chandler's vision of the California he knew and wrote about. Chandler is widely regarded as an author who raised crime fiction to a higher level and enabled this genre to transcend its traditional separation from mainstream fiction. Chandler's deeply felt combination of cynicism and sentimentalism, anarchy and justice, fraud and truth offered more profound insights than had been previously attained in the detective novel. Marlowe appears as a latter-day knight-errant casting his quizzical gaze over the corrupt world he works in. Chandler's most famous works are *The Big Sleep* (1939), *Farewell, My Lovely* (1940), and *The Long Goodbye* (1953).

Chandler was born in 1888 in Chicago of Irish-American parentage. His mother was an Irishwoman from Co. Waterford who married an American engineer of Irish descent, so the young Chandler was at least half Irish by blood. Chandler's parents divorced when he was still a young boy, and his mother returned to England with him in 1895. They settled in South London, where Chandler was educated at Dulwich College, a noted English public school. Chandler's benefactor in these years was a wealthy Irish uncle called Ernest Thornton, a solicitor in Co. Waterford. Chandler spent his summer holidays there, and these experiences may have helped develop his sharp eye for social nuance and social distinctions. In California, the rigidities of class and religion counted for little, and Chandler's novels reflect this. But as a man he could express snobbish attitudes, and he had a lifelong aversion to the dogmatic Roman Catholicism he witnessed in Ireland as well as an involuntary association of Irish-American identity with working-class Catholicism and poverty. For this reason he did not see himself as Irish American.

His uncle, however, was Protestant, and Chandler was equally suspicious of the ossified gentility of his uncle's household and class. The freedom of California and the relatively egalitarian nature of American society with regard to race and religion were, to Chandler, a welcome contrast to the cloistered and claustrophobic world of Ireland in particular and, to a lesser extent, his public school milieu.

America was the country of Chandler's birth and his adoptive country of residence. He returned there in 1912, working briefly in St. Louis and Omaha before finally moving to California. He left to serve in the Canadian Army during World War I but

returned in 1919, spending most of the remainder of his life living in California, aside
from some later trips to England. It is here,
with the support of his wife (Pearl Cecily
Hulbert), that Chandler began writing and
perfecting the hard-boiled detective style
that was to characterize his art. He was a slow
writer who, unfortunately, suffered from
bouts of heavy drinking (which became
more frequent with the death of his wife in
1954), but his best works stand as testament
to the art of detective fiction. Chandler died
of pneumonia on March 26, 1959, in the
Scripps Clinic in La Jolla, California.

All of Chandler's fiction is located in and
around Los Angeles, California. He uses a
taut, fiery American vernacular in a highly
original prose style. Although Chandler's
work contains a smattering of characters
with Irish names and occasional allusions to
Ireland or the Irish, there is no more Irishness
to be found than is appropriate to his American settings. However, Chandler's European
and Irish experiences may have sharpened
his insight into crime, corruption, and sleaze,
which he depicts so brilliantly. He wrote
with the insider's knowledge of the terrain
and the outsider's appreciation of its sordid
and treacherous nature.

Benjamin Keatinge

References
Chandler, Raymond. *The Big Sleep and Other
    Novels.* London: Penguin, 2000.
Hiney, Tom. *Raymond Chandler: A Biography.*
    London: Chatto and Windus, 1997.
Hiney, Tom, and Frank MacShane, eds. *The
    Raymond Chandler Papers: Selected Letters
    and Non-Fiction 1909–1959.* London:
    Hamish Hamilton, 2000.
MacShane, Frank. *The Life of Raymond
    Chandler.* London: Jonathan Cape, 1976.
Skinner, Robert E., ed. *The Hard-Boiled
    Explicator: A Guide to the Study of Dashiell
    Hammett, Raymond Chandler and Ross
    Macdonald.* Metuchen, NJ: The Scarecrow
    Press, 1985.

CHERISH THE LADIES (FORMED 1983)

It began with several nights of concerts in
New York City in 1983, "and I didn't really
think anyone would come," said flute and
whistle player Joanie Madden, who had
been asked by folklorist Mick Moloney to
help organize several shows featuring Irish-
American women musicians. He had no-
ticed that although female musicians were
winning awards in prestigious All Ireland
musical contests and other competitions,
the main bands and solo artists—the ones
receiving public notice and recognition—
were all men. Those first shows sold out,
which led the National Endowment for the
Arts to fund the production of an album
featuring more than a dozen women musicians. The recording was called *Cherish the
Ladies,* taking its name from an Irish jig,
and was chosen by the Library of Congress
as the best folk album of 1985.

That recording also led to the birth of
a band, a group that over twenty years and
a number of personnel shifts still continues
to explore traditional and contemporary
Celtic music and create new interpretations
as well as new songs in the Celtic tradition.
Madden as bandleader shepherded the
change from an endowment-funded ensemble to an "in-the-trenches working
band," whose venues have included clubs,
pubs, arts events, the Kennedy Center, the
Celtic Connections Festival, and the 1996
Summer Olympics, and who have been
named best musical group of the year by
the BBC, and top North American Celtic
Act by the National Public Radio program
Thistle and Shamrock. In the early days,
though, it was not easy going. "People
thought we were the Celtic Spice Girls,"
Madden recalls, "a group of women put
together for show." Once audiences and

Portrait of Irish folk music group Cherish the Ladies in a field of wildflowers. (Corbis)

promoters began actually hearing the musicianship of Madden on flute and whistle, Mary Coogan (who had also played on the original recording) on guitar and banjo, Maureen Doherty on accordion, Siobhan Egan and Eileen Ivers on fiddle, and Cathie Ryan on vocals and bodhran, they realized this group was an important and unique pesence in Celtic music.

The women toured constantly, offering a mix of jigs, reels, airs, and songs, often with the addition of step dancers. Their work reached wider audiences with the release of the first band recording, *The Back*

Door, in 1992. By that time Ivers had left the group (though she coproduced the record) to be replaced by fiddler and step dancer Winifred Horan, and Ryan was establishing herself as a writer: the title track was an emigration song she had written. The eclectic selection of music on this collection underlined the fact that these were not just women together as a band, but talented, thoughtful musicians with creative views of what they could contribute to Celtic music. In addition to Ryan's original song, which in the liner notes she dedicates to "all undocumented Irish aliens," there's

"Character Polka," composed by Madden, Horan, and Egan and played in a set with a traditional strathspey and two reels, a hornpipe and reels that are suited to step dancers; "Maire Mhor," a traditional song about an independent, spirited woman that Ryan sings in Irish; the play party song "Coal Quay Market"; and "Carrigdhoun," a poem of the Irish landscape set to a traditional air.

Changing membership in the group through the years has brought out different colors and emphases in their music. It has also been a seedbed for talent: Horan went on to help form the group Solas; Ivers played with Riverdance and now fronts her own band; Aoife Clancy, who replaced Ryan as lead singer, now has a well-respected solo career of her own; and Ryan has established herself as a top singer and songwriter in Ireland and America.

The current membership of the group, all of whom appear on the band's most recent release, *Woman of the House,* comprises Heidi Talbot on vocals and bodhran, Roisin Dillon on fiddle, and Mirella Murray on accordion, along with Madden on flute and whistles and Coogan on guitar and banjo. The group has changed, too, from a group of women who were the first or second generations of their families in America to include musicians born in, and/or living in, Ireland alongside Irish Americans, a natural evolution of seeking the best musicians, Madden says. Their music retains the variety and independent spirit common through the band's history. On *Woman of the House,* an original reel composed by Madden, "Bonkers in Yonkers," stands in a set with the traditional "Rascal in the Haystack"; "Carolan's Favorite Jig" kicks off a set of lesser-known tunes, which show the women in fast-flying musical conversation;

Talbot trades leads with guests Kate Rusby and Karen Matheson on the Appalachian traditional ballad "Fair and Tender Ladies"; and both sides of the Irish and American equation join as the women support Talbot's quiet singing on the emigration song "Green Fields of Canada."

Kerry Dexter

See also: CHIEFTAINS, The; CLANCY BROTHERS, the; RYAN, Cathie

Discography

Cherish the Ladies. *At Home* (sound recording) RCA, 1999

Cherish the Ladies. *The Back Door* (sound recording). Green Linnet, 1992

Cherish the Ladies. *On Christmas Night* (sound recording). Rounder, 2004

Cherish the Ladies. *Out and About* (sound recording). Green Linnet, 1993

Cherish the Ladies. *Woman of the House* (sound recording). Rounder, 2005

References

Madden, Joanie. Telephone interviews, September 1, 2005, and April 17, 2006.

Parrish, Michael. "Cherish the Ladies," Dirty Linen no. 120, October/November 2005, 36–39.

Winich, Steve. "Cherish the Ladies," Dirty Linen no. 59. August/September 1995, 48–53, 115.

CHIEFTAINS, THE (FORMED 1962)

Originally members of Seán Ó Riada's group Ceoltóiri Chualann, which was formed in the late 1950s, the Chieftains made their first recording in 1963. They quickly became popular in Ireland and by the 1970s were touring the United States, where they played a major role in creating an interest in Irish traditional instrumental music. While many bands have followed in their wake, The Chieftains remain the best-known Irish traditional group, not only in America but also around the world.

When formed to make a recording for Garech Browne's new Claddagh Records in Dublin, the group consisted of Paddy Moloney on uilleann pipes, Seán Potts on tin whistle, Michael Tubridy on flute, and Martin Fay on fiddle. Although they had no interest in pursuing Ó Riada's original idea of developing a form of modern Irish music based on traditional elements, The Chieftains continued to pursue the composer's experiments in creating a new type of folk ensemble using traditional instruments.

Until Ó Riada formed Ceoltóiri Chualann, ensemble playing, beyond informal combinations of a few local musicians, had been dominated by ceilidh bands. Created initially by the Irish in England to provide dance music for large halls, these bands mixed fiddles, flutes, and sometimes uilleann pipes with piccolos, accordions, pianos, and drum sets borrowed from the jazz band. The emphasis was on the melody with a strong rhythm pounding away for the dancers. The Chieftains followed Ó Riada's example in dropping the less traditional instruments (they also dispensed with Ó Riada's harpsichord), replacing the modern drum set with the bodhran, an Irish goatskin, single-frame drum. They slightly expanded Ó Riada's use of harmony and occasional countermelodies and made other nontraditional attempts to arrange the music for a new urban audience. Like Ó Riada they included slow airs along with traditional dance pieces. A smaller group with no duplication of instruments, The Chieftains developed a crisp, clean style of playing, alternating a warm ensemble sound with opportunities for virtuoso solo playing. The resulting untraditional approach to traditional music caught the attention of Irish audiences just as the country was beginning to urbanize.

The group began to tour abroad in the 1970s, first to Britain, then to North America. By the 1980s they were traveling the world, following their trademark custom of playing, whenever possible, with local musicians. Sometimes this resulted in unusual recordings, preserving encounters with musicians in Brittany, Galicia, and even China. Other musical combinations were better guaranteed to provide income and publicity for the group, which took on a full-time professional status after 1975. The Chieftain's leader, Paddy Moloney, has been adept at getting international rock stars and American country musicians to record with the group. Film scores and television appearances have also helped keep the band busy.

Over the years Potts and Tubridy left the group as other musicians joined; fiddler Seán Keane, flautist Matt Molloy, singer and percussionist Len Graham, and harpist Derek Bell. Bell brought to the ensemble performance of Irish music the sound that Ó Riada's harpsichord was intended to suggest. The addition of the harp, never really a folk instrument, took The Chieftain's sound to a new level. Except for their crossover recordings, their music was still traditional, but the band's professionalism and their arrangements placed them far from the house and crossroads dances where the music had once been played. The Chieftains put the music on stage and took it into urban concert halls around the world.

The success of the band helped open the doors to other Irish folk bands, such as The Bothy Band, De Dannen, and Planxty. However, only the Boys of the Lough (originally made up of performers from Ireland, England, and Shetland) have had anything like the staying power of The Chieftains, whose tours have taken the band into the twenty-first century.

William H. A. Williams

See also: CLANCY BROTHERS, The; Ó RIADA, Seán

Reference
Meek, Bill. *Paddy Moloney and the Chieftains,* Dublin: Gill and Macmillan, 1987.

CHOPIN, KATE (1850–1904)

Biographers of American author Kate Chopin (born Katherine O'Flaherty) often allude to her French background when they attempt to explain the influences that created such a scandalous figure. Her very young mother, Eliza Faris, to whom Chopin was extraordinarily close, was from a poor Creole family, and was the source (along with Guy de Maupassant) of Chopin's relatively sophisticated and liberal thinking. But Chopin was half Irish as well; her father, Thomas O'Flaherty, was born in Galway in 1805 and traveled to America in 1823, at a time when many still viewed the Irish as less than desirable. Though the family initially met with some success in St. Louis, Missouri, Chopin often found herself on the fringes of whatever society she was in because of the influences of both French and Irish cultures. As a five-year-old, she was a boarder at Sacred Heart Academy at an unusually young age. When her father died suddenly that same year in a railway accident, she was raised in a community of strong women, including her great-grandmother, an influence that is perhaps the reason biographers downplay her Irish background over her French. When she married Oscar Chopin, an older man who later became a cotton factor, she moved to New Orleans and then to Natchitoches

Parish, Louisiana; in both places, her accent, her background, and her lack of Southern sensibilities created problems for her with her contemporaries. Despite having six children (five boys and one girl), Chopin was never content to be a homemaker, preferring instead to explore the world (often at night and with a cigarette in hand) and to watch people. Through her explorations, she became an important American writer.

Many of her characterizations were taken from life, and occasionally her attempts to veil identities were transparent enough that she got into trouble for them, creating some lifelong enemies. Some of those enemies included the wife of the man she was purportedly having an affair with (though it remains unclear whether the affair was going on while Chopin's husband was still alive), the editor of a local newspaper, and the parish priest, all of whom were parodied in her stories. Such behavior on Chopin's part, while eminently amusing, did not win her friends in her town, and she was not a favorite there, failing to understand that things were done differently in the South.

While Chopin's short stories, especially "The Storm" and "The Story of an Hour," are included in many literature anthologies and frequently taught in English classes, her novel, *The Awakening* (1899), is her most widely read and controversial work. Though it has quite a reputation, it was in fact never banned, but simply neglected because of the scathing reviews of the time and was only revived when women's rights movements grew in strength in the 1960s. Her contemporaries' objections, as with "The Storm," (not published until 1969), had to do with the scandalous subject matter of unapologetic adultery, too daring for most publishers to tackle. The reviews at the time, in focusing on the subject of sex, generally missed the much larger (and potentially more transgressive) point that Chopin was making in many of her stories, including in her first short story collection, *Bayou Folk:* women are about more than marriage and children, and their perspective is more complicated than most writers allowed.

Kathleen A. Heininge

See also: NEW ORLEANS

References

Chopin, Kate. *Chopin: Complete Novels and Stories,* edited by Sandra Gilbert. New York: The Library of America, 2002.

Toth, Emily. *Kate Chopin.* New York: William Morrow, 1990.

Toth, Emily. *The Unveiling of Kate Chopin.* Jackson: The University Press of Mississippi, 1999.

CLANCY BROTHERS, THE (FORMED 1956)

Although born and raised in Ireland, the Clancy Brothers and Tommy Makem established themselves as ballad singers in the United States in the 1960s. In doing so they single-handedly revived interest in Irish ballads and contributed greatly to the post–World War II enthusiasm for folk music on both sides of the Atlantic.

The Clancys came from Carrick-on-Suir in Co. Tipperary. The elder brothers—Tom (1923–1990) and Pat (1923–1998)—had served in the Royal Air Force during the war and had then emigrated to the United States where they pursued careers in acting. Young Liam was also interested in acting. However, he fell in with Diane Hamilton (née Guggenheim), who was touring Ireland, recording folk songs. When he left Ireland in 1955 to join his brothers in New York City, Liam continued to work for a time with Hamilton's Tradition Records. Although short lived, the record company produced a few classic albums of field recordings made in Ireland and in the American South as well as the first recording of the Clancys with Ulster singer Tommy Makem.

Makem was born into a musical family in Keady, Co. Armagh. His mother, Sarah, had a repertory of some 500 songs and was well known to folk song collectors. Makem had become friends with Liam Clancy, during the latter's collecting trips through Ulster with Diane Hamilton. Makem and Liam later emigrated to America at the same time. When the Clancy brothers began singing in New York bars for rent money between acting assignments, Makem helped them tap into a broader field of Irish folk song besides "rebel" songs.

By the late 1950s the folk music revival was well on its way in America, and Makem and the Clancys, boosted by their first Tradition recording, *The Rising of the Moon* (1959), began to attract attention. As they became more professional, their singing never quite lost the boisterous, improvisational edge of enthusiastic pub singers. With their bouncy rhythms, shouts of encouragement to each other, and occasional harmonies—not to mention rugged good looks—they added zest and excitement to a folk scene that usually featured nasal-voiced guitar pickers and flutey sopranos with long, straight, ironed hair. By the time they had appeared on the popular Ed Sullivan television show on the CBS network and on the stage at Carnegie Hall, the Clancy Brothers and Tommy Makem had become a folk music phenomenon.

Irish traditional music group the Clancy Brothers perform in 1970. (Getty Images)

In the United States they managed to reintroduce Irish traditional English-language ballads to Irish Americans, who had long proclaimed their ethnic identity through Tin Pan Alley songs like "My Wild Irish Rose" or "Mother Machree." At the same time they almost single-handedly introduced Irish folk music to Americans, regardless of ethnic background. One did not have to be Irish to enjoy the Clancys. They also helped to open the door through which other Irish groups, vocal and instrumental, would enter.

In Ireland eyes and ears were opened by the fact that a bunch of country lads could put Ireland on the international musical map with a parcel of pub songs. Many of those then involved in salvaging and reviving interest in traditional Irish music did not always welcome the sudden emergence of scores of ballad bands with their guitars, tin whistles, and shouts of "fine girl you are." When 76,000 young people, many with guitars and backpacks, turned up for the 1966 Fleadh Cheoil in Boyle, Co. Roscommon, the Comhaltas Ceoltóirí Éireann, fearful that Ireland's pure musical tradition would be contaminated, decided to hide subsequent Fleadhs in the more remote parts of western Ireland. The Comhaltas need not have worried. Most of the Irish ballad bands that sprouted in the wake of the Clancy Brothers' success faded quickly. However, some groups, such as The Dubliners and The Wolftones, established themselves in Ireland's own folk revival. Even the success of instrumental groups, such as the Chieftains, owed something to the power of the Clancy Brothers and Tommy Makem in helping to make Irish folk music interesting to the rising generation of urban Irish.

Eventually, age and death ended the careers of the older Clancys. However, Liam and Tommy, with the help of young generations of Clancys and Makems, have continued to perform into the twenty-first century.

William H. A. Williams

See also: CHIEFTAINS, The

Reference
Clancy, Liam. *The Mountain of the Woman: Memoirs of an Irish Troubadour.* New York: Doubleday, 2002.

Portrait of Confederate Army Major General Patrick Ronayne Cleburne. (Library of Congress)

CLEBURNE, PATRICK RONAYNE (1828–1870)

Patrick Ronayne Cleburne rose to fame as a Confederate major-general and the highest-ranking Irish-born military leader in American history. He was born in Ovens, Co. Cork, on March 16, 1828, at Bride Park Cottage. His father, Joseph Cleburne, was a doctor at the local dispensary. His mother was Mary Anne Ronayne Cleburne, the daughter of landowner Patrick Ronayne of Annebrook on Great Island. She died when Cleburne was eighteen months old, and his father remarried Isabella Stewart, the children's tutor.

Cleburne received his early education at the boarding school of the Reverend William Spedding nearby. When he was eight, the family moved to Grange Farm, outside Ballincollig. However, when Dr. Cleburne died in November 1843, the young man's future changed drastically. He was sent to Mallow for a two-year apprenticeship to Dr. Thomas Justice, and there were plans to enroll him in Apothecary Hall in Dublin so that he could follow his father's profession. However, upon arriving in Dublin in February 1846 and taking the entrance exam, Cleburne promptly failed. Too humiliated to return a family failure, the seventeen-year-old enlisted in the 41st Regiment of Foot of Her Majesty's army, expecting to be sent to India. His attempt at running away was foiled when the regiment was instead shipped to Mullingar for duties in Ireland associated with the crisis of the Famine.

For the next three and a half years, Cleburne spent his army service posted at barracks in Limerick, Tarbert, Buttevant, and Spike Island in Cork Harbor. He served during the turbulent months of the 1848 Young Ireland Rebellion and received a promotion to corporal on July 1, 1849.

After years of being estranged from his family, he obtained leave to visit Grange Farm. He found a desperate situation. The farm was in arrears for six months' rent, and his stepmother suggested that the oldest four children emigrate.

On November 5, 1849, Cleburne, his older sister Anne, and his brothers William and Joseph boarded the *Bridgetown* for America and landed in New Orleans, Louisiana, on Christmas Day. Employment was a priority, and while his siblings headed up the Mississippi River to Cincinnati, Cleburne obtained the situation of druggist at Nash and Grant's Drugstore in Helena, Arkansas, arriving in April 1850. For the next decade, Cleburne pursued the study of law, and eventually passed the Arkansas bar examination in 1856. Around this time, the rest of his family moved to America and settled in Newport, Kentucky, near Cincinnati.

Pat Cleburne left turbulent times in his own country only to find himself in the middle of the road to civil war in his new homeland. His politics mirrored those of the Southern states, which sought freedom from what they considered the oppression of the North and a trampling of their constitutional rights. While Cleburne never owned slaves, and voiced outright opposition to the institution, he valued the right and desire of a section of the country to govern itself. The local plantation owners and well-respected citizens formed a militia company called the Yell Rifles. Cleburne was elected captain, and the company was thoroughly drilled under the skills he learned in the British Army. Arkansas seceded in April 1861 and joined the Confederate States of America. The Yell Rifles became part of the 1st Arkansas Volunteer Infantry Regiment.

On his own merit, Cleburne swiftly rose through the ranks. Elected colonel of the 1st Arkansas, his command was attached to what became known to history as the Army of Tennessee, the main Confederate army in the western theater. Cleburne was promoted to brigadier general in March 1862, less than a year into the war. His brigade exhibited exceptional bravery and competence at the Battle of Shiloh in April and in the Kentucky Campaign during the summer. At the Battle of Richmond, Cleburne was wounded in the face by shrapnel and forced to leave the field, but not before he put into motion a strategic plan leading to a Confederate victory. He was back in action for the Battle of Perryville in October. However, the Confederate army was forced to withdraw from Kentucky later that year.

In December 1862, Cleburne was promoted to major general, and he commanded a division at the Battle of Murfreesboro in East Tennessee. Though his command attained its battlefield objectives, the army once more retreated to middle Tennessee by spring 1863, with a schism in its command. The constant retreats under General Braxton Bragg had begun to affect the army's morale. Cleburne joined a group of officers led by General William J. Hardee in voicing their opinion that Bragg should resign for the sake of the army.

Throughout 1863, Cleburne was present at some of the most famous battles of the war: Chickamauga in September and Missionary Ridge in November. On November 27, 1863, Cleburne's division made a stand at Ringgold Gap, Georgia, as the rearguard protecting the retreating Confederate army while it fled south from Chattanooga. Here, 4,000 effectives (soldiers fit and available for service) under

Cleburne's careful direction held at bay 15,000 Union troops under General Joseph Hooker. Cleburne received a congressional citation from the Confederate capital for his victory. His fame spread throughout the South. He determined to use this confidence in his position to discuss a proposal he had long been considering. The southern army was short on supplies and, more important, men. Cleburne knew their only hope came from abroad and from the support of England and France. But both nations, though sympathetic, held the slavery issue up as a deterrent for official recognition of the Confederacy and economic support. Cleburne suggested that if the slaves in the South were offered military service in exchange for their freedom, the foreign support and personnel issues would be resolved, as well as the slavery dilemma, but his idea did not come to fruition.

In January 1864, Cleburne met and fell in love with Susan Tarleton of Mobile, Alabama, when he attended the wedding of his commander, General Hardee. The two became engaged, and Cleburne returned to the front at Dalton, Georgia. In May 1864, the Atlanta Campaign began when Union General William T. Sherman launched a dogged assault, over four months, with a series of battles beginning at Resaca, Georgia. The summer was spent in heavy fighting, at Pickett's Mill, Kennesaw Mountain, Peachtree Creek, and finally Jonesboro. Atlanta fell in September. While General Sherman cut a 60-mile-wide swath through Georgia on his way to Savannah, General John Bell Hood in command of the Confederate army proceeded north to Nashville to attack the Union army there under General George H. Thomas. Cleburne's division led the vanguard into Tennessee. They encountered a small Union force at Spring Hill, Tennessee, late on the afternoon of November 29, 1864. Confusion ensued, and the Union force pulled back and regrouped at the fortified town of Franklin, 17 miles to the north. That night, Hood ordered an assault on Franklin. It would be a disaster.

Again, Cleburne's division led the charge. Fighting commenced at 4:00 p.m., just before sunset. When it ended five hours later, Patrick Cleburne was dead. He died leading a charge of his old regiment, mostly composed of Irish immigrants, on Union breastworks. That night the Union army pulled out of Franklin. At dawn Cleburne's body was found in the Union lines. He was mourned by his troops and buried in a small churchyard cemetery at St. John's Church in nearby Columbia. Later, in 1870, his body was reinterred in Helena, Arkansas. He was 36 years old.

Mauriel Joslyn

See also: ABOLITIONISM AND SLAVERY; AMERICAN CIVIL WAR

References
Buck, Irving S. *Cleburne and His Command.* Jackson, TN: McCowat-Mercer Press, 1957.
Joslyn, Mauriel P. *A Meteor Shining Brightly: Essays on Maj. Gen. Patrick R. Cleburne.* Milledgeville, GA: Terrell House Publishing, 1998.
Purdue, Howell, and Elizabeth Purdue. *Pat Cleburne: Confederate General.* Hillsboro, TX: Hill Junior College Press, 1973.
Sword, Wiley. *Embrace an Angry Wind.* New York: Harper Collins, 1992.

CLINTON, WILLIAM JEFFERSON (1946–)

William Jefferson Clinton, forty-second president of the United States, was a champion of the Northern Ireland peace process during the 1990s. By paying three official

President Bill Clinton (second from left) stands with British Prime Minister Tony Blair (right), Northern Ireland's First Minister David Trimble (left), and Deputy First Minister Seamus Mallon on the steps of Parliament in Belfast, Northern Ireland, on December 13, 2000. Clinton urged residents of Northern Ireland to protect the progress made toward peace and to build on it. (AP/World Wide Photos)

visits to Ireland, Clinton personally shaped and directed his administration's Northern Ireland policy. He has described the Irish peace process as one of the great passions of his presidency. Born in Hope, Arkansas, on August 19, 1946, Clinton served as president between 1993 and 2001. In unseating the Republican Party incumbent George H. W. Bush, Clinton became the first Democratic Party president since Franklin D. Roosevelt to serve two terms. He is married to Hillary Rodham, and they have one child, Chelsea. Clinton's presidency combined many successes in foreign and domestic policy with personal scandals. On the domestic front, Clinton is credited with generating

economic prosperity and eliminating the public spending deficit. Apart from Northern Ireland, his foreign policy successes include the Middle East and Bosnia.

These successes were, however, overshadowed by allegations of sleaze and corruption. Most notably, in 1998 Clinton became the first president since Andrew Johnson in 1868, to be impeached by the House of Representatives. In a highly charged political party atmosphere, the House impeached Clinton for perjury and obstruction regarding investigations into events surrounding extramarital relationships with a White House intern, Monica Lewinsky, and an Arkansas state employee,

Paula Jones. Subsequently, the Senate found him not guilty of the charges leveled against him. During the impeachment crisis his approval ratings remained very high.

He appointed Madeleine Albright as the first female secretary of state in 1997, and his presidency sought to include minority groups. Clinton's passion for Ireland did not end after he left the White House during January 2001. On the contrary, he has maintained strong connections with Ireland.

Clinton was born into a lower-middle-class family background, and his father died shortly before his birth. He excelled in school and college, becoming the first member of his family to be conferred a university degree. In 1963 he was selected as a Washington, D.C., delegate for the Boys Nation Leadership Camp. During his trip to Washington he famously shook hands with President John Fitzgerald Kennedy. The moment was captured on film and provided an emotional and sentimental backdrop to the 1992 Democratic Party Convention in New York City.

During 1966, Senator William Fulbright employed Clinton as a researcher for the Senate Foreign Relations Committee. Clinton attended both Georgetown and Yale Universities, and between 1968 and 1970 he was a Rhodes Scholar at Oxford. Qualifying as an attorney in 1973, his focus was firmly on a political career. At the age of twenty-eight he made a failed bid for the U.S. House of Representatives. Elected attorney general of Arkansas in 1976, he only had to wait a further two years before being elected governor. Showing an early interest in Irish affairs, he declared Saint Patrick's Day 1978 Irish Human Rights Day in Arkansas. However, near political catastrophe befell the future president in

1980. Defeated in the gubernatorial election, Clinton was suddenly without political office. However, two years later he was reelected governor and served until 1992.

Clinton declared his candidacy for the White House during 1991. However, his strategic preparations had begun many years before his formal announcement. Placing a strong emphasis on networking, he gradually created a base within the Democratic Party, becoming a key figure in the National Governors Association. During the 1992 presidential primaries, the support of Democratic Party governors would prove to be of enormous electoral benefit to Clinton. He was also an important player in the Democratic Leadership Council founded during 1985 with the aim of making Democrats more electable by moving toward the political center. Similarly, Clinton cultivated Hollywood support.

Nevertheless, as a little-known Arkansas governor, Clinton's chances of winning the party nomination, let alone the presidency, were slim. However, Clinton's skills as a quality candidate emerged at an early stage of his campaign. In particular, he possessed strong public-speaking skills, which allowed him to connect with audiences. Equally important, he loved mingling with crowds. But it was not all plain sailing for the future president. Allegations about serious flaws in his character soon emerged. It was suggested that Clinton had had a string of extramarital affairs. Similarly, he was accused of smoking marijuana during his student days. Most seriously for the future commander-in-chief of the United States military he was accused of being a draft dodger in the Vietnam War. Despite these allegations he emerged as the Democratic Party's choice in 1992. In an effort to court the more conservative southern vote,

Tennessee Senator Albert Gore was chosen as the party's vice presidential candidate.

Clinton faced an uphill battle to unseat the incumbent President George H. W. Bush. Bush's approval ratings remained high, as he had recently enjoyed military victory in Kuwait and Iraq. The presence of independent candidate Ross Perot on the ticket complicated the race further. In the lead up to the 1992 election, Clinton adopted a clear strategy. First, sensing voter dissatisfaction with Bush's economic policies, he focused on the economy. Second, adopting a centrist approach to economic policy, he tried to woo more conservative voters to support him. Third, relying on his communications and interactive skills. he adopted a different campaign style. Appearing on late-night television shows, he tried to appeal to a broader audience, particularly younger voters.

Capitalizing on perceptions that President Bush was out of touch with the needs of ordinary citizens, Clinton kept emphasizing economic issues. As November 1992 approached, it was becoming evident that the obscure governor from Arkansas was on the verge of unseating the incumbent. On election day, Clinton secured 42 percent of the popular vote, Bush 37 percent and Perot 19 percent. In the electoral college this meant that Clinton secured 370 votes to Bush's 160. Clinton was reelected for a second term four years later. On this occasion he secured 49 percent of the vote, which gave him a total of 379 Electoral College votes. The Republican Party's candidate, Robert Dole, secured 41 percent of the vote, which translated into 159 electoral college votes.

After twelve years of Republican occupation, Clinton and Gore entered the White House in January 1993, the first

Democrats since Jimmy Carter and Walter Mondale to do so. Being the first president born after World War II, Clinton's presidency signaled a generational shift. During Clinton's eight years in the White House the American economy grew significantly. While his presidency is associated with economic growth and prosperity, he nevertheless brought public spending under tight control. He inherited a fiscal deficit of $290 billion. By 2000 he had converted the deficit into a surplus of $167 billion.

During his presidency Clinton highlighted the themes of opportunity, responsibility, and community. According to Clinton, with freedom came responsibility. Calling for a New Covenant, he emphasized that citizens were entitled to state support only if they gave something in return. Thus, Clinton sought to increase labor market participation and decrease reliance on welfare payments. His controversial welfare reforms were designed to meet these twin objectives. Unsurprisingly, left-wing democrats interpreted his welfare reforms as an attack on the poorer citizens of the United States. Electorally, Clinton's political strategy was designed to increase the appeal of the Democratic Party beyond its traditional constituencies.

Enjoying a majority in both Houses of Congress, Clinton immediately advocated radical reform in health policy. His Health Care Bill, which sought to provide health care for all Americans, was subjected to a massive anti-lobby by the health insurance industry. Their efforts succeeded. As his first term's flagship policy proposal, its ultimate collapse was a significant political failure, although many point out that the policy proposal was drawn up under the personal direction of First Lady Hillary Rodham Clinton. Clinton's majority in both houses of Congress disappeared in November 1994. The Republican Party gained 53 house seats and 9 senate seats. The Republican landslide was an almost fatal blow to Clinton's presidency. Speaker Newt Gingrich, who had engineered the Republican landslide, launched a full-scale assault on the president's program. Despite the speaker's strong position, Clinton's political tactics ultimately outmaneuvered him. Forcing the shutdown of federal services, the Republican Party got most of the blame for the budgetary crisis.

In the foreign-policy sphere, Clinton was operating in a radically transformed international setting. With the collapse of Soviet communism, a bipolar world order had ceased. By the 1990s the United States was the world's only superpower. Clinton faced a number of significant foreign policy challenges during his two terms. The most significant was the Bosnian crisis, which resulted in the return of genocide and wide-scale human rights abuses on the European continent. A new phrase, "ethnic cleansing" entered the vernacular.

Initially, Clinton struggled to come up with a meaningful response to the Bosnian crisis. By 1995, however, Clinton began to assert his authority. On the urging of his United Nations ambassador, Madeleine Albright, he authorized air strikes against the Serbs. Four years later, because of Serbian repression of the Kosovars, Clinton authorized full-scale military action under the auspices of the North Atlantic Treaty Organization. Clinton also sought to end the crisis through peace negotiations. He appointed Special Envoy Richard Holbrooke, and all participants were eventually brought to Dayton, Ohio, for crucial negotiations. Applying considerable personal pressure, Clinton secured an agreement in 1995. Known as the Dayton Accords, along with the Middle East and Northern Ireland agreements, it ranks as one his most significant foreign policy successes.

Clinton's involvement in the Northern Ireland peace process has helped define him as a truly international statesman. Clinton was very committed to bringing peace to Northern Ireland. Few would dispute the assertion that he was a central actor in the negotiations that led to the signing of the Good Friday Peace Agreement on April 10, 1998. The Good Friday Agreement was a truly historic political compromise. Apart from establishing inclusive and non-majoritarian institutional structures in Northern Ireland, it legally recognized an all-Ireland dimension to Northern Ireland's future governance. Crucially, on May 22, 1998, the Good Friday Agreement was approved in referenda both in Northern Ireland and the Republic of Ireland. In the Republic of Ireland the agreement was approved by 94 percent of voters while in Northern Ireland 71 percent voted in favor. Throughout the night preceding the agreement, Clinton had telephone conversations with all the main players. His final conversation of the night took place at 5 a.m. with Gerry Adams, leader of the Irish Republican Army's (IRA) political wing, Sinn Fein. Many commentators consider this late-night conversation between Clinton and Adams to have sealed the agreement. Clinton made a number of key decisions, which facilitated successful negotiations. First, in January 1994, he granted Adams a visa. Adams was working with Social Democratic and Labour Party leader John Hume to create the political conditions for an IRA cease-fire. It was hoped that a cease-fire would create a space for all-party peace negotiations to commence. However, Adams and Hume were acutely aware that republican supporters in the United States needed to be convinced of the merits of a cease-fire. Clinton's decision to grant the visa allowed Adams to canvass his American constituency. In granting Adams's visa, Clinton went against the strong advice of State Department officials. In particular, Secretary of State Warren Christopher opposed the granting of a visa because he believed it would damage the United States' special relationship with Britain. While the decision greatly perturbed both the British government and his own State Department, it was a crucial ingredient in a chain of events that led to the IRA cease-fire of August 31, 1994.

Second, Clinton made two crucial appointments. Former U.S. senator George Mitchell was initially appointed as an economic envoy to Northern Ireland in deference to British political sensibilities. Mitchell ultimately became chairman of the multiparty talks that led to the Good Friday Agreement. Mitchell's negotiating skills achieved what many commentators believed would be impossible. A multiplicity of different parties coming from radically different sides of the Northern Ireland conflict agreed to a set of institutional structures for the future governance of Northern Ireland. Known as the Good Friday Agreement, it has transformed Northern Ireland politics. Mitchell also formulated the Mitchell Principles, which required parties to commit themselves to the pursuit of politics by exclusively democratic and peaceful means. Clinton also appointed Jean Kennedy Smith as U.S. ambassador to Dublin. Sister of the assassinated John F. Kennedy, she proved a crucial link between the Irish government and the White House. Kennedy Smith strongly encouraged Clinton to grant Adams's visa in January 1994.

Apart from specific decisions and appointments, Clinton demonstrated an unswerving personal commitment to the Northern Ireland peace process. The White House operated a virtual open-door policy to representatives of all parties. Clinton's Saint Patrick's Day parties in the White House became legend within political and journalistic circles. Crucially, he established good working relationships with successive Irish and British governments. He worked closely with three successive Irish prime ministers, Albert Reynolds, John Bruton, and Bertie Ahern. Despite huge setbacks, such as the temporary collapse of the IRA cease-fire in February 1996, Clinton remained firmly focused on the possibility of achieving a durable peace. The murder of twenty-eight civilians by a dissident republican group in Omagh on August 15, 1998, increased Clinton's determination to make the then four-month-old Good Friday Agreement work.

Clinton had a particularly close relationship with Irish Foreign Minister Dick Spring. Spring enjoyed a level of direct access to Clinton that was the envy of other European foreign ministers. Clinton also developed a good working relationship with British Prime Minister Tony Blair. Blair's New Labour project incorporated much of Clinton's third-way ideology. Blair's huge parliamentary majority ensured that he could deliver on agreements reached with Clinton and the Irish government. Clinton's commitment combined with Blair's commanding parliamentary majority were crucial factors in facilitating the evolving peace talks.

Clinton's commitment to the peace talks was clearly illustrated by the fact that he made three official visits to Ireland. His first two visits in 1995 and 1998 were working trips designed to move the peace process forward. His final visit, during December 2000, took place when he only had a few weeks left in office. As an outgoing president his role as a facilitator was diminished. As such, his final official visit as president was a victory lap in recognition of his previous efforts. It provided parties both in the Republic of Ireland and Northern Ireland with the opportunity to applaud Clinton for his efforts in the peace process. During all three visits Clinton brought thousands of well-wishers onto the streets. He made particularly memorable visits to Ballybunion Golf links in Co. Kerry and Dundalk, Co. Louth. Clinton of course was not the first sitting president to visit Ireland. However, apart from John F. Kennedy's famous 1963 visit, none matched those of Clinton. It is no exaggeration to state that Clinton earned the affection of the Irish people during the 1990s as Kennedy had done in the 1960s. However, in tangible terms Clinton's commitment and input into Irish affairs immeasurably surpassed those of Kennedy.

How can Clinton's commitment be explained? A variety of factors were at play. As a student at the Jesuit-managed Georgetown University he came into contact with the Boston–New York Irish. Perhaps more crucially, his period as an Oxford University Rhodes Scholar coincided with the emerging violence of Northern Ireland politics. The conflict would have been a major topic for political debate during his two years in Oxford. Having noted this, it is surprising to learn that he only paid one weekend trip to Ireland during this period. The Kennedy influence cannot be lightly disregarded. The Kennedy family's Irish roots were no doubt important to the formative thinking of Clinton. Electoral

factors were undoubtedly a major consideration, too. Clinton knew that in states like New York, the Irish-American vote would be of tremendous importance. In this regard he attended a crucial meeting of the Irish American Caucus in January 1992. Held in New York City during the rough and tumble of presidential primaries, this meeting proved to be a watershed for Clinton. Those in attendance included future Republican Congressman Peter King; Niall O'Dowd, editor of *The Irish Voice;* and senior representatives of New York's Democratic Party. It was at this meeting that the then Governor Clinton gave his controversial undertaking to appoint a White House special representative to Northern Ireland should he be elected president in November 1992. While the proposal would inevitably alienate the British government, it had the effect of giving a boost to New York Democrats. The meeting appeared to have sealed Clinton's commitment to the Northern Ireland Peace Process.

Finally, the British Conservative Party, under the leadership of Prime Minister John Major, pushed Clinton closer to the Irish vote. During Clinton's bid for the White House, two Conservative Party officials joined the flagging Bush campaign. Proposing what amounted to an anti-Clinton smear campaign, the officials alienated the future president. Clinton was slow to forgive the Conservative Party both for its interference and the tactics employed. Despite these explanatory factors the scale of his commitment remains somewhat mysterious. Time and time again he defied official advice. During the crises surrounding the issuing of visas to Gerry Adams and Joe Cahill, Clinton went out on a political limb. He exposed relationships with the

John Major–led government in London to profound risk. In short, Clinton took political risks, which can only be explained on the basis that he was personally committed to the Irish peace process.

During May 2001, the then ex-president paid a private visit to the Bally-bunion Golf Links in Co. Kerry. During July 2003 he signed an agreement to combat AIDS (acquired immunodeficiency syndrome) with Prime Minister Bertie Ahern. And during 2004 he returned to Dublin for the Irish launch of his autobiography, *My Life.* Thousands of Clinton admirers queued for his book-signing event at O'Connell Street, Dublin. Clinton remains a hugely popular figure with the Irish public.

Anthony O'Halloran

See also: KENNEDY, John F.; MITCHELL, George J.

References

Adams, Gerry. *Hope and History: Making Peace in Ireland.* Dingle, Ireland: Brandon, 2003.

Clinton, Bill. *Between Hope and History: Meeting America's Challenges for the 21st Century.* New York: Random House, 1996.

Clinton, Bill. *My Life.* London: Hutchinson, 2004

Coakley, John, and Michael Gallagher. *Politics in the Republic of Ireland.* London: Routledge, 2005.

Conason, Joe, and Gene Lyons. *The Hunting of the President: The Ten-Year Campaign to Destroy Bill and Hillary Clinton.* London: Channel 4 Books, 2001.

Drew, Elizabeth. *On the Edge: The Clinton Presidency.* New York: Simon and Schuster, 1994.

Mitchell, George. *Making Peace.* London: Heinemann, 1999.

O'Clery, Conor. *The Greening of the White House: The Inside Story of How America Tried to Bring Peace to Ireland.* Dublin: Gill and Macmillan, 1996.

Patrick, John A., Richard M. Pious, and Donald A. Ritchie. *The Oxford Essential Guide to the U.S. Government.* New York: Berkley Books, 2000.

Posner, Richard A. *An Affair of State: The Investigation, Impeachment, and Trial of President Clinton.* Cambridge, MA: Harvard University Press, 1999.

Stewart, James B. *Blood Sport: The President and His Adversaries.* New York: Simon and Schuster, 1996

Walker, Martin. *Clinton: The President They Deserve.* London: Vintage, 1997.

COCKRAN, WILLIAM BOURKE (1854–1923)

William Bourke Cockran, a noted orator and U.S. Representative from New York, was born in Carrowkeel, Ireland, on February 28, 1854. He was the third son of Roman Catholics Martin and Harriet Knight Cockran. When Martin Cockran, a prominent farmer, died in a horseback riding accident in 1862, the family moved to Sligo. At the age of nine, Cockran went to France to study at the Institute des Petits Fréres de Marie at Beuchamp. At 14, Cockran returned to Ireland to continue his schooling. He wanted to become an attorney but jobs for lawyers were few in Ireland. In 1871, Cockran immigrated to the United States to better his prospects. He loved the gaiety and excitement of life in New York City and, despite difficulties finding work, resolved to stay, although he briefly returned to Ireland in 1875 as a reporter for a New York newspaper. On September 15, 1876, Cockran passed the New York Bar and became an attorney.

Cockran specialized in charming juries with his oratorical skills. He initially focused on criminal cases but his reputation as a trial attorney steadily won him new clients. He gained recognition in civil litigation and became well known among leaders of the financial district. Cockran amassed a substantial fortune but his runaway success did not extend to his personal life. Cockran married three times but remained childless. In 1876 he married Mary Jackson, who died in childbirth in 1877; in 1885 he married Rhoda Mack, who died in 1895; and in 1906 he married Anne L. Ide, who would survive him. In 1887 he bought an estate, the Cedars, at Sands Point, Long Island, which remained his chief residence.

Cockran's public speaking on behalf of the Democratic Party brought him to political prominence. One of the best speakers of his age, Cockran would entertain crowds of people for hours. Habitually speaking without a written text, Cockran employed classical and historical allusions, expansive logical arguments, and a rich vocabulary. His facial expressions and gesticulations added drama to the event. More importantly, in an age that lacked microphones, Cockran could project his Irish brogue into the farthest reaches of the largest amphitheaters.

Cockran joined the Tammany Hall political organization in 1884. Although consulted by Tammany leaders, Cockran never played a major role in the organization, probably because of his independent tendencies. One Tammany leader, George Washington Plunkitt, admired Cockran's speaking skills but condemned him as an unreliable politician. Aloof and too patrician to be comfortable with the working-class base of Tammany, Cockran nevertheless played a crucial part in Democratic state and national conventions, rallies, and other party functions, particularly in drafting such legal documents as platforms and resolutions.

Cockran was elected to Congress from New York City's Twelfth Congressional District in 1886 and was in and out of Congress over the next thirty-five years (1887–1889, 1891–1895, 1904–1909, 1921–1923). When he was out of favor with Tammany, Cockran was out of office. As a minority member during most of his career, his opportunities to influence important legislation were few.

Cockran used his powers of oratory to comment on the major issues of his day. On most economic issues Cockran sought only a very limited role for government. He denounced income tax, municipal ownership of public utilities, and the protective tariff as socialism. In 1900, Cockran denounced the imperialistic activities of the United States and opposed annexation of the recently acquired Philippine Islands. Perhaps making a connection to the history of Ireland, Cockran saw imperialism as a hostile act that imposed a foreign government on a conquered land and was contrary to American principles. Cockran's political views were also heavily influenced by his Long Island neighbor, Theodore Roosevelt. In 1912 Cockran deserted the Democrats to join the Progressive party and support Roosevelt's presidential bid.

Cockran returned to the Democratic Party as World War I created new political issues. Unsympathetic to British interests, he supported neutrality in the early stages of the conflict. He would later support the declaration of war against Germany. The domestic attacks against hyphenated Americans as the war progressed disturbed Cockran, who was immensely proud of his Irish heritage. He opposed Prohibition, in company with many Irish Catholics who saw the proposed legislation as an attack upon their culture and customs. Cockran died of a brain hemorrhage in Washington, D.C., on March 1, 1923.

Caryn E. Neumann

See also: TAMMANY HALL

Reference
McGurrin, James. *Bourke Cockran: A Free Lance in American Politics.* New York: Charles Scribner's Sons, 1948.

COFFEY, BRIAN (1905–1995)

Brian Coffey was a noted figure in Irish poetic modernism whose career seemed to embody the emigré status of experimental writers in post-Independence Ireland. Born in 1905 to an affluent, Roman Catholic family, Coffey attended Clongowes Wood College before moving to the Continent to complete his secondary education with a baccalaureate. He returned to Ireland and studied sciences at University College Dublin, where his father was president of the College. Here he met fellow Irish modernist poet Denis Devlin, and together they published *Poems* (1930). Devlin joined the Irish diplomatic service, but Coffey returned to Paris to undertake postgraduate work, initially in physical chemistry. He became acquainted with exiled Irish writers such as Thomas MacGreevy and Samuel Beckett, and his poetry was much influenced by French models, notably those of Apollinaire, Mallarmé, and Verlaine, some among the many French poets Coffey would translate. Coffey's Catholicism drew him to the Institut Catholique de Paris where he wrote a doctoral thesis on St. Thomas Aquinas under the supervision of noted Thomist philosopher Jacques Maritain. Meanwhile, he published his first sole-author collection, *Third Person* (1938), which fellow expatriate George Reavey saw through his Europa Press, the same press that had published Beckett's *Echo's Bones* in 1935.

Following the successful conclusion of his doctoral research in 1947, Coffey moved to the United States to take up a position as assistant professor at St. Louis University in Missouri. Here he brought his growing family and wife, Bridget Rosalind Baynes, whom he had married in 1938, and they settled in a farmhouse in Jefferson County, Missouri. Never a prolific poet, Coffey had remained largely silent since the publication of *Third Person*. But in 1952 this silence was broken when he composed perhaps his most memorable poem, *Missouri Sequence,* a long meditative poem that highlights Irish-American identity and Coffey's own immigrant status. Drawing attention to the "Many Irish souls" who inhabit Missouri, people who "drifted in here from the river,/Irish, German, Bohemian,/more than one hundred years ago,/come to make homes," Coffey reminds us of the migrations that have created American society. Acutely conscious of his outsider status, Coffey makes a virtue of his exile and explores its implications for his family and for himself as a poet. Coffey's sense of the Missouri landscape and climate, of Irish-American history, and of his place within them, all contribute to a poetics of identity suffused with local color. His Missouri sojourn ended in 1954 when the Coffey family returned to Europe.

Settling in England and working as a schoolteacher, Coffey continued writing and produced dense, cryptic works, such as the long poems *Advent* (1975) and *Death of Hektor* (1979). These brought him some recognition in Irish literary circles and led to the 1991 publication of *Poems and Versions 1929–1990,* introduced by noted Irish scholar and Coffey advocate J. C. C. Mays. Always a minority interest, Coffey's poems are seen, in the eyes of some critics, to constitute an authentic avant-garde voice in the often claustrophobic and provincial Irish literary scene. Along with Denis Devlin, Thomas MacGreevy, and the more celebrated Samuel Beckett, Coffey's work can be said to form part of an alternative line of development within post-Independence Irish writing. Brian Coffey died at his home in Southampton, England in 1995.

Benjamin Keatinge

See also: BECKETT, Samuel; MISSOURI

References

Coffey, Brian. *Poems and Versions 1929–1990.* Dublin: Dedalus Press, 1991.

Coughlan, Patricia, and Alex Davis, eds. *Modernism and Ireland: The Poetry of the 1930s.* Cork: Cork University Press, 1995.

Morgan, Jack. "*Missouri Sequence:* Brian Coffey's St. Louis Years, 1947–1952," *Éire-Ireland* 28, no. 4 (Winter 1993): 100–114.

Moriarty, Donal. *The Art of Brian Coffey.* Dublin: University College Dublin Press, 2000.

Smith, Michael, ed. *The Lace Curtain: A Magazine of Poetry and Criticism* 4 (Summer 1971).

COGHLAN, EDUARDO AQUILIO (1912–1997)

Eduardo Coghlan was born on October 29, 1912, in the province of Corrientes, son of Patricio Coghlan (1883–1952) and María Dolores Jantus. He was the grandson of Joseph Coghlan (1853–1892), from Ballylarkin, Co. Wicklow, and Elisa Byrne. In 1937 Coghlan graduated from the School of Law at the University of Buenos Aires. After a career in public service that included positions in the public records office and the national welfare system, Coghlan was appointed to the federal court of Buenos Aires in 1957. He retired as a judge of appeals in 1978.

In 1979–1980 Coghlan was the president of the Argentine Genealogical Institute, during which time he published more than fifty articles about Irish and other families in Argentina. He was also vice president of the Irish-Argentine Federation and a member of the Irish Catholic Association.

As a judge, Eduardo Coghlan was appointed to the national court of appeals during the military dictatorship of 1976–1983. For this reason he is sometimes criticized by human rights organizations and included in lists of accused members of the Argentine judicial system. However, Coghlan's activity as a magistrate focused exclusively on civil law, voting for example in cases of currency impacts of inflation (*La Amistad v. Iriarte,* September 9, 1977). During his career in public service, Coghlan published many technical papers and articles, for instance, "Hacia la Seguridad Social en la Argentina: Una Comparación Sugestiva" (1943) and "Los Resultados del Censo Escolar Ponen en Evidencia la Necesidad Urgente del Censo General de la Nación" (1944). ("Towards Social Security in Argentina: an Indicative Comparison" [1943] and "The Results of the Education Census Stress the Urgent Need for a National General Census" [1944].)

Many Irish Argentines are in Coghlan's debt as his research enabled them to pinpoint their Irish relations and often the county, parish, and townland from which their great-grandparents left for Argentina. Coghlan cooperated closely with Bill Meek of the Irish national radio service (RTÉ), when he visited Argentina in 1987 and produced a successful radio documentary series about the Irish Argentines. Coghlan's pioneering research in public archives and records of Irish births, marriages, and deaths, which was published in the *Southern Cross* and the *Standard,* allowed him to establish a massive family history database. During an official appointment at the Archivo General de la Nación (Argentine public records office), Coghlan was able to transcribe arrivals to Buenos Aires and census data that referred to thousands of Irish immigrants and their families. He recorded persons with Irish names, people that were certain to be Irish born, and their children born in Argentina. Coghlan undertook a detailed and painstaking research over a lifetime of Irish emigrants and their descendants from the date of their arrival in Argentina through the succeeding generations.

Coghlan published the following works about the Irish in Argentina: *Fundadores de la Segunda Época: Los Irlandeses* [*Founders of the Second Period: the Irish*] (1967), *Los Irlandeses* [*The Irish*] (1970), "Orígenes y Evolución de la Colectividad Hiberno-Argentina" in the *Southern Cross* ["Origins and Evolution of the Hiberno-Argentine Community" in the *Southern Cross*] (1975), *Andanzas de un Irlandés en el Campo Porteño 1845–1864* [*An Irishman's Adventures in the Countryside of Buenos Aires, 1845–1864*] (1981), *Linajes Argentinos de Origen Irlandés* [*Argentine Families of Irish Descent*] (several articles between 1982 and 1985), *El Aporte de los Irlandeses a la Formación de la Nación Argentina* [*The Irish Contribution to the Formation of the Argentine Nation*] (1982), and the vast genealogical catalog of the Irish-Argentine community, *Los Irlandeses en la Argentina: Su Actuación y Descendencia* [*The Irish in Argentina: Their Participation and Descendants*] (1987). Coghlan's master work, however, is his *Los Irlandeses en la Argentina* [*The Irish in Argentina*], a 963-page directory including detailed records of 4,350 Irish-born immigrants and their families up to the third and often fourth generation. Entries are arranged alphabetically by family name. Other contents include a chronicle of the Irish in Argentina, sketches of 413 livestock brands owned by Irish-Argentine ranchers (reproduced from Estevan Parle's 1885 *Registro de Marcas de Hacienda de la Provincia de Buenos Aires* [*Cattle Brands Register in the Province of Buenos Aires*]), the article "La Heráldica Irlandesa" by Félix F. Martín y Herrera, and 182 Irish family coats of arms. There are also press clippings, photographs, and documents. The book was published privately, with contributions from the Cultural Relations Committee of the Irish Department of Foreign Affairs and private supporters (who are listed in the final pages). Although the book is largely focused on the traditional segment of Catholic rural landowners and does not include a vast majority of re-emigrations to other countries, *Los Irlandeses en Argentina* is a key source of information for most studies of this particular migration. In 1987 the Irish Ministry of Foreign Affairs approved the purchase of copies of Coghlan's genealogical catalog to be distributed to county libraries and institutions abroad. Eduardo Coghlan died on August 1, 1997.

Edmundo Murray

See also: ARGENTINA

Reference

MacLoughlin, Guillermo. "The Forgotten People: the Irish in Argentina and other South American Countries. In Memory of Edward A. Coghlan." Paper delivered at The Scattering of Ireland and the Irish Diaspora: A Comparative Perspective Conference, University College Cork, Ireland, September 24–27, 1997.

COHALAN, DANIEL F. (1865–1946)

The Irish nationalist, politician, and judge Daniel Cohalan, was one of the most influential Irish-American nationalist leaders of the early twentieth century. Born in 1865

Portrait of Irish nationalist Daniel F. Cohalan. (Library of Congress)

in Middletown, New York, Cohalan graduated from Manhattan College in 1885 and went on to study law, ultimately being admitted to the New York bar in 1888. By 1900, Cohalan was heavily involved with the Democratic Party, serving as a delegate to both the 1904 and 1908 national conventions. Meanwhile, he became an influential adviser to New York's Tammany Hall boss Charles F. Murphy and subsequently became the grand sachem of the Tammany Society from 1908–1911. Appointed an associate justice to the New York Supreme Court in 1911, Cohalan retained this post until his resignation in 1924.

Cohalan and John Devoy collaborated in reuniting Clan na Gael in 1900. The Clan was a secret Irish-American revolutionary organization dedicated to the use of physical force to achieve full Irish independence and allied to the Irish Republican

Brotherhood in Ireland. Devoy and Cohalan also helped organize the Irish Race Convention of March 4–5, 1916, in New York City. The Friends of Irish Freedom (FOIF) was formed at this convention. Founded as an open organization that protested British actions in Ireland and publicized Ireland's case from within the United States, FOIF became a crucial fund-raising body for the Irish nationalist movement in America. Cohalan was a staunch isolationist, and his persistent support for the Irish cause during and after World War I, and his vigorous opposition to the League of Nations, drew the ire of President Woodrow Wilson.

From June 1919 to December 1920, Eamon de Valera undertook a tour of the United States on behalf of the recently formed Dáil Éireann. His goal was to raise funds for the new government and to obtain diplomatic recognition for it from the United States. From the very beginning, de Valera clashed with Cohalan and Devoy because of his belief that he should have direct control of Irish and Irish-American efforts for Ireland. Specifically, Cohalan and Devoy argued that the money raised, more than $5 million, should remain in America and be used to promote Ireland's cause in the United States and to resist the founding of the League of Nations. Cohalan and de Valera further clashed when both men led delegations to the 1920 Republican Convention in Chicago in an effort to obtain a plank (a fundamental part of a political program) on Irish freedom in the party's platform. Their effort ultimately failed because of their inability to compromise on the wording for a resolution.

The split with de Valera in 1920, and the outbreak of civil war in Ireland, would lead to a state of fractious and divided

Irish-American nationalist politics in the 1920s and 1930s. Cohalan died on November 12, 1946.

Ely Janis

See also: De VALERA, Eamon; DEVOY, John; MURPHY, Charles Francis

References
Carroll, Francis M. *Money for Ireland: Finance, Diplomacy, Politics and the First Dáil Éireann Loans, 1919–1936.* Westport, CT: Praeger Publishers, 2002.
Funchion, Michael, ed. *Irish American Voluntary Organizations.* Westport, CT: Greenwood Press, 1983.
Tansill, Charles. *America and the Fight for Irish Freedom 1866–1922.* New York: The Devin Adair Co., 1957.
Ward, Alan. *Ireland and Anglo-American Relations 1899–1921.* Toronto: Toronto University Press, 1969.

COHAN, GEORGE M. (1878–1942)

Although his birth certificate states that he was born on July 3, his mother always said that George M. Cohan was born on the 4th of July, and a mother ought to know. Anyway, given Cohan's deft ability to knock off Tin Pan Alley and Broadway flag-waving hit songs, such as "Yankee Doodle Dandy" and "You're A Grand Old Flag," the convergence between parturition and patriotism is close enough.

Back in Cork the family name had been Keohane, but it was changed to Cohan when George's grandfather emigrated to America in the early nineteenth century. Jerry Cohan, the songwriter's father, had been bitten by the theatrical bug early in life. He pursued blackface minstrelsy until 1874, when he organized a Hibernicon, a sort of Irish variety show, which for one glorious moment featured the great uilleann pipe virtuoso Patsy

Touhey. Jerry Cohan moved on to writing and performing, with his wife, Nellie, in a series of comic Irish shows. Gradually, Jerry and Nellie worked their children, Josephine and George, into their acts.

Josephine turned out to be a graceful skirt dancer, and she was sometimes in greater demand than the rest of the family. For his part young George substituted athleticism for grace. He would finish up a solo clog with a run up the sides of the proscenium arches. Part of his famous stiff-legged tap style was the result of an accident, when the conductor in the pit substituted a slow piece in two-four time for Cohan's customary six-eight "essence" dance. The exaggerated steps the dancer was forced to improvise were a hit with the audience and were incorporated into his later acts. Something of his unique dance style can be seen in James Cagney's impersonation of Cohan in the 1942 bio-film *Yankee Doodle Dandy.*

In 1891 Jerry Cohan made the important decision to go beyond Irish-American theater. The Four Cohans, as they billed themselves, performed *Peck's Bad Boy and His Pa.* Soon they were part of B. F. Keith's expanding vaudeville circuit. George began to take over from his father the task of writing material, and he soon had some modest success with several vaudeville sketches. However, it was his 1904 musical, *Little Johnnie Jones,* that launched him on his career.

Apart from theater-savvy advice from his father, Cohan's main influences were Dion Boucicault and Edward Harrigan. Cohan admired Harrigan's work and gave him a musical tip of the hat in a 1908 song, "Harrigan." *Little Johnnie Jones,* with its overly complicated plot and endless puns, has all the earmarks of a Harrigan musical, without the Irish-American setting and themes. However, it was the songs for the show that demonstrated that Cohan had mastered the new Tin Pan Alley idiom. Two of his most famous songs, "I'm a Yankee Doodle Dandy" and "Give My Regards to Broadway," came out of his first theatrical hit.

Many other successes followed. In 1906 he formed a partnership with Sam Harris, and together they produced all of Cohan's musicals, reviews, and plays until 1920. Until then Cohan had paid little attention to Irish America. Perhaps it was the success of *Abie's Irish Rose* in 1920s that encouraged him to revisit the Irish-American musical. Whatever the reason, Cohan wrote *Little Nellie Kelly* (1922), *The Rise of Rosie O'Reilly* (1923), and *The Merry Malones* (1927). All three were essentially celebrations of the Irish-American girl, a popular icon in the early decades of the twentieth century.

Although Cohan had begun his career on the vaudeville stage as a song-and-dance man, over the years he developed considerable skill as an actor. In addition to appearing in his own plays, serious works as well as comedies, he received critical acclaim when he played Nat Miller in Eugene O'Neill's *Ah, Wilderness* (1933), and Rodgers and Hart tapped him to play the presidential role in *I'd Rather Be Right* (1937).

By the mid-1920s Cohan's musicals and plays had begun to lose their appeal for Broadway audiences. With the exception of a few of his dramatic works, Cohan had never excelled at, or even shown much interest in, his plots. If anything, he made fun of the conventions of the musical by using his songs to call attention to his creaky plot devices. The lines he gave his characters were slangy and unmemorable. However, no one else better caught the brash, audacious, and energetic mood of early twentieth-century American.

Diagnosed with stomach cancer in 1940, Cohan died on November 5, 1942.

William H. A. Williams

See also: CAGNEY, James; HARRIGAN AND HART

References

Cohan, George M. *Twenty Years on Broadway and the Years It Took to Get There*. 1925. Reprint, Westport, CT: Greenwood, 1971.

McCabe, John. *George M. Cohan: The Man Who Owned Broadway*. New York: Doubleday, 1973.

COLEMAN, MICHAEL (1891–1945)

Through his recordings, Sligo fiddler Michael Coleman, who immigrated to America as a young man, became the best known and most influential performer of traditional Irish music in the twentieth century. His recordings shaped the playing style of many fiddlers on both sides of the Atlantic.

Coleman was born in Knockgrania in the Killavil district of southern Co. Sligo, which, by the late nineteenth century, had become an intensely musical area. Taking advantage of this situation, Coleman, from an early age, learned traditional Irish music from various skilled neighbors, uilleann pipers as well as fiddlers. Even as a boy he was considered talented. He was a good step dancer, as well as a fiddler. As he got older, Michael and his older brother, James, were in great demand to play for house dances.

Like most farms in the area, the Coleman holding was small, and Michael, as the youngest of seven children, eventually had to leave home to seek a living. For a time he moved back and forth between England and Sligo. However, with his overriding interest in music, he picked up no particular trade or craft. Coleman finally immigrated to America in 1914. He lived for a time with an aunt in Boston, working at odd jobs. However, New York City, with its larger audience for Irish music, soon attracted him.

There, the easiest and steadiest money for an Irish musician came from playing in the bands that performed in the city's many Irish dance halls. However, Coleman, confident of his talent, was determined to be a solo artist. He played everywhere, from weddings to the vaudeville circuit. The resulting hand-to-mouth existence was eased a bit when he began to record in 1921. Very quickly, Coleman became established as the most popular Irish fiddler in America. Even after the Depression resulted in cutbacks by the record companies, Coleman was able to resume recording between 1934 and 1936. In all, Coleman cut some 80 sides, often for major labels, such as Victor, Columbia, and Decca. However, all of his records, along with those of hundreds of other Irish musicians, were aimed primarily at the Irish-American market.

Coleman's fiddling was grounded in the style of his native Sligo. His fast, smooth, long-bow style with its rapid ornamentations made him popular, especially after 1925, when the new electrical recording technique provided better fidelity than the original acoustical methods. Of course, Coleman was not the only talented fiddler from the region to have a successful recording career. James Morrison and Paddy Killoran, fellow Sligo immigrants, were also

popular recording artists. As a result, the Sligo style became virtually *the* fiddling style for Irish Americans living in the great industrial cities.

Popular as Coleman's recordings were in America, they caused even greater excitement as they began to appear back in Ireland. Until then, traditional music had been primarily a local affair, dominated by regional playing styles. The repertory of tunes was also local, broadened only by the visits of occasional traveling musicians from outside of one's area. Suddenly, coming out of the windup gramophones was the sound of a highly skilled, professional, his music propelled by the percussive sound of the piano.

Major regional fiddling styles survived in Ireland, but the influence of Coleman and the other Sligo musicians was everywhere. Coleman's stamp on the music is demonstrated by the extent to which tunes he recorded became the standard versions throughout much of the country. Indeed, the combination of the American recordings and Francis O'Neill's printed tune collections resulted in a certain standardization within Irish traditional music. Nevertheless, the fact that the old music was being disseminated by the newest technology helped to valorize the music for the rural Irish. And if some tunes and local playing styles were lost, recordings such as Coleman's helped raise the bar for the standards of musicianship and injected much excitement in a form of music that was facing the growing pressures of twentieth-century popular culture.

A talented musician, Coleman lacked the business skills that might have enabled him to increase his income and build for the future. The constant traveling and playing for parties took a toll on his family and, eventually perhaps, on his health. He died in New York City in 1945 at the age of 54.

William H. A. Williams

See also: O'NEILL, Francis; MUSIC IN
    AMERICA, IRISH

Reference

Bradshaw, Harry. *Michael Coleman:
    1891–1945*. Dublin: Viva Voce, 1991.

COLOMBIA

The only South American country with coasts on both the Pacific and the Atlantic oceans, Colombia was part of the Spanish viceroyalty of New Granada. The United States of Colombia, including also Panama, Venezuela, and Ecuador, was proclaimed in 1819 by Simón Bolívar, when he crossed the Andes and defeated the royalist forces at the Battle of Boyacá. In 1822 the four countries were united as Gran Colombia, which collapsed in 1830 with the separation of Venezuela and Ecuador. The republic of Colombia was established in 1886, but Panama separated in 1903, after the U.S.-encouraged War of the Thousand Days (1899–1902).

Irish soldiers fought in Colombia during the War of Independence with Spain in 1816–1822. They were recruited in Dublin, London, and other cities by John Devereux, James T. English, William Walton, and others. The Irish Legion sailed from Liverpool in July 1819. Some of the officers were Major F. Anthony L'Estrange, Francisco Burdett O'Connor, and William Aylmer. They arrived at the island of Margarita, where they suffered hardships, sickness, and loss of life. In March 1820 the Legion sailed to Río Hacha, and after the attack on this city, their standard displaying the harp of Ireland was raised instead of the Spanish royal ensign. Weakened by lack of

pay and proper food, and complaining about the native officers, some of the Irish mutinied, got drunk, and began to ransack the city for booty. The mutineers were transported to Jamaica and turned over to the British authorities. O'Connor's lancers continued the campaign and reached Cartagena by the end of 1822, and they effectively assisted Bolívar at the decisive battle of Boyacá. The chief responsible for forming the Irish Legion, John Devereux, did not arrive at South America until 1821. He never took part in a single engagement with the legion, but he made a pretty profit in organizing it. However, Bolívar absolved Devereux from any blame and in 1822 attached him to the general staff at Bogotá. In 1823 John Devereux was appointed Colombian envoy to the courts of northern Europe.

Some of the soldiers of the Irish Legion remained in Colombia after the War of Independence. After the battle of Boyacá, Daniel Florence O'Leary (1801–1854) was appointed Bolívar's aide-de-camp and served in Venezuela, Panama, Ecuador, Peru, and Bolivia. In 1828 O'Leary married Soledad Soublette in Bogotá and lent valuable services to Colombia and Venezuela. His memoirs, published posthumously by his son Simón Bolívar O'Leary, remain a basic reference for students of the South American Wars of Independence. Beatriz O'Connell, who was related to the Liberator Daniel O'Connell, married Manuel Pombo in 1795 in Madrid, and in 1819 was living in Bogotá. Other Irish settlers in Colombia related to the Wars of Independence were Thomas Murray (d. 1823), who married Estrada Callejas; John Hands; Francis O'Farrell (known as Francisco Puyana); Joseph Boylan; Robert Lee; James Rooke; and the physicians Hugh Blair Brown (surgeon of the Arthur Sandes's Rifles in Peru), John Kennedy, Thomas Williamson, and Dr. McEwen.

Among the visitors to Colombia who left detailed travel accounts, William John Duane (1780–1865), of Clonmel, Co. Tipperary, family, embarked in 1822 on a journey through Colombia and Venezuela. The product of these travels was *A Visit to Colombia in the Years 1822 & 1823* (Philadelphia: Thomas H. Palmer, 1826), a book detailing a rather leisurely trip from Caracas to Cartagena de Indias, via Bogotá. A convinced supporter of South American independence from Spain, Duane used the trip to study the situation of the places he visited, and he made a number of interesting observations about contemporary social conditions and politics in Gran Colombia.

Almost 150 years later, a new type of legion arrived in Colombia, though this time peacefully. In 1953 the Catholic lay movement Legion of Mary sent Seamus Grace and Alphie Lamb (1932–1959) to Bogotá to expand their mission in Colombia. From the capital, Grace and Lamb established many legion branches (*praesidia*) in other parts of the country. They visited bishops and obtained permission to set up in their dioceses. The legion flourished around Colombia, especially among the poor, and then expanded to Ecuador, Venezuela, and throughout South America.

The most recent chapter in the history of Colombian-Irish relations connects the Irish Republican Army (IRA) and the Revolutionary Armed Forces of Colombia (FARC). On August 11, 2001, Jim Monaghan, Niall Connolly, and Martin McCauley were arrested at Bogotá's airport and accused of being IRA members providing explosives training to the FARC in the demilitarized zone of San Vicente del Caguán in southern Colombia. Established in 1964 as the military wing of the Colombian Communist Party, the FARC is the largest irregular army in Latin America. Washington accuses the FARC and other "narco-terrorists" of profiting from the illegal drug production and distribution business. The three Irishmen were traveling on false passports. At first they said they were bird-watching but later added that they were studying the Colombia peace process. Their initial acquittal in April 2004 was overturned by a higher court, which imposed sentences of seventeen years on each of them. They escaped from Colombia and in August 2005—a week after the IRA proclaimed the end of its military operations—they arrived safely in Ireland. The Colombian authorities have formally requested their extradition.

Edmundo Murray

See also: DEVEREUX, John; MURRAY, Thomas; O'CONNOR, Francis Burdett; O'LEARY, Daniel Florence; VENEZUELA

References

Barnwell, David. "William Duane and his 'Visit to Colombia' of 1823." Paper presented at the CAIS annual conference, Maynooth, June 22–26, 2005.

Hasbrouck, Alfred. *Foreign Legionaries in the Liberation of Spanish South America.* New York: Columbia University, 1928.

Kirby, Peadar. *Ireland and Latin America: Links and Lessons.* Dublin: Trócaire, 1992.

COLUM, MARY (1884–1957)

Mary Catherine Gunning Maguire was born in 1884, in Collooney, Co. Sligo. The early deaths of her parents left her under first a grandmother's care, then under the care of an aunt who resented being burdened by the young girl. When the aunt also died, Mary was sent to a boarding school in Monaghan, the Convent of Saint Louis. She disliked the regimentation there, but obtained a strong education, which she augmented by incessant reading. Her interest in, and facility with, languages distinguished her from an early age.

Upon graduating from St. Louis she moved to Dublin, where she began studying at the National University, the precursor of the modern University College Dublin. Here she studied for, and obtained, a degree in modern languages; she was later to note that she and James Joyce had followed essentially the same curriculum at the university and had read many of the same textbooks. Although she enjoyed her coursework, the greater stimulus to Mary was that of Dublin itself, particularly its theatrical life. She formed a University theater appreciation club, and thereby met one of her heroes, William Butler Yeats, and saw another, John M. Synge.

Upon graduation Mary decided to remain in Dublin, and she took a position at St. Enda's School, one of Padraig Pearse's inventive nationalist schools. She appears to have been happy there, and admired Pearse, through whom she met many other prominent nationalist leaders (such as Thomas MacDonagh). She also befriended another young teacher, and aspiring writer, Padraic Colum. In 1912, despite fears of being trapped in a routine or oppressive marriage, Mary wed Colum, and their marriage survived until her death. Although her memoirs describe their courtship in strangely unromantic terms, and despite her affair with the writer Van Wyck Brooks (of which Padraic may never have known), they seem to have enjoyed a companionable, if not engrossingly passionate, marriage.

One result of their marriage was an opportunity to visit relatives in the United States. This trip is not thought to have been intended to be permanent, but they quickly decided to settle in America, once there. After moving in rapid succession from New York to Pittsburgh to Chicago, they moved again to New York City, where they began to establish themselves as teachers and essayists. It was in these dual roles that Mary showed her greatest skills. Having written numerous critical reviews for the press in Dublin—and having been praised as a critic by Yeats himself—she began writing reviews, essays, and critical appreciations that were published in both newspapers and magazines. Her personal knowledge of important literary figures, as well as her knowledge of several leaders of the 1916 Rising, gave her an unusual authority in American literary and political journals. This influence she often used, particularly in her reviews, to promote Irish writers whose work she admired to American audiences.

In 1930 Mary and Padraic moved briefly to France, first living in Paris, then in Nice. During this extended stay the Colums met often with another of Mary's literary heroes, James Joyce. She particularly relished trading words in odd languages with him, and recollecting National University professors whom they had both known. Mary also helped the Joyces tremendously by providing their daughter Lucia with friendship and sympathy as her mental difficulties became ever more difficult for Lucia and her family. On occasion she took Lucia into their home, giving her a place where she felt safe, and where Joyce and his wife Nora trusted Mary as Lucia's guardian. Mary's memoirs of Joyce were incomplete at the time of her death, but

Padraic edited them in with his own, and the combined volume *Our Friend James Joyce* is an appealing, if slightly starstruck, view of the great writer.

Upon returning to the United States, Mary and Padraic settled again in New York City. She continued her reviewing and essay work, and became even more influential than she had been earlier, as many of the writers she had championed earlier (Yeats, Joyce) were now entering their posthumous widespread American appreciation. She also published two well-regarded books: *From These Roots* (1937), a critical introduction to the ideas of modern literature, and *Life and the Dream* (1947), an autobiography. From 1946–1948 she served as a chancellor of the Academy of American Poets. Long-term ill health, however, made her last years of life difficult, and she was frequently weakened by persistent anemia. She died in 1957.

Although now almost wholly overshadowed by her husband, Mary Colum may have been the better literary mind—she simply lacked Padraic's lyrical gift. Despite the interest of her three major book publications (including the posthumous Joyce memoir), her real contribution to Irish-American relations lay in her articulate and perceptive advocacy of Irish writers who were just beginning to make names for themselves in the United States. Because of her interest and ability to explicate difficult literature, she helped writers, even those of Joyce's stature find a greater reading public in the United States.

Andrew Goodspeed

See also: COLUM, Padraic; JOYCE, James Augustine Aloysius; YEATS, William Butler

References

Colum, Mary. *From These Roots.* New York: C. Scribner's Sons, 1938.

Colum, Mary. *Life and the Dream.* London: Macmillan, 1947.

Colum, Mary, and Padraic Colum. *Our Friend James Joyce.* Garden City, NY: Doubleday, 1958.

Sanford Sternlicht. "Declaration of Independence: Mary Colum as Autobiographer." *Syracuse University Library Associates Courier* 32 (1997): 25–33.

COLUM, PADRAIC (1881–1972)

Padraic Colum was born Patrick Collumb on December 8, 1881, in Columbkill, Co. Longford. The Longford landscape and local speech were important to Colum, and to his work, throughout his life. His father was the master of the Longford Workhouse, and Padraic therefore met many downtrodden people who were experiencing difficulties in life; it is perhaps from these early experiences that he developed the gentleness and sympathy with the unhappy that distinguishes his works.

Colum studied for a time at St. Michael's Boys' National School in Longford, then at Glasthule National School when his father became rail manager of the station at Sandycove, in the outer suburbs of Dublin. His father resigned this position and left in a doomed pursuit of wealth in the Colorado gold mines; during his absence Padraic and his family lived in his mother's family home in Co. Cavan. They returned to Dublin when his father returned goldless from America.

Colum originally became a clerk for the Irish Railway Clearing House. Just after the turn of the century he began to write and publish poems, which gave him a local fame as a skilled young poet. Later, his abilities attracted an American patron (Thomas Hugh Kelly), who paid for him to attend University College Dublin. At this time he also became interested in theater and started to write plays. His 1902 play, *The Saxon Shillin'*, won a prestigious Cumann na nGaedheal drama prize. As it addressed the recruitment of Irishmen into the British army, it was precisely the type of drama that Dublin's major dramatists desired: topical, somewhat controversial, and written by an Irishman. Colum found himself a success in Dublin's theatrical society, and routinely associated with some of the artists he most admired: W. B. Yeats, Lady Augusta Gregory, and John M. Synge. He was an original founder of the Abbey Theatre in 1904, and the Abbey produced several more of his plays to considerable approbation: most notable of these were *Broken Soil* (1903), *The Land* (1905), and *Thomas Muskerry* (1910). His early dramas are generally considered his best, and subsequent plays did not fulfill the full promise of his earlier work. Later in life, however, he experimented skillfully with the Japanese Noh tradition (*Moytura: A Play for Dancers* [1963]).

Colum was fascinated by the Irish cultural and linguistic revival; he joined the Gaelic League in 1901, and began to call himself not "Patrick Collumb" but "Padraic Colum." He was also a supporter of Arthur Griffith (founder and first leader of Sinn Féin), and supported a policy of national independence. Although he was in the United States at the time of the Easter Rising in 1916, he published a volume of Irish Revolutionary Brotherhood poems in honor of the dead.

In 1912 Colum married Mary Maguire, a thoughtful teacher who was just beginning a distinguished career as a reviewer and critic. He remained devoted to her for the rest of his life. Their early years together were troubled by financial difficulties, which may account for their decision to remain in the United States when they were on a vacation there in 1914. Some scholars believe they decided to emigrate permanently before leaving Ireland.

Colum and Mary were to spend most of the rest of their lives in the United States (with the three-year exception of 1930–1933, when they resided in France and renewed their friendship with James Joyce; Colum occasionally helped Joyce by typing portions of *Finnegans Wake*). They were to become instrumental figures in the Irish-American literary world; their personal knowledge of Irish writers and their ability to review the writers' works clearly and sensitively gave them many opportunities to promote Irish writing. Among much other work, Colum wrote a particularly sensitive preface to the separately published installment of *Finnegans Wake, Anna Livia Plurabelle*.

Settling in New York, both Colums taught and lectured. Mary became the more prominent critic, but Padraic began to find new creative strengths in his writings. He started to write a children's column in a local newspaper, and found that writing for children was perhaps his strongest literary ability. He was pleased when, in 1922, the Legislature of Hawaii commissioned him to write a children's book about Hawaiian folklore. He visited the islands, conducted researches, and produced several books, the best of which is likely *The Bright Islands* (1925).

Colum's skill as a writer of books for children ensured a small, steady income, and he became highly prolific. He was particularly interested in reinterpreting mythology for children, and many of his works involve mythological heroes:

The Adventures of Odysseus (1918); *The Children of Odin* (1920); *The Golden Fleece and the Heroes who Lived Before Achilles* (1921). He also continued to write poetry for adults. His verse is particularly strong in traditional ballad modes, and he wrote several poems that have been set to music effectively. His "She Moved Through the Fair" is still widely known in Ireland, as is "The Old Woman of the Roads." His poems reveal a sensitivity to age, poverty, weariness, and sadness that is perhaps most closely comparable with elements of James Stephens's work. (Stephens and Colum were close friends).

After returning from their visit to France, the Colums again settled into Manhattan, where they began teaching at Columbia University. They later became American citizens. In 1957 Colum published his strongest novel, *The Flying Swans.* Padraic was heartbroken by Mary's death in 1957, and set himself to editing her memoirs of Joyce with passages he had written: this was published in 1958 as *Our Friend James Joyce.* A year later he published his long-planned biography of Arthur Griffith, *Ourselves Alone.* In his last years Colum continued to publish prolifically and lecture often. He became something of a genial paternal figure to a younger generation of writers and frequently visited Ireland. He received numerous honors in both America and Ireland and served as a chancellor of the Academy of American Poets (1950–1951). Although Padraic died in Connecticut on January 11, 1972, he is buried in Dublin, with Mary.

Colum was one of the major figures of Irish-American literature. Although much of his best work was done while still in Ireland, he remained a practicing poet of distinction in New York, and his books for children were works written with skill in a difficult genre. In his frequent role as critic, lecturer, or reviewer, he promoted Irish writing in the United States and offered particularly strong and thoughtful advocacy of James Joyce. He also edited an anthology of Irish verse that was popular in the United States.

Andrew Goodspeed

See also: COLUM, Mary; JOYCE, James Augustine Aloysius; YEATS, William Butler

References

Bowen, Zack. *Padraic Colum.* Carbondale: Southern Illinois University Press, 1970.

Colum, Padraic. *Collected Poems.* New York: Devin-Adair, 1953.

Colum, Padraic. *The Flying Swans.* New York: Crown, 1957.

Colum, Padraic. *Selected Plays of Padraic Colum.* Syracuse, NY: Syracuse University Press, 1986.

Sternlicht, Sanford. *Padraic Colum.* Boston: Twayne, 1985.

CONN, WILLIAM DAVID (1917–1993)

Born in East Liberty, Pennsylvania, on October 8, 1917, William David Conn was the oldest son of William Robert Conn, a steamfitter for the Westinghouse Corporation, and Irish-born Margaret McFarland Conn. Conn, who went by Billy instead of William, dropped out of the Sacred Heart Parochial School to pursue a boxing career at age seventeen. He had learned how to box as a means of self-defense at age sixteen, taking lessons from his father's friend and former boxer, Johnny Ray, who eventually became his manager.

Conn, who never boxed as an amateur, immediately entered the professional ranks as a light heavyweight, winning eight of his first fourteen fights. Although he lost his first bout against Dick Woodward, in Fairmont, West Virginia, on June 28, 1934, he won his second fight against Johnny Lewis, in Charleston, South Carolina, on July 20, 1934, by a knockout in the third round. Beginning September 9, 1935, Conn won twenty-seven consecutive bouts, including three knockouts and one decision. All of these fights occurred in Pittsburgh, Pennsylvania, where he acquired the moniker, the "Pittsburgh Kid." Notable fighters, such as Vince Dundee, Babe Risko, Teddy Yarosz, and Fritzie Zivic, succumbed to Conn's winning streak. His winning streak came to an end on August 13, 1937, in the tenth round of a fight against Young John Corbett III in San Francisco, California. Conn avenged his loss to Corbett on November 8, 1937, in Pittsburgh, Pennsylvania, winning in the tenth round.

By the spring of 1939, Conn was considered to be a leading contender for the light heavyweight world title. On February 4, 1939, Melio Bettina defeated Tiger Jack Fox for the light heavyweight world championship, a title recently vacated by Joe Louis, who had held the heavyweight title since June 22, 1937. Conn entered the ring against Bettina for the light heavyweight world title in New York, on July 13, 1939. He won the title on points, after going the entire fifteen rounds against Bettina. On September 25, 1939, Conn defended his title against Bettina, again winning a fifteen-round bout on points in Pittsburgh, Pennsylvania. Gus Lesnivich challenged the Pittsburgh Kid for the world light heavyweight title on November 17, 1939, in New York. Conn defended his title against Lesnivich in a fifteen-round bout decided on points. Conn's bout against Lesnivich, his last of 1939, marked the end of the year

in which he won the Edgar J. Neil Trophy, awarded to the person who had done the most to advance the sport of boxing during the year by the nation's boxing writers.

Conn remained the world's light heavyweight champion through the spring of 1941. On June 5, 1940, he defended his title for the last time against Lesnivich, winning a fifteen-round bout on points in Detroit, Michigan. Conn's next fight, on September 6, 1940, against Bob Pastor, was his first as a heavyweight. He won the fight, knocking Pastor out in the thirteenth round. Conn continued to fight as a heavyweight through the spring of 1941. In seven matches against the heavyweights, the light heavyweight champion remained undefeated, winning four bouts by knockouts. Conn, who won *The Ring* Magazine Merit Award in 1940, relinquished the world light heavyweight title in May 1941, in anticipation of challenging Joe Louis for the world heavyweight title. On June 18, 1941, he fought Louis for the world heavyweight title in New York, losing on points in the thirteenth round. Although a rematch against Louis was scheduled for October 12, 1941, in Yankee Stadium, in New York, Secretary of War Henry Stimson canceled the bout, ordering all boxers back to their respective service units. For Conn, that meant serving in the United States Army from 1942 to 1946. Much anticipated, the bout between Conn and Louis occurred on June 19, 1946, with Louis winning in the eighth round. Conn, who did not enter the ring in 1947, fought three times in 1948, before retiring from the sport after a six-round exhibition against Louis in Chicago, Illinois, on December 10, 1948.

Conn, who earned $700,000 alone from his second fight with Louis, retired from boxing in good financial shape. By investing his savings wisely in oil, automobile, and other enterprises, he supported his wife and three sons comfortably. An inaugural inductee into the International Boxing Hall of Fame in 1990, Conn died of pneumonia in a Veterans Hospital in Pittsburgh, Pennsylvania, on May 29, 1993.

Adam R. Hornbuckle

See also: PENNSYLVANIA

References

Grasso, John. "Conn, William David."
Biographical Dictionary of American Sports: Basketball and Other Indoor Sports, edited by David L. Porter. Westport, CT: Greenwood Press, 1989: 367–368.

Menke, Frank G. *The Encyclopedia of Sports.* Rev. ed. New York: A. S. Barnes and Company, 1969.

Sammons, Jeffrey T. *Beyond The Ring: The Role of Boxing in American Society.* Urbana: University of Illinois Press, 1988.

Portrait of 1896 Olympic track and field gold medal winner James Brendan Connolly. (Library of Congress)

CONNOLLY, JAMES BRENDAN (1868–1957)

James Connolly was born in South Boston, Massachusetts, on October 28, 1868, one of twelve children of John and Ann O'Donnell Connolly, both Irish-born Catholics; his father worked as a fisherman on the "T" wharf of the Boston waterfront. Educated at the Notre Dame Academy and the Mather and Lawrence Grammar School, Connolly did not graduate from high school, but instead went to work as a clerk at a Boston insurance company. In 1892 he secured employment with the United States Army Corps of Engineers in Savannah, Georgia; his brother, Michael, who already worked for the Savannah District Army Corps of Engineers, helped James get a job at the Corps of Engineers, where he worked as a clerk, recorder, and inspector for three years.

In Savannah, Connolly became involved in local sports as a participant, organizer, and writer. He organized the Catholic Library Association (CLA) track and field and football teams, and as football captain, led CLA to a 36–0 win over the Young Hebrew Association, scoring three touchdowns himself. As the captain of the CLA cycling team, Connolly promoted cycling through the Savannah Wheelmen. His enthusiasm for cycling did not go unnoticed, as Savannah mayor John J. McDonough, proclaimed "that Mr. James B. Connolly is well and favorably known to me as the leader in Savannah in cycling and general athletic circles and that his reputation for integrity is unquestioned." In addition to his work with the CLA and Savannah Wheelmen, Connolly also helped develop the Savannah Baseball Club and the Savannah Football Team, and he managed

Pat Ready, a local prizefighter. Finally he wrote a weekly sports column for the *Lamplighter*.

Despite not graduating from high school, Connolly continued his education through correspondence courses and, in 1895, passed the entrance examination to Harvard University. After a tryout for the Harvard football team resulted in a broken collarbone, he turned his attention to track and field, specializing in the triple jump. No novice to the triple jump, Connolly had won the U.S. national championship in the event in 1890, representing South Boston's Trimount Athletic Club. With the revival of the Olympic Games in 1896, he requested a leave of absence from Harvard to compete in Athens, Greece. Harvard granted a leave of absence to Ellery Clark, a senior honors student, to join the U.S. Olympic team, but denied Connolly's request. Informed that he would have to resign from the university to compete in the games and then apply for readmission, Connolly replied, "I am not resigning and I'm not making application to re-enter on my return. I am through with this college right now. Good day." Winning the triple jump, he became the first Olympic champion of the modern era. Connolly also finished second in the high jump and third in the long jump in 1896 and second in the triple jump in 1900.

In 1898 Connolly fought in the Spanish-American War as a member of the Ninth Massachusetts Infantry, formerly known as the Irish Fighting Ninth during the Civil War. The *Boston Globe* published his accounts of the war as *Letters from the Front in Cuba*. Connolly, who attended the 1904 Olympic Games as a journalist, became a prolific writer of maritime stories, many of which were based on his own experience working on ships and docks. Connolly also ran unsuccessful campaigns for the U.S. Congress as a Progressive in 1912 and 1914. As the commissioner for the American Committee for Relief in Ireland, Connolly spent much time in Ireland and became closely associated with the Irish Republican Army, which fought for independence from Great Britain.

Adam R. Hornbuckle

See also: BOSTON; IRISH REPUBLICAN ARMY

Reference

Wilcox, Ralph C. "'The English as Poor Losers' and Other Thoughts on the Modernization of Sport: The Literary Works of James Brendan Connolly, First Modern Olympic Victor." www.rms-republic.com/connolly.html (accessed June 30, 2007).

COOKE, JOHN WILLIAM (1920–1968)

Politician and ideologue of the Peronist movement, John William Cooke was born on November 14, 1920 (although 1919 has also been suggested) in La Plata, capital city of the Buenos Aires province. John William and his brother David were sons of Juan Isaac Cooke (1895–1957) and María Elvira Lenci. Juan Isaac Cooke, the son of a Dublin-born immigrant, was a distinguished member of the Junta Renovadora faction within the Radical Civic Union party, which supported Juan Domingo Perón's standing in the 1946 presidential elections. Cooke's father, Juan Isaac, was minister of foreign affairs, national member of parliament (MP), and ambassador to Brazil.

From an early age John William Cooke was familiarized with political debate, so it was natural for him to be a politically committed student in secondary school.

He studied in the school of law at the University of La Plata, and graduated in 1943. During his student years Cooke joined the radical forces of the Intransigent University Union, as well as FORJA *(Fuerza de Orientación Radical de la Joven Argentina),* an important nationalist and anti-imperialist political hub of its time. In 1946, at the early age of twenty-five, Cooke was elected MP for Junta Renovadora and would continue to serve in parliament up to 1951. Cooke was appointed secretary of the Peronist group of MPs and member of the Executive Committee of Partido Único (a coalition of the Labour Party, the Independent Party, and Junta Renovadora, which would become the Peronist Party). The Antitrust Act was one of the parliamentary projects submitted by John W. Cooke. In opposition to his own political party, he voted against the Chapultepec Act and the San Francisco Convention of 1945, which he considered against national sovereignty. Cooke coauthored with Ricardo Guardo one of the constitutional amendment projects that was proposed for voting. Additionally, he was a professor of political economics and constitutional law at the University of Buenos Aires.

In 1950 Cooke joined the Juan Manuel de Rosas Historical Society, the most important meeting point for revisionist historians in the country, and in 1954 he was appointed its vice president. He edited the weekly paper *De Frente* and adopted a national stand opposing the contracts with the Standard Oil Company. After a failed revolt against Perón in June 1955, Cooke was offered the post of secretary of technical affairs, but refused and was therefore appointed to head the Peronist Party in Buenos Aires. Owing to the unstable political context he recommended the organization of popular militias to defend the democratic regime against a coup d'état.

The coup took place on September 16, 1955, when the so-called Revolución Libertadora, led by Eduardo Lonardi, overthrew the Peronist rule. Juan D. Perón was exiled in Paraguay and later in Venezuela and Spain, and the Peronist Party (and even the word "Perón") was banned. Cooke escaped and went into hiding for a time until he was seized and imprisoned in Buenos Aires and later in Patagonia. On November 2, 1956, Perón wrote the famous letter that entitled John W. Cooke, "who is now jailed for his loyalty to our cause and our movement, to represent myself in any circumstance or political activity. His decision will be my decision, and his word will be my word" (Perón to Cooke, 2 November 1956). Perón appointed Cooke his political envoy, a responsibility held by Cooke until 1959, and the Peronist movement's head in case of Perón's death.

After 1955 Cooke became a key player of Resistencia Peronista, the organization created to recover the democratic government from the military rulers. From prison, Cooke led different efforts among students and workers, including strikes, sabotage, and operations using homemade bombs. In 1957 Cooke and other Peronist activists escaped from the prison of Río Gallegos and settled in Chile. That year Cooke married Alicia Graciana Eguren (1924–1977), a writer and professor of literature. She was abducted on January 26, 1977, by an Argentine Navy death squad and became one of the *desaparecidos.*

Cooke's correspondence with Perón was initiated in 1957 and did not end until 1966, when their relations began cooling off. Cooke was one of the negotiators of a secret pact between Perón and the leader of

Unión Cívica Radical Intransigente (UCRI), Arturo Frondizi, who in the 1958 presidential elections obtained the Peronist votes in exchange for several appointments and other concessions to the Peronist movement. Once in power—acting between military and labor union pressures—Frondizi was reluctant to fulfill his commitment, and a series of strikes was organized. In January 1959 Cooke was an active leader in the actions against the privatization of Lisandro de la Torre meat-packing plant. After this he was banished to Uruguay.

Cooke had an influential part in creating the first Argentine rural guerrilla Uturunco group, in the province of Tucumán. The group was responsible for the attack and capture of a police station at Christmas 1959. In 1960 Cooke settled in Havana, Cuba, and established a lifetime relation with Ernesto "Che" Guevara. On April 17, 1961, Cooke participated in the battle at Playa Girón (or Bay of Pigs, as it is referred to in the United States). Cooke wanted to make Peronism known in Cuba and to bring the Cuban revolution to Peronism. A project arranged by Cooke in 1962 included Fidel Castro's proposal to Perón that he could permanently reside in Cuba. However Perón failed to answer Castro's invitation.

One of Cooke's revolutionary undertakings was Acción Revolucionaria Peronista. In 1962 Cooke and Che Guevara backed the People's Guerrilla Army of Jorge Ricardo Massetti, which engaged in attacks in Salta until 1964. In 1967–1968, Cooke organized guerrilla groups at Taco Ralo. When Guevara went to Bolivia, Cooke was fighting on the Argentine side of the border, presumably to unite with Guevara's forces. In his last years, Cooke had a radical perspective that included direct action, and he was an important theorist of the left side within the Peronist movement. Cooke's ideology was popular and inspiring among Argentine and other Latin American activists, in particular those who recognized labor movements like Peronism as the most efficient channels for class struggle and the fastest approach to attain the dictatorship of proletariat. Many of his books were published or reprinted posthumously, among them *La Lucha por la Liberación Nacional. El Retorno de Perón. La Revolución y el Peronismo* (1971), *Correspondencia Perón-Cooke* (1972), *Apuntes para la Militancia* (1973), and *Peronismo y Revolución. El Peronismo y el Golpe de Estado. Informe a las Bases* (1973). Cooke died of cancer in Buenos Aires on September 19, 1968.

Edmundo Murray

See also: BAXTER, José Luis; GUEVARA LYNCH, Ernesto "Che"; MURRAY, Luis Alberto; WALSH, Rodolfo.

References

Adelchanow, Melina Natalia. "John William Cooke y su Visión del Pasado Argentino. Reflexiones Entre la Historia y la Política." Postgraduate dissertation, Universidad de Belgrano, Buenos Aires, 2005.

Caro Figueroa, Gregorio. "John William Cooke: Ignorado, Condenado y Luego Mitificado. *Todo es Historia* 288 (June 1991): 8–9.

Chávez, Fermín. *John William Cooke, el Diputado y el Politico.* Buenos Aires: Círculo de Legisladores de la Nación, 1998.

Galasso, Norberto. *Cooke: de Perón al Che. Una Biografía Política.* Rosario: Homo Sapiens, 1997.

Gillespie, Richard. *J. W. Cooke: el Peronismo Alternativo.* Buenos Aires: Cántaro Editores, 1989.

Goldar, Ernesto. "John William Cooke: De Perón al Che Guevara." *Todo es Historia* 288 (June 1991): 10–40.

Mazzeo, Miguel. *Cooke, de Vuelta. El Gran Descartado de la Historia Argentina.* Buenos Aires: La Rosa Blindada, 1999.

COSTA RICA

Although Christopher Columbus did land on the coast of what became Costa Rica, it did not become an administrative unit until 1868 when it became a province under the "audiencia" of Guatemala. At that time it was known as Nuevo Cartago, and in 1821, as the Republic of Costa Rica, it gained its independence from Spain. After becoming a member of the Central American Federation from 1823 until 1838, it then became an independent republic. Costa Rica's geographical position between Panama (to the south) and Nicaragua (to the north) has meant that it has been involved in disputes in both countries. The first of these was the attempts by the American William Walker to seize control of Nicaragua. Using volunteers to make up a mercenary army, Walker's soldiers included a number of Irish adventurers.

As it has long been relatively poor, Costa Rica was underpopulated and in the mid-nineteenth century encouraged settlers to take up land in the country. A large number of Germans had successfully settled in Costa Rica, but attempts by Irish activist Thomas Meagher to encourage Irish settlement in the country failed. When, on an exploratory expedition to Central America, Meagher visited the Costa Rican capital of San José in 1858, he found that the man in charge of the local hospital, Dr. Hogan, was Irish, and one of his patients was a seventeen-year-old Canadian soldier of Irish ancestry. The boy had come to Central America with William Walker but had been captured when Walker's men had been overwhelmed in battle by the Costa Ricans. Meagher later advertised in New York newspapers for the teenager's parents but none were traced. Meagher soon

decided that Irish migration to Costa Rica was not practicable.

During the early twentieth century there was still somewhat of an Irish presence in Costa Rica. Some Britons of Irish descent worked for the Anglo-Costa Rican Bank (founded 1863); and in 1937 the president of the Rotary Club in San José was an Irishman, Daniel Molloy. In addition, the botanist Paul Carpenter Standley (1884–1963) wrote *Flora of Costa Rica,* which was published in four volumes in Chicago in 1937–1938—Standley's mother was of Irish descent. Kenneth Strachan, whose grandmother was a Beamish from Cork, worked as a missionary with the Latin American Mission, and was the subject of a biography, *Who Shall Ascend,* by Elisabeth Elliot. From the 1980s because of its beaches, climate, and wildlife, Costa Rica became a popular destination for tourists, including some from Ireland. Arguing that Costa Rica should concentrate on high-technology industry, Eva Paus wrote *Foreign Investment, Development, and Globalization: Can Costa Rica Become Ireland?,* which was published by Palgrave Macmillan in New York in 2005. She urged that Costa Rica could develop in the same way that Ireland had transformed itself during the 1980s from a largely agricultural country to a modern economy by taking advantage of globalization.

Mention should also be made of the French-Italian film *Viva Maria!* (1965), which relates the fictional story of an Irish nationalist who flees England after bombing an army base and a London club in 1907. He arrives in a Central American republic (possibly Costa Rica, Nicaragua, or Honduras) where he and his daughter continue attacking British interests. The man is killed soon afterwards but his daughter,

Maria, joins with another girl also called Maria (played by Brigitte Bardot) to stage a revolution.

Justin Corfield

See also: MEAGHER, Thomas Francis; NICARAGUA; PANAMA

References

Elliot, Elisabeth, *Who Shall Ascend: The Life of R. Kenneth Strachan of Costa Rica,* London: Hodder & Stroughton, 1968.

Meagher, Thomas Francis. *Vacaciones en Costa Rica,* San José: Tipgrafia Trejos Hermanos, 1923.

COTTER, WILLIAM (DATES UNKNOWN)

Following the Brazilian scheme to encourage European immigration, mercenaries and colonists were recruited in the 1820s in Germany and Ireland. In 1823, the German governments forbade emigration to Brazil to neutralize the enterprise of Gregor von Schäffer, a colonel in Brazil who enlisted as many as 2,000 soldiers and 5,000 colonists from northern and western Germany. Dom Pedro I, the Brazilian emperor (1798–1834), who in 1822 had proclaimed Brazil's independence from Portugal, then turned to Ireland, with equally poor results. William Cotter, an Irish-born colonel in the service of the Brazilian army, proved as unscrupulous as Schäffer. In October 1826, he was sent to Ireland and once in Cork hired between 2,400 and 2,800 Irish farmers with no military experience of any kind. The immigrants who sailed from Cork to Brazil (Rio de Janeiro, Espirito Santo, and São Paulo) in ten ships included 2,450 men, 335 women, 123 young men and women, and 230 children. Most were army recruits who enlisted because the contract promised them pay and allowances equal to one shilling per day and victuals, as well as fifty acres of land after five years of service in the army.

They arrived in Rio de Janeiro between December 1827 and January 1828. Learning that the men would be press-ganged in Brazil's Imperial army and realizing that Cotter's promises were a bunch of lies, the immigrants complained to the British ambassador, Robert Gordon, who logged a strong protest about the unfair treatment of the families before Brazilian authorities to no avail. Fortunately, the diplomat did not give up and kept applying pressure on the Brazilian government on the Irishmen's behalf. This resulted in minor improvements in their situation and allowed most to refuse enlistment. Eventually, only less than 400 of the men joined the Imperial army, and any thoughts of creating an Irish Legion had to be abandoned. Too few to become a separate unit, the Irishmen were integrated into the 3rd (German) Battalion of Grenadiers. This put them in contact with men who were as unhappy as themselves.

War with Argentina over Banda Oriental (today known as Uruguay) had broken out in 1826, but the Irishmen never made it to the front. In 1827 Argentina and the rebellious province of Banda Oriental defeated the Brazilian forces. The British mediated the conclusion of the conflict, and the province became independent Uruguay. The Irish remained in Rio de Janeiro on garrison duty, but living conditions were precarious and many died of illness. Applications for medicines directed to the Brazilian officials fell upon deaf ears. Doctors Dixon and Coates of the British Legation provided medicines for the sick, largely at their own expense.

The African slaves—called *moleques*—who formed the majority of the population of the Imperial capital profoundly disliked the German and Irish mercenaries. Being themselves the poorest class of people in Brazil, they took a fiendish delight in tormenting the Irish at every opportunity, and they called them *escravos brancos.* There were constant scuffles and brawls in the streets. The Irish were unarmed, and when they were attacked by the armed slaves they had only sticks and their fists with which to defend themselves.

On March 15, 1828, Irish men, women, and children, 101 families in all of the Cork emigrants, left Rio on the *Victoria* for Salvador, a town on the Atlantic coast. They arrived on March 28 and in August 3 settled as farm laborers in Taperoa, near Valença. For those who remained in Rio, the sorry saga came to an end when in June 1828 seventy or eighty Irishmen serving the 3rd Grenadier Battalion mutinied. The mutineers took to the streets, where many Irish civilians swelled their ranks. Alcohol was flowing freely in a matter of minutes, and there was an orgy of destruction in the center of Rio, where the black slaves took advantage of the chaos to settle scores with the hated foreigners. In desperation, the authorities issued arms to the civilian population, including the slaves. Ferocious street combat followed and lasted for a whole day and night. Eventually, the mutineers withdrew to their barracks. Brazilian troops were rushed to the capital, and the authorities asked the British and French naval commanders to land sailors and marines to help them. On June 12 and 13 the rebel barracks were put under siege. The episode ended in carnage, with as many as 150 soldiers of fortune (both German and Irish) killed during the mutiny.

Many of the Irish recruited by William Cotter (both military and civilian) were repatriated in July 1828, and it is known that at least 1,400 of them returned to the British Isles. The voyage home was organized at the insistence of Robert Gordon and was paid for by the Brazilian government. Perhaps as many as 400 others stayed in Brazil as farmers and eventually settled in the southern provinces of Santa Catarina and Rio Grande do Sul. This leaves 600 Irish unaccounted for, most of whom probably died. The emperor Dom Pedro blamed the whole incident on the war minister, Barbozo, whom he accused of inciting the mutiny and doing nothing to suppress it. Barbozo was dismissed from his office. There were no further accounts of William Cotter.

Edmundo Murray

See also: ARGENTINA; BRAZIL; URUGUAY

References

Basto, Fernando L. B. *Ex-combatentes Irlandeses em Taperoá.* Rio de Janeiro: Editorial Vozes, 1971.

Rodriguez, Moises Enrique. *Freedom's Mercenaries: British Volunteers in the Wars of Independence of Latin America.* Vevey: Author's Edition, 2004.

Sullivan, Eileen A. "Irish Mercenaries in Nineteenth-Century Brazil." http://gogobrazil.com (accessed March 28, 2005).

Von Allendorfer, Frederic. "An Irish Regiment in Brazil, 1826–1828." *The Irish Sword* 3 (1957–1958): 28–31.

COUGHLIN, FATHER CHARLES EDWARD (1891–1979)

A Catholic priest who acquired large popularity in the 1930s with his Sunday radio sermons, Father Charles Coughlin became one of the most controversial figures of the New Deal era for his anti-Semitic pronouncements. Born in Canada of Irish-American parents, Coughlin founded a

Father Charles Edward Coughlin at a microphone in New York in 1933. Coughlin gained controversial popularity for his anti-Semitic sermons. (Library of Congress).

parish in 1923, the Shrine of the Little Flower, in Royal Oak, Detroit. In 1926 he began radio preaching, focusing initially on exclusively religious topics but gradually shifting to topical subjects such as communism, prohibition, and especially the Depression, as he railed against the "banksters" and the Hoover administration. The interest of the subjects and Coughlin's talent for broadcasting attracted an audience of about 10 million regular listeners and growing donations to his "radio parish," the Radio League of the Little Flower.

Coughlin was an early and enthusiastic supporter of Franklin D. Roosevelt (FDR), but his esteem was one-sided, and after the 1932 election he was not invited to join the president's entourage. Coughlin's disappointment with FDR became more and more vocal until, in 1936, he announced the formation of the Union Party (thus called after Lincoln's antislavery party), a coalition of the main opponents to the New Deal. Coughlin's partners in this were Gerald L. K. Smith (formerly one of Huey Long's lieutenants) and Dr. Francis Townsend, and their presidential candidate was William Lemke. The campaign was characterized by extreme verbal violence and had some climactic moments but, ultimately, the Union Party received fewer than 900,000 votes in the election, about one-tenth of the outcome they expected.

After this, Coughlin retired from broadcasting, but in early 1937 he resumed his Sunday lectures, gradually turning the anti-Semitic tones that had previously remained in the background into rabid tirades that escalated to a climax in 1938–1939. In that period, Coughlin made a series of speeches in which he minimized the gravity of *Kristallnacht* and defined Fascism and Nazism as "defense movements" against "Jew-dominated Communism"; spoke, and was acclaimed, at a rally of the German-American Bund (an openly pro-Nazi organization) at Madison Square Garden in New York; and encouraged the foundation of the Christian Front, a pro-Fascist paramilitary organization that engaged in boycotts and attacks against Jewish shops and people.

All of these activities were supported throughout by *Social Justice,* the weekly newspaper Coughlin had founded in 1936, whose circulation reached an estimated 300,000 copies and whose contributors included European fascists and champions of isolationism, anti-immigration movements, and anti-Semitism. Between August and November 1938, *Social Justice* published the notorious *Protocols of the Elders of Zion,* introduced and annotated by Coughlin himself.

Coughlin's tirades, however, gradually alienated a public increasingly supportive of American intervention in World War II. Contributions and subscriptions collapsed, and in 1940 Coughlin abandoned broadcasting. He continued to publish until April 1942, when strong pressure from his ecclesiastic superiors forced him to return to his parish duties. He retired in 1966 and died of a heart attack in 1979. Coughlin, whose message sprang mainly from populism and social Catholicism, is widely considered to be the forefather of modern televangelism and hate radio.

Lucilla Cremoni

See also: CATHOLIC CHURCH, the; MICHIGAN

References
Brinkley, Alan. *Voices of Protest: Huey Long, Father Coughlin and the Great Depression.* New York: Vintage Books, 1982.
Cremoni, Lucilla. "Antisemitism and Populism in the United States in the 1930s: The Case of Father Coughlin." *Patterns of Prejudice* 32, no. 1 (January 1998): 25–38.
Warren, Donald. *Radio Priest: Charles Coughlin, the Father of Hate Radio.* New York: The Free Press, 1997.

COWELL, HENRY DIXON (1897–1965)

A second-generation Irish American, Henry Cowell was a composer, pianist, writer on music, and teacher. One of the greatest innovators in early twentieth-century art music, Cowell pioneered new techniques of piano playing that became avant-garde standards and combined these with elements of Irish traditional music and references to Celtic legends. He was born in Menlo Park, California, on March 11, 1897, the son of Harry Cowell, an immigrant Irishman, and the writer Clarissa Dixon Cowell. He grew up in a nonconformist social environment with a constant lack of financial resources. The musical talents of the widely read boy were discovered by two professors from Stanford University who enabled Cowell to take courses there (1914–1917) despite his lack of a formal education. Cowell's first acknowledged compositions for the piano date from 1910, preceding his musical studies at Stanford with Charles Seeger.

Apart from his father's influence, Cowell's interest in Irish culture evolved from his association with John Varian, a theosopher and translator of Irish mythological verse. Some of Cowell's early music was written to accompany Varian's plays and

Composer Henry Cowell tuning a piano. Combining traditional Irish music with avant-garde arrangements, Cowell was one of the greatest innovators in early twentieth-century art music. (Bettmann/Corbis)

was later arranged as concert pieces. Among them is *The Tides of Manaunaun* (ca. 1912), the earliest piece involving his new technique of tone clusters—blocks of notes played simultaneously using the fist or the elbow. Another of his inventions is the play on the open strings of the piano, by stroking or plucking the strings in combination with silently pressed-down keys to change the sound spectrum. Important works using this technique were *Aeolian Harp* (1923) and *The Banshee* (1924) for solo piano and the *Irish Suite* (1929) for string piano and small orchestra. These techniques aroused great attention in musical circles in America and Europe, where he gave many recitals and lessons between 1922 and 1932. Often his critics focused on the techniques only, describing his extraordinary style of playing with fists, elbows, and stirring inside the body of the instrument, and ignored his actual music. Cowell's book *New Musical Resources* (1930), however, confirmed his reputation as an innovative and highly individual thinker on contemporary art music. His creative ideas were admired by Bartók, Schönberg, and other leading musical figures of his time.

Following a court case on moral misconduct to which he pleaded guilty, Cowell was imprisoned in San Quentin from 1936 to 1940. On his release he moved to White Plains, New York, where he married the folklorist and photographer Sidney Hawkins Robertson in 1941. He made music broadcasts for the Office of War Information and later taught at Columbia University (1949–1965). He never stopped composing, even in difficult circumstances, and his enormous list of works includes 21 symphonies, 34 stage works, 42 choral works, over 100 songs, and hundreds of chamber music and solo instrumental pieces. In his later years he was increasingly occupied by his other great musical interest, ethnological studies of Asian music, which resulted in a number of research travels, commissioned by the Library of Congress and the Smithsonian Institution, to Iran, India, and Japan. Cowell survived seven strokes and serious heart disease and eventually died of cancer in Shady, New York, on December 10, 1965.

Axel Klein

See also: MUSIC IN AMERICA, IRISH

References

Lichtenwanger, William. *The Music of Henry Cowell: A Descriptive Catalog.* New York: Institute for Studies in American Music, 1986.

Mead, Rita H. *Henry Cowell's New Music, 1925–1936: The Society, the Music Editions, and the Recordings.* Ann Arbor, MI: UMI Research Press, 1981.

Nicholls, David, ed. *The Whole World of Music: A Henry Cowell Symposium.* London: Routledge, 1998.

Sachs, Joel. *Henry Cowell, a Biography.* New York: Oxford University Press, 2005.

Saylor, Bruce. *The Writings of Henry Cowell: A Descriptive Bibliography.* New York: Institute for Studies in American Music, 1977.

CRAIG, JOHN (1709–1774)

John Craig was born on August 17, 1709, into a middle-class family in the parish of Donegore, Co. Antrim, in the north of Ireland. His parents' ancestors had helped set up the Donegore Presbyterian church during the first Ulster Plantation. The young Craig grew up feeling both indebted to these previous generations who had protected the church during turbulent periods of rebellion and persecution, and guilty that he had been born at a time of relative calm. Craig would later look to the American frontier as a place to prove his spiritual worth.

Craig was educated in Ulster for nine years and completed his studies at the University of Edinburgh, taking an MA in 1732. However, Craig instead resolved secretly to study medicine. But his guilt at turning away from the church led him to attempt suicide, pleading with God that if by some miracle he should survive, he would do anything God wished. After six months Craig had recovered sufficiently to resolve to emigrate and seek ordination in America.

In 1734, Craig apparently traveled alone to Pennsylvania where he studied theology under the Irish-born Reverend John Thomson of Chestnut Level. In 1738 Craig was licensed to preach by the Presbytery of Donegal, which then covered most of Pennsylvania west of Philadelphia and the whole southwestern frontier. After two years in temporary ministries in western Pennsylvania, Maryland, and Virginia, in 1740 Craig accepted a position at the Scotch-Irish settlement at Augusta County, Virginia. Augusta County had only just been established, making Craig the first permanently settled clergyman west of the Blue Ridge Mountains.

Craig preached and farmed in Augusta County, which was spread over 1,800 miles, for the rest of his life; he would preach on alternate Sundays at two churches, the Augusta Stone church near Staunton and the Tinkling Spring church near Fishville, which were 10 miles apart. He also established thirteen churches in western Virginia and North Carolina. Despite relinquishing the Tinkling Spring ministry in 1764, Craig continued to preach into old age, remaining at the Augusta Stone church until his death in 1774.

From its very beginnings, the Presbyterian church of colonial America was reliant on foreign ministers, particularly those who, like Craig, were Ulster born and Scottish educated. Yet whereas in Ireland Presbyterian ministers received a regular stipend from the crown, clergymen in colonial America relied on the generosity of their parishioners. Craig struggled unsuccessfully to secure a regular salary from a disparate parish whose inhabitants had received little religious education back in Ulster. He also became entangled in a power struggle between two ruthless Tinkling Spring parishioners, John Lewis and James Patton.

But difficult parishioners were the least of Craig's problems. Between 1741 and 1748 the first Great Awakening, colonial America's first wave of religious enthusiasm, split the Presbyterian Church in two, the revivalists making up the "New Side" and the traditionalists, like Craig, the "Old Side." In 1741 Old Side clergymen Craig, Francis Alison, and John Thomson signed a protestation that expelled the New Side evangelists led by Gilbert Tennant, Samuel Blair, and Samuel Finlay from the Philadelphia Synod. Thomson and many other Old Side clergy were eventually expelled from their pulpits. However, Craig was able to retain control of his own churches, probably because the newly established parishes of the Western frontier were less ethnically and ideologically mixed than eastern congregations. Ironically, the threat of the French-Indian war (1755–1763) allowed Craig to

strengthen his ministry further by using his own money to fortify his churches.

However these upheavals only heightened Craig's sense of isolation and self-doubt, affecting his fragile mental state. In 1745 Craig suffered an acute depression in which he considered abandoning his family, church, and faith. But it was his faith that restored him once again. Indeed, Craig's faith continued to inspire him in later life: first to become a champion of human rights during a crisis in colonial-British relations from 1763, and second to write his memoir, an invaluable account of Scotch-Irish communities on the American frontier in 1769–1770.

Tara Stubbs

See also: ETHNIC AND RACE RELATIONS (Irish and Indigenous Peoples), PRESBYTERIANISM, SCOTS-IRISH CULTURE, SCOTS-IRISH AND MILITARY CONFLICT

References

Craig, John. *Memoir* (1769–1780). In the Historical Foundation of the Presbyterian and Reformed Churches, Montreat, North Carolina.

Craig, L. K. *Reverend John Craig, 1709–1774*. New Orleans: Accurate Letter Company, 1963.

Miller, Kerby A., Arnold Schier, Bruce D. Boling, and David N. Doyle, *Irish Immigrants in the Land of Canaan— Letters and Memoirs from Colonial and Revolutionary America, 1617–1815*. Oxford: Oxford University Press, 2003.

CREAGHE, JOHN "JUAN" (1841–1920)

John "Juan" Creaghe, an international revolutionary anarchist whose name is most often associated with anarchism in England and Argentina (though he was also active in the United States in support of exiled Mexican anarchists), helped pioneer a movement of critical importance to Argentine and South American labor history. Born in 1841 in Limerick, Creaghe took up his medical practice at Mitchelstown, Co. Cork, a year after qualifying as a physician in 1865 at the Royal College of Surgeons in Dublin. He was fully licensed as a medical practitioner in 1869 from the King's and Queen's Colleges of Physicians in Ireland. Creaghe remained in practice in Mitchelstown until 1874, when he emigrated to Buenos Aires, Argentina, and quickly became a follower of anarchism. It is likely that he became an anarchist at least in part under the influence of Errico Malatesta (1853–1932), the seminal anarchist thinker and activist.

By 1890, Creaghe had relocated to Sheffield, where he worked in a poor, working-class district of the English city, which was populated by a great many Irish immigrants from Dublin. He soon involved himself with the local branch of the famous designer William Morris's Socialist League, but they broke away early in 1891 to form a specifically anarchist group in Sheffield. The *Sheffield Anarchist* newspaper was founded by Creaghe and Fred Charles.

In 1892 Creaghe left Sheffield and traveled to Liverpool, London, Barcelona, and finally, Buenos Aires. Once there, he began another publishing venture with *El Oprimido* (1893–1897), which became *La Protesta Humana* (1897–1903), and the hugely influential *La Protesta* (1903 to present day). In each case, Creaghe invested considerable time, energy, and money into these propagandist ventures that would eventually bear fruit in the form of the *Federación Obrera Regional Argentina* (FORA), the mighty anarcho-syndicalist union that won the hearts and loyalties

of 20,000 Argentine workers by the time of the events of the Tragic Week of January 1919, when the army fired against the crowd on strike and killed about 1,000 persons in eight days. Creaghe was also heavily involved in the Free School movement in Buenos Aires and was director of the Rationalist School in Luján, an anarchist educational experiment along the lines of those founded by the Spanish anarchist Francisco Ferrer (1859–1909). Creaghe also rallied to the defense of a young Polish immigrant who killed the chief of police in Buenos Aires at an anarchist demonstration in 1909. At the same time, he worked as a doctor from his base in Luján, combining easily the roles of local physician and anarchist militant.

Creaghe took to his travels again in 1911, settling eventually in Los Angeles, California, among Mexican anarchists. He took part in producing yet another influential anarchist newspaper, *La Regeneración*, and struck up a good friendship with the leading Mexican anarchist, Ricardo Flores Magón (1874–1922), who eventually died in Leavenworth Federal Penitentiary in Kansas. Magón, along with Creaghe, was involved in the Baja, California, revolt of 1910 and gave support to the fragmented anarchist movement in Mexico in the years after the start of the Mexican revolution of 1910–1914. Creaghe died in utter poverty in Washington, D.C., on February 19, 1920.

Edmundo Murray

See also: ARGENTINA

References

Ó Catháin, Máirtín. "Dr. John O'Dwyer Creaghe: Irish-Argentine Anarchist (1841–1920)." www.irlandeses.org (accessed December 11, 2004).

Pasini, Fransico José. *Anecdotario Lujanero.* Luján: Librería de Mayo, 1977.

CREIGHTON, EDWARD CHARLES (1820–1874)

Edward Charles Creighton gained wealth and fame as the builder of the transcontinental telegraph. The construction of telegraph lines entailed the use of draft animals and wagons; thus, the entrepreneurial Creighton established thriving enterprises in the related businesses of freighting, street grading, preparing railroad rights-of-way, and raising draft animals. Once wealthy, he ventured into real estate, banking, mining, and railroading.

Creighton was born on August 31, 1820, in Belmont County, Ohio, near the town of Barnesville. He was the fifth child of James and Bridget (Hughes) McCrarin (as he acquired land and worked to build the National Road through Ohio during the 1820s, James copied his brother Christopher, who had married a Methodist and changed his surname to a Scottish form, Creighton). Edward attended public elementary school and began work as a cart boy at age fourteen. Four years later, his father provided him with a wagon and a team of horses, and his career as a freighter commenced; he hauled goods between Cumberland, Maryland, and Cincinnati, Ohio. In 1847, Creighton observed two Irish Americans erecting telegraph lines for a company owned by Irish immigrant Henry O'Reilly. The ethnic connections presented satellite business opportunities. For the next decade and a half, he superintended the construction of telegraph lines crisscrossing the area between the Appalachian Mountains and the Missouri River. The work put him in partnership with the people who eventually organized the Western Union Company. Ultimately, Creighton single-handedly surveyed the route for the transcontinental telegraph, and between

July 2 and October 17, 1861, he oversaw the construction of the segment from Julesburg, Colorado, to Salt Lake City, Utah (six days later the builders of the western portion reached the town).

Creighton's street grading, railroad roadway preparation, and telegraph construction businesses had brought him to the frontier town of Omaha in 1856. That same year, he married Lucretia Wareham of Dayton, Ohio. They had a son, Charles, who died as a toddler (1859–1863). From his new hometown, Creighton established a lucrative freighting business, supplying miners beginning with the Pike's Peak gold rush, as well as Mormons established in the Salt Lake City area. Subsequently, the Montana mines increased the operation, which lasted for decades until the railroads supplanted wagons for long-distance hauling. Edward used the profits (1,600-mile expeditions from Omaha to Salt Lake City to Virginia City, Montana, and return to Omaha, netted between $30,000 and $50,000) to enter the banking business. He began making personal loans in Omaha during the Panic of 1857 and entered into a partnership with the Kountze brothers to provide credit to the gold rushers in Colorado. They established the Colorado National Bank in Denver and the Rocky Mountain National Bank in Central City. In 1863, with Creighton as president, they chartered the First National Bank in Omaha.

Creighton also invested in railroads and real estate; he came to own thirteen lots in Omaha and several thousand acres in eight counties in eastern Nebraska. However, greater fame and fortune came from the "possession" of tens of thousands of acres of open-range land (owned by the federal government) in the unorganized areas of western Nebraska, Wyoming, Utah, and Montana on which he raised cattle, oxen, horses, and sheep (on free prairie grass). According to legend, Creighton spawned the cattle industry on the northern Great Plains; supposedly, a snowstorm trapped him (or one of his employees; the myth has several versions) around Laramie, Wyoming, and he had to abandon teams of oxen, while making his way back to Omaha. Returning in the spring, he found the animals fat and healthy, proving bovines could survive the harsh winters. Undeniably, he became the leading stockman in the United States and was subsequently inducted as a charter member of the National Cowboy Hall of Fame.

Creighton's career ended suddenly; on November 3, 1874, he collapsed at his office at the First National Bank. He did not regain consciousness and died at home two days later. Virtually all business activity ceased in Omaha during his funeral. He had established himself as the city's leading entrepreneur and philanthropist, and the state's wealthiest citizen. While he lived, he gave generously to the poor and endowed a Catholic convent, hospital, and cathedral in Omaha. He had spoken of starting a school; therefore, in his honor and memory, his wife used part of his estate to endow a university that bears his name, Creighton University.

Dennis Milehich

See also: CREIGHTON, John Andrew

References

Johnson, Allen, and Dumas Malone, eds. *Dictionary of American Biography.* New York: Charles Scribner's Sons, 1930.

Mullens, P. A. *Biographical Sketches of Edward Creighton, John A. Creighton, Mary Lucretia Creighton, Sarah Emily Creighton.* Omaha, NE: Creighton University, 1901.

Nielson, P. Raymond. "Edward Creighton and the Pacific Telegraph." *Mid-America: An Historical Review* 24 (January 1942): 61–74.

CREIGHTON, JOHN ANDREW (1831–1907)

John Andrew Creighton was an entrepreneur and philanthropist, count of the Papal Court, and benefactor to many Catholic institutions in Omaha, Nebraska. His success as a wholesale and retail merchant, cattleman, and banker established him as Omaha's leading businessman, and his investments in mining and real estate propelled him to the position of Nebraska's wealthiest citizen. His legacy transformed a small school, established in honor of his brother Edward, into Creighton University, a Jesuit-operated complex of five professional and undergraduate colleges (currently nine).

John Andrew, born on October 15, 1831, was the ninth and final child of James and Bridget (Hughes) McCrarin. John attended public school and studied for two years at St. Joseph's College (Dominican) at Somerset, Ohio. In 1854, he abandoned higher education to join the flourishing freighting, street grading, and telegraph construction business established by his brother Edward. He worked as a crew chief during the construction of the transcontinental telegraph and subsequently became a wagon master for long-distance hauling to the mining areas of the West. In 1862, after leading an expedition that consisted of 35 four-oxen wagons on a 117-day trek to Virginia City, Montana, Creighton remained there for five years, becoming a leading merchant and banker.

In 1868, he returned to Omaha and married Emma (Sarah Emily) Wareham (a younger sister of brother Edward's wife); they had a daughter Lucretia, who died in infancy (1870). The brothers and sisters then resided together until the deaths of the older siblings in 1874 and 1876, respectively. John received a $300,000 bequest from Edward and served as an executor for Lucretia's estate. He supplanted his brother as Nebraska's wealthiest citizen, and his investments in banking, industry, railroads, mining, cattle, the Omaha Stockyards, and real estate far surpassed previous accumulations. He became a prodigious philanthropist, endowing the Good Shepherd Home for Troubled Girls, the Poor Clares Convent, St. John's Church, and St. Joseph's Hospital. For his benevolence, in 1895, Pope Leo XIII named him a count of the Papal Court.

After the death of his wife on September 30, 1888, John Andrew adopted the fledgling school established in honor of his brother Edward as his child. As a tribute to his wife, he built a new Creighton Memorial St. Joseph's Hospital, which became the teaching facility for the medical school he established as a part of Creighton University; both opened in 1892. Subsequently, he built a medical facility in 1895 and a School of Dentistry in 1905. In the latter year, he initiated a College of Pharmacy and, in 1907, erected for it a building attached to the medical school. In the meantime, he added L-shaped wings to the Arts College (1899–1900), built a library and auditorium (1902), and financed the construction of a law school (1904) and the erection of a dormitory (1906). Thus, by his death on February 7, 1907, he had officially become a cofounder of Creighton University, which received 40 percent of his $2.7 million estate. His benefice transformed a struggling institution, a college in name only, into a five-school university—a monument to the memory of his brother Edward, and Lucretia and Sarah Emily Wareham, as well as a testament to the entrepreneurial skill and philanthropy of John Andrew Creighton.

Dennis Milehich

See also: CREIGHTON, Edward

References
Dowling, M. P. *Creighton University: Reminiscences of the First Twenty-Five Years.* Omaha, NE: Press of Burkley Printing Company, 1903.
Johnson, Allen, and Dumas Malone, eds. *Dictionary of American Biography.* New York: Charles Schribner's Sons, 1930. 535–536.
Mullens, P. A. *Biographical Sketches of Edward Creighton, John A. Creighton, Mary Lucretia Creighton, Sarah Emily Creighton.* Omaha, NE: Creighton University, 1901.

CROKER, RICHARD (1841–1922)

Richard Croker, a leader of Tammany Hall and boss of New York City, was born in Blackrock, Dublin, Ireland on November 24, 1841. After immigrating with his Episcopalian Scots-Irish parents to New York in 1846, Croker never finished school. At thirteen, he became an apprentice machinist for the Harlem Railroad and later worked in the shops of the New York Central Railroad. A burly, bearded man well-known for being good with his fists, Croker joined and soon led the Fourth Avenue Tunnel Gang. Attracting the attention of Tammany Hall Democrats, he became a boss "repeater," directing members of his gang to vote repeatedly in elections. In 1865, Croker voted seventeen times in local elections. Fourth Avenue Tunnel Gang members would often battle political

Portrait of Richard Croker, politician and leader of New York City's Tammany Hall. (Library of Congress)

opponents in the streets, in an effort to block rival repeaters from casting ballots.

Croker's success in winning elections for Tammany Hall earned him rewards from the Democratic Party. In 1868, he was elected alderman and joined the reform faction of Tammany that opposed the corrupt rule of Boss William Tweed. An 1874 trial for shooting a political opponent in a street brawl almost derailed his career, but the trial resulted in a hung jury. Croker always denied responsibility for the murder, claiming that he preferred fists over firearms. After the incident, Croker could not find work and fell into poverty before Tammany Hall came to his aid. He served as coroner in 1876 and then as fire commissioner beginning in 1883. A protégé of "Honest" John Kelly, Croker replaced Kelly as boss of Tammany Hall upon his retirement in 1886. He now commanded an army of 90,000 Tammany party workers and thirty-five Tammany district leaders.

As boss, Croker essentially ran New York City, serving as unelected mayor. He became a master in graft. He gave city jobs to supporters, told municipal judges to rule for his friends and interests, and pressured businesses to grant him favors. As he once publicly stated, Croker's chief concern was his pocket, and he spent every moment looking for ways to increase his wealth. Croker made a fortune as boss but the city did not fare that well. A brief reform movement in the mid-1890s cost Croker control of City Hall. Mounting public dissatisfaction with corruption in the police department and the mayor's office resulted in Tammany's defeat in the election of 1901. The electoral loss cost Croker control of the Tammany organization and of New York City politics.

Croker had already spent considerable time in England for health reasons, and he retired to his English manor. Having inherited a love of horses from his blacksmith/veterinarian father, Croker owned a stable of horses. One of his animals won the English Derby, the most famous horse race in England, in 1907. Croker died in Glencairn, Ireland, on April 29, 1922.

Caryn E. Neumann

See also: KELLY, "Honest" John; TAMMANY HALL; TWEED, William "Boss"

References

Hammack, David C. *Power and Society: Greater New York at the Turn of the Century.* New York: Russell Sage Foundation, 1982.

Stoddard, Lothrop. *Master of Manhattan: The Life of Richard Croker.* New York: Longmans and Green, 1931.

CROSBY, BING (1903–1977)

Born Harry Lillis Crosby in Tacoma, Washington, in 1903, Crosby was nicknamed "Bing" at elementary school. On his father's side he was descended from a signatory of the Mayflower Compact, while his mother's family, the Harrigans, had emigrated from Co. Cork to Canada in 1831. While still a student in Spokane, Washington, Bing Crosby began performing with a local dance band, the Musicaladers, and in 1925, with Al Rinker, he went on the vaudeville

American singer Bing Crosby performs on NBC in 1940. (Library of Congress)

circuit. The next year the duo joined up with the highly popular Paul Whiteman band; from 1927, Crosby, Rinker, and Harry Barris were featured with Whiteman's orchestra as the Rhythm Boys. In 1931 Crosby was offered and accepted a contract to do a radio show by the Columbia Broadcasting System. The Crosby radio show, first broadcast in September 1931, was an instant and lasting success (with contractual and format changes it continued until 1962), establishing him as a solo artist, and indeed as a star. Crosby's status as a radio star was the cornerstone of his success as a recording artist and in movies.

Between 1926 and 1977, Crosby recorded a total of around 2,000 titles and was by far the most successful recording artist of his era and, with sales of more than 400 million disks, arguably the most successful ever. His twenty-two gold records included "Too-Ra-Loo-Ra-Loo-Ral (That's an Irish Lullaby)," "McNamara's Band" and "Galway Bay."

Crosby's film career began in 1930, but it was only after he teamed up with Bob Hope and Dorothy Lamour in 1940 to make *The Road to Singapore* that he became a major box-office attraction. *The Road to Singapore* initiated a highly successful series of Road films, ending in 1952 with *The Road to Bali* (there was also an ill-advised attempt at a revival in 1962 with *The Road to Hong Kong*). Even more successful were *Going My Way* (1944) and *The Bells of St. Mary's* (1945) in both of which Crosby played a Roman Catholic priest, Father Chuck O'Malley; *Going My Way*, which also starred Irish actor Barry Fitzgerald, won Crosby an Oscar for best actor. Crosby also worked with Fitzgerald in *Top o' the Morning* (1949)—in which he played an insurance investigator sent to Ireland to look into the theft of the Blarney Stone. Any account of Crosby's career in films must also mention his two major musicals of the 1950s: *White Christmas* (1954) and *High Society* (1956).

Although Crosby did not, as a performer, dominate the new medium of television as he had earlier dominated radio and movies, by any standards other than his own, he did enjoy a successful television career; he made his television debut in 1948 and from the mid-1960s until his death starred in (and produced) a highly popular Christmas show. He also owned a television production company that was responsible for a number of hit series (for instance, *Ben Casey* and *Hogan's Heroes*). Crosby's earnings from records and films, and his judicious investments in oil, real estate and television (among other things) made him a rich man and allowed him to indulge his passion for sport, particularly golf and horse racing. Crosby's first wife, Dixie Lee, died in 1952, and in 1957 he married Kathryn Grant; he had four children by his first wife and three by his second. Crosby died of a heart attack in October 1977 on a Spanish golf course.

When Bing Crosby paid the first of a number of visits to Ireland in September 1961 he was met at Dublin airport by the Artane Boys Band. Most of his subsequent visits were golf or racing related but in 1966 he did, at the instigation of his friend and associate George O'Reilly, record an hour-long program for RTÉ, ("A Little Bit of Irish"). His last visit to Dublin, in July 1976, was for a charity performance at the Gaiety Theatre.

Although, throughout his career, Irish, and even stage Irish, material was a significant element in Crosby's repertoire, he was never a narrowly 'Irish' act. Rather, he was always very much in the mainstream of twentieth-century American popular music; indeed, for a time he was the mainstream. One of the first generation of singers to have learned to sing into a microphone, Crosby realized that technology had made possible a more relaxed, subtly phrased, intimate, and vernacular vocal idiom that came to be called "crooning." Crosby greatly influenced Frank Sinatra who took up and developed the style; the Crosby-Sinatra duet in *High Society* ("Well, Did You Evah!") is both an epitome and virtuoso exhibition of twentieth-century American popular vocal technique. Posthumous allegations of drinking, infidelity, and harsh (even violent) treatment of his children, although clearly at odds with the carefully crafted public image of the equable and easygoing pipe-smoking Bing, have apparently done little to diminish his still very considerable popularity.

Stephen Wilson

See also: FITZGERALD, Barry

References

Crosby, Bing. *Call Me Lucky: Bing Crosby's Own Story.* Cambridge, MA: Da Capo Press, 1993.

Giddins, Gary. *Bing Crosby: A Pocketful of Dreams.* Boston: Little, Brown, & Co. 2001.

CROUCH, FREDERICK NICHOLLS (1808–1896)

A composer, Frederick Nicholls Crouch was known as the "Irish Lecturer" and spent almost fifty years of his life in America. Born in London, in 1808, the son of a musician, Crouch's talents as a child prodigy were apparent from the age of nine. He was a violoncellist and a vocalist and as a child he played in the Royal Coburg Court Orchestra. Around 1822, he attended the Royal Academy of Music. Later he joined the orchestra attached to the Theatre Royal, Drury Lane. He also played in the Royal Italian Opera orchestra in London and became musical supervisor to D'Almaine & Co., a leading London music publisher.

Although Crouch was born in England he seemed to associate with things Irish more than English when it came to composing music. Around 1838 he organized a series of programs on the Songs and Legends of Ireland. As a result he became known as the "Irish Lecturer." The series included a large number of songs, and one of the series, published around 1840 by *D'Almaine,* was called *The Echoes of the Lakes.* This group included the song "Kathleen Mavourneen," which became immensely popular. Another song in the group, "Dermot Astore," also gained prominence. The words for both of these works were by the Cavan-born poet, Julia Crawford (ca. 1800–1855), whose poetry had also been used by other composers.

Much of the success of Crouch's "Kathleen Mavourneen" can be attributed to the Irish soprano Catherine Hayes (1818–1861), who included it in almost every one of her concerts around the world in the mid-nineteenth century. She performed it as an encore for Queen Victoria and 500 guests in Buckingham Palace in 1849 and sang it in Dublin, Limerick, New York, Boston, Philadelphia, Savannah, New Orleans, San Francisco, Sydney and Melbourne. The song has also been recorded by many great singers, such as soprano Adelina Patti and tenor John McCormack.

In 1849 Crouch arrived in America, where he conducted orchestras in Philadelphia, Pennsylvania, Washington, D.C., and

Richmond, Virginia. He also became a music critic in New York. He later joined the Confederate army and served in the First Regiment Richmond Greys during the Civil War. After the war he returned to composing music. He wrote two operas, neither of which was successful. He also composed a number of Irish songs, such as "The Emigrant's Lament," "The Exile of Erin," and "Sing to Me, Nora," which were included in a successful book, *Songs of Erin.* As the years progressed, Crouch remained active as a vocalist, even singing "Kathleen Mavourneen" at a banquet given in his honor when he was 84 years old in Portland, Maine. He died in Baltimore, Maryland, in 1896. Like many other nineteenth-century songwriters his output was prodigious. However, "Kathleen Mavourneen" is the only one of his many works occasionally heard today, primarily in Ireland.

Basil Walsh

See also: HAYES, Catherine

References

Adair-Fitzgerald, S. J. *Stories of Famous Songs.* London: John C. Nimmo, 1898.

Baltzell, W. J. *Dictionary of Musicians.* Boston: Oliver Ditson Company, 1891.

Brown, J. D., and S. S. Stratton. *British Musical Biography.* Birmingham, England: S. S. Stratton, 1897.

CURLEY, JAMES MICHAEL (1874–1958)

James Michael Curley was a renowned New England politician who held the position of governor of Massachusetts from 1935 to 1937. Born in Boston on November 20, 1874, Curley was the son of Irish-Catholic immigrants from Co. Galway. After leaving public school at age 14, he educated

Portrait of James Michael Curley, Governor of Massachusetts (1935–1937). (Library of Congress)

himself at the public library and worked as a salesman.

Active in local Roxbury Democratic politics, Curley began a long and tumultuous political career when he was elected to the Boston Common Council in 1900. He then served in the Massachusetts legislature (1902–1903), as a Boston alderman (1904–1909), and as a Boston city councilor (1912–1914). Elected to the House of Representatives (1912–1914), he resigned to serve as mayor of Boston (1914–1918), an office he also held in 1922–1926 and 1930–1934. His considerable oratorical skills and biting wit made the tall, handsome, and elegant Curley a dangerous opponent in debates. Unlike the Massachusetts ward boss politicians, he built a multiethnic political machine as a lone wolf in the Bay State Democratic Party.

Curley was one of the few big-city Democratic leaders to abandon Alfred E. Smith to support Franklin D. Roosevelt for president in 1932. After breaking with President Roosevelt, who offered him the post of ambassador to Poland, much to Curley's disdain, he served as governor of Massachusetts (1935–1937). Curley fashioned his own state New Deal program of extensive and expensive public works to cope with the Great Depression. Unsuccessful in campaigns for the Senate (1936) and for mayor (1938 and 1942), he was elected to the House of Representatives (1943–1947) and again as mayor (1946–1950). Sentenced to federal prison for mail fraud, Curley was paroled in 1947 after serving six months and was pardoned by President Harry Truman in 1950. Curley returned to the mayor's office in triumph.

Unsuccessful in "last hurrah" campaigns for mayor (1950 and 1954), the "Mayor of the Poor" retired to write his memoirs, *I'd Do It Again* (1957), and bask in the reflected glory of Edwin O'Connor's subtle and sophisticated best-selling novel (1956) and John Ford's film (1958), both called *The Last Hurrah,* said to be based loosely on his career. Curley threatened a lawsuit, but soon he adopted the charismatic Governor Frank Skeffington as his literary alter ego. He is fondly recalled as an ingenious rogue in Joseph Dineen's biography *The Purple Shamrock* (1949) and in Thomas P. "Tip" O'Neill's memoirs, *Man of the House.* Jack Beatty's biography, *The Rascal King* (1992), is a more critical assessment.

Although suspected of graft and corruption while in office, Curley was not wealthy when he died in Boston on November 12, 1958. His body lay in state at the State House in Boston as large crowds waited to pay their last respects. Curley's funeral at the Cathedral of the Holy Cross was followed by burial at Mount Calvary Cemetery in Boston. His colorful and controversial career obscures his legacy as a resourceful and innovative municipal leader during a time when Yankee Republicans were abandoning the deteriorating city. Two statues of Curley are located near Boston City Hall, and his elegant Jamaica Plain home is preserved by the city.

Peter C. Holloran

See also: BOSTON; O'CONNOR, Edwin; FORD, John

References

Beatty, Jack. *The Rascal King: The Life and Times of James Michael Curley, 1874–1958.* Reading, MA: Addison-Wesley, 1992.

Curley, James M. *I'd Do It Again: A Record of All My Uproarious Years.* Englewood Cliffs, NJ: Prentice-Hall, 1957.

Dinneen, Joseph F. *The Purple Shamrock: The Hon. James Michael Curley of Boston.* New York: Norton, 1949.

O'Neill, Thomas P., Jr., and William Novak. *Man of the House: The Life and Political Memoirs of Speaker Tip O'Neill.* New York: Random House, 1987.

CURRAN, MARY DOYLE (1917–1981)

Mary Doyle Curran was a novelist, poet, short story writer, and teacher. Her novel *The Parish and the Hill* (1948) depicts the experiences of Irish Americans who lived and worked in the mill town of Holyoke, Massachusetts, between the two world wars. Curran traces how issues of ethnicity, gender, and class affect the narrator's family as its Irish-born generation gives way to its American-born offspring. The third-generation narrator, Mary O'Connor, negotiates between the community-oriented "shanty" values and poverty of the first generation and the exclusionary aspirations of the "lace curtain" second generation as she struggles to find her voice within the restrictive community. The novel's 1986 republication by the Feminist Press drew the attention of Curran's Irish studies and feminist colleagues alike, who have recognized it as an important portrayal of Irish-American experience in the early twentieth century.

Curran was born Mary Rita Doyle on May 10, 1917, in Holyoke, Massachusetts, known at that time as the "Paper City," which is the title for one of Curran's later short stories. Her parents, Edward Doyle and Mary Sullivan Doyle, both worked in local mills. Irish-born Edward was employed as a skilled wool-sorter while American-born Mary was one of the few Irish-American mothers of the period who worked outside the home. Curran had four older brothers but no sisters. She was the first in her family to attend college, and she worked her way through as a waitress, library assistant, and pay clerk in the mill before her graduation from Massachusetts State College in 1940. She earned a master's degree in 1941 and a PhD in 1946, both from the State University of Iowa. Curran taught at Wellesley College from 1946 to 1955 and then at Queens College, New York, where she founded an Irish studies program. She remained at Queens College until 1967, when she became a professor of English and director of Irish studies at the University of Massachusetts, Boston. Curran continued to write throughout her career and spent time at the Yaddo artists' community during the 1950s. Curran married naval officer John Curran in 1942, although the couple divorced ten years later. She never remarried. Curran had no

children and died of lung cancer in 1981. She left behind many unpublished novels, poems, and other projects.

Kelly J. S. McGovern

See also: MASSACHUSETTS

References

"Curran, Mary Doyle." *Directory of American Scholars.* Vol. 2. 8th ed. Lancaster, PA: Science Press, 1982.

Halley, Anne. Afterword to *The Parish and the Hill,* by Mary Doyle Curran. New York: The Feminist Press, 1986.

CUSACK, CYRIL (1910–1993)

A stage and screen actor and a recognizable face of Hollywood films from 1960 to 1990, Cyril Cusack was born in South Africa in 1910 but moved to Ireland with his mother at the age of six. His first movie role, in

Portrait of actor Cyril Cusack, who appeared in over 100 films and television shows from 1960 to 1990. (Corbis)

1918, was in the silent film *Knocknagow,* in which he played a starving child during the Irish famine. He studied history and politics at University College Dublin, but soon found himself involved in the Abbey Theatre. In the 1930s and early 1940s, Cusack appeared in more than sixty plays at the Abbey; his roles included Christy Mahon in *The Playboy of the Western World* and Fluther Good in *The Plough and the Stars.* Many of his performances took him to the London stage. In 1944, Cusack formed his own theater production company and continued to act and direct plays. A fluent speaker of Irish Gaelic, Cusack wrote and staged the play *Tar Éis an Aifrinn* (*After the Mass*) in 1942, and composed poetry in both Irish and English. He has three collections of published poetry: *Timepieces* (1970), *Poems* (1976), and *"Between the Acts" and Other Poems* (1990). He won the 1961 International Critics' Award at the Paris Festival for his productions of *Arms and the Man* and *Krapp's Last Tape.* He has also won awards in Britain and the United States for his radio and television work.

Cusack had a lively film career, particularly in the United States and England, but almost always in supporting roles. From 1960 to 1990, he appeared in more than 100 films and television shows. His most significant film appearances include Carol Reed's *Odd Man Out* (1947), François Truffaut's *Fahrenheit 451* (1967), *The Day of the Jackal* (1973), *My Left Foot* (1989), and *Far and Away* (1992). One of his briefest but most notable screen appearances is in the 1971 cult comedy hit *Harold and Maude.* Cusack worked mostly in Ireland, the United Kingdom, and the United States, but in the late 1960s and early 1970s, he made a series of Italian movies,

playing his first film lead in 1969's *Galileo.* He was involved in the breakthrough Irish film *Poitín* (1978)—Cusack played the poitín-maker. The film presented the west of Ireland in a starkly realistic, de-romanticized manner that stood in contrast to many Hollywood images of Ireland. In addition to stage, film, and television acting, Cusack also worked extensively in audio recordings of several Shakespeare plays, James Joyce novels, Sean O'Casey plays and the poetry and plays of William Butler Yeats.

Although Cusack was a staple of Hollywood and European filmmaking, his stage career is considered more significant. He worked with the Royal Shakespeare Company and the Old Vic, in addition to his noteworthy Abbey performances. On stage, Cusak played melodrama, comedy, tragedy, and farce with equal talent. In 1990, Cusack appeared to critical acclaim with his daughters Sinéad, Sorcha, and Niamh onstage in Anton Chekhov's *Three Sisters* at London's Royal Court Theater and Dublin's Gate Theater.

Danine Farquharson

See also: JOYCE, James Augustine Aloysius; YEATS, William Butler

References

Cusack, Cyril. *"Between the Acts" and Other Poems.* 1970. Reprint, London: Colin Smythe, 1990.

Rockett, Kevin, Luke Gibbons, and John Hill. *Cinema and Ireland.* London: Routledge, 1987.

Welch, Robert. *The Abbey Theatre, 1899–1999: Form and Pressure.* Oxford: Oxford University Press, 1999.

CUSACK, MARGARET ANNA (1829–1899)

Also known as "the Nun of Kenmare" and Sister Mary Francis, Margaret Cusack led a life characterized by religious fluctuations between Anglicanism and Catholicism and a few brief flirtations with other Protestant faiths. She lived in Ireland, England, and the United States and visited other countries, too. Cusack was a controversialist who ran into trouble with church administrators throughout her religious career. She was also a prolific writer, a political commentator, and a businesswoman.

Cusack was born in Coolock, Dublin, on May 6, 1829, the year of Catholic Emancipation, to Sarah and Dr. Samuel Cusack. She had one brother, Samuel. When she was in her early teens she moved with her mother and brother to England, after the breakup of her parents' marriage, and went to boarding school in Exeter. When Cusack's fiancé, Charles Holmes, died prematurely, she went into a depression and subsequently into an erratic yet productive religious and writing career.

In 1852, Cusack became an Anglican nun after becoming interested in the Oxford Movement, a reform movement within that church. She communicated with significant members of the movement such as John Henry Newman and Edward Pusey. However, failing to find satisfaction after nearly five years in the Anglican sisterhood, she converted to Catholicism in 1858, and became a nun in that church. She joined the St. Clare convent in Newry, Co. Down, in 1860. The following year, she was sent to Kenmare, Co. Kerry, with five others to start up a Poor Clare Order there.

During her twenty-year sojourn in Kerry, Cusack wrote a number of books and set up her own press, Kenmare Publications. Her dozens of publications over the course of her life included lives of Irish saints, advice manuals, religious treatises, nationalist works, histories, political and social commentaries, novels, letters to the newspapers, biographies, and autobiographies. One of the books she wrote at this time was a biography of Daniel O'Connell, *The Liberator: His Life and Times, Political, Social and Religious* (1872). She had access to the O'Connell family papers in nearby Derrynane. Another popular work that helped financially support her convent was *An Illustrated History of Ireland; From the Earliest Period* (1868).

Cusack was also a social activist, a path that often led her into controversy. She considered herself an Irish nationalist, was a supporter of Home Rule and the Land League, and was a vocal critic of absentee landlords. After the bad harvests of the late 1870s, she organized a famine relief fund in 1879 and raised £15,000. Although Cusack wrote about women and their work and education (*Woman's Work in Modern Society* appeared in 1872), she was not concerned with women's rights per se. She subscribed to prevailing contemporary assumptions concerning their biology and intellectual abilities.

Shortly after the first apparitions of the Virgin Mary at Knock (1879), Cusack moved to Mayo intending to establish a convent that would provide accommodation for visiting pilgrims. However, after she claimed the virgin was speaking to her and appeared to be increasingly difficult to deal with, she ran into problems with the local priest and local archbishop.

Cusack subsequently left Knock and went back to England. After receiving a dispensation to leave the Poor Clare nuns in 1884, Cusack founded the order of the Sisters of St. Joseph of Peace (with the permission of Pope Leo XIII). She then went to New Jersey where she opened a hostel for Irish immigrant girls in 1885 in Jersey City.

This was not a new concern for her; she had already written *Advice to Irish Girls in America* (1872). In Jersey City, however, she once again encountered controversy, this time by coming into conflict with the local Catholic hierarchy over funding and because she publicly supported a suspended priest. When she left the United States in the early 1890s, she also left the Catholic Church and wrote a number of anti-Catholic books, including *The Black Pope: A History of the Jesuits* (1896). Her own record of her life is found in her two auto-biographies: *The Nun of Kenmare* (1888) and *The Story of My Life* (1893). She died back in the Anglican faith in 1899 in Leamington, England.

Cliona Murphy

See also: CATHOLIC CHURCH, the; GREAT FAMINE, The; LADIES' LAND LEAGUE; O'CONNELL, Daniel

References

Cusack, Mary F. *Advice to Irish Girls in America*. New York: McGee, 1872.

Cusack, Mary F. *The Story of My Life*. London: Hodder and Stoughton, 1891.

French Eager, Irene. *Margaret Anna Cusack, a Biography*. Cork: Mercier Press, 1970.

Luddy, Maria. Introduction to *The Nun of Kenmare, Irish Women's Writing, 1839–1888*. Vol. 6. London: Routledge/Thoemmes Press, 1998.

Vidulch, Dorothy A. *Peace Pays a Price, A Study of Margaret Anna Cusack, The Nun of Kenmare*. Dublin: Center for Peace and Justice, 1975.

D

DAILEY, DAN (1913–1978)

Born on December 14, 1913 (or 1917, as some sources give), in New York City, the son of a hotel man, Daniel James Dailey, Jr., began his show business career as a child in minstrel shows and vaudeville, appearing with Minsky's burlesque troupe. Known for his stylish and affable personality, Irish good looks, and natural song-and-dance abilities, Dailey made his Broadway debut in 1937, playing a small part in the chorus of Rodgers and Hart's *Babes in Arms*. After a lead role in *Stars in Your Eyes* (1939), starring Ethel Merman and Jimmy Durante, Dailey was signed by MGM, though he was first miscast as a Nazi in *The Mortal Storm* (1940).

After World War II, where Dailey served as a lieutenant in the U.S. Army, he returned to Hollywood and began to get starring roles. Although he was highly acclaimed in such dramatic roles as Dizzy Dean in *Pride of St. Louis* (1956), it was in movie musicals, such as *Mother Wore Tights* (1947), opposite Betty Grable; *Give My Regards to Broadway* (1948); *There's No Business Like Show Business* (1954), also starring Ethel Merman, Donald O'Connor, and Marilyn Monroe; *It's Always Fair Weather* (1955), directed by and starring Gene Kelly; and *Meet Me in Las Vegas* (1957) that Dailey devoted most of his time and talent. Dailey was nominated for an Academy Award for *When My Baby Smiles at Me* (1948), though he lost the Oscar to Laurence Olivier.

When the popularity of big-budget musicals waned, Dailey worked as a stage actor, in cabaret rooms, and in various dramatic and comedic roles; he also directed films and television shows and appeared in numerous television episodes and miniseries, both as himself and in dramatic roles. Dailey starred in three television series in the last three decades of his career: *The Four Just Men* (1959), *The Governor and J. J.* (1969–1972), and *Faraday and Company* (1973–1974). For his best-known role, that of Governor William Drinkwater in *The Governor and J. J.*, Dailey won a Golden Globe in 1970.

Dailey was married and divorced three times, first to Esther Rodier, then Elizabeth Hofert, and then to Gwen Carter O'Connor. One son, Dan Dailey III, committed suicide in 1975, at the age of 28. Marital problems and heavy drinking led to a breakdown, and Dailey spent four months in a psychiatric hospital. A fall from the stage in the mid-1970s left Dailey with a slight limp; he retired, became somewhat of a recluse, and continued to drink heavily.

Dan Dailey died of anemia at the age of 64 on October 6, 1978, in Los Angeles, California. He is buried in Forest Lawn Cemetery in Glendale, California.

Gary Kerley

See also: NEW YORK CITY

References

Carzo, Eileen. "Dailey, Dan." *The Encyclopedia of the Irish in America,* ed. Michael Glazier. Notre Dame, IN: University of Notre Dame Press, 1999.

Curran, Joseph M. *Hiberian Green on the Silver Screen: The Irish and American Movies.* Westport, CT: Greenwood Press, 1990.

Quinlan, David. *Quinlan's Film Stars.* 5th ed. Washington, DC: Brassey's, 2000.

Walker, John, ed. *Halliwell's Who's Who in the Movies.* 5th ed. New York: HarperCollins, 2003.

DALY, "JOHN" AUGUSTIN (1838–1899)

Born in Plymouth, North Carolina, Augustin Daly moved to New York City at an early age with his mother when his father died. There, Daly developed his life-long love of the theater. His first professional engagement with the theater was as a drama critic when he was 21. He wrote for five different New York periodicals: *Sunday Courier,* 1859–1867, *Express,* 1864–1867, *Sun,* 1866–1867, *Citizen,* 1867, and *Times,* 1867–1869. During this time he also began writing and adapting his own plays. Throughout his playwriting career, Daly was assisted by his brother Joseph, whose contribution was significant, but rarely acknowledged publicly. Daly had his first success with *Leah the Forsaken.* This work, liberally adapted from the German play *Deborah* by Salomon Hermann Ritter von Mosenthal, opened at the Howard Athenaeum in Boston in 1862 and then moved to New York where it was similarly well received. Daly's next major success was with his original play, *Under the Gaslight,* which opened at the New York Theatre in 1867. Although a typical melodrama, this work drew wide acclaim with its series of sensational effects, each more thrilling than the last, including one in which the heroine saves a man who is strapped to railroad tracks as the train thunders near. By the end of his career, Daly saw more than 90 of his plays and adaptations performed throughout the world. Despite his prolific-ness, Daly produced no masterpieces. He was, however, effective at fulfilling his audi-ence's desire for special effects, sensational melodramas, and sentimental comedies. His most successful productions include *A Flash of Lightning* (1868), *Frou-Frou* (1870), *Horizon* (1871), *Divorce* (1871), *Article 47* (1872), *Needles and Pins* (1880), *Dollars and Sense* (1883), *Love on Crutches* (1884), and *The Lottery of Love* (1888).

Daly was also an important theater manager and director. In 1869, he rented the Fifth Avenue Theatre in New York and established his own company, which included such notable actors as Fanny Davenport, Mrs. George Gilbert, and James Lewis. In 1873, the Fifth Avenue Theatre burned down, and Daly leased the New York Theatre, renaming it Daly's Fifth Avenue Theatre. For a time, Daly conducted this theater, the Grand Opera House, and the New Fifth Avenue Theatre which he built on Twenty-eighth St. However, he found the effort of maintaining three the-aters too great and decided to focus his efforts exclusively on the newly built play-house. Financial hardship and a difficult theatrical market forced Daly to give up the New Fifth Avenue Theatre in 1877, but in 1879 he took over the Old Broadway

Theatre, renovated it extensively, and renamed it Daly's Theatre. In this space, Daly maintained a consistently outstanding repertory company, including a group of actors known as the "Big Four": John Drew, Ada Rehan, James Lewis, and Mrs. George H. Gilbert. In 1884, Daly's company visited Europe, playing in London, Berlin, and Paris. After two additional trips in 1886 and 1890, Daly opened his own theater in London in 1893. Daly maintained his theaters in New York and London until his death in 1899.

The merit and success of Daly's shows derived largely from his demand that actors in his troupe work toward an ensemble effect, with no single individual receiving star billing. Consequently, Daly was able to maintain uniformly high standards of production and has come to be recognized as one of the first American directors or régisseurs.

Robert I. Lublin

See also: NEW YORK CITY

References

Daly, Augustin. *Plays,* edited by Rosemary Cullen and Don B. Wilmeth. New York: Cambridge University Press, 1984.
Daly, Joseph. *The Life of Augustin Daly.* New York: Macmillan, 1984.
Felheim, Marvin. *The Theater of Augustin Daly.* Cambridge, MA: Harvard University Press, 1956.

DALY, MARCUS (1841–1900)

Born in Ballyjamesduff, Co. Cavan, Marcus Daly spent his early years as a farm laborer before immigrating to the United States in 1856. He spent five years working in New York City and then moved to California to join his sister. After working in the California mines for a few years, he moved to Virginia City, Nevada, in 1865 and worked his way up through the ranks at the Comstock mine, until the mine was shut down after a fire in April 1869. In 1870 Daly was hired by the Walker Brothers to manage the Emma mine in Alta, Nevada, and later, to manage Walker Brothers mines at Ophir and Dry Canyon. While employed by the Walker Brothers, he met and married Margaret Evans (in 1872), who bore him two girls in Nevada, and later, another girl and a boy. Daly became a U.S. citizen in 1874.

In 1876 the Walker Brothers sent Daly to the small enclave of Butte, Montana, to investigate purchasing a mine. Daly enthusiastically promoted the development of the Alice mine, to the point of putting up some of the money to buy it. It was in Butte that Daly made his name and his fortune. With the money he earned from the Alice mine, in 1880 he purchased the Anaconda mine and converted it from silver to copper mining. Very rapidly he built up the copper mine, bought adjoining property and other mines, built a large smelter to support the mine, and eventually, built the town of Anaconda to support the smelter. Some of his contemporaries had disdained his emphasis on copper mining (arguing that silver was more valuable), but his timing was perfect: he owned significant copper mining capabilities just as new demands for copper—for use in electrical, telegraph, and telephone wires—took off.

In a short time Daly amassed a great fortune, and he became known as one of the "copper kings" of Butte. His contemporaries remembered Daly as a good businessman and a warmhearted and generous Irishman. He was known for hiring Irish miners to work in his mines, and as he became more famous, he helped spur a great deal of Irish immigration to Montana, and particularly, to Butte. He joined the Butte and Anaconda divisions of the Irish Catholic Ancient Order of Hibernians, and was nominated for membership in the Robert Emmett Literary society.

Daly dabbled in state politics, although primarily to foil another Irishman, W. A. Clark, with whom he quarreled. The Clark-Daly feud, as it was known, centered on their competition for influence in state and national politics and their fight over the location of the new state capital. Both Irishmen spent millions of dollars in their efforts, which included using local newspapers as personal soapboxes (Daly had to start a newspaper—*The Anaconda Standard*—to battle Clark's own *Butte Miner*), purchasing political influence, and buying votes for their causes. The feud between the two millionaires only ended with Daly's death in 1900.

Daly was known for his bloodstock horse farm. Over the course of many years, he purchased several racehorses and built up a well-known and respected stable. Among his most famous horses was Tammany, which won several races, including the Great Eclipse Stakes and the Jerome Handicap. His legacy, however, remains with his achievements in copper mining. By the time of his death the Anaconda Company was the largest producer of copper in the world.

Korcaighe P. Hale

See also: ANCIENT ORDER OF
   HIBERNIANS

References

Emmons, David. *The Butte Irish: Class and Ethnicity in an American Mining Town, 1875–1925.* Chicago: University of Illinois Press, 1990.

Glasscock, C. B. *The War of the Copper Kings: Builders of Butte and Wolves of Wall Street.* New York: Grosset and Dunlap, 1935.

Marcosson, Isaac F. *Anaconda.* New York: Dodd, Mead and Co., 1957.

Shoebotham, H. Minar. *Anaconda: Life of Marcus Daly the Copper King.* Harrisburg, PA: The Stackpole Company, 1956.

Works Projects Administration. *Copper Camp: Stories of the World's Greatest Mining Town, Butte, Montana.* New York: Hasting House, 1943.

DAVIN, NICHOLAS FLOOD (1840–1901)

Baptized Nicholas Francis, Nicholas Flood Davin was a journalist, lawyer, politician, and writer. Born January 13, 1840, in Kilfinane (Republic of Ireland), he was the eldest child of Nicholas Flood Davin and Eliza Lane. Davin's early years in Ireland and England remain hidden in mystery because of his own efforts to disguise his past. He changed his middle name and concealed his Roman Catholic upbringing. Following the death of his father, Davin was raised with his Protestant uncle. He was apprenticed to an ironmonger at age 18. Six years later he spent one term at Queen's College Cork.

Like many of his contemporaries, Davin joined the stream of Irish migrants to London, where he studied law. He was called to the bar in 1868. Although he kept a legal practice in London during these years, he made his living as a journalist working for several different newspapers in England and Northern Ireland. He arrived in Toronto in 1872, ostensibly on an assignment to investigate the possibility of Canada's annexation to the United States.

Davin's first noteworthy public appearance came in 1873. Accepting the invitation of the Saint George's Society of Toronto, Davin gave a spirited lecture in which he strongly criticized American society while promoting what he saw as the superior type of British civilization. Although called to the bar in Ontario in 1876, he made his mark more as a lecturer and a writer. After the publication of a few rather minor pieces, Davin wrote what is generally considered his most significant addition to Canadian literature, *The Irishman in Canada* (1877). In this lengthy example of ethnic self-gratification, he deliberately ignores the Protestant-Catholic, Orange-Green divide among the Irish in the country, divisions he considered irrelevant to Canada

A founding member of the Toronto Young Men's Liberal-Conservative Association in 1876, Davin shortly thereafter stood for elected office for the Conservative party in the strong Liberal riding of Haldimand (Ontario) and lost by a very small margin. This near victory brought him a brief appointment in 1879 to examine industrial schools for native children in the United Sates. In his report later that year, Davin recommended that Canada adopt a similar course for its aboriginal population. However, his career as political journalist soon brought him to the western prairies.

With the financial support of the Conservative party in the form of a series of Canadian Pacific Railroad lots in the town of Regina, Davin founded the *Regina Leader* in 1883. Although the paper got off to a good start, both the founder-editor and the paper soon fell upon hard times, which were only briefly relieved by Davin's appointment as secretary of the royal commission on Chinese immigration. With news of the rebellion in the west in 1885 and especially the trial of its leader, Louis Riel, the nation's eyes were focused on Regina. Davin even succeeded in obtaining an interview with Riel on the eve of his execution by entering the prison disguised as a priest. With such attention, the *Leader's* circulation increased. During this period of relative prosperity, Davin began his liaison with Kate Simpson Hayes, which produced a son and a daughter, both of whom were "placed" outside Regina.

In the general election of 1887, Davin easily won Assiniboia West for the Conservative party. Although he would be re-elected in 1891, the much sought-after cabinet position eluded him. Yet his personal popularity was such that he was the only Conservative in the territories to be returned to Parliament in 1896. Davin sold the *Leader* in 1895 and married Eliza Jane Reid. From 1896 to 1900, from the opposition's side of the House, he remained the imperialist he had always been, as is evidenced by his urging Canada to support Britain in its South African war. Defeated in the general election of 1900, Davin took his own life in his hotel room in Winnipeg the following year.

Although Davin's was a tragic life marked by alcoholism, Davin nonetheless had some literary talent. In addition to *The Irishman in Canada,* he also wrote some poetry and a novel. Yet he will likely be most remembered for his attempt to foster a national sentiment in the new territories of the west, a sentiment which he personally found intertwined with the larger imperial project.

Robert J. Grace

See also: ONTARIO

References

Koester, C. B., *Mr. Davin, M.P.: A Biography of Nicholas Flood Davin.* Saskatoon: Western Producer Prairie Books, 1980.

Thompson, John Herd. "Davin, Nicholas Flood." In *Dictionary of Canadian Biography.* Vol. 13. Toronto: University of Toronto Press, 1994.

DAVITT, MICHAEL (1846–1906)

The Irish nationalist, agrarian radical, and journalist Michael Davitt was one of the most influential leaders of Irish nationalism during the nineteenth century as well as a founder of the Irish National Land League. Born in 1846 in Straide, Co. Mayo, Davitt was the son of small farmers. In 1850 they were evicted from their home and immigrated to the industrial town of Haslingden in England. Davitt left school at the age of nine to work in the local cotton mills, but at the age of eleven he was the victim of an industrial accident that cost him his right arm. After his disability, Davitt was able to receive an education and obtained a job in the local post office

In 1865, Davitt joined the Fenians, a secret Irish revolutionary organization dedicated to the forceful overthrow of British rule in Ireland. Three years later, in 1868, Davitt became the organizing secretary of the Irish Republican Brotherhood (IRB) for England and Scotland. In 1870, Davitt was caught in Britain attempting to export arms to Ireland and was sentenced to fifteen years of penal servitude. During the seven and a half years of his sentence, he was subject to poor conditions and abusive treatment. He managed to smuggle out an account of his imprisonment, which was published widely in British and Irish newspapers. Because of outside pressure on the British government, Davitt was released on parole in December of 1877.

After his release, Davitt began to reformulate his earlier ideas about the usefulness of physical force, moving instead toward a belief in the need for cooperation between constitutional and physical force nationalists. Because of his rural background, he was also concerned about the plight of tenant farmers and the rural poor in Ireland. He undertook a tour of America in 1878 and came into contact with the American Clan na Gael leader, John Devoy. Devoy and Davitt began a discussion that would eventually lead to a shift in the Irish and Irish-American nationalist movement. The "New Departure" was an informal alliance among constitutional and physical force nationalists to work together peacefully under the leadership of Charles Stewart Parnell.

A severe crop failure and falling prices in 1879 led to rising agrarian discontent in the west of Ireland. A series of protest meetings was quickly organized in Co. Mayo, and Davitt was able to enlist Parnell's aid in the struggle. On October 21, 1879, the Irish National Land League was formed with Parnell as president and Davitt as secretary. The Land League attempted to achieve the immediate reduction of rents and the eventual establishment of tenant ownership. Davitt also convinced Parnell to support the creation of a Ladies' Land League under the leadership of Anna Parnell, Charles Parnell's sister. As the Land League grew, agrarian disorder and conflict with the British government increased, and Davitt was arrested for violating his parole on February 3, 1881. The Land League movement ended when William Gladstone and Parnell concluded an informal pact in April of 1882, commonly known as the "Kilmainham Treaty," to end rural agitation in Ireland in exchange for British concessions on tenants' rights.

Upon his release from prison in May of 1882, Davitt, with the encouragement of Henry George and Patrick Ford, briefly thought of embarking on a radical new phase of land agitation by pushing for land nationalization, but in the face of severe criticism from Parnell and others, he put the idea aside. For the rest of the 1880s, Davitt supported Parnell's attempts to achieve Home Rule for Ireland. In 1887, Davitt defended Parnell's and his own record before the Special Commission on Parnellism and Crime. When news of Parnell's affair with Katherine O'Shea became public during her divorce proceedings in 1890, Davitt felt personally betrayed and called for Parnell's resignation. After Parnell's death in 1891, Davitt sided with the anti-Parnellite section of the now split Irish Parliamentary Party.

During the 1890s, Davitt continued to work for various causes. He was elected to Parliament for North-East Cork in 1893 and for South Mayo in 1895. Throughout his life, he was actively engaged in labor activism, drawing praise not only from Irish but also from British working-class leaders. Eschewing only middle-class concerns, Davitt tried to connect the plight of the urban and rural laborers. In 1895, Davitt traveled to Australia, Tasmania, and New Zealand on a seven-month lecture tour and published *Life and Progress in Australasia* (1895). With the outbreak of the Anglo-Boer War in 1899, Davitt resigned his seat in protest. Davitt traveled widely from 1900 to 1906, visiting South Africa, the United States, and Russia. He briefly served as a war correspondent in South Africa for William Randolph Hearst's *New York American Journal.* He also published several books: *The Boer Fight for Freedom* (1902), *Within the Pale: The True Story of Anti-Semitic Persecutions in Russia* (1903), and *The Fall of Feudalism in Ireland* (1904), his account of the Land War. Davitt died on May 30, 1906.

Ely Janis

See also: DEVOY, John; FENIANS; FORD, Patrick; IRISH REPUBLICAN BROTHERHOOD; LADIE'S LAND LEAGUE

References

Cashman, D. B. *The Life of Michael Davitt.* Glasgow: Cameron, Ferguson, & Co., 1882.

Davitt, Michael. *The Fall of Feudalism in Ireland: Or, the Story of the Land League.* New York: Harper & Brothers, 1904.

King, Carla. *Michael Davitt.* Dundalk: Dundalgan Press, 1999.

Moody, T. W. *Davitt and Irish Revolution, 1846–1882.* Oxford: Clarendon Press, 1981.

Sheehy-Skeffington, Francis. *Michael Davitt: Revolutionary, Agitator, and Labour Leader.* London: T. F. Unwin, 1908.

DAY, DENNIS (1916–1988)

Born Owen Patrick Eugene Dennis McNulty in the Bronx, New York, on May 21, 1916, Dennis Day was a successful popular singer, actor, and entertainer. He had a distinguished career in radio, film, and television, particularly in the 1940s and 1950s. In his best days, Day was known as "America's Favorite Irish Tenor." Day's father hailed from Co. Armagh, and his mother (née Mary Grady) was from Charlestown, Co. Mayo. A former choir member of Saint Patrick's Cathedral in New York City, he developed a lyrical tenor voice and made his radio debut on the *Jack Benny Show* on October 8, 1939. Day became a popular attraction on the show, where he used to play a naive teenager known for his tagline "Gee, Mr. Benny!" Day followed Benny in his move to the television screen in 1950 and reappeared on the show occasionally until 1974. From 1946 to 1952 Day had his own radio show, *A Day in the Life of Dennis Day,* and the short-lived *Dennis Day Show* on television

(1952). In the same year he also traveled to Ireland, performing August 1 in the parochial hall of his mother's native town in Mayo.

In the 1940s and 1950s Day starred in a number of Hollywood movies, including *Music in Manhattan* (1944), *Melody Time* (1948), and *Golden Girl* (1951), and he lent his voice to the Warner Brothers movie on Chauncey Olcott's life, *My Wild Irish Rose* (1947), songs from which were released on an RCA album set. For much of the 1950s and 1960s Day disappeared from public view, but he returned in the mid-1970s in a number of minor television and film roles. His sound recordings were also republished on records. Day died of Lou Gehrig's disease in Bel Air, California, on June 22, 1988.

Axel Klein

See also: OLCOTT, Chauncey; SAINT PATRICK'S CATHEDRAL

DAY-LEWIS, DANIEL (1957–)

Daniel Michael Blake Day-Lewis was born in London on April 29, 1957. He is the son of Irish-born poet, Cecil Day-Lewis (b. 1904 in Co. Laois), and Jill Balcon (b. 1924), daughter of leading British film producer, Sir Michael Balcon. Although Daniel and his sister Tamasin (b. 1953) were raised largely in London, the family has always maintained its Irish roots— Cecil Day-Lewis was best known for his collection of poems, *The Whispering Roots,* which alluded to his Irish lineage, and the family spent their summer holidays in the west of Ireland.

Daniel Day-Lewis was educated at Invicta Junior School and Sherington

Junior Boys School in London before becoming an unhappy student at the Sevenoaks Boarding School in 1968; he transferred to another school, Bedales, in 1970, the year his father became Britain's poet laureate. During his time at Sevenoaks Boarding School Day-Lewis became interested in acting and appeared in a number of student productions. In 1971 he was cast in a bit part in John Schlesinger's film, *Sunday Bloody Sunday,* and, following his father's death in 1972, he joined the National Youth Theatre. After two years there he entered the Old Vic Bristol Stage School and began to appear in their productions after completing three years of training. Day-Lewis first attracted critical attention in 1980 when he played a troubled adolescent in a production of Nigel Williams's play, *Class Enemy;* he followed this with a role as a mentally challenged man in Mike Stott's *Funny Peculiar.*

Day-Lewis's performance in the Little Theatre's production of John Osborne's classic "angry young man" play, *Look Back in Anger,* was received with mixed reviews but undoubtedly helped to raise his profile among critics and the public. His next performance, the title role in Christopher Bond's production of Stoker's *Dracula,* also brought him publicity and interest from the BBC: soon after, he was cast in a supporting role in a BBC drama, *Artemis 81,* by David Rudkin.

From 1980 Day-Lewis balanced film and television work with theater work. He was featured in a minor role in Richard Attenborough's *Gandhi* and could also be seen on television in one episode of the popular detective show *Shoestring* and in a 1982 BBC production of Antonia White's *A Frost in May.* He traveled to Ireland to appear in a screen version of Jennifer Johnson's *How*

Many Miles to Babylon? (1982) and to New Zealand to act in a big-budget remake of *Mutiny on the Bounty* (renamed *The Bounty*) starring Mel Gibson and Anthony Hopkins.

On stage Day-Lewis won critical acclaim for his role in Julian Mitchell's *Another Country*, based on the life of British spy Guy Burgess (and later made into a film starring Rupert Everett) and appeared in the Royal Shakespeare Company's touring productions of *A Midsummer Night's Dream* and *Romeo and Juliet*.

Day-Lewis's screen and theater work in this period certainly demonstrated his versatility and range as an actor, but it was his performance as a homosexual skinhead in Stephen Frears's film of Hanif Kureshi's script *My Beautiful Laundrette* that proved his willingness to essay challenging and controversial roles. Released in 1985, *My Beautiful Laundrette* was a scathing attack on the values of Thatcher's Britain and is generally regarded as one of the most important British films of the 1980s, winning the BAFTA (British Academy of Film and Television Arts) award for Best Film in 1986.

Day-Lewis's next film part was a complete change from Frears's film: he took on a historical role in the 1985 Merchant-Ivory production of E. M. Forster's *A Room with a View*. Playing Cecil Vyse, the priggish suitor of Helena Bonham-Carter's Lucy Honeychurch, he gave a finely nuanced performance that helped to transform his character from an object of audience contempt to a figure of some poignancy.

Following a brief return to theater to appear as the poet Vladimir Mayakovksy in Richard Eyre's production of *The Futurists*, he took on a role in an Anglo-French film, *Nanou* (1986), which received mixed reviews. In 1987 he was cast in a major film,

Philip Kaufman's *The Unbearable Lightness of Being* (1988), based on the novel by Milan Kundera. In preparing for his role as Tomas, a Czech doctor, Day-Lewis conducted extensive research on the historical period and even learnt some Czech. This meticulous preparation underlined his commitment to his craft and his belief in immersing himself entirely in the role at hand, qualities that would become even more pronounced in later films such as *My Left Foot* and *In the Name of the Father*.

His next film role was in an American production of William Boyd's novel, *Stars and Bars* (1988), which was directed by Irish director Pat O'Connor. The film was not well received and soon after Day-Lewis took a break from acting, retreating to Ireland (he had held an Irish passport since 1987). While he was living in Ireland he was approached by theater director Jim Sheridan with a script for a proposed film on the life of disabled Dublin writer Christy Brown. Sheridan had worked in theater in Ireland and America for almost a decade but this was to be his debut as a film director. Day-Lewis accepted the role as Christy in *My Left Foot* and immersed himself completely in it—on set he remained in character and in a wheelchair, and the result was a heartfelt, deeply authentic performance in a film that largely avoided excessive sentiment. It was said that Christy Brown's friends and family were overcome when they saw the film, such was the effectiveness of his performance. Audiences in Europe and America embraced *My Left Foot*, and the film was nominated for a variety of awards, including the BAFTAs (winning awards for Day-Lewis and Ray McAnally) and the Academy Awards (nominated for five Oscars, it won two, for Day-Lewis and Brenda Fricker).

Soon after filming *My Left Foot,* Day-Lewis took on another Irish role, a traveling dentist called Fergus O'Connell, in a film shot by Argentinean director Carlos Sorin. *Eversmile, New Jersey* was released in 1989 but failed to win the critical and commercial success that had been enjoyed by *My Left Foot.*

Riding high on his film successes, Day-Lewis returned to the theater to take the lead role opposite Judi Dench in a prestigious production of *Hamlet,* directed by Richard Eyre for the National Theatre in London. During the play's run, Day-Lewis suffered a nervous breakdown and withdrew from the production. Undoubtedly, the breakdown was brought on by the strain of his hectic work schedule, although rumors circulated that he had suffered a collapse after seeing his father's ghost on the stage!

Following a two-year hiatus from both theater and film work, Day-Lewis re-emerged as an unusual action hero in Michael Mann's film of *The Last of the Mohicans* (1992). Playing Hawkeye, the English settler gone native in James Fenimore Cooper's wilderness tale, Day-Lewis won critical acclaim and commercial success. The role also established his credentials as a romantic lead, and this was underlined with his casting as Newland Archer in Martin Scorsese's lavish film of Edith Wharton's novel, *The Age of Innocence.* The film was released in 1993 to somewhat mixed reviews, but both actor and director enjoyed the collaboration and would work together again in *The Gangs of New York* (2002).

Day-Lewis teamed up with another favorite director, Jim Sheridan, on two films in the 1990s: the first, *In the Name of the Father,* told the story of Gerry Conlon, one of the Guildford Four wrongly imprisoned for fifteen years by the British government

Actor Daniel Day-Lewis (right) speaks with director Jim Sheridan (left) on the set of In the Name of the Father *in 1993. (Universal/The Kobal Collection)*

on bomb charges; the second, *The Boxer* (1997) featured Day-Lewis as Danny Flynn in an archetypal boxing story of ambition, success, and failure. Of the two, *In the Name of the Father* sparked the most controversy and critical acclaim when it was released in 1993, and it further aligned Day-Lewis with Irish cinema. Although both films involved meticulous research and training, it was his grueling preparation for the role of Gerry Conlon—which involved starving himself in a bid to replicate the debilitating physical state experienced by Conlon on hunger strike—that proved his adherence to method-style acting. During this time Day-Lewis reaffirmed his Irish roots by purchasing Castlekevin, a Georgian mansion in Co. Wicklow once owned by playwright J. M. Synge. Henceforth, he would divide his time between there and New York.

While making a film version of Arthur Miller's *The Crucible* (1996) in America Day-Lewis met and married Rebecca Miller, the daughter of the playwright. Day-Lewis retreated again from the public eye, refusing roles in such high-profile films as *Interview with a Vampire, Shakespeare in Love,* and *Philadelphia.* Since 1997 he has appeared in only two films: *The Gangs of New York* (2002), Scorsese's ambitious epic of Irish and English gangs in New York of the 1860s, and *The Ballad of Jack and Rose* (2005), written and directed by his wife, Rebecca Miller.

Day-Lewis divides his time between America and Ireland and has three children: Gabriel-Kane Adjani (b. April 9, 1995, from a relationship with the actress Isabelle Adjani), Ronan Cal Day-Lewis (b. June 14, 1998), and Cashel Blake Day-Lewis (b. May 2002).

Gwenda Young

See also: SHERIDAN, Jim

References

Barton, Ruth. *Irish National Cinema.* London: Routledge, 2004.

Caughie, John, and Kevin Rockett. *The Companion to British and Irish Cinema.* London: British Film Institute, 1996.

Jenkins, Garry. *Daniel Day-Lewis: The Fire Within.* New York: St. Martin's, 1994.

DE CHASTELAIN, JOHN (1937–)

Born in Romania to a Scottish father and an American mother (both of whom had been involved in covert activities on behalf of the Allies during World War II), John de Chastelain was educated in Scotland and immigrated to Canada with his parents as a teenager. After military training, de Chastelain rose through the ranks of the Canadian Army to become chief of Defence Staff from 1989–1993. He also served as Canadian ambassador to the United States from 1993–1994 and was recalled to serve once again as chief of Defence Staff in 1994–1995.

De Chastelain was appointed head of the Independent International Commission on Decommissioning in 1997. Alongside former U.S. Senator George Mitchell and former Finnish Prime Minister Harri Holkeri, de Chatelain was part of an international team that played a key role in brokering the Good Friday Agreement (1998). Disagreements between the armed groups, principally the Irish Republican Army and assorted loyalist paramilitaries, and elected representatives in Northern Ireland, Britain, and the Republic of Ireland resulted in a protracted stalemate over the status of paramilitary arms, partly resolved by IRA decommissioning in 2005.

De Chastelain's leadership of the Commission has not been without controversy. Initially selected because of his perceived impartiality, de Chastelain attracted criticism from Unionist, Loyalist, Nationalist, and Republican quarters as initial high hopes for a speedy disarmament of paramilitaries (or the placement of their arms "beyond use") were repeatedly disappointed. He is widely recognized as one of the major international figures engaged in the peace process in Northern Ireland.

Kevin James

See also: MITCHELL, George

References

MacGinty, Roger, and John Darby. *Guns and Government: The Management of the Northern Ireland Peace Process.* London: Palgrave Macmillan, 2002.

Peatling, Gary K. "Conflict and Ireland, 1829–2003: Canadian and American Stories." *Canadian Journal of Irish Studies* 31, no. 1 (Spring 2005): 52–59.

DE VALERA, EAMON (1882–1975)

Eamon de Valera was an American-born politician and statesman who fought for Irish freedom and later became one of the main architects of the Irish state. He valued Ireland's links with the United States and was convinced that, without the moral support of American opinion, the state could not have come into existence. Nevertheless, his call in the 1930s for League of Nations intervention in the Chaco War displeased Washington. And during World War II the Roosevelt administration strongly disapproved of his policy of Irish neutrality. Earlier, when he had toured the United States to win support for the fledgling Irish republic, he antagonized leading Irish Americans and left a legacy of division among

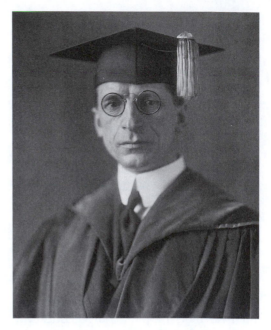

Portrait of Eamon de Valera, President of Ireland (1959–1973). (Library of Congress)

the American friends of Ireland. He was proud to welcome President John F. Kennedy to Ireland in June 1963, the first such visit by a serving American president. At the invitation of President Lyndon Johnson he made his last visit to the United States in 1964, during which he addressed a joint session of Congress. The people of Ireland, he said, had constantly looked to the United States as the champion of human liberty, the liberty of nations, and the liberty of individuals.

Born in New York to Catherine Coll and Vivion Juan de Valera, he was raised by relatives in Bruree, Co. Limerick. He was educated by the Christian Brothers in Charleville, Co. Cork, and by the Holy Ghost Fathers at Blackrock College, Co. Dublin. He graduated with a degree in mathematics from the Royal University, after which he taught at St. Patrick's College, Maynooth. He married Sinéad Ní Fhlannagáin in 1910.

A member of both the Irish Volunteers and the oath-bound Irish Republican Brotherhood, he commanded the Boland's Mill garrison in the 1916 Rising. Though he was sentenced to death by the British authorities, representations were made on his behalf, citing his American citizenship. The death penalty was commuted to life imprisonment, but de Valera was released in 1917, the year in which he was elected member of parliament for East Clare. Arrested during the anti-conscription campaign and imprisoned in Lincoln Jail, he was reelected to Westminster in the Sinn Féin landslide of 1918. With the help of Michael Collins, he escaped from prison and was elected Príomh Aire (First Minister) of the Irish Republic in April 1919.

To let Irish Americans know who was boss, de Valera styled himself president of the Irish Republic for his visit to the United States in 1919. His mission was to raise funds and gain recognition for the Republic. On a coast-to-coast tour he addressed audiences totaling more than 500,000 people in venues such as Fenway Park, Boston, Madison Square Gardens, New York, and Soldier Field, Chicago, raising more than $5 million. But he clashed with Irish-American leaders Judge Daniel Cohalan and John Devoy, over his handling of the recognition issue, contending that they were not seeking formal recognition of the republic, as he was, but were merely calling for recognition of the Irish people's right to self-determination. And de Valera caused a furor when he unilaterally offered Britain a guarantee similar to the Platt Amendment, which gave the United States the right to intervene in Cuba's affairs. He further antagonized Cohalan and Devoy by attempting to establish himself as a power broker in U.S. politics. Portraying himself as the man

who could deliver Irish-American support for the League of Nations, de Valera also gave the impression that he could influence the Irish-American vote in the 1920 presidential election. But when he went to lobby Republicans at their convention in Chicago, he was refused a hearing. The election of Warren G. Harding ended any hope of recognition.

On de Valera's return to Ireland he disagreed with Michael Collins over the conduct of the War of Independence, arguing that the Irish Republican Army (IRA) should fight a conventional war rather than use guerrilla tactics against the British. He insisted Collins should attend the treaty negotiations while he remained in Dublin. He then opposed the treaty, proposing instead document No. 2, a version of the external association model that the British had previously rejected. His opposition centered not on partition but on the Oath of Allegiance. The Dáil voted in favor of the treaty and pro-treaty candidates won an overwhelming majority in the 1922 general election. However, continued opposition by republican hardliners led to a civil war (1922–1923) in which 3,000 people died, among them Michael Collins. De Valera spent most of the war in prison followed by a further four years in the political wilderness.

In 1926, having failed to overturn Sinn Féin's abstentionist policy, he and his followers left the party to form Fianna Fáil. The party entered the Dáil in 1927 and quickly became a well-organized, highly disciplined political machine that enjoyed the tacit support of the IRA. Members of the Dáil were required to take the Oath of Allegiance, which de Valera now dismissed as an empty formula.

Between 1927 and 1929 de Valera was busy fund-raising in the United States, and in 1931 he used American bonds to launch the *Irish Press*. After the 1932 general election, he was elected head of a government pledged to an independent, self-sufficient rural republic. Committed to ending free trade, de Valera sought to foster indigenous industries, but sufficient private investment was not forthcoming, thereby forcing the state to increase its involvement in industry. Some modest progress was made, but the home market was too small to enable domestic industry to expand significantly. Exports were uncompetitive because of high costs. His abolition of the Oath of Allegiance and removal of the governor-general led to the economic war with Britain, exacerbating the problems caused by his protectionist policies. The cattle trade in particular suffered, which in turn contributed to the emergence of the Blueshirts, who fought street battles with both the IRA and members of Fianna Fáil. De Valera's government neutralized the Blueshirts and in 1936 banned the IRA.

In 1937 de Valera unveiled a new constitution. It reflected his firm belief that Ireland was a Catholic nation. Certainly, it included elements of the liberal tradition, but Catholic social teaching was to the forefront, and a vocational dimension was most in evidence in the composition of the senate. The constitution recognized "the special position of the Holy Catholic and Apostolic Roman Catholic Church as the guardian of the faith professed by the great majority of its [Ireland's] citizens." It defined the national territory as the whole island of Ireland and distinguished the jurisdiction of the twenty-six-county state from the territory of the nation, "pending the integration of the national territory." Fidelity to the nation was demanded of citizens, Irish was nominated as the first official language,

women's place was in the home, and marriage was indissoluble. (In 1972 the Article relating to the Catholic Church was deleted by referendum; a wafer-thin majority voted in 1996 to remove the prohibition on divorce; and Articles 2 and 3 defining the national territory were amended in 1998 as a result of the referendum on the Good Friday Agreement.) The constitution was adopted by a majority of 56.5 percent of the vote to 43.5 percent on a turnout of 75.8 percent.

The ending of the economic war in 1938 made it possible for the seaports that had been retained by Britain under the terms of the treaty to be placed under Irish control. This was essential to maintaining Irish neutrality in World War II. The policy enjoyed all-party support in the Dáil, but the IRA took the opportunity to declare war on Britain. During the Emergency de Valera cracked down on militant republicans. Six IRA men were executed, three died on hunger strike, 500 were interned, and 600 were committed under the Offences against the State Act. Censorship was tightened to an extraordinary degree so that war news was effectively blacked out in Irish newspapers. De Valera accepted the assurance of the German minister in Dublin, Edouard Hempel, that Germany would respect Irish neutrality. Aware that U.S. President Franklin D. Roosevelt had little sympathy for Ireland's position, he welcomed the formation in 1940 of the American Friends of Irish Neutrality. When the United States expressed its support for British efforts to obtain the use of the Irish ports, de Valera sent Frank Aiken to explain to Roosevelt why he could not oblige. In an acrimonious meeting Roosevelt rejected the explanation.

From 1941 onwards, David Gray, the American envoy to Dublin, was increasingly outspoken in his criticism of de Valera, on one occasion appealing to a group of cabinet ministers to abandon neutrality. When the United States entered the war, Roosevelt pointedly said that Ireland's freedom was also at stake. De Valera ruled out the possibility of U.S. bases being located in Ireland and expressed disapproval of bases in Northern Ireland, causing much anger in the United States—even among Irish Americans. Nonetheless, the Irish defence forces continued to supply valuable intelligence information to the Office of Strategic Services. De Valera attracted widespread criticism when he visited the German Legation in Dublin to express condolences on the death of Hitler. As the war drew to a close, a *New York Times* columnist commented that de Valera's conduct had cost him U.S. political support in his quarrel with the British.

On losing office in 1948, de Valera embarked on a four-week tour of the United States to campaign against partition, complaining that British behavior in Northern Ireland was worse than that of communist regimes in Eastern Europe. He had told Gray that people in Northern Ireland who objected to a united Ireland should be physically transferred to the country to which they wished to adhere. He later modified his position, saying that unionists would be given the choice of staying or moving to Britain.

The British government responded to Ireland's 1948 declaration of the republic by guaranteeing that Northern Ireland would remain a part of the United Kingdom so long as a majority of its population so desired. Fianna Fáil governed between 1951 and 1954. Having spent a further three years (1954–1957) in opposition, de Valera returned to serve his last term as taoiseach. In 1958, the introduction of the First Programme for Economic Development marked the end of economic nationalism. De Valera resigned as Taoiseach a year later. In 1959 he was elected president, but his party's proposal to abolish proportional representation (which would have permanently tipped the electoral balance in favor of Fianna Fáil) was defeated in a referendum.

De Valera served two terms as president, leaving public life in 1973. He died on August 29, 1975. His primary political aims, the political unification of Ireland and the restoration of the Irish language, are no longer actively pursued by any major political party.

Patrick Gillan

See also: COHALAN, Daniel; DEVOY, John; GRAY, David; IRISH REPUBLICAN ARMY; IRISH REPUBLICAN BROTHERHOOD

References
Brown, Terence. *Ireland: A Social and Cultural History 1922–79*. London: Fontana, 1981.
Cronin, Seán. *Irish Nationalism: A History of Its Roots and Ideology*. New York: Continuum, 1980.
Lee, J. J. *Ireland 1912–1985: Politics and Society*. Cambridge: Cambridge University Press, 1989.
Ryle, Dwyer T. *De Valera: The Man and the Myth*. Dublin, Ireland: Poolbeg, 1991.

DELANTY, GREG (1958–)

Born in Cork City, Ireland, on July 19, 1958, Greg Delanty was educated at Colaiste Chriost Ri and at University College Cork, where he received his bachelor's degree in English literature and history in 1980, followed by a higher diploma in 1982. During his time at university, he edited the arts magazine and published his first poems in *The Examiner* newspaper. In 1983 Delanty received the Patrick Kavanagh Memorial Award for poetry. In total he has published six collections of poetry. His first poetry collection, *Cast in the Fire,* was published by Dolmen Press in 1986. In the same year Delanty left his native Cork to settle in America. Much of his work since his first volume has concentrated on the experience of exile. This preoccupation continued with *Southward* (1992), his second collection, which includes some of the poems included in his first volume. Poems such as "Epistle from a Room in Winston-Salem, North Carolina" and "The Emigrant's Apology," which is dedicated "to my mother," reflect this growing awareness of America. However, there is also a consciousness of his native Cork in a poem such as "Home from Home." The presence of America reaches its height with *American Wake* (1995), his third collection. The title, with its evocation of the rural communal gatherings that were held before people emigrated from Ireland to America, directly refers to the sense of exile and loss engendered by emigration. Poems such as "The Fifth Province," "Economic Pressure," "America," and "On the Renovation of Ellis Island" explore the history of emigration from Ireland to America, while the poem "In the Land of the Eagle" relates this history to the experience of Irish immigrants to America in the 1980s.

In addition to the importance of America and the experience of the emigrant, Delanty has returned to the theme of printing and the role of the printer. He was born into a family of printers—his father, grandfather, uncles, and cousins all worked in the trade. Delanty worked in the Eagle Printing Company in Cork, and this awareness of the trade is reflected in his poetry. It is first visible in "The Master Printer," a poem from his debut collection. However, it is in his fourth book, *The Hellbox* (1998), that this becomes a dominant theme with poems like "The Compositor," "The Composing Room," "Striped Ink," and "The Printer's Devil." In 1986, the year his first volume of poetry was published, Delanty was awarded the Allan Dowling Poetry Fellowship in the United States. He received the Austin Clarke Centenary Poetry Award in 1997, and two years later he was a prizewinner in the National Poetry Competition. He has also received an Irish Arts Council Bursary. Delanty's work has been widely anthologized in publications such as *Poetry Ireland Review, The Southern Review,* and *The Irish Times.* With Nuala Ni Dhomhnaill, he edited *Jumping Off Shadows: Selected Contemporary Irish Poets.* He also edited *The Selected Poems of Patrick Galvin* with Robert Welch. He has translated Aristophanes' *The Suits,* Euripides' *Orestes,* and *Selected Poems of Kyriakos Charalambides.* His most recent publication is the volume *Collected Poems 1986–2006* (2006).

Delanty currently lives with his American wife, Patricia Ferreira, in Vermont, where he teaches at St. Michael's College. He ran for the Vermont Green Party in the U.S. elections. For three months each year he returns to his Irish home in Derrynane, Co. Kerry.

David Doyle

See also: EMIGRATION

References
Delanty, Greg. *Collected Poems 1986–2006.* Manchester: Carcanet, 2006.
Hearon, Todd. "Greg Delanty." In *The Encyclopedia of the Irish in America.* Ed. Michael Glazier. Notre Dame: University of Notre Dame, 1999.

DELAWARE

Before European contact and settlement, the region was inhabited predominantly by the Delaware tribe. The British explorer John Cabot laid claim to the area in 1497, but the first settlements were Dutch and subsequently Swedish before the British reasserted their initial claim in 1664.

Presbyterian Scots-Irish were the first Irish settlers, and immigration was steady in the late seventeenth and early eighteenth centuries. The numbers spiked in the 1720s, the early 1740s and 1760s, and finally in the years immediately preceding the Revolution, when approximately 30,000 people left Ulster, and large numbers sailed from Northern Ireland ports of Belfast, Londonderry, Larne, and Portrush.

Many of the Scots Irish would leave in family groups, many as indentured servants, and would settle in the Delaware estuary; their numbers spread across both Delaware and, especially, Pennsylvania. Presbyterian churches were established regionwide from the early 1700s

The Mason-Dixon Line was surveyed between 1764 and 1767 to resolve standing disputes over borders involving what would become Delaware. The Scots Irish contributed significantly to the Revolutionary War for the patriot cause. Also prominent in the area's contribution was John Dickinson, "penman of the Revolution" and Delaware's regiment, the Blue Hen Chickens. Delaware subsequently became the first of the original thirteen states to ratify the Constitution and is thus known as the First State.

From the late eighteenth century, Irish Catholics began to settle in northern Delaware, many drawn to the gunpowder factory established by E. I. DuPont in 1802. The DuPonts regularly contributed to costs of migration, assisted with low-cost housing, and provided savings accounts and widows' pensions.

The Know-Nothing campaigns of the 1850s, based on a raw appeal to anti-immigration and anti-Catholicism, had success in Delaware as elsewhere. Peter Causey was elected on the nativist ticket as governor of the state from 1855 to 1859 but proved unpopular, not least because he introduced prohibition.

Delaware was a slave state (with relatively very few slaves) but did not vote to secede from the Union, and the majority of men fought for the state, but many crossed the border to fight with Virginia. The last Union general killed in the war was Irishman General Alfred Smyth from Co. Cork, who had emigrated to Delaware in 1854.

Largely because of the influence of the DuPont family, the Republican party was politically dominant for much of the twentieth century until more recent gubernatorial victories by the Democrats. DuPont is the second largest chemical company in the world because of its success in developing polymers. Because of the very strong Scots-Irish roots, followed by Irish Catholic arrivals, and coupled with the fact that many Germans settled in the nearby Pennsylvania area, Delaware is one of three states in the country in which Irish is today the leading ancestry group.

Sam Hitchmough

References

Doyle, David Noel, and Owen Dudley Edwards, eds. *America and Ireland, 1776–1976: The American Identity and the Irish Connection.* Westport, CT: Greenwood Press, 1980.

Kenny, Kevin. *The American Irish,* Longman, 2000.

Miller, Kerby A., *Emigrants and Exiles: Ireland and the Irish Exodus to North America.* Oxford: Oxford University Press, 1988.

Mulrooney, Margaret M. *Black Power, White Lace: The Du Pont Irish and Cultural Identity in Nineteenth-Century America.* Durham: University of New Hampshire, 2002.

DEMPSEY, GEORGE T. (1943–)

Born in 1943, George Dempsey was educated at St. Pius X Seminary in Sacramento, the University of California at Berkeley, Harvard University, and St. John's College of Oxford. He joined the U.S. diplomatic service in 1973 because he was "seduced by George F. Kennan," the diplomat with the greatest impact on American cold war strategy. Dempsey often cited Kennan as his professional and ideological role model, expressing a desire to write about his six host capitals (Madrid, Vienna, Geneva, the Hague, Dublin, and Caracas) with the same precision as Kennan had addressed his Soviet posting. Dempsey's formal diplomatic career in Ireland (as first secretary for political affairs) lasted only four years (1988–1992), but his association with the island and its polity was much longer. He lived in Blackrock, Co. Dublin from 1994 to 2003, before an unbearable disgruntlement with the Irish political class and media forced him back to Sacramento, California.

Dempsey's contribution to Irish-American diplomatic relations lay in his recurrent advocacy of a less hostile approach to Washington's global posture. He was chargé d'affaires beginning during the 1991 Gulf War. Throughout this conflict, a central concern of U.S. diplomats in Dublin, Dempsey later wrote, was to check "a certain Irish governmental inclination toward pusillanimity in the face of public disquiet." The Irish ministers would support the American government often in private, little in public. This frustrated Dempsey greatly.

In 1993 he sparred with Taoiseach Charles Haughey, who complained that the British Foreign Office had been running the U.S. State Department for years. "Fair's fair," replied Dempsey, "Iveagh House [the Irish Department of Foreign Affairs] has taken over the American Embassy." Despite considerable, and not untypical, State Department reservations over Clinton's tolerance of Sinn Féin ("They were the dark side of the moon"), Dempsey remained cautiously optimistic about the Northern Ireland peace process. Indeed, he saw it as a good illustration of how the United States did its business. Why, he puzzled, did the Irish trust American intentions toward Northern Ireland and yet persist in believing the worst of American foreign policy elsewhere?

In several respects, Dempsey's post-diplomatic career in Ireland, rather than his formal tenure in the U.S. embassy, offers the more reliable barometer of what he saw as a "reflexive" Irish anti-Americanism: "a determination . . . to brush aside both complexities and simple truths and to cast the United States as a sinister villain." His trenchant retrospective (*From the Embassy: A U.S. Foreign Policy Primer,* 2004), written "from the perspective of a working-level professional diplomat," is a case-by-case study of what he saw as a wilful misrepresentation of America by the "vociferous nutters [who] dominated the public foreign policy debate in Ireland." He is particularly harsh about *The Irish Times*' "resident moralizer," Fintan O'Toole, who, observed Dempsey in the wake of the 9/11 terrorist attacks, saw a moral equivalency between al Qaeda and the United States. Such thinking revolted him: "The hatred of America which drove the suicidal terrorists," said Dempsey, "doesn't flourish in a global vacuum."

Dempsey's increasing disaffection was fueled by his self-identification as ethnically Irish (he was, he claimed proudly, "one of the tens of millions of Americans with Irish ancestry"). He had arrived in Dublin in 1988 "with a sense of anticipation akin to a homecoming." This soon gave way to a deep pessimism when he realized "that the prevailing attitude in Ireland towards American foreign policy was not the friendly understanding and support I had every right to expect but an overtly-expressed contempt." Dempsey labored to change this state of affairs—with limited success, confirming his belief that anti-Americanism was innate to Irish political discourse.

A regular speaker, broadcaster and society dinner guest, until his self-imposed exile in 2003, Dempsey never fought shy of defending American policies and condemning their distortion in the Irish media. He was a man of considerable erudition and classical learning, and the foreclosure of "rational debate" in Ireland inspired him to open it—and forced on him the regrettable admission that he could not.

Timothy J. Lynch

See also: CLINTON, William Jefferson; FOREIGN POLICY, IRISH

Reference

Dempsey, George. *From the Embassy: A U.S. Foreign Policy Primer.* Dublin: Open Republic Institute, 2004.

DEMPSEY, JACK (1895–1983)

Jack Dempsey was born William Harrison Dempsey on June 14, 1895, in Manassa, Colorado, to Hyrum Dempsey, a rancher

Portrait of boxer Jack Dempsey. Considered one of America's first great sports heroes, Dempsey held the world heavyweight title between 1919 and 1926 (Library of Congress)

and shopkeeper, and Mary Celia (Smoot). Jack was one of eleven children, and the family moved from one western mining community to another, so that Jack (who was known as Harry until he began fighting professionally) never went to school beyond the eighth grade. Dempsey began his career as a saloon fighter, challenging all patrons to a fight. From 1911 to 1916, he tramped across the western United States, never earning more than was needed for basic survival. By late 1914 he was fighting professionally in Salt Lake City under the pseudonym "Kid Blackie." Known as "the Manassa Mauler," Dempsey quickly gained a reputation as a knockout artist and feared pugilist.

In 1916 Dempsey married Maxine Cates, a piano player and sometime prostitute fifteen years his senior; the union ended in divorce in 1919. In 1917 and 1918, Dempsey won a number of bouts against highly regarded heavyweights and signed on with Jack Kearns, an ex-fighter who became Dempsey's manager. Kearns took Dempsey east and introduced him to boxing promoter Tex Rickard, who recognized the potential windfall Dempsey could produce.

Dempsey would soon become one of America's first great sports heroes; his savage style captivated the public and made him as popular a figure as Babe Ruth or Red Grange. His legend was secured on July 4, 1919, at an outdoor arena in Toledo, Ohio, when Dempsey beat heavyweight champ Jess Willard. Temperatures in the ring reached 100 degrees that day, as Dempsey knocked the champ to the canvas seven times in the first round. The fight ended when Willard, nursing a broken jaw and two broken ribs, failed to answer the bell for the fourth round. Dempsey's reign as heavyweight champion had begun. A title defense against Georges Carpentier is widely regarded as boxing's first million-dollar gate. Profiled as a match between the Frenchman's civilized urbanity and Dempsey's savage ferocity, the bout was an instant sellout. A giant stadium constructed for the event housed seats for 80,000 who watched Dempsey dispatch the challenger in four rounds.

On September 14, 1923, Dempsey faced Argentina's Luis Angel Firpo at the Polo Grounds in New York. Known as the "Wild Bull of the Pampas," Firpo was dropped seven times in the first round; he gave as good as he got, though, flooring Dempsey twice in the first three minutes. But before the first round ended, the challenger sent Dempsey through the ropes

with a single right hand, silencing the 80,000 in attendance. Dempsey made it back into the ring, barely beating the ten-count. The fight ended 57 seconds into the second round with Dempsey a knockout winner.

Dempsey was a tremendously popular commodity, who cashed in on his fame and good looks by starring in several Hollywood movies. A constant fixture on the celebrity pages, Dempsey toured Europe and marketed himself as well as any contemporary athlete. In 1925, he moved to Los Angeles, where he met and married the actress Estelle Taylor. Their complicated and stormy relationship, coupled with Dempsey's growing independence, led to a split with Kearns.

After three years of inactivity, Dempsey defended his title against Gene Tunney on September 23, 1926, in Philadelphia. Rusty from the layoff, the six-foot-one-inch and 180-pound Dempsey received fewer points than the larger, more tactical Tunney. In a rematch on September 22, 1927, before the largest crowd ever to see a fight, Dempsey and Tunney met in Chicago's Soldier Field. For six rounds Tunney bested Dempsey, but in the seventh, a smashing punch sent the champ to the canvas. Instead of retiring to a neutral corner, Dempsey stood over the fallen Tunney, delaying the referee's count and allowing the champ precious time to recover. After some 17 seconds, the fight resumed and Tunney regained sufficiently to win the contest. This was Dempsey's last bout, and the controversy over the long count remains one of the most famous in the history of professional boxing.

Dempsey lost most of the fortune he had amassed in boxing during the stock market crash of 1929; for the next twelve years he eked out a meager existence by boxing in exhibitions and refereeing amateur bouts. He divorced his wife in 1930; three years later he married Hannah Williams. They had two daughters before the union dissolved in 1940. During World War II, Dempsey joined the Coast Guard, earning the rank of commander and directing that unit's physical fitness program. After the war, he retired to New York City, where he owned and operated a restaurant. Married to Deanna Piatelli in 1959, he lived happily with her until his death on May 31, 1983. In his 78 bout career, Dempsey compiled 49 knockouts, 25 of them in the first round. Elected to the International Boxing Hall of Fame in 1990, Dempsey is arguably the most well-known boxer of all time.

Tim Lynch

See also: TUNNEY, James Joseph "Gene"

References

Kahn, Roger. *A Flame of Pure Fire: Jack Dempsey and the Roaring Twenties.* New York: Harcourt, 1999.

Roberts, Randi. *Jack Dempsey: The Manassa Mauler.* Urbana: University of Illinois Press, 2003.

DERRANE, JOE (1930–)

Joe Derrane was born in Boston, Massachusetts, in 1930 to Irish immigrant parents. With a father from Inis Mór (the Aran Islands) and a mother from Roscommon, he exhibited a love for the accordion and traditional Irish music from a very early age. Around 1940, his parents sought tutelage for him on the ten-key melodeon with Jerry O'Brien (1899–1968), an accordionist who had immigrated from Kinsale, Co. Cork in the early 1920s. By the time Derrane was fourteen years old, O'Brien was bringing him along to perform at Irish "kitchen rackets"—a euphemism for popular parties of that time, held in homes or apartments, where dancing was usually confined to linoleum-floored kitchens to avoid damage to rugs or hardwood floors. By age 17, he had purchased a two-row chromatic diatonic instrument and had begun to perform steadily in the legendary ballroom scene in Roxbury, which boasted five dance halls dotting Dudley Street. He was also performing regularly on WVOM's original "Irish Hour," a live Sunday night radio program hosted by impresario Tommy Shields. His performances came to the attention of Justus DeWitt, owner of the Copley Records label, who invited him to make a recording. This would be the first of 16 solo sides on 78 rpm media. The recording series began at Ace Recording Studios on Boylston Street, Boston, while Derrane was still a senior at Roxbury's Mission High School. He also recorded with his accordion teacher, Jerry O'Brien, and with the All-Star Ceili Band, and the Irish All-Stars, which also featured his younger brother George (1932–2003) on tenor banjo.

By the late 1950s the showband era had taken hold, and a mass exodus to the suburbs had siphoned off a great portion of the former dance hall patrons. By 1960, the dance hall scene had all but collapsed, resulting in a major income drop for Derrane. With few venues left, and unwilling to perform in barrooms, Derrane sold his button box, took up piano accordion, and quickly adapted to new styles. He soon found himself solidly entrenched in the pop music field. By 1980, however, the piano accordion had lost its appeal to many people, and Derrane again had to make a transition, this time to piano/synthesizer keyboards in the Top 40 idiom. He and his son, Joe Jr., formed Nightlife, a popular group that featured Joe Jr. on bass guitar and vocals. Around 1990, Derrane retired from music altogether.

In 1993, Rego Records bought the rights to Derrane's 78 rpm recordings and reissued them on CD and cassette, sparking a new wave of interest in his music. He was invited to perform on button accordion at the prestigious Wolf Trap Irish Folk Festival in Vienna, Virginia. He had not performed on button box for more than thirty years; indeed, he did not even have one. Using a 15-key Walters (D/C#) recently given to him by his friend Jack Martin, he set about preparing a limited repertoire of eight tune medleys (with a few more in reserve) for what he viewed as one last performance for old times' sake, to be performed with the great piano accompanist Felix Dolan. On May 29, 1994, his stage performance at Wolf Trap before approximately 1,200 people drew standing ovations, and a career was reborn. His return to the button accordion is widely recognized as the greatest comeback in the history of Irish music. Since then, Derrane has recorded six new albums: *Give Us Another* and *Return To Inis Mor* for the Green Linnet label; *The Tie That Binds* for the Shanachie label; *Ireland's Harvest* with Frankie Gavin, *The Boston Edge* with Seamus Connolly and John McGann, and *The Man Behind The Box* with John McGann for the Mapleshade label.

In 1998 Derrane was inducted into the Comhaltas Ceoltoiri Eireann North American Province Hall of Fame in recognition of his impact on, and contribution to, Irish traditional music. In 2000, he was chosen by Chicago's *Irish-American News* as the Best Male Musician of the Decade 1990–2000 for outstanding achievement in Irish traditional music. In 2004, the National Endowment for the Arts chose Derrane as a National Fellowship recipient.

Susan Gedutis Lindsay

See also: MUSIC IN AMERICA, IRISH

Reference
Gedutis, Susan. *See You at the Hall: Boston's Golden Era of Irish Music and Dance.* Boston: Northeastern University Press, 2004.

DEVEREUX, JOHN (1778–1860)

Wexford-born John Devereux, thought by some to be a veteran of the 1798 rising at New Ross, was living in the 1810s in the United States in voluntary exile and as a US citizen. He joined a business firm in Baltimore, Maryland, from which he ran a cargo of coffee through the British blockade to France in 1812. In 1815, Devereux arrived in Cartagena, Colombia, from the United States with a cargo of arms just as Simón Bolívar was going into exile. Devereux then made an offer to the patriots to obtain support for them in Britain, where he alleged that he had many friends in parliament, and to raise an Irish Legion of 5,000 men with the requisite arms, ammunition, and military stores. He was to be paid $175 for each soldier he imported into Venezuela. Devereux untruthfully boasted that he was a general in the Irish army and had led the Irish Catholics in the fight for Emancipation. After a visit to Buenos Aires, where he tried to convince the authorities he could raise a loan of 2 million pesos backed by the U.S. government, he arrived in Haiti to stay with Robert Sutherland, a British merchant in Port au Prince. In July 1817 Sutherland forwarded to Bolívar "General" Devereux's offer to raise the Irish Legion, which he strongly recommended. Bolívar accepted the offer, and Devereux went to Ireland in 1818 and started recruitment for his legion.

Although many of the noncommissioned officers and privates recruited by Devereux were veterans, little care was exercised in selecting the best candidates, and nearly all who applied were accepted. The force was noted more for its bravery than for its discipline. Thousands of returned soldiers from the British army in France enlisted for service in Venezuela. They sought not only the certainty of an immediate livelihood but also the prospect of further excitement and adventure, and a chance of making their fortunes in South America. With Daniel O'Connell's support and the aid of the Irish Friends of South American Independence, Devereux sold commissions in his legion by forging a letter from Bolívar to give him the authority. O'Connell's son Morgan and a near relative from Ennis, Maurice, were among the officers.

The first contingent of Devereux's Irish Legion landed in Margarita between September and December 1819, and the rest arrived in Angostura (today's Ciudad Bolívar) in April and May 1820. From the beginning the expedition was plagued with problems as they were given little food and no pay. They suffered a number of mutinies, particularly after an attack on the Legion at Rio Hacha soon after they landed. This left huge casualties and afterwards most of the Irish were evacuated to Jamaica for shipment home.

The commander of the Irish Legion, Devereux himself, remained behind his men in England and Ireland, living sumptuously on the contributions of his dupes, until the return of some of those whom he had cheated exposed him to danger of being arrested or shot, so that he was forced at last to go. He landed on Margarita Island many months after his legion had departed. The Irish blamed the Venezuelan authorities for the terrible hardships they were forced to endure, but the responsibility should have been placed entirely on Devereux, who sent his troops off without making any arrangements for their reception, designated Margarita as their destination without consulting or notifying the military authorities of Venezuela, and above all, failed to accompany his men to look after their needs.

In Margarita, Devereux was received with great distinction by the governor Juan Bautista Arismendi. At a banquet in his honor, Devereux is reported to have spoken for two hours, promising that all Ireland was aroused in the cause of the South American patriots. It was an eloquent speech; however, its effect was somewhat marred by the fact that Devereux spoke in English, which none of his hearers was able to understand. In 1821 Bolívar confirmed Devereux in the grade of major general. He remained in military service for two years longer, and in December 1823 he was appointed Colombian envoy extraordinary to the courts of northern Europe. In 1825 he was arrested by the Austrian authorities and confined in Venice on charges of spying for the British. Devereux was eventually released, and he returned to the United States, where he lived upon a pension he received from the government of Venezuela. He returned to live in London, and died on February 25, 1860.

Edmundo Murray

See also: COLOMBIA; O'CONNELL, Daniel; O'LEARY, Daniel Florence; VENEZUELA

References

Hasbrouck, Alfred. *Foreign Legionaries in the Liberation of Spanish South America.* New York: Columbia University, 1928.

Lambert, Eric. "Irish Soldiers in South America, 1810–30." *The Irish Sword* 26, no. 62 (1984): 22–35.

DEVOY, JOHN (1842–1928)

Born in Kill, Co. Kildare, on September 3, 1842, Devoy joined the Irish Republican Brotherhood (IRB) at age eighteen. A year later, he enlisted in the French Foreign Legion and spent a year in Algeria. Upon his return to Ireland, Devoy was appointed the chief Fenian organizer for the British army, his mission being to recruit disaffected Irish soldiers from the British army in Ireland. He also arranged for the escape of the Fenian leader James Stephens from an English prison. In February 1866, however, Devoy was arrested and sentenced to 15 years penal servitude. He was released five years later on the condition that he settle outside the United Kingdom, so on January 18, 1871, Devoy arrived in New York City aboard the SS *Cuba* along with four other Fenian exiles, including Jeremiah O'Donovan Rossa.

Shortly after arriving in New York, Devoy got a job as a reporter for the *New York Herald* and later became its foreign editor. He also joined the Clan na Gael, a secret Irish-American revolutionary organization dedicated to achieving Irish independence. He quickly moved through the ranks, and in 1874, Devoy became chairman of a Clan na Gael rescue committee whose purpose was to free Fenian prisoners in Australia. To carry out this plan, Devoy purchased the whaling ship *Catalpa* and, on April, 1875, set out for Australia. On

Portrait of Fenian leader John Devoy. (Library of Congress)

April 18, 1876, six Fenian prisoners boarded the *Catalpa* and escaped their British captors, arriving in New York four months later. Upon their arrival, the escaped convicts were greeted with much fanfare, and this public defiance of British authority greatly boosted Clan na Gael's reputation.

Michael Davitt, the Irish radical agitator, undertook a tour of the United States in 1878 and was befriended by Devoy. Davitt and Devoy began a discussion that would eventually lead to a shift in the Irish and Irish-American nationalist movement. The "New Departure'" was an informal alliance among constitutional and physical force nationalists to work together peacefully under the leadership of Charles Stewart Parnell. In 1882, Devoy founded the newspaper, the *Irish Nation,* and published the *Land of Eire,* his account of the Land League movement in Ireland and America. He also devoted himself to several other projects, including financing the construction of the *Fenian Ram,* a failed experimental submarine by John Holland, the later inventor of the first modern-day submarine. Devoy and Clan na Gael were racked by internal strife and faction throughout the rest of the 1880s and 1890s.

In 1900, Devoy, together with longtime ally Daniel Cohalan, reorganized the Clan na Gael. Devoy founded the newspaper the *Gaelic American* in 1903 and for the next 20 years, he would remain at the forefront of Irish-American nationalism, contributing and participating in every major effort and campaign for Irish freedom. Thomas Clarke, the former Fenian, came to New York in 1901 and worked for Devoy before returning to Ireland to begin reorganizing the IRB in 1907. Devoy also provided financial support for Arthur Griffith's *United Irishman* and contributed to Patrick Pearse's school, St. Edna's.

With the outbreak of World War I and the belief that "England's difficulty was Ireland's opportunity," Devoy was at the forefront of the conspiracy that led to the Easter Rising of 1916. Devoy, together with Sir Roger Casement, came into contact with the German ambassador to the United States and was able to obtain a promise of 20,000 German rifles to support the rebellion. However, a miscommunication between Devoy and those in Ireland led to the arms languishing off the coast of Ireland for two days on the German ship *Aud* before the captain scuttled the boat and arms after being discovered by a British patrol. Despite this failure, the leaders of the rebellion carried through with their plans, but were eventually crushed by the British. After the establishment of Dáil Éireann and the outbreak of the Anglo-Irish War in 1919, Devoy welcomed the president of the Dáil Éireann, Eamon de Valera, on his fund-raising tour to America. Relations between the two men quickly soured because of de Valera's belief that he should have direct control of Irish and Irish-American efforts for Ireland. Specifically, de Valera and his supporters wanted the money raised during his tour to be sent directly to the Dáil while Devoy and Cohalan favored using the money to win support for Ireland in the United States and to oppose Woodrow Wilson's League of Nations. After the signing of the Anglo-Irish Treaty in 1921, Devoy supported the treaty, seeing it as a necessary first step in the movement toward Irish independence.

Devoy visited Ireland in 1924 as a guest of the Irish Free State. He died on September 29, 1928, in Atlantic City, New Jersey, unmarried and nearly penniless. His remains were taken to Ireland, and he was buried in Glasnevin Cemetery, Dublin.

Ely Janis

See also: CASEMENT, Roger; COHALAN, Daniel; DAVITT, Michael; DE VALERA, Eamon

References

Devoy, John. *Recollections of an Irish Rebel.* New York: Chase P. Young & Co., 1929.

Golway, Terry. *Irish Rebel: John Devoy and America's Fight for Irish Freedom.* New York: St. Martin's Press, 1998.

Ryan, Desmond. *The Phoenix Flame: A Study of Fenianism and John Devoy.* London: A Barker, 1937.

Ryan, Desmond, and William O'Brian, eds. *Devoy's Post Bag, 1871–1928,* 2 vols. Dublin: Fallon, 1948.

DILLON, PATRICK JOSEPH (1842–1889)

Born 1842 in Tuam, Co. Galway to John Dillon and Julia Rign(e)y, Patrick Joseph Dillon went to school in Banagher and then entered All Hallows in Dublin to study for the priesthood. He was ordained in Dublin on October 25, 1863, and arrived in Argentina a few weeks later. Initially, he was appointed the Irish chaplain in Merlo and later in Cañuelas. At the end of 1865, Father Dillon traveled on mission to the Falkland/Malvinas Islands to attend the Catholic residents. A year later, he was appointed as professor of theology, canon law, and sacred scripture in the diocesan seminary. In 1869 Dillon was made canon of the cathedral of Buenos Aires and accompanied Archbishop Escalada as a theological consultant to Rome and the first Vatican Council. He returned to Argentina and in 1871 replaced Anthony Fahy, O.P., as principal Irish chaplain in Buenos Aires. Dillon opened St. Brigid's chapel in La Choza in 1872, and a year later was named chaplain of the Irish Hospital in Buenos Aires and of the Irish Sisters of Mercy. In 1876 he founded St. George's school for boys of Irish and other English-speaking families.

The first issue of the *Southern Cross* was distributed in Buenos Aires on January 16, 1875, and was characterized by its founder, Dillon as "Catholic and Irish." The main English-language paper at the time, the *Standard,* was British-oriented despite being owned by Irish-born brothers Edward and Michael G. Mulhall. Therefore, Dillon decided to create a paper to represent Irish-Catholic interests. Since 1875 the *Southern Cross* has served as the main record of the Irish-Argentine community. Dillon remained its editor until 1882.

Dillon participated in several political activities and groups, all of them within the social circles of the growing Irish-Argentine landed elite. On March 1, 1879, during a meeting led by Dillon, the General Brown Club was founded to put forward candidates at the provincial and national elections. Some of the club's goals were economic reform, encouragement of European immigration, and the moral restoration of the gauchos (the cowboys of the pampas). With the sponsorship of the most conservative political forces, Patrick J. Dillon and Eduardo Murphy were elected members of parliament in the province of Buenos Aires. In 1883 Dillon was elected national senator representing Buenos Aires province. Some historians argue that Dillon was more popular with the rich than with the poor among the Irish in Argentina. He is also accused of having been too much involved in politics for a priest. Dillon had to face conflicts with a group of women in the community who wished to have independent management for Irish charities. In 1879 Mary Brennan (née Colclough), of the Ladies' Irish Beneficent Society, complained that Dillon refused to turn over a large sum of money belonging to the society. Others disapproved of his maneuvering to auction the properties of the St. Patrick's Society. In all of these cases the *Southern Cross* was effectively used to support Dillon's position.

Through his influential positions in politics, the press, and official religion, Dillon played an important role in the government policy to attract massive immigration from Europe to Argentina in the 1880s. On April 18, 1881, parliament commissioned Dillon to promote emigration from Ireland. He went to Europe on an official mission and returned in January 1882.

His recommendations to the government included the payment of tickets to attract emigrants, as well as granting lands and facilitating internal transport. Dillon committed himself to travel back to Ireland to personally guarantee the success of the project. As a result, with the support of President Juarez Celman, the government decided to grant 50,000 free or assisted tickets to European emigrants. In this context occurred the tragic episode that would become known as the Dresden Affair of 1889. Dillon's role in the Dresden Affair is unclear. His brother, John Stephen Dillon, was appointed as one of the immigration agents in Ireland and was paid a bonus plus commissions from the shipping companies. The steamer *City of Dresden* was crowded with poor emigrants mainly from Irish cities. They arrived at Buenos Aires on February 1889, but many of them died during the crossing, while others re-emigrated or vanished after a few years in Argentina.

Early in 1889, Dillon returned to Ireland because of ill health, and died in Dublin on June 11, 1889. He was buried in Glasnevin, near Daniel O'Connell's monument.

Edmundo Murray

See also: DRESDEN AFFAIR; FAHY, Anthony; FALKLANDS/MALVINAS ISLANDS; PRESS, THE IRISH IN LATIN AMERICA; MULHALL, Michael George

References

Coghlan, Eduardo A. *Los Irlandeses en la Argentina: Su Actuación y Descendencia.* Buenos Aires, 1987.

Marshall, Oliver. *The English-Language Press in Latin America.* London: Institute of Latin American Studies, 1996.

Murray, Thomas. *The Story of the Irish in Argentina.* New York: P. J. Kenedy & Sons, 1919.

"Número del Centenario." Special issue. *The Southern Cross* (1975).

"Special Golden Jubilee Number 1875–1925." Special issue. *The Southern Cross* (1925).

DIPLOMATIC RELATIONS, IRISH–LATIN AMERICAN

Relations between Irish authorities and Latin American governments have been driven by consular, economic, political and, more recently, trade factors. The lack of an articulated Irish policy on Latin America until the last decades of the twentieth century is evidence of the changing priorities of foreign affairs in Ireland.

During the nineteenth century and the first years of the twentieth century, Ireland's foreign affairs were handled by the English government. Therefore, the diplomatic representation of the Irish throughout Latin America was in the charge of British consuls. The British presence in the area intensified during the independence period (1806–1825), and the consuls had to deal with a diversity of situations, in particular the protection of English subjects and their property, as well the delicate relations with the weakening Spanish colonial administrations. Irish settlers in the River Plate and Brazil, and ex-soldiers in Venezuela, Colombia, Ecuador, and Mexico were increasingly relating to other English subjects through the consuls, who issued passports, arbitrated disputes, and registered some private events (such as birth, marriage, and death records, a responsibility of the Roman Catholic, Anglican, and other churches). The network of British consulates and vice consulates was extended in the second half of the nineteenth century with the development of railways, mining companies, cold-storage plants, and other British-owned businesses.

Among the Irish-born British consuls, Robert Gore (1820–1854), of Saunders Court, Co. Wexford, was appointed chargé d'affaires at Montevideo (1846) and Buenos Aires (1851) and played an important role during the last years of Juan Manuel de Rosas's government in Buenos Aires. Thomas J. Hutchinson, vice consul in Montevideo and then in Rosario, had a heroic role as a physician during the cholera outbreak of 1867. Hutchinson published geographical and economic essays about Argentina, Paraguay, and Peru. In 1906, Roger Casement (1864–1916) accepted the consular post in Rio de Janeiro and other Brazilian cities until 1911. He investigated and made charges against the Peruvian Amazon Company and its brutal exploitation of Putumayo indigenous people in Amazonian Colombia, Ecuador, and Peru. Casement calculated that in the first decade of the twentieth century at least 30,000 natives had been directly murdered or killed by deliberate starvation. He was knighted for his services.

When the young American republics developed their diplomatic representations in Europe in the mid-nineteenth century, some of them established honorary consulates in Dublin and Liverpool under the supervision of the ambassadors in London. In the early 1860s, the consul of Buenos Aires in Dublin was Michael O'Brien, who returned to Argentina in May 1864. In the 1880s, at the time of the Dresden Affair, the Argentine embassy in the United Kingdom had consuls in Dublin and Cork, who worked together with government agents to sign up immigrants to Argentina.

In the first decades of the twentieth century the Irish declared their independence from England. Swiftly, the new government procured direct diplomatic relations with the United States and Argentina. The members of the first Dáil Éireann (1919–1922) recognized that in both countries, probably owing to the existence of influential Irish communities, it would be relatively easier to obtain international recognition and financial support, as well as to develop direct trade for the new state. On May 6, 1919, Eamon Bulfin (1892–1968) was appointed as representative to the government of the Argentine Republic; this was the first-ever mission of the Irish diplomatic service. Bulfin, who began working in Buenos Aires in March 1920, established a contact network with government officials and Irish-Argentine leaders. He also launched the Irish Fund to raise funds for Ireland, and negotiated shipments of ammunitions for the Irish Republican Army. In 1921 the Republic had eight representatives, two of them in Latin America (Bulfin in Argentina and Frank W. Egan in Chile). On July 25, 1921, Laurence Ginnell (1852–1923) arrived in Buenos Aires to help raise a loan for the Republic. He met with the Argentine foreign minister, Honorio Pueyrredon, and effectively campaigned among Irish Argentines in Buenos Aires and the provinces. Ginnell remained in Argentina until April 1922, when he joined the second Dáil as the only anti-Treatyite member. Patrick J. Little was the third diplomatic envoy to South America, after his mission in South Africa. He visited Argentina, Chile, and Brazil. In his report of December 4, 1921, Little observed that the Irish in South America were prejudiced against diplomatic missions from Ireland, because there was a shared belief that the Irish only went there for money and did not care about what happened to the emigrants.

In Chile, Frank Egan was an effective representative to the authorities. He had good connections in government and society and actively used Irish propaganda in the Chilean press. Both in Chile and Argentina, the Irish envoys had to counterbalance the strong British influence in railways, meat exports, mining, and trade. Patrick J. Little also reported a network of unofficial representatives and informers in Latin American countries, including Donald Buckley and John Tobin in Brazil, Richard Nicholls in Bolivia, James O'Durnin in Paraguay, and William Morgan in Uruguay.

In 1923, Ireland's representative to the League of Nations, Michael MacWhite, intensively cultivated Irish–Latin American historical links. He was successful in this policy, and by 1930 Ireland was able to canvas support from the Latin American republics at Geneva and was elected to the League of Nations as a nonpermanent member. However, formal diplomatic relations between Ireland and Latin America were not established until 1947, when an Irish commercial mission led by L. H. Kerney went to Argentina to buy wheat. A chargé d'affaires, Matthew Murphy, was appointed in December 17, 1947. In early 1964, the mission was upgraded to ambassador level, and Michael Leo Skentelberry was appointed as the first ambassador. One of the most complete and detailed reports on the Irish Argentines that exists (July 22, 1958) was sent to Dublin by Timothy Horan, the chargé d'affaires in 1955–1959; it included a complete description of the community and their attitudes and social divisions. Among the Argentine envoys in Ireland, Lorenzo McGovern was the first Irish Argentine to be appointed to the mission in Dublin (1955).

Peadar Kirby remarked that the opening of relations with Argentina had more to do with historical links with that country than with any particular Irish interest in Latin America. In fact, it was not until the Irish foreign service was expanded after European Community (EC) membership in 1973 that Ireland established diplomatic relations with Brazil (1975) and Mexico (1977). Exceptions to the fluctuating Irish policy in Latin America have been the support to human rights solidarity groups in Nicaragua and El Salvador in the 1980s and the support to removing EC economic sanctions on Argentina during the Falklands-Malvinas War in 1982. When it failed to get a unified EC decision, Ireland (together with Italy) broke ranks in refusing to continue with the sanctions, a stand warmly welcomed and still remembered in Argentina.

Edmundo Murray

See also: BULFIN, Eamon; CASEMENT, Roger; DRESDEN AFFAIR; FALKLAND/MALVINAS ISLANDS

References

Ferns, H. S. *Britain and Argentina in the Nineteenth Century.* Oxford: Clarendon Press, 1960.

Kennedy, Michael. "'Mr. Blythe, I Think, Hears from him Occasionally': The Experiences of Irish Diplomats in Latin America, 1919–23." In *Irish Foreign Policy 1919–1966: From Independence to Internationalism,* edited by Michael Kennedy and J. M. Skelly. Dublin: Four Courts Press, 2000: 44–60.

Kirby, Peadar. *Ireland and Latin America: Links and Lessons.* Dublin: Trócaire, 1992.

DOMESTIC SERVANTS, IRISH

During the nineteenth century, an expanding American middle class led to a greater demand for female domestic servants. As a result, English-speaking immigrant women without any training or experience could readily find employment in American homes. The majority of domestic servants in the United States during the nineteenth century were either African Americans (slaves in the southern states before Emancipation, and free blacks in the Northern states) or Irish immigrants. Domestic servants contributed essential labor to the household and, equally important, were also a symbol of social status for their employers. While conditions varied among employers and from rural to urban households, Irish domestic servants often worked in isolation, and the treatment they received in the households where they lived underscored their low social status.

Although some Irish women had worked as domestics in Ireland before immigrating, they were unfamiliar with American household practices and unprepared for the frequent isolation of their new life. (Male Irish immigrants were rarely employed as domestic workers; male domestic servants in nineteenth-century America were usually African American.) Many Irish women came from a background of rural poverty and were accustomed to a very limited diet, to preparing food on a turf fire, and to living with sparse furnishings in a tiny home. They did not have the knowledge required to cook in middle-class American kitchens or to clean multiple rooms filled with elaborate Victorian knickknacks and furnishings. Their employers, almost invariably Protestants, were often uncomfortable with, if not hostile to their hires' Catholicism and were sometimes unwilling to allow Irish employees time to attend Catholic services.

Nonetheless, the benefits of "living out" or "going into service" far outweighed the downsides for most Irish female immigrants. Historian Hasia R. Diner has noted that nineteenth-century white domestics could earn 50 percent more than saleswomen and 25 percent more than textile works; did not have to pay for food, housing, shelter, heat, water, or transportation; and lived in comfortable, pleasant homes as opposed to the overcrowded, unsanitary tenements occupied by factory workers. As a result of their relatively high pay and low living expenses, Irish women could save up to several thousand dollars as domestics, most of which they sent home to their impoverished families. In fact, most of the money remitted by Irish immigrants to post-Famine Ireland came not from men but from women, many of whom were also able to earn enough to later establish their own households in the United States. This, in addition, gave Irish women a greater degree of autonomy than many female immigrants from other countries, who not only lacked English skills but also were often discouraged or prevented by their families from working outside the home. The Catholic Church in the United States also benefited from the piety and industriousness of these women—many Catholic churches were built in large part with donations from the earnings of Irish female domestics.

Such was the demand for female domestics that most American employers were as dependent upon their Irish servants as these women were upon them. In fact, in many cases, it was the Irish domestic who held the upper hand, aware of the demand for her labor. Nineteenth-century households were usually large, and for any woman who could afford to hire help, shouldering the huge burden of cleaning, cooking, laundry, and child-rearing on her own was not practical. As Irish domestics became an all but ubiquitous fixture of middle- and upper-class American homes, employers were forced into the often uncomfortable position of having to tolerate members of an alien culture and religion living under the same roof. Many Americans also grumbled about their hires' self-importance. One employer complained that when her sister was ill, their Irish maid refused to bring the woman her meal on a tray, saying that she had not been hired as a nurse. It was not uncommon for women's magazines of the era to carry articles advising how to cope with the incompetence and quirks of one's Irish maid or cook, as well as short stories and jokes lampooning "Bridget's" shortcomings as a housekeeper, her quaint Irish accent and turns of phrase, and her "superstitious" Catholic practices. American magazines of the era, such as *Godey's Lady's Book,* and popular domestic novels with titles such as *That Bridget of Ours!,* generally portrayed Irish domestics as garrulous and good-hearted, but also dim-witted and incompetent.

It is worth contrasting briefly the attitudes of American employers toward African-American domestics as opposed to Irish servants. Not surprisingly, some employers preferred to hire African-American domestics, not only because they would work for less pay but also because black servants were often perceived as more "cheerful," "obedient," and "agreeable" by employers than their Irish coworkers. The African-American scholar and activist W. E. B. DuBois, in an 1899 study of black domestic servants in Philadelphia, quoted one employer: "If you get a good class of colored people they are the most faithful, honest and biddable servants in the world." DuBois observed, "This docility which is a recognized trait of the Negro character has doubtless been developed by slavery, and it is not unlikely that it has been still further cultivated in these later days by their knowledge that losing their places in service may mean inability to get work of any kind for an indefinite period." Unlike African-American domestics, Irish women knew that they generally had more choices and could demand more pay; consequently, many refused to tolerate poor treatment.

As might be expected, Irish female domestics themselves had a very different view of their work experiences than their employers. The Irish-born author Mary Anne Sadlier drew on her experiences as a domestic in American homes in her novels such as *Bessy Conway: or, an Irish Girl Living in New York.* Sadlier, a deeply devout Catholic, used her novels to warn her readership of the potential pitfalls they faced in their new homeland, including such temptations as missing Mass, drinking alcohol, or going dancing rather than attending to their employers' needs. "The father and mother who suffer their young daughters to come out unprotected to America in search of imaginary goods," said Sadlier, "would rather see them laid in their graves than lose sight of them, did they know the dangers which beset their path in the New World." While Sadlier's words were doubtless somewhat hyperbolic, her novels reveal that Irish female domestics were keenly aware of their lower social status and the necessity not only of learning to thrive in a new, alien culture but also of keeping their traditional values and religious faith intact as a source of strength. Unlike their American employers, who often viewed hiring an Irish domestic as an unwelcome necessity, for Irish immigrant women going into service was a welcome opportunity to better their lives and those of their loved ones in Ireland.

Eventually, as the Irish became further assimilated to the larger American culture and had more opportunities open to them, fewer Irish women chose to go into service. The United States' eventual entry into World War I was the biggest factor in the decline in the number of domestic servants generally, not because middle-class women did not continue to clamor for servants, but because the war opened up a wider range of occupations to female workers, such as clerical work. As the twentieth century progressed, the decline in domestic servants was also furthered by the proliferation of domestic appliances. However, the decline in the numbers of all women entering domestic service can be attributed mostly to the advantages the new types of employment offered women over domestic work: higher wages, more independence, often better working conditions, and more interesting and challenging work.

Danielle Maze

See also: EMIGRATION

References

Diner, Hasia R. *Erin's Daughters in America: Irish Immigrant Women in the Nineteenth Century.* Baltimore, MD: Johns Hopkins University Press, 1984.

DuBois, W. E. B. *The Philadelphia Negro.* New York: Lippincott, 1899.

Milner, Nina. "Savoir Faire: Documenting the Immigrant Experience." Canada Library and Archives. www.collectionscanada.ca/ bulletin/015017–0101–11–e.html (accessed January 7, 2004).

Morris, Charles R. *American Catholic.* New York: Vintage, 1997.

Wilson, Harriet. *Our Nig: or, Sketches from the Life of a Free Black.* Boston: Rand & Avery, 1859.

DONGAN, THOMAS (1634–1715)

Thomas Dongan was the first Irish Catholic governor of New York. Born in 1634, at Casletown Kildrought, now Cellbridge, Co. Kildare, Thomas Dongan was the youngest son of Sir John Dongan, baronet and member of the Irish Parliament. Devoted to the Stuarts, after the death of Charles I, the family removed to France, where Thomas served in an Irish regiment of the French army under Turenne, rising to the rank of colonel in 1674. After the Treaty of Nimeguen (1678), he returned to England and, through the influence of the Duke of York—a fellow officer under Turenne—was appointed lieutenant governor of Tangiers.

In 1682, with the province of New York bankrupt and in a state of rebellion, James, Duke of York, appointed Dongan as its governor. Arriving in 1683, Dongan was well received by Manhattan's Anglo-Dutch oligarchs, who, it seems, admired his "knowledge, refinement, and modesty." Dongan began his administration by convening the first representative assembly of New York Province on October 14, 1683. The eighteen assembly members met for three weeks at Fort James; their main accomplishment being a "Charter of Libertyes and Privileges." This charter defined the form of government for the colony, recognized basic political and personal rights (such as trial by jury and no taxation without representation), and affirmed religious liberty for Christians. It also divided the colony into twelve "shires" or counties and, as in England, these were to be the basic units of local government. Dongan further issued a new charter for the government of New York, known as Dongan's Charter, which made New York a self-governing corporation, one of little more than a dozen communities ever incorporated in British America. In 1685, with the Duke of York's ascension to the throne as King James II, he would form a new super-colony incorporating all of New England, plus New York, New Jersey, and Pennsylvania, thus disallowing New York's Charter of Libertyes and its provincial legislature. However, the charter's presence would continue to be felt throughout the eighteenth century, as New York colonists used its system of government as a program for continuous political agitation. Indeed, many of its principles passed into the framework of American federal government.

Dongan also established the boundary lines of the New York colony by settling disputes with Connecticut on the east, Canada on the north, and Pennsylvania on the south. And, in 1684, in a treaty with the Indians at Albany, New York, Dongan obtained the written submission of the Iroquois to the Great Sachem Charles, and outlined the policy that would keep the Five Nations friends of England and a barrier between French and English possessions in North America. However, by this time, there was growing unrest toward Dongan in New York. Not only was he giving baronial land grants to a select group of favored insiders, and lining his own pockets along the way (in Manhattan he used dummy partners to accumulate hefty slices of real estate along both sides of the city wall), but his public demonstration and support of his Catholic faith rankled the largely Protestant citizenry. Several Jesuit priests had accompanied Dongan to New York and, for the first time in the city's history, mass had been celebrated in Fort James. Further, Dongan had appointed Catholics to strategic positions in his administration and authorized Jesuits to open a Roman Catholic school.

However, before any of this began to seriously affect Dongan's administration, Sir Edmund Andros (a former governor of the New York colony) returned to New York in 1688; on the authority of King James II, he removed Dongan from office, broke the provincial seal, seized all provincial records, and hoisted the flag of New England over the fort. Refusing command of a regiment with the rank of major general, Dongan retired to his estate on Staten Island until anti-Catholic prejudice (after the overthrow of James II in 1689) forced him to flee to England. With the death of his brother in 1698, Dongan became the second earl of Limerick. However, failing to recover his ancestral lands from anti-Catholic confiscation, Dongan died a poor man on December 14, 1715.

James P. Byrne

See also: NEW YORK CITY

References
Burrows, Edwin G., and Mike Wallace. *Gotham: A History of New York City to 1898.* New York: Oxford University Press, 1999.
Driscoll, John T. "Thomas Dongan." From the *Catholic Encyclopedia.* www.catholicity.com/encyclopedia/d/dongan,thomas.html (accessed June 30, 2007).
Harrell, Joy. "Dongan, Thomas." In *The Encyclopedia of the Irish in America.* Ed. Michael Glazier. Notre Dame, IN: University of Notre Dame Press, 1999: 219.

DONLEAVY, J. P. (1926–)

James Patrick Donleavy was born on April 23, 1926, in Brooklyn, New York, to parents who were Irish immigrants. After serving in the United States Navy during World War II, Donleavy applied to a number of American colleges, but because of his poor academic record he was turned down. Eventually accepted by Trinity College Dublin, he spent three years there, ostensibly studying microbiology but in reality spending much of his time frequenting Dublin's pubs and meeting many of its literary figures, among them the writer

Portrait of author J. P. Donleavy, who is best known for his first novel The Ginger Man. *(Library of Congress)*

Brendan Behan. Training as a painter before he became a writer, he exhibited paintings in several Dublin galleries. In 2006 a sixty-year retrospective of his paintings was held at the Molesworth Gallery in Dublin. As well as his own Irish ancestry, Donleavy said that one of the principal reasons for his settling in Ireland and becoming an Irish citizen in 1967 was because of the country's policy of exempting writers from paying income tax.

Donleavy is best known for his first novel *The Ginger Man* (1950). Set in Ireland just after World War II, it tells the story of Sebastian Dangerfield, a young American of Irish descent who is a thinly fictionalized version of Donleavy himself. Like the author, Dangerfield is a student at Trinity College Dublin where he leads a rowdy, drunken existence based on fornication and philosophizing. In his autobiographical *The History of the Ginger Man* (1994),

Donleavy recounted how his friend Gainor Stephen Crist was also one of the models for Dangerfield. In the same book, Donleavy detailed the complex circumstances of the novel's publication. Because of its bawdy content, Donleavy had trouble finding a publisher for the novel. On Behan's advice, he submitted it to Maurice Girodias at the Olympia Press, a Parisian publishing house, which as well as publishing writers such as Henry Miller and Samuel Beckett also published pornographic novels. Donleavy was shocked to find his novel published as part of the Traveler's Companion Series, the publisher's series of pornographic novels. Because of the damage being associated with such novels might do to his career, Donleavy sued the publishers. The case was settled twenty-two years later when Donleavy purchased Olympia Press. Upon its publication, the novel was banned in Ireland and the United States because of obscenity. Since it was first published the novel has sold more than 45 million copies in two dozen languages, and it was included in the Modern Library's Best 100 Novels of the 20th Century. In 2005 it was reprinted in its first Irish-only edition.

Although Donleavy's reputation mainly rests on his debut novel, he has written many other works. His other novels include *The Saddest Summer of Samuel S* (1966), *The Beastly Beatitudes of Balthazar B* (1970), *The Onion Eaters* (1971), and *The Destinies of Darby Dancer, Gentleman* (1977). Another novel, *A Fairy Tale of New York*, is frequently cited as being the inspiration for the popular Christmas song of the same name, which was recorded by The Pogues and Kirsty MacColl. He has also published nonfiction, including *The Unexpurgated Code: A Complete Manual of Survival & Manners* and *De Alphonse Tennis:*

The Superlative Game of Eccentric Champions. Several of his novels have been adapted for the stage, and a collection of his short stories, *Meet My Maker the Mad Molecule,* has also been published. He wrote, narrated, and was featured in a television documentary entitled *J. P. Donleavy's Ireland in All Her Sins and Graces* (1992) which was coproduced by the Discovery Channel and the Irish national broadcaster RTÉ. Based on his book of the same title, the documentary featured the author traveling around Ireland and reading passages from his work. The documentary won the Worldfest Houston Gold Award in 1992 and a Cine Golden Eagle in 1993.

Donleavy currently lives alone in Levington House, an old mansion on the outskirts of Mullingar, Co. Westmeath. Dressed in his tweed suits, he has long been a recognizable figure in Ireland. After previous failed attempts, a film adaptation of "The Ginger Man" starring Johnny Depp and directed by Laurence Dunmore is said to be in the works.

David Doyle

References
Donleavy, J. P. *The Ginger Man.* New York: Atlantic Monthly Press, 1988.
Donleavy, J. P. *The History of the Ginger Man.* New York: Houghton Mifflin, 1994.
Ryan, John. *Remembering How We Stood: Bohemian Dublin at the Mid Century.* New York: Taplinger, 1975.
Shea, Peter G. "J. P. Donleavy." In *The Encyclopedia of the Irish in America.* Ed. Michael Glazier. Notre Dame: University of Notre Dame, 1999.

DONOVAN, GERARD (1959–)

Gerard Donovan was born in 1959 in Wexford, Ireland, and grew up in Galway. Donovan studied at Trinity College Dublin, and at Johns Hopkins University in Baltimore, Maryland. He has taught at Johns Hopkins and the University of Arkansas and is currently teaching at Southampton College in New York, dividing his time between New York and Ireland. Best known as a poet, Donovan has also published numerous short stories and two intriguing novels. The collections are published by Salmon Press and include *Columbus Rides Again* (1992), *Kings and Bicycles* (1995), and *The Lighthouse* (2000). The latter collection was short-listed for the prestigious *Irish Times* Literature Prize.

Donovan's poems are difficult to classify and cover a range of topics and approaches. While some are distinctly grappling with the conflict of belonging to two different nationalisms ("They Write," "On a Trawler to the Mainland," "Suitcase Poems"), others are historical ponderings about the postcolonial condition ("Columbus Rides Again," "Caribbean Queen," "The Reykjavik Wife"). Some are deeply personal ("The Fate of Mothers," "Having Forgotten to Water the Anniversary Flowers," "Anniversary: To a Father") while others speak of place ("Two Seasons in Connemara," "Long Island Rush Hour Report," "Mr. Henderson's Bicycle Shop"). In *The Lighthouse,* however, Donovan has framed the collection with poems that have differing perspectives about lighthouses, and somehow the lighthouses come to represent the border between the elements he considers to be at work in his life. The lighthouses are the space between countries, between land and sea, between those who travel and those who are immobile, between light and dark. Their position as bookends, with such a variety of poems in between, serves to nicely define the way that Donovan situates his poetry.

Donovan's novels have much of the poetic about them. His first novel,

Schopenhauer's Telescope (2003), is an unusual and unsettling book that demonstrates Donovan's interest in the overlap between the mundane and the horrible. Set during a civil war somewhere in Europe, the two characters speak while one of them digs a hole in a field in the middle of winter; the purpose for the hole is veiled but sinister. The Baker and the Teacher discuss the relevance of history, telling details of historical tales via various narrative devices, while they are watched by a group of citizens who are held at gunpoint on the field's edge. The novel won the Kerry Group Irish Fiction award, and was long-listed for the Booker Prize.

His second novel, *Dr. Salt* (2005), is a satirical look at the way American culture deals with emotions (or refuses to deal with emotions) and the way pharmaceutical companies try to erase any possible emotions with chemicals. Alternately hilarious, horrifying, and sad, the book follows the life of a character who has never been allowed to grieve for the events of his life, and whose efforts to find help through doctors and drugs have all failed.

In all of his work so far, Donovan takes us through the range of emotions himself, so that we laugh at the same time that we think, and we cry while we relish the manipulation of the words on the page. It is not work to be skimmed through, but to be carefully considered. Rather, it is, as he says, in "The Body Lights," as the lighthouse: "Its steel steps draft short breaths."

Kathleen A. Heininge

References

Donovan, Gerard. *Columbus Rides Again*. Co. Clare: Salmon Press, 1992.

Donovan, Gerard. *Dr. Salt*. Great Britain: Scribner, 2006.

Donovan Gerard. *Kings and Bicycles*. Co. Clare: Salmon Press, 1995.

Donovan Gerard. *The Lighthouse*. Co. Clare: Salmon Press, 2000.

Donovan Gerard. *Schopenhauer's Telescope*. Great Britain: Scribner, 2003.

DORSEY, THOMAS FRANCIS "TOMMY" (1905–1956)

Thomas Francis "Tommy" Dorsey was a prominent swing/big band leader who helped to define the genre and became one of its most successful practitioners. Dorsey was born in 1905 to Thomas Francis Dorsey, Sr., and Theresa Langton Dorsey. Thomas Sr., in addition to being a coal miner, was also the town bandleader in Lansford, Pennsylvania, and acted as a music instructor to his sons, Tommy and Jimmy. Tommy and his brother experimented with several instruments before Tommy focused on the trombone and Jimmy focused on the cornet and saxophone. The brothers began to form various outfits to showcase their talents, including such acts as Dorsey's Novelty Six and Dorsey's Wild Canaries in the early 1920s. Their paths, although sometimes separated, would continue to cross often over the next three decades.

Together the brothers first garnered widespread attention as The Dorsey Brothers Orchestra, recording for Okeh Records in the late 1920s. Before this the two brothers had relocated to New York City as session musicians. In 1934 they signed to Decca Records, where they enjoyed several hits, including "Lullaby of Broadway," which featured Bob Crosby, Bing's younger brother; the Dorseys had worked with Bing on "Let's Do It (Let's Fall in Love)." Tommy left the band in the spring of 1935 to embark on a solo career.

Recording mostly for RCA Victor, Dorsey would find incredible success as a

Portrait of Tommy Dorsey playing the saxophone.
(Corbis)

solo act throughout the remainder of the decade, with such hits as "Marie" and "On Treasure Island." Over the years his orchestra would feature such names as Gene Krupa, Buddy Rich, Jack Leonard, Connie Haines, and Frank Sinatra. Dorsey also successfully hosted a radio program, "The Tommy Dorsey Show" in which he was faithfully introduced as '"the Sentimental Gentleman of Swing," a moniker that would stay with him throughout the rest of his career. Despite a musicians' strike that prevented acts from recording in the early 1940s, Dorsey still managed to score numerous top-ten hits with songs recorded before the strike, including "There Are Such Things." Dorsey was also featured, along with an ever-changing lineup in his orchestra, in such motion pictures as *Las Vegas Nights, Ship Ahoy, Presenting Lily Mars,* and *Girl Crazy* in the 1940s and 1950s.

Dorsey would also find fame on television. His brother Jimmy joined Tommy's orchestra in 1953, which was soon again billed as the Dorsey Brothers Band. In 1954 they were given the opportunity to host their own television show, *Stage Show.* Along with featuring the brothers and their orchestra, the show was a national showcase for numerous acts, including, in 1956, the first nationally broadcast appearances of Elvis Presley.

Dorsey passed away in 1956 at the age of 51; his brother Jimmy died at the age of 53 the following year. Throughout his career Tommy Dorsey became one of the most successful names in the big band era. Dorsey proved to be one of the most commercially viable practitioners of the genre, while also acting as a mentor of sorts for artists who would become influential in the following decades, like Sinatra and numerous others. Dorsey's combination of jazz and sentimentality made him famous not only in his own lifetime but also long after; like others such as Benny Goodman, Count Basie, and Glen Miller, Dorsey became one of the legendary names of big band music.

Mathew Joseph Bartkowiak

See also: CROSBY, Bing

References
Sanford, Herb. *Tommy and Jimmy: The Dorsey Years.* New Rochelle, NY: Arlington House, 1972.
Stockdale, Robert L. *Tommy Dorsey: On the Side.* Metuchen, NJ: Scarecrow Press, 1995.

DOUGLASS, FREDERICK (1817–1895)

Frederick Douglass was the most famous African-American abolitionist, social reformer, and political leader of the nineteenth century. Douglass, who escaped from slavery

Portrait of Frederick Douglass, leader in the abolitionist movement (1817–1895). (Library of Congress)

at the age of 21, devoted his entire life to fighting slavery and race prejudice in all its forms. In 1845, after the publication of his autobiography made his return to slavery a real possibility, Douglass embarked on a two-year lecture tour of Great Britain, which included an extended visit in Ireland. While there Douglass spoke out against slavery at a series of well-attended events. Despite anti-black feeling among Irish Americans, Douglass refused to return the animosity, arguing that the poor Irish in America and African Americans were natural allies, not enemies. He also rejected the anti-Catholic sentiment popular at the time. He remained active in Irish affairs right up until his death in 1895.

Douglass had little knowledge of his age and family. The reality that he had been a slave was the central fact of Douglass' life. Douglass never knew his father (although he believed him to be his white master), and his knowledge of his mother, who worked on a plantation twelve miles away, was very scanty. Douglass was raised by his grandparents and then lived in Baltimore, Maryland, for seven years, first working as a house servant and then as an unskilled laborer in a shipyard. Life in Baltimore was far superior to anything Douglass had previously experienced. Douglass saw that the path to freedom lay in knowledge—in learning to read and write and in learning as much as possible about the world outside of slavery.

Eventually, Douglass was returned to the plantation, and he had a difficult time adjusting to the strictness of slave life on the plantation after the relative freedom of living in the city. In September 1838, Douglass escaped to freedom and moved to New Bedford, Massachusetts. Soon, he was speaking out at local antislavery meetings and attracting notice from area abolitionists. On August 9, 1841, he attended the annual meeting of the Bristol Anti-Slavery Society held in New Bedford. He spoke that night and was heard by William Lloyd Garrison and made an enormously positive impression on the older man. Within three days Douglass was asked to become an agent for the American Anti-Slavery Society.

In 1845 Douglass published his autobiography to much acclaim and public attention, in the North and the South. With this notoriety, Douglass's friends feared that his owners might take legal action to return him to slavery. It was agreed that he would travel to Great Britain for an extended speaking tour, as black American abolitionists had been well received in England. Plans were also made for him to spend time in Ireland. As slavery had been abolished in

Britain in 1833, it had become a relatively common practice for black American abolitionists to travel there on speaking tours. The antislavery lobby in Great Britain had begun working to end slavery in America once it had been abolished at home. Douglass's tour was a turning point in his life for a variety of reasons. It was also quite successful as he gave countless lectures, 50 in Ireland alone, and met all the leading Irish reformers of his day. It was almost two years before he returned to the United States.

Although often overlooked in modern works on the abolitionist cause, a lively abolitionist movement existed in Ireland. The Hibernian Anti-Slavery Society was founded in Dublin in 1837, and one of its most prominent members was Richard Davis Webb, a printer, publisher, and Quaker. One of the main reasons for Douglass's visit to Ireland was to confirm the details of Webb's plan to publish an Irish edition of his autobiography. While there he spoke on a variety of topics, including temperance. Douglass argued the one of the main causes of poverty in Ireland was the abuse of alcohol, and he personally made the pledge to abstain from alcohol to Father Theobald Mathew, the famous Irish temperance leader. But he would always link his topic back to his main interest—the eradication of slavery. When he arrived in Ireland, the Great Irish Famine had already begun, although it had by no means reached its worst levels. Douglass was well aware of the suffering of the Irish peasants and the hypocrisy of Irish abolitionists who stepped around the starving poor even as they made their way into one of his lectures about the evils of slavery in America.

Douglass's visit to Ireland gave him an opportunity to meet one of his heroes—the great Irish nationalist Daniel O'Connell. O'Connell was responsible for the Great Irish Address of 1841, a petition signed by 60,000 people in Ireland calling for Irish Americans to oppose slavery in America. Douglass had an extremely positive view of O'Connell, which was only strengthened by the warm reception he received from the older man during his Ireland visit. O'Connell returned the admiration, calling Douglass the "black O'Connell."

Douglass's links to O'Connell and Mathew might lead one to see him as mainly connected to the nationalist movement, but his closest contacts were with evangelical Protestants, who were most active in supporting reform movements in Ireland and America. An important aspect of the tour for Douglass was the fact that he was almost universally treated as an equal by the people with whom he came into contact. The freedom to ride the train or walk into any restaurant was an exhilarating experience for the young reformer. The memory of this treatment, along with the suffering he had witnessed among the poor Irish Catholics, goes far in explaining Douglass's sympathy with the Irish in their attempts to gain independence from Great Britain. He consistently saw the treatment of Irish Catholics as analogous to the treatment of blacks in America, and as late as 1883 he responded to a Supreme Court decision denying blacks the right to be served in any public establishment by saying, "We want no black Ireland in America" (McFeely 1991, 318).

Despite the antagonism of many Irish Americans toward both freed and enslaved blacks, with whom they were competing for jobs at the low end of the economic scale, Douglass refused to criticize Irish Catholics as a group. While he would recognize the color prejudice of many Irish Americans, he was very aware of the abuses that group had suffered in Ireland and, indeed, in the United States.

Douglass remained politically active for the rest of his life, recruiting black troops for the Union in the Civil War, working for the Civil War amendments to the Constitution, and speaking out against prejudice and bigotry toward any group of people. A major supporter of the Republican Party, Douglass was rewarded after the Civil War with posts as United States marshal, and then later as the recorder of deeds of the District of Columbia. In the late 1880s, Douglass served as consul to Haiti and played a key role in helping prevent American annexation of the island nation.

To the end of his life, Douglass remained engaged with events in Ireland. On a trip there in 1886 he lamented the oppressed state of the Irish. When Charles Stewart Parnell came to America seeking support for his Home Rule campaign, Douglass appeared on platforms with him and spoke in favor of the program. Unfortunately, Douglass did not live to see either black equality in America or Irish independence, but he devoted his remarkable life to these goals, among many others, and helped as much as any one individual in making them a reality.

William B. Rogers

See also: ABOLITIONISM AND SLAVERY; MATHEW, Father Theobald; O'CONNELL, Daniel; WEBB, Richard Davis

References

Douglass, Frederick. *The Life and Times of Frederick Douglass: Written By Himself.* New York: Pathway Press, 1941.

McFeely, William. *Frederick Douglass.* New York: Norton, 1991.

Rogers, William B. *"We Are All Together Now": Frederick Douglass, William Lloyd Garrison, and the Prophetic Tradition.* New York: Garland, 1995.

Rolston, Bill. "Frederick Douglass: A Black Abolitionist in Ireland." *History Today* 53, no. 6 (June 2003): 45–51.

DOWNEY, MORTON (1901–1985)

Morton Downey was a singer, composer, and businessman of Irish immigrant parentage. As a broadcaster and entertainer, his performances were popular on the stage as well as on radio and during the early television years. Born in Wallingford, Connecticut, on November 14, 1901, Downey began his singing career in a Greenwich Village movie theater and became a vocalist with the Paul Whiteman Orchestra. His first commercial recordings were made in 1923 for Edison Records, and he also recorded for the Victor and Brunswick (1920s), ARC and Decca (1930s), and Columbia (1940s) companies. In 1927 he toured Europe, appearing in London, Paris, and Berlin. Downey became a popular radio singer as well, voted the U.S. "Radio Singer of the Year" in 1932. His mainly (pseudo-) Irish repertory earned him the nickname "Irish Nightingale." His most successful numbers were "All I Need is Someone Like You," "California Skies," "In the Valley of the Roses," "That's How I Spell Ireland," and "Wabash Moon." In 1963, he published a collection of *Morton Downey's Favorite Irish Songs* for voice and piano, which included a number of popular traditional tunes.

From 1929, Downey appeared occasionally on the movie screen, starring as Danny O'Neill in *Dublin in Brass* (1935). In 1950–1951 he hosted the television show *Star of the Family*. Later, he entered a successful business career and became a member of the board of Coca-Cola and other corporations. He married the dancer Barbara Bennett in 1929, but they divorced in 1941. His son, Morton Downey Jr. (1933–2001), was a popular talk show host (known as "Television's Ultimate Loudmouth"). Morton Downey died in Palm Beach, Florida, on October 25, 1985.

Axel Klein

See also: MUSIC IN AMERICA, IRISH

Reference

Official Morton Downey Jr. Website. http://mortondowneyjr.com (accessed May 4, 2004).

DOYLE, RODDY (1958–)

Born in Kilbarrack, North Dublin, on May 8, 1958, Roddy Doyle was raised with two sisters and a brother by his lower middle-class parents. He attended National School in Kilbarrack before going on to a National School in Raheny and St. Fintan's Christian Brothers School in Sutton, Co. Dublin. Doyle graduated from University College Dublin with a bachelor's degree in English and geography and a higher diploma in education. During his time at university, Doyle traveled to communist Poland and joined the Socialist Labour Party, a sociopolitical engagement that is obvious in both him and his work. From 1980 to 1993 he taught English and geography at Greendale Community School in Kilbarrack, retiring from the profession once he was successful enough to earn a living from his writing.

Doyle has been celebrated as one of contemporary Ireland's greatest social analysts. This is apparent in his depiction of the urban poor, alcoholism, drug addiction,

and the treatment of women. His work is most defined by a dark portrayal of poor working-class life that simultaneously delights in a rambunctious and often profanity-laced humor. This is most evident in his earliest works, the novels of *The Barrytown Trilogy* (*The Commitments, The Snapper,* and *The Van*) and the Booker Prize–winning *Paddy Clarke Ha Ha Ha.* This last book brought him international fame, along with Alan Parker's popular film adaptation of *The Commitments,* which also spawned a hit soundtrack. In later years Doyle's work has been the source of some controversy, from the public outcry at the domestic violence and drug addiction of his television drama *Family,* which became the source for his novel *The Woman Who Walked into Doors,* to the revisionist history of *A Star Called Henry.* This last work has formed the beginning of a second trilogy, *The Last Roundup,* which also includes *Oh, Play That Thing.* Though he is best known as a novelist, Doyle has also written plays, short stories, film scripts, and children's books.

Doyle has been particularly adept at noting the influence of America and American culture on Irish society. In *The Commitments,* an aspiring rock band dreams of fame and fortune through the medium of rhythm and blues music from the 1960s, specifically that produced by Motown and the band's hero, James Brown. While relating to American blacks through the memorable phrase that "the Irish are the niggers of Europe, Dubliners the niggers of Ireland, and Northsiders the niggers of Dublin," the group fuses American black culture into a localized, hybrid American pop culture. This same culture also defines characters in his other works, such as the young Paddy Clarke's identification with

Geronimo as opposed to Daniel Boone. American multinational corporations and transnational capital, and the coming wave of change and financial growth that would mark the Celtic Tiger, are implicitly blamed for the unemployment of the men in *The Van.* In his play *Brownbread,* Doyle satirizes not only American pop culture but also American politics: when a few local lads, bored from their daily life, kidnap a priest, they are attacked by the American marines when it is discovered that the priest is an American citizen by birth. Doyle finally leaves Dublin and Ireland behind in *Oh, Play That Thing,* taking his protagonist, Henry Smart, on the run from the Irish Republican Army and post-independence forces, to America where he identifies and associates with American blacks, most notably as Louis Armstrong's right-hand man. It is interesting that it is always the specter of America that lurks in the background of Doyle's work and, save for a few moments, rarely England.

In recent years, Doyle has been actively involved with the publishers of *Metro,* a multicultural publication edited by Nigerian immigrants that confronts, among other issues, race and citizenship in Ireland. In addition to his writing, Doyle has also been a prominent activist, most vocally during the divorce referenda of 1986 and 1995 and in campaigns for immigrant and minority rights.

Brad Kent

See also: LITERATURE, AMERICAN CHILDREN'S

References
McCarthy, Dermot. *Roddy Doyle: Raining on the Parade.* Dublin: The Liffey Press, 2003.
White, Caramine. *Reading Roddy Doyle.* Syracuse, NY: Syracuse University Press, 2001.

DRAFT RIOTS

Over five days in the summer of 1863, from July 13 to 18, New York and America were rocked by a riot that was more than just an uprising of the mob; it threatened to overthrow the city, the state, and national order. Represented on one level as a race riot enacted by poor, Irish-Catholic immigrants upon freed blacks, the Draft Riots were much more than this; they were the outpourings of an impoverished and destitute American working class against a system and a representative government that they believed further victimized their already miserable existence.

Although rioting had been increasing as a form of social demonstration since the middle of the century—there had been ethnic riots, race riots, working-class riots, theater riots, and Orange riots—nothing of the scale and devastation of the Draft Riots had ever been experienced by the people of New York. The spark that would ignite the Draft Riots was the federal Conscription Act passed by Congress in March 1863. This act was designed to reinforce a hemorrhaging Union Army at a low point in Northern fortunes in the Civil War. The law was an attempt to sustain the flow of men into the army; it made all men between the ages of twenty and thirty-five and all unmarried men between thirty-five and forty-five liable for enlistment. Names were collected from a house-to-house census and then a lottery in each congressional district determined who went to war. The act contained a provision, however, that allowed drafted men who presented an "acceptable substitute" or paid $300 to be exempt. Effectively, this meant that the burden of the Act fell on the poor working-class immigrant population, and the freed black population was exempt from

Rioters sack the Brownstone Houses in New York during the Draft Riots of 1863. The riots erupted during the Union Army's attempt at drafting individuals (primarily poor immigrants) during the American Civil War. (Library of Congress)

conscription because of the call for draftees to be "citizens of the United States." Consequently, the destitute population of lower New York would see themselves as opposed to the wealthier classes above Broadway and the blacks who lived among them.

The draft lottery began on Saturday, July 11, in the uptown Ninth District and passed without incident. By Sunday, however, the first plans of resistance had been formed as the people gathered in saloons and on street corners to discuss the resumption of the lottery on Monday. Specifically, several Irish members of the Black Joke Volunteer Fire Company, learning that that the name of one of their own had been drawn on Saturday, began to conspire to prevent Monday's resumption of the draft

process and to destroy any records of selection. By 8:00 on Monday morning, a large, angry crowd had begun to make its way uptown toward the draft office. They cut down telegraph poles, pulled up train tracks, and attacked several policemen on the way.

Draft selection began in the Ninth District Office at 10:30 a.m. After about 50 names had been drawn, the Black Joke Engine Company arrived, burst into the office, destroyed the selection wheel, and set fire to the building. By 11:30 a.m. orders had been given to suspend the draft, but by now the mob had swelled to more than 12,000 and had begun to spread out toward sites at which they could vent their anger against emblematic agents of the war and proponents of the draft, such as Horace Greeley's *Tribune* (the voice of abolition) and the Republican *Times* (an ardent supporter of Lincoln's campaign). Along the way they burned and plundered at will, meeting little resistance as the army was away fighting the war at Gettysburg. What began as an antidraft demonstration quickly turned into groups of marauding mobs, largely Irish, rampaging and burning at will throughout the city: the Armory on Twenty-First Street, the Harlem Temperance Room, the Magdalene Asylum for Aged Prostitutes, and Brooks Brothers on Fifth Avenue. By the afternoon they had begun to turn their attention toward those they viewed as opposed to them and their rights; they began to loot and burn the homes of police officials, prominent Republicans, and the wealthy of New York. They attacked both well-dressed gentlemen on the street and the houses of the wealthy at Gramercy Park and other places. They also turned their attention toward a less fortunate group of New Yorkers they held symbolically responsible for their situation—the blacks; after all, with the Emancipation Act at the beginning of the year this had become a war about slavery and its abolition. A mob attacked a nine-year-old black boy on the corner of Broadway and Chamber Street; another set fire to the Colored Orphan Asylum on Fifth Avenue (home to more than 200 African-American children; luckily they all escaped). By nightfall, America's leading metropolitan city had fallen into anarchy.

By Tuesday the riot had entered a new phase; from a somewhat organized demonstration against conscription it soon became a war raged along working-class and racial lines. Many of the early antidraft demonstrators of Monday morning had, by now, repudiated the violence of the mob and were engaged in protecting property and suppressing the riot. The volunteer fire companies, prominent in the antidraft demonstration of early Monday morning, were now actively engaged in protecting their local districts against the rioters. On an ethnic level, the prominence of German immigrants in Monday's demonstration had, by Tuesday, given way to largely Irish and Catholic mobs. As the make-up of the rioters changed, so did its focus, on Eighth Avenue a mob of 5,000 men went from house to house in search of black men and interracial couples. On Roosevelt Street, tenements that housed black families were torched, and their furniture was burned in street bonfires; by midweek, the harbor front had been virtually emptied of people of color by rioters. Laborers, largely Irish, attacked and hanged black men, such as James Costello and Abraham Franklin, on the streets. They also continued their assault on what they saw as representatives of Republican power: the police, the militia, the Union Steam Works, and houses and offices of prominent Republicans and abolitionists. By midweek, the rioters began to cordon off waterfront neighborhoods from the bourgeois districts in the center of the island. This was, in part, a response to the arrival of the army in the city; the 56th New York regiment—the first Union reinforcements—arrived in the city on Wednesday night, and the 7th New York regiment arrived the next morning. By Thursday the tide had begun to turn, and the city had begun to be reclaimed by the forces of law and order. Like the police, a lot of the Union soldiers were, in fact, local boys of Irish families who were ordered to fire on their own.

By Friday, New York was completely occupied by Federal troops, but the city lay in ruins. Hundreds of buildings were burned or demolished and the cost of property damage was estimated at $5 million. The death toll from the riots can never be accurately estimated—some claim that as many as 2,000 died—but there were at least 119 verified deaths: 18 African Americans, 16 soldiers, and 85 rioters (most of them Irish).

Although not the only ethnic community involved in the Draft Riots, the disproportionate number involved, killed, and arrested (of 184 people of known ethnicity arrested, 117 were Irish) ensured that the Irish became synonymous with the riots. The Irish involvement in the Draft Riots would undo a lot of the goodwill generated toward them by their impressive service and immense sacrifice in the Civil War.

James P. Byrne

See also: AMERICAN CIVIL WAR; NEW YORK CITY

References

Bernstein, Iver. *The New York City Draft Riots: Their Significance for American Society and Politics in the Age of the Civil War.* Oxford: Oxford University Press, 1990.

Burrows, Edwin G., and Mike Wallace. *Gotham: A History of New York City to 1898.* New York: Oxford University Press, 1999.

Cook, Adrian. *The Armies of the Streets: The New York City Draft Riots of 1863.* Lexington: University Press of Kentucky, 1974.

DRESDEN AFFAIR

On February 15, 1889, the steamer *City of Dresden* arrived in Buenos Aires with 1,774 passengers on board, most of them from Ireland. They had been enticed to make the trip by an immigration scheme promoted by the Argentine government and executed by members of the Irish community in that country. The project was a complete failure, and several immigrants died or had to re-emigrate in the few years after their arrival. This immigration brought a fresh influx of Irish domestic service and laborers to affluent households and ranches in Buenos Aires. However, for the Irish in Argentina, the Dresden Affair represented a significant loss of prestige in the political and institutional arena. Furthermore, the negative reports from the government and Roman Catholic Church in the British Isles put an end to organized emigration from Ireland to Argentina.

Father Patrick Dillon, chaplain of the Irish in Buenos Aires since 1863, was elected the member of parliament for Buenos Aires province in 1880. Dillon advocated in parliament for the assisted immigration of European settlers, and in April 18, 1881, he went on an official mission to Ireland to establish an immigration scheme. Back in Argentina, he recommended that the government pay free or assisted tickets and grant land to new immigrants. The administration of President Juarez Celman actively encouraged immigration, and approved the granting of 50,000 assisted passages to prospective emigrants. They also established a network of resident agents in Europe, who received a commission of about £5 for every emigrant landed in Buenos Aires, plus commissions from the shipping companies. In 1887, Irish Argentines Buckley O'Meara and John Stephen Dillon, brother of Father Dillon, were appointed immigration agents in Ireland. To get their commissions they overlooked the government rules regarding the desirable characteristics of immigrants, and they lied to prospective emigrants, telling them they would receive land, houses, machinery, and seed. Therefore, they managed to collect all the people needed to fill a large steamer, the *City of Dresden.*

The *Dresden,* a new 4,527-ton steamer, weighed anchor on January 25, 1889, in Cobh (formerly Queenstown), Co. Cork. The ship carried the largest number of immigrants ever to arrive in Argentina from any one destination and in any one vessel. Though the immigrants were in general young laborers and servants from poorer urban districts in Dublin, Cork, and Limerick, there were also several large families, aged people, prostitutes, and convicts undergoing terms of imprisonment in Limerick and Cork jails. Some of the passengers died at sea, probably due to nontreated sicknesses.

When the immigrants landed in Buenos Aires, they were accommodated in the old *Hotel de Inmigrantes,* which did not have enough room for them. Most children were naked. Sickness, hunger, and exhaustion were appalling. The food provided by the officials of the Immigration Department was insufficient. The Irish and English communities, as well as the British consulate, immediately formed a British Immigrations Committee to provide better conditions and, eventually, jobs to the newly arrived immigrants. Among the committee members were John Drysdale, Samuel Hale, Eduardo Casey, Father Matthew Gaughren, Edward Mulhall of *The Standard,* and Michael Dineen of *The Southern Cross.* Some families were moved to the filthy stables in Paseo de Julio and then to a hotel near the Southern Railway station in Plaza Constitución. Some of the young single women were sent to the Irish Convent, where ladies could hire them as domestic service. But others began the long tradition of Irish prostitution in Buenos Aires.

Father Matthew Gaughren, O.M.I., who was in Argentina on a fund-raising mission, aided the immigrants and worked to improve their circumstances in Buenos Aires and later in the Irish Colony in Bahía Blanca. He published several letters in the newspapers to collect funds and personally accompanied them in their distressful situation in Bahía Blanca.

Peter A. Gartland, an ex-soldier of the American Civil War, together with John S. Dillon, offered to let the immigrants occupy 40-hectare parcels in Naposta, a remote place near Bahía Blanca (400 miles south of Buenos Aires). Seven hundred were carried by railway to Naposta station. When they arrived, their luggage was lost. There were no houses to live in, and no way to build them, because Gartland did not have enough funds to finance the project. Families lived in tents, under the trees, or in ditches. The death rate reached 100 in two years; children were particularly affected. In March 1891 the Irish Colony was broken up and 520 colonists trekked the 400 miles back to Buenos Aires.

The effects of the Dresden Affair on further Irish immigration to Argentina were devastating. Tim Healy (1855–1931) denounced the affair in the British parliament and created a negative perception among English officials and diplomatic envoys in South America. In 1889, Thomas W. Croke, Archbishop of Cashel, wrote in a letter published by *The Freeman's Journal* (and quoted in Michael Geraghty's "Argentina: Land of Broken Promises" [1999]) about the corrupt scheme implemented by Argentine government officials and agents: "I most solemnly conjure my poorer countrymen, as they value their happiness hereafter, never to set foot on the Argentine Republic." Among the immigrants, the survivors encountered many difficulties in adapting to the country. A few years after the *City of Dresden* arrived in Buenos Aires, as it was impossible to find favorable economic situations in the country, most of the emigrants returned to Ireland or re-emigrated to the United States, Australia, and other countries. Because of the lack of recognition from the larger part of the Irish-Argentine community, those who stayed had a higher rate of integration in the local society.

Edmundo Murray

See also: CASEY, Eduardo; DILLON, Patrick Joseph; GAUGHREN, Father Matthew

References

Gaynor, Juan Santos. *The Story of St. Joseph's Society.* Buenos Aires: The Southern Cross, 1941.

Geraghty, Michael. "Argentina: Land of Broken Promises." *The Buenos Aires Herald,* March 17, 1999.

Murray, Thomas. *The Story of the Irish in Argentina.* New York: P. J. Kenedy and Sons, 1919.

DUGGAN, THOMAS (1827–1913)

Thomas Duggan, a businessman and benefactor of the Irish-Argentine community, was reputed in Argentina to be one of the wealthiest Irish-born persons of his time. He was born on November 18, 1827 in Ballymahon, Co. Longford, the son of Hugh Duggan and Jane Kelly. Duggan emigrated to Argentina in 1859, as did his brothers Michael, John, Daniel, and Hugh as well as several members of his family and neighbors. They worked together in sheep farming, and as wool and hides agents, and made an immense fortune that was chiefly invested in land in San Antonio de Areco, Chacabuco, and Lincoln (departments of Buenos Aires province). In total they owned more than 300,000 hectares of the best land. La Primavera, one of their ranches in Lincoln, alone had an extension of 65,000 hectares. Duggan Brothers storehouses of Buenos Aires were in Calle Victoria, Constitución, and Once.

Duggan married Marcela Casey (1845–1922) in 1869 and was a visible representative of the Irish community in Argentine public life. In 1876 he was a member of the education council in Balvanera. One year later he was present at the reconciliation banquet celebrated after the political agreement between Buenos Aires governor Adolfo Alsina and president Nicolás Avellaneda. In 1879 Duggan supported the establishment of the Passionist Fathers in Argentina, though later he led the campaign against their Italianization of the order, that is, their links with the Italian immigrant community. In 1889 and 1892 he was invited to the banquet of the ecclesiastical council presided over by the apostolic nuncio, and in the latter year he was also honored during the Saint Patrick's Day celebrations. Duggan owned the property occupied by the Irish orphanage, which was sold in 1897. Together with his brothers, Duggan was one of the most generous donators to charity among the Irish in Argentina, and he was a great benefactor of the Irish hospital and other works developed by the Sisters of Mercy. He was also very active in supporting Catholic charities in Ireland and England.

As a businessman and risk capitalist Thomas Duggan was a partner of Eduardo Casey, his brother-in-law, in many undertakings. The construction of a central market in Barracas, Buenos Aires, in 1887 was one of their most important undertakings. Once erected in 1889, the building was the largest public market in the world. They also invested in Sindicato Argentino, a company in Buenos Aires and Uruguay with interests in banks, mining, cattle ranching, railways, immigration, building, and the press. Gradually, these businesses became more speculative, and in August 1890 a crisis of the Montevideo stock exchange deeply affected the company. Duggan was forced to obtain fresh cash using his eighteen ranches as collateral for a loan, which creditors did not allow to be longer than ten years. Daniel and Michael Duggan died in 1888 and 1896, respectively, leaving their brother Thomas a fortune calculated of at least £6 million sterling. Immediately the creditors asked Duggan to cancel the total debt, but he answered that since they did not give him extended credit when he needed it he would take the time of the loan to repay the capital. The creditors had to wait until the end of the ten-year term to recover their capital. Duggan used to entertain visitors to the central market in Barracas telling them that every brick in that building represented a dollar in his pocket.

In contrast to his brothers and to most of the large Irish landowners in Argentina, Thomas Duggan favored Irish nationalism. For this reason he avoided doing business with English-owned banks and cold-storage plants. Roger Casement was invited to his ranch in San Antonio de Areco. In 1888 Duggan bought Shorthorn bulls and cows in Sittyton, Scotland, and established a breeding ranch in Argentina. Thereafter, Duggan's Sittyton ranch was awarded the Grand Award in Palermo's rural fair twenty-eight times. Thomas Duggan owned more registered Shorthorn, Hereford, and Angus breeding cattle than any other Argentine breeder. On September 18, 1896, Thomas

Duggan sold forty-one hectares of his land in San Antonio de Areco to the Western Railway Company. A station was built and the town that grew up nearby was named "Duggan." Thomas Duggan died on June 8, 1913.

Edmundo Murray

See also: CASEMENT, Roger; CASEY, Eduardo

References
Coghlan, Eduardo A. *Los Irlandeses en la Argentina: Su Actuación y Descendencia.* Buenos Aires: Author's Edition, 1987.
Murray, Thomas. *The Story of the Irish in Argentina.* New York, P. J. Kenedy & Sons, 1919.

DUNNE, FINLEY PETER, (1867–1936)

Newspaper columnist Finley Peter Dunne created a cast of fictional characters in order to express his political and social views more forcefully. Most famous of these was Martin J. Dooley, a saloonkeeper with strong opinions on everything and everyone. Dunne's columns vividly portrayed the turn-of-the-century Irish-American world while advocating a progressive political agenda. The columns grew to be nationally popular, and many of them were reprinted in book collections.

Born in Chicago of Irish immigrants, Dunne took a job as an errand boy at the *Chicago Telegram* at the age of 16. Over the next few years he worked at a variety of newspapers, gradually working his way up the journalistic ladder. At the age of 21, he surprised everyone by becoming the city editor of the *Chicago Times.* In 1893, at the age of 26, Dunne started his column in the *Evening Post,* commenting on society and politics using Martin J. Dooley and the

Portrait of newspaper editor and columnist Finley Peter Dunne. (Library of Congress)

other invented residents of Archey Road to express his opinions. Dooley and the other characters spoke with strong Irish accents as can be seen in Dooley's view of school: "Childher shudden't be sint to school to larn, but to larn how to larn. I don't care what ye larn thim so long as 'tis onpleasant to thim. Tis thrainin' they need, that's all. I never could make use iv what I larned in colledge about thrigojoomethry an'—an'—grammar an' the' welts I got on the' skull fr'm the schoolmasther's cane I have never been able to turn to anny account in the' business, but 'twas th' bein' there and havin' to get things to heart without askin' th' meanin' iv thim an' goin' to school cold an' comin' home hungry, that made th' man iv me ye see before ye" (*The Education of the Young*). Dooley, with his distinctive Irish brogue and humorous outlook on life,

could get away with social commentary on Dunne's Chicago and America that the columnist often couldn't risk when writing as himself. For example, he had Dooley say, "Big business is much like murder," and "The Supreme Court follows the election returns." Dooley's honesty, cynicism, and humor made Dunne a major spokesman for the little guy in American society.

Dunne used Dooley and the lively action at his South Side saloon to expose hypocrisy and scandals in politics, poke fun at the self-centered egotism of politicians and robber barons, and provide a voice for the opinions of the common man. He also promoted a consistently progressive message, whether concerning the right of organized labor, women's suffrage, or tolerance toward the masses of new immigrants flooding into the country. The Pullman Strike of 1894 particularly stirred Dunne's efforts. Sometimes, in essays like "When the Trust is at Work" and "The Idle Apprentice," he went beyond humor into a new tragic dimension in his compassion for the sufferings of the poor, but more frequently he made use of the just as potent weapon of comedy and satire. Dunne became nationally famous when several papers began carrying Dooley's hilarious observations of Admiral George Dewey's victory at Manila Bay ("On His Cousin George") in 1898 at the start of the Spanish-American War. Dunne was opposed to the imperialism he saw in Theodore Roosevelt before and during the war, and he had Mr. Dooley launch a campaign against it. By 1899 the country had gone crazy for Dooley: popular songs were being written, college presidents were quoting him, and no less a social commentator than Henry Adams was recommending him to his friends.

The column became hugely popular and a fixture of American culture during its long run. In all Dunne wrote more than 700 columns, many of which were reprinted in nine books of collected works. There was wisdom as well as laughter in the Dooley columns, and some critics at the time recognized this. Both William Dean Howells and Van Wyck Brooks admired Dunne's writing. Brooks argued that Dunne was one of the writers responsible for creating a distinctive American form of the English language, separate from England's. Dunne is also important because he is one of the first successful Irish-American authors to use unabashedly—even proudly—his ethnicity in his writing. Dunne retired Dooley early in the 20th century, turning instead to more serious writing when he joined the editorial staff of *The American Magazine*. Many critics see these writings as his most profound writings, but the public wanted Dooley. Dunne refused to revive him, even for World War I. After he retired in 1927, when a bequest made it possible for him to do so, he wrote very little.

William B. Rogers

See also: ETHNIC AND RACE RELATIONS (Irish and African Americans)

References

Dunne, Finley Peter. *Mr. Dooley in Peace and War.* Urbana: University of Illinois Press, 2001.

Dunne, Finley Peter. *Observations by Mr. Dooley.* Whitefish, MT: Kessinger Publishing, 2005.

Ellis, Elmer. *Mr. Dooley's America: A Life of Finley Peter Dunne.* New York: Knopf, 1941.

Fanning, Charles. *The Irish Voice in America: Irish-American Fiction from the Eighteenth Century to the Present.* Lexington: University Press of Kentucky, 1999.

DUNNE, IRENE MARIE (1898–1990)

Irene Marie Dunne was born on December 20, 1898, in Louisville, Kentucky, the daughter of Joseph and Adeline Dunne. Joseph died when Dunne was 12, and mother and daughter then lived with relatives. Dunne inherited her mother's artistic talent and became a trained singer and pianist. She toured with a theatrical company in 1920, and made her Broadway debut in *The Clinging Vine* in 1922. Thereafter, she obtained a number of roles in a variety of musicals. Dunne earned a scholarship and graduated from the Chicago Musical College in 1926. However, she failed her audition with the prestigious Metropolitan Opera Company because of her inexperience.

Dunne married dentist Dr. Francis Griffin in 1928. The staunchly Roman Catholic couple remained happily married and adopted a daughter named Mary Frances. Dunne was spotted by Florenz Ziegfeld, who cast her in *Showboat* in 1929. She was awarded a contract by RKO in 1930 and relocated to Hollywood. She appeared in *Leathernecking* in 1930 and won a Best Actress Academy Award nomination for *Cimarron* in 1931. *Back Street* in 1932 was followed by *Magnificent Obsession, Sweet Adeline* and *Roberta* in 1935, and *Show Boat* in 1936.

Dunne's career took a major turn when she began accepting comedic roles. She appeared in *Theodora Goes Wild* in 1936 and received a Best Actress Academy Award nomination. This success was followed by Best Actress Academy Award nominations for *The Awful Truth* in 1937, *Love Affair* in 1939, and *My Favorite Wife* in 1940.

Dunne appeared in *Penny Serenade* in 1941, *The White Cliffs of Dover* in 1944,

Irene Dunne was a motion picture actress who achieved fame during Hollywood's golden era. Her work in film ranged from melodramas to screwball comedies and earned her five Academy Award nominations for best actress. (Hulton Archive/Getty Images)

Anna and the King of Siam in 1946, and *Life with Father* in 1947. She received an Academy Award nomination for *I Remember Mama* in 1948 and yet another Academy Award nomination for *The Mudlark* in 1950. Her last film was *It Grows on Trees* in 1952.

Dunne retired from acting in films in 1952 but appeared in a variety of television programs. By this time Dunne had become wealthy because of sound investments. She was a devoted Republican and served on numerous political and socially oriented boards and became active in philanthropic endeavors. Dunne was one of five alternate members to the United Nations. She was

also a member of the board of Technicolor. Dunne's husband, Dr. Griffin, died in 1965. Dunne never remarried.

Dunne received a Lifetime Achievement Award at the Kennedy Center Honors in 1985 but did not attend the event because of ill health. Dunne was 91 when she died on September 4, 1990, in Beverly Hills, California, where she is buried in the Calvary Cemetery. Dunne has a star on the Hollywood Walk of Fame.

Annette Richardson

References

Gerhring, Wes D. *First Lady of Hollywood.* Lanham, MD: Scarecrow Press, 2003.

DiBattista, Maria. *Fast-talking Dames.* New Haven, CT: Yale University Press, 2001.

DURCAN, PAUL (1944–)

Paul Durcan was born in Dublin in 1944. His childhood was divided between the family home in Ranelagh and summer vacations with his aunt and maternal grandmother in the west of Ireland. The importance of these and other key locales is a definitive feature of Durcan's poetry and informs a poetics of place that includes Russia, Australia, and the Americas. After graduating from Gonzaga College Dublin in 1962, Durcan enrolled in economics and history at University College Dublin. During the following year he established lasting friendships with a group of writers and intellectuals, including Michael Hartnett, Leland Bardwell, Macdara Woods, John Moriarty, and most importantly in terms of his writing, Patrick Kavanagh. An initial collection of poetry, *Endsville,* was published in 1967. After a short period in London, Durcan married Nessa O'Neill, and the couple returned to Ireland with their two daughters to live in Cork. In 1974 he graduated with first-class honors in archaeology and medieval history from University College Cork, and in the same year was the recipient of the Patrick Kavanagh Award, an honor that enabled him to publish his first major collection, *O Westport in the Light of Asia Minor* (1975). Over the past 30 years, Durcan has published 18 volumes of poetry, each one charting new territory in terms of its attitude to form and subject matter.

While he is frequently regarded as an iconoclastic social critic of Irish, and latterly American, social, political, and religious institutions and hypocrisies, Durcan is as much a poet of praise as he is a satirist. Complex, incantatory hymns laud society's unacknowledged "holy souls" and extol exemplary individuals, many of them women. Durcan's recitals of his work, a unique blend of oratory and theatrics, rapidly gained him a wide audience in Ireland and Europe during the 1980s. A residency at the Frost Place at Franconia, New Hampshire, in May 1985 followed by reading tours in Canada, the United States, and Brazil, introduced him to a new and enthusiastic readership. In 1989 he received the Irish American Cultural Institute Poetry Award and in 1995 was a recipient of the Heinemann Award. Durcan has been writer in residence at Trinity College Dublin (1990) and University College Dublin (2003), and in 2004 he was appointed to the prestigious Ireland Chair of Poetry.

While the focus of Durcan's poetry is Ireland, he is equally attuned to international politics and social change, and his engagement with all things American, in particular, has been passionate and lifelong. As he confirmed in a recent radio broadcast: "since I saw my first Charlie Chaplin and Laurel and Hardy films, I have been a devotee at the shrine of American culture." This devotion is manifest in his poetry in a number of ways. Formally, his long lines and open, variable metrics salute Walt Whitman and Allen Ginsberg, while his bluesy refrains and lyrics of social protest owe as much to Robert Johnson and Howlin' Wolf as they do to Bob Dylan and Johnny Cash. In terms of subject matter, early poems such as "Were He Alive" and "Black Sister" implicitly engage with the civil rights movement of the 1960s, championing as they do humanist values and racial equality. Later works show an acute awareness of the painful legacy of Irish emigration to the Americas, poems such as "Backside to the Wind"; "The Girl with the Keys to Pearse's Cottage," which speaks of a Connemara postman's daughter who "was America-bound at summer's end. / She had no choice but to leave her home"; and "Loosestrife in Ballyferriter" which voices one woman's plaintive keen— "Iowa doesn't want me and I don't want Iowa. / Why must I forsake Ireland for Iowa?" Whether chronicling his trans-Atlantic crossings ("EI Flight 106: New York-Dublin," "Flying Over the Kamloops"), evoking media figures from Bugs Bunny to Ronald Reagan, or comically positioning himself in Dublin as "the centre of the universe," phone-counseling acquaintances as far away as Los Angeles, São Paulo, and New York, Durcan has built up a network of connections between Ireland and the Americas that bespeaks a rich and complex postmodern fabric of cultural exchange.

It is in *Greeting to Our Friends in Brazil* (1999), however, that Durcan enters into his most full-blown poetic dialogue with North and South America. As the title poem signals, the volume is a plea for inter-cultural communication and, by extension, the kinds of conversations that destabilize fixed notions about gender, race, and nationality. A reading tour of Brazil in the spring of 1995 occasioned the opening sequence, which explores literary, social, and religious connections between Ireland and Brazil. The book also includes a series of self-portraits, among them "The Chicago Waterstones," a characteristically humorous recollection of a reunion with the young woman who was the poet's monitor at the Frost Place, but also a frank account of the frequently fraught discourse between men and women. The book's final section, devoted as it is to the years of Mary Robinson's presidency, contains three poems honoring Jean Kennedy Smith, American ambassador to Ireland from 1993 to 1998. While paying tribute to Kennedy Smith, Durcan also aligns her role as ambassador with that of the poet: "A poet . . . is an ambassador / Who is the carrier of the significant messages / Across frontiers, checkpoints, walls, controls." Throughout his writing career Durcan has sought to convey that imperative precisely. His indignation at the Bush administration's foreign policy in the Middle East, the invasion of Iraq, and the incarceration of political prisoners at Guantanamo Bay constitute his harshest criticism of, and his most sustained engagement with, the United States to date. At the same time, he is as magnanimous in his admiration for a Manhattan Yellow Cab driver and the courteous customs of the citizens of St. John's, Newfoundland, as he is in his respect for the pacifist politics of the American Jesuit theologian John Courtney Murray.

Kathleen McCracken

See also: KENNEDY FAMILY; ROBINSON, Mary

References

Durcan, Paul. *Cries of an Irish Caveman.* London: Harvill, 2001.
Durcan, Paul. *Greetings to Our Friends in Brazil.* London: Harvill, 1999.
Durcan, Paul. *Paul Durcan's Diary.* Dublin: New Island Books, 2003.
Durcan, Paul. *A Snail in My Prime: New and Selected Poems.* London: Harvill, 1993.
Tóibín, Colm, ed. *The Kilfenora Teaboy: A Study of Paul Durcan.* Dublin: New Island Books, 1996.

EATON, TIMOTHY E. (1834–1907)

Preserved now only in name, the T. Eaton Company was Canada's foremost retailer through most of the twentieth century. Its founder, Timothy Eaton, was born into a rural heartland of Presbyterian Ulster, the ninth child of the recently widowed Margaret Craig Eaton. The Presbyterian Church, the family farm and a network of kin and neighbor were deeply interwoven into the fabric of community in rural Mid Antrim. Eaton began his retailing career by tapping into this culture, apprenticing in dry goods retail to a distant relative in the village of Portglenone, in an area west of Ballymena notorious for sectarian conflict. Although spared the worst ravages of the Famine that visited other parts of Ireland in the late 1840s, the experience of distress in Mid Antrim was nonetheless acute, and the prosperity of the New World enticed many people to leave Ireland, especially those with the means to emigrate who had family connections capable of providing assistance on their arrival. In 1854, Timothy Eaton followed a brother and three sisters, as well as members of his extended family, to Canada, becoming a clerk in Glen Williams, outside Georgetown, Canada West (now Ontario), where a number of his relatives had settled. Eaton was not a Famine immigrant of popular imagination, but rather a more typical Irish immigrant to British North America—possessing some capital and goods and arriving with £10, a new suit, and a silver watch. Building on his retail experience, Eaton took up the grocery and dry goods trade, opening two stores in Kirktown, near St. Mary's, in 1857 in partnership with his brother James.

Retail in small-town Canada West revolved around structures of personal credit: retailers purchased goods from wholesalers on credit, sold the goods in their shops, and the value of articles was negotiated through bargaining. Retailers serving a wider agricultural community frequently extended credit to customers on a seasonal basis and were often compelled to accept payment in kind: the fortunes of the retail trade were intimately connected to those of the land. Under these delicate and at times trying circumstances, Timothy Eaton's brothers, Robert and John, suffered a series of setbacks with their retail partnership in St. Mary's. In 1860–1861, one of Timothy's enterprises failed—a bakery that ceased trading in St. Mary's only a few months after opening.

Eaton married Mary Beattie—a woman of Ulster Protestant stock—in 1862. In 1869 he entered into a retail partnership briefly on Front Street in Toronto; later that year, he purchased the assets of the Britannia House on Queen Street in the city, and he opened a dry goods store on the small premises. Although often erroneously identified as the originator of cash-only retail in Canada, Timothy Eaton was undoubtedly a pioneer in adopting fixed prices and cash payments—departures from the practices of retail in the small villages and towns where he had learned the trade. "Goods satisfactory or money refunded" was another policy adopted by Eaton—an innovation facilitated by mandating cash-only purchases. This fledgling Queen Street concern, later relocated to larger premises, became the cornerstone of a nationwide retailing empire—two years younger than Canada itself—which progressively expanded through the last decades of the nineteenth century, although facing stiff competition from a neighboring business owned by the Scots immigrant Robert Simpson.

Although he hailed from a rural area of strong Presbyterian sympathies, Eaton became a Methodist soon after his arrival in Canada and was one of the denomination's most generous local benefactors. In his business life, Eaton became famous for exerting a resolutely paternalist and strictly Sabbatarian influence over his company's business practices, banning the sale of playing cards, tobacco, and liquor and progressively limiting shopping hours, which were long through much of the nineteenth century, often stretching from eight o'clock in the morning until late into the evening. At Eaton's store, however, store opening was reduced to daylight hours Monday to Saturday (closing on Saturday afternoons in the summer months). On Sundays, the store curtains were drawn in deference to the stricture of Sunday observance widely followed in Toronto and especially promoted by Eaton himself.

In a city profoundly shaped by the culture of Ulster Protestantism and often described as the "Belfast of the New World," Ballymena immigrants, and Protestants particularly, were rumored to find work easily in departments of Timothy Eaton's expanding concern. Indeed, the company's officers retained links to the region of Timothy's birth. On his death, Timothy Eaton was succeeded as company president by his son John (later Sir John) Eaton. Sir John was in turn succeeded by his cousin Robert Young Eaton, who had been born in the Ballymena area and had immigrated to Canada to help run the Eaton family business. Before his death, Sir John visited the district of his father's birth and paid for the refurbishment of his grandparents' graves in the local cemetery. Such strong personal and cultural identifications with a world across the Atlantic informed the development of Canada's foremost retail chain and were part of a broader narrative of Protestantism, commerce, and Empire in which connections between an Ulster family and the district from which it hailed shaped the retail culture of Toronto and the new Dominion.

Kevin James

See also: EMIGRATION; GREAT FAMINE, The

References

Macpherson, Mary Etta. *Shopkeepers to a Nation: The Eatons.* Toronto: McClelland and Stewart, 1963.

Santink, Joy L. *Timothy Eaton and the Rise of his Department Store.* Toronto: University of Toronto Press, 1990.

The Life Story of Canada's Greatest Merchant. Toronto, 1907.

EGAN, DESMOND (1936–)

An Irish poet with a substantial critical reputation in the United States, Desmond Egan was born July 15, 1936, in Athlone, Ireland, to Thomas and Kathleen (Garland) Egan. He was educated by the Marist Brothers of Athlone, graduated with a BA from Maynooth University, and received an MA in 1965 from University College Dublin. He married the writer Vivienne Abbot, and they have two daughters. He taught at Mullingar (Greek and English) secondary school, then at Newbridge College.

One of the founders of the Goldsmith Press, Egan originated and edited *Era,* a quarterly magazine of the arts from 1974–1984. His first volume, *Midland* (1972), announced a modern minimalist (somewhat like e. e. cummings) who disdained rhyme or punctuation, dramatizing deep images augmented by inward meditation and contextualized by transience and informal phrasing. With Michael Harnett he edited *Choice* (1973), an anthology of contemporary Irish poetry. *Leaves* (1974) chronicles a failed love affair. In modernist fragments, *Siege!* (1976) examines the pathology of politics in Ireland as it connects to a kidnapping. *Woodcutter* (1978) features a tribute to Ezra Pound. *Athlone?* (1980) puts an empathetic magnifying lens to Egan's neighborhood. *Snapdragon* (1983) articulates tender poems of love tempered by loneliness amid the vagaries of time and memory. *Seeing Double* (1983) exhibits a postmodern simultaneity; poems are presented in a double-column format, and the echoing motif creates an unexpected musical harmony or dissonance. This volume also contains memorable elegies for Eugene Watters and Francis Ledwidge. In 1983 Carroll F. Terrell, describing Egan as "the finest Irish poet since Patrick Kavanagh," awarded Egan the National Poetry Foundation of America Prize, a breakthrough that earned him a wider audience and led to the appearance of *Collected Poems* (1983). That same year he won the Muir Award. In 1987 Egan won the American Society for Poetry Award and the Chicago Haymarket Award, and in 1988 the Farrell Literary Award.

Sean McBride penned the introduction for Egan's *Poems for Peace* (1986). *A Song for My Father* (1989) contains the polyphonic title sequence and a haunting poem about the tenor John McCormack. *Peninsula* (1992) meditates on the landscape of Dingle with poems of haiku-like elegance and beauty addressing a tragic event of the sixteenth century. Hugh Kenner edited *Selected Poems* in 1992. *In the Holocaust of Autumn* (1994) laments the Jewish tragedy with heartfelt anguish. *Famine* (1997) plunges into the Irish historical disaster. *Elegies* (1997) contains poems selected by the author. *Music* (2000) provides subtle Leopardi-like meditations on various modalities of the art, high and low. *The Outdoor Light* (2005) is an impassioned, extended elegiac sequence that achieves epic scope.

In 1993 Egan received an honorary doctorate of letters from Stanford University and another from Washburn University in 1996. He received the Bologna Literary Award in 1998 and the Literature of Macedonia Award in 2004. Since 1988 Egan has been the artistic director of the Gerard Manley Hopkins International Summer School. Egan has published translations of Euripides' *Medea* and Sophocles' *Philoctetes;* his poems have been published in French, Dutch, Italian, German, Japanese, Czech, Hungarian, Russian, Polish, Greek,

Bulgarian, and Albanian. He often reads at international poetry symposiums. John Hunter has made a one-hour video documentary, *Through the Eyes of a Poet* (1995), and the CD *Needing the Sea* (2001) records the author's voice. For more than two decades he has made spring reading tours in America.

As a writer Egan's strength is twofold: intimate poems that display sensitive musical phrasing with a simplicity possessing the lyric quality of Schubert's music and a robust capacity for public elegy that touches a raw, emotional nerve in the audience. Nearly all of his books offer poems arranged in a disciplined sequence. Several of his double-column sequence poems from 1989 and later are not meant to be read on the page, but are scripts for performance pieces featuring three or four voices that pay particular attention to the blending of voices and rhythms, as in chamber music. Egan is an accomplished tenor with a substantial repertoire of folk songs; he remains a knowledgeable fan of progressive jazz and classical music. More recently, he has been painting.

Kevin T. McEneaney

See also: GREAT FAMINE, The;
    McCORMACK, John

References

Arkins, Brian. *Desmond Egan: A Critical Study.* Little Rock, AR: Milestone Press, 1990.

Egan, Desmond. *The Death of Metaphor: Selected Prose.* New York: Barnes & Noble, 1986.

Kenner, Hugh, ed., *Desmond Egan.* Orono, ME: Northern Lights, 1990.

EIRE SOCIETY OF BOSTON, THE

Founded in 1937, The Eire Society of Boston was organized and functions for the purpose of spreading awareness of the cultural achievements of the Irish people. The Eire Society promotes knowledge of Irish culture through the encouragement of study in the arts, sciences, literature, language, and history of Ireland; the contributions to civilization made by the Irish and those of Irish ancestry; networking between all Irish and Americans; and raising awareness of the Irish people's actions in advancing American ideals. The Eire Society, by its constitution, is nonsectarian and nonpolitical: no individual holding or seeking public office may serve as an officer or member of the board of directors.

The Eire Society was established by a group of 82 adults who had just completed a 16-lecture Irish history course presented by the Massachusetts Department of Education. After the conclusion of lecture series, alumni met on May 11, 1937, for a $1.50 a plate dinner, during which the Eire Society was formally launched. The Society was formed to complement other Irish organizations, such as the Charitable Irish Society, the Ancient Order of Hibernians, the Clover Club—while consciously distancing itself from things stereotypically Irish. It has never held a function on Saint Patrick's Day, and its letterhead is printed in black or royal blue. Today, the Eire Society touts that it is "more than green beer and shamrocks," and it provides the Boston community with events and resources that celebrate the true contributions of Irish heritage and culture to the world.

The Eire Society has historically been very active in Boston. Monthly meetings are held September through June, and it hosts an annual Gold Medal dinner. Its official periodical, published several times a year, is the *Bulletin*. It also maintains a website, www.eiresociety.org. Society meetings provide a forum for Irish singers, musicians, fashion designers, dancers, artists, actors, poets, filmmakers, writers, and statesmen. Eamon de Valera, former taoiseach and president of Ireland, appreciated the Society and its work and welcomed members to Áras an Uachtaráin (The Irish presidential home). Honored guests have included Hugh Leonard, Sean McBride, Michael MacLiammoir, Desmond Guinness, Roy Johnston, Thomas McAnna, Brian Friel, Brendan Behan, Grainne Yeats, Mary Manning, John Montague, Thomas Flanagan, Charles Bowen, and Thomas Kinsella.

Each year, the society offers a gold medal to an individual whose efforts have significantly fulfilled society ideals. Past recipients have included scholars, architects, teachers, lawyers, sportsmen, politicians, philanthropists, critics, and artists. Past members and gold medal honorees have included John F. Kennedy, Seamus Heaney, the Chieftains, John Hume, Siobhan McKenna, Sean McBride, George Mitchell, John Huston, William Bulger, Thomas "Tip" O'Neill, Maureen O'Hara, John Ford, Padraic Colum, Joseph Cannon, John W. McCormack, Eugene McCarthy, and Mary Lavin. The *Bulletin* series amounts now to several volumes, which are archived with the Eire Society's records, at the Honorable John J. Burns Library of Rare Books and Special Collections at Boston College.

Throughout its history the Eire Society has hosted nearly 1,000 lectures, screenings, opening nights, and receptions, cooperated with four decades of Irish consular and diplomatic missions, and given its support to numerous Irish hospitals, educational ventures, ecumenical and peace-seeking projects, and creative enterprises. In 1978, during its 41st season, the society and other local Irish organizations supported the exhibit called *Irish Legacy: 1500 BC/1500 AD* at Boston's Museum of Fine Arts. In January 1980, the society arranged a special viewing for members and friends of the John F. Kennedy Presidential Library on Boston's Columbia Point.

To mark the Eire Society's 50th anniversary, five gold medals were awarded, and the society commissioned the Irish artist Val McGannto to create a painting of Joyce's Tower. Dedicated to the people of Massachusetts, the painting now hangs in the reading room of the State House. In 1989 the Eire Society presented a facsimile of The Book of Kells to the Irish collection at the Burns Library at Boston College.

The society has been a charitable, nonprofit organization since its inception. In 1945, the society donated $1,000 to Boston's Museum of Fine Arts to purchase ancient gold Celtic ornaments, and in 1950, it presented $1,000 to Richard Cardinal Cushing, archbishop of Boston. Cardinal Cushing endorsed the check to Ireland's Muintir na Tire for use in its back-to-the-land movement. In 1953, the Society presented three Fergus O'Ryan oils to local institutions: one each to the Boston Public Library, Harvard's Fogg Museum, and Boston College High School. Boston College received works of literature, history, and law (including $2,300 worth of Irish legal documents in facsimile), as well as several portraits and landscapes of Mountmellick and Tramore Bay. Harvard University accepted an eighteenth-century Perry violin in addition to $5,000 to underwrite acquisition of treasures on microfilm from the National Library of Ireland. The society donated a rare A. J. Potter score to the Boston Symphony Orchestra to fund a tour of Europe in Dublin and Cork. In 1966, the society formed a delegation for Dublin to march in the Easter Sunday parade of 1966, which is depicted in Cuimhneachan, the official record of Ireland's commemoration of the 1916 Rising.

Susan Gedutis Lindsay

See also: DE VALERA, Eamon; FORD, John; HEANEY, Seamus; HUSTON, John; MONTAGUE, John

Reference

History of the Eire Society: Adapted from the work of the late George E. Ryan. www.eiresociety.org/esmission.html (accessed July 27, 2007).

EL SALVADOR

Although Ireland has had historical links with many countries in Central America and South America, its connections with El Salvador only came to the fore during the 1980s. From 1979, El Salvador had been experiencing a bloody civil war in which the government forces were fighting against left-wing rebels of the Farabundo Marti National Liberation Front (FMLN). This was at a time when President Ronald Reagan had declared the Soviet Union to be "the evil empire" and when he thought its influence was spreading across Latin America. This was true not only of Cuba and later of Grenada, but also of El Salvador's neighbor Nicaragua, where the Sandinistas toppled the Somoza regime in 1979.

To counter Soviet and Cuban influence in the region, Reagan began to supply anticommunist governments with arms and money. The El Salvadoran military, because the country was in a civil war against rebels said to be receiving support from the Soviet Union, became the recipient of large amounts of military and financial aid from the United States. One of the critics of this arrangement between America and the El Salvadoran government was Oscar Romero, the archbishop of San Salvador, who criticized the El Salvadoran government's abuse of human rights in many of his weekly homilies at Mass. In this way he became a focus for some of the discontent against the government, and he began to attract international attention because of his statements. Once, at a sermon delivered at a mass in the city's cathedral, he called on soldiers in the army to disobey orders that oppressed the human rights of others. The next day, while he was celebrating Mass in a chapel near the cathedral in the capital, he was assassinated. It was suspected, and later confirmed by a United Nations report, that his assassination had been ordered by Major Roberto d'Aubisson, a vehemently anticommunist army officer who had received some military training in the United States and was the head of military intelligence. The funeral of Archbishop Romero, as well as being attended by thousands of El Salvadorans, was also attended by Bishop Eamonn Casey, the bishop of Galway in Ireland and the head of the Catholic charity Trócaire. A charismatic figure, who had been appointed as a bishop at a relatively young age, he later gave an emotional account on Irish television of being in the crowd when the crowds at the funeral were fired upon by government troops.

President Ronald Reagan's visit to Ireland in 1984 was surrounded by more controversy than the visit of any other American president. There were large demonstrations opposed to his visit. Most of this opposition was due to U.S. foreign policy in Latin America, particularly in El Salvador and Nicaragua, and U.S. support to military and undemocratic governments there. As well as visiting the ancestral home of his family in Ballyporeen, Co. Tipperary, Reagan was awarded an honorary degree by University College Galway. However, the bishop of Galway, Eamonn Casey, refused to meet Reagan, citing America's support for military regimes, in particular Reagan's support for the Nicaraguan contras and El Salvador's military government.

The connections between Ireland and El Salvador continued in November 1989 when six Jesuit priests, who had been working in the Universidad Centroamericana José Simeón Cañas in San Salvador, were taken out and shot dead along with their housekeeper and her daughter. Although it was made to look as if they had been killed by left-wing guerrillas, death squads linked to the El Salvadoran army were suspected. As a result of these killings, there were commemorations held in Ireland by the Jesuits and in the schools which they administered.

David Doyle

Winners of the National Book Award in 1960, (left to right) for poetry, Life Studies, *Robert Lowell; for biography,* James Joyce, *Richard Ellman; and for short novels,* Goodbye Columbus, *Philip Roth. (Bettmann/Corbis)*

References

In Memoriam: The Jesuit Martyrs of El Salvador. CIIR: Trócaire, 1990.

Jesuit Communication Centre. *El Salvador: Chronicle of a Cover-Up: Jesuit University Murders, 16th November 1989.* Swords, Ireland: Irish El Salvador Support Committee, 1991.

ELLMAN, RICHARD DAVID (1918–1987)

Richard Ellmann was born on March 15, 1918, in Highland Park, Michigan, where he spent his youth. After obtaining both his BA and MA degrees from Yale, he taught for a year at Harvard. In 1943 he began war service, working in both the Office of Strategic Services (the wartime precursor to the Central Intelligence Agency) and the U.S. Navy's construction battalions (popularly called the "Seabees"). While on assignment to London, Ellmann took time off to visit the Anglo-Irish poet W. B. Yeats's widow George, who gave him primary access to her husband's manuscript materials. Ellmann's study of these resulted in two influential interpretations of the poet, *The Man and the Masks* (1948)—which was essentially his 1947 PhD thesis at Yale—and *The Identity of Yeats* (1954).

After teaching for several years at Harvard, Ellmann taught from 1951 to 1968 at Northwestern University. In 1959 he published his most highly acclaimed work, a biography of *James Joyce,* which he revised in 1982, and he also edited important collections of Joyce's letters and critical writings. He taught again at Yale from 1968 to 1970, after which he accepted a post at New College of Oxford University, which he held from 1970 to 1984. From 1982 until 1986 he also taught at Emory University. With the exception of Harvard (where he was employed as instructor and assistant professor), all of Ellmann's postwar appointments were professorships or named professorships. He was one of America's most influential and internationally renowned scholars of modern Irish literature. Ellmann's works on Yeats and Joyce helped establish them as subjects in American academia, and his interpretations of their work continue to attract widespread concurrence. His biographies of James Joyce and Oscar Wilde are notably accomplished, blending astute artistic criticism with enormous biographical comprehensiveness. His critics suggest that he displays an excessive interest in his subjects' sexual peculiarities, and that his fascination with his subjects occasionally leads him to an unscholarly acceptance of their views (as in his antagonistic depiction of Oliver St. John Gogarty in *James Joyce*). Nevertheless, his works remain the touchstones from which other critics depart, and which even detractors acknowledge to be important contributions to scholarship. Ellmann died on May 13, 1987.

Andrew Goodspeed

See also: GOGARTY, Oliver St. John; JOYCE, James Augustine Aloysius; YEATS, William Butler

References

Dick, Susan, et al., eds. *Essays for Richard Ellmann: Omnium Gatherum.* Quebec and Gerrards Cross, ON: McGill-Queens University Press and Colin Smythe, 1989.

Ellmann, Richard. *Four Dubliners.* Washington, DC: Library of Congress, 1986.

Ellmann, Richard. *Oscar Wilde.* New York: Knopf, 1988.

EMIGRATION

Emigration refers to leaving one's country of residence to assume residency in another land. It usually implies an extended period abroad, but it is not strictly dependent on the permanency of the departure. The primary sense of emigration, however, most often describes an attempt to live in another country and to attain citizenship there. It is also commonly held to refer to leaving one's native land, yet may exceptionally apply to one leaving a country in which one has resided, but which was not the country of one's birth.

The term *emigration* may refer to the actions of an individual, a family, or a larger social group. Forced abandonment of one's country, either through coercive expulsion or judicially imposed exile, is a form of emigration, but the terms more commonly used in these instances are *expulsion* or *exile*. (Judicial exportation has also been referred to as "transportation," but that term has now an almost exclusively historical usage.) A person who lives abroad by choice, but who retains the citizenship of the land of his or her birth, is frequently referred to as an expatriate. These distinctions, however, are fluid, and the strict application of the terms *emigrant, exile,* and *expatriate* often depends on the person's self-identification.

Ireland is famously a nation of emigrants. A strong sense remains of "the Irish" as incorporating both the native-born residents of Ireland and the emigrants and descendants of emigrants (sometimes known as the "Irish Diaspora"). Yet there are immediate complications inherent in the notion of the Irish as an emigrant nation. Ireland has long been a home to many who were not born there: repeated attack, settlement, and intermarriage have brought large numbers of non-Irish to Ireland, tremendously complicating the notion of what it means to be Irish or to settle abroad. The Ireland-born descendants of such migrants have historically struggled with questions of Irish identity and divided notions of homeland. Evidence suggests that the native-born Irish (of whatever descent) have been similarly migratory. As just one example, the initial Viking settlers of Iceland encountered hermits who are thought to have been religious eremites from Ireland who had come to Iceland seeking solitude. The early migration patterns of Irish settlers are difficult now to reconstruct; what seems certain is that the early Irish were not isolated and must have settled outside the island in appreciable numbers, just as numerous outsiders came to Ireland and stayed.

However one defines Irish identity, it is indubitable that emigration has long taken residents of Ireland away from the island. Mass movements of people, of course, are a commonplace of history; Ireland, therefore, ought not be seen as unique, but as an unusual extreme in the extent of its emigratory patterns. Yet the numbers of emigrants from Ireland can be difficult to establish. The main body of mass Irish emigration is commonly considered to belong to the years 1800–2000 (dates chosen more for their general utility than for exact historical delineations). Reputable guesses frequently suggest that 5 or 6 million Irish emigrated during this period, and several responsible estimates have reached as high as 7 or 8 millions. Whatever the exact number may be, the emigratory depletion of Ireland between 1800 and 2000 is one of the most significant nonmilitary depopulations in modern history. Perhaps the single most important mass emigration during this period was caused by the Potato Famine of 1845–1849. The terrible conditions of starvation, sickness, and poverty that followed upon the failure of the potato crops produced a grim and astonishing modern exodus. Although exact numbers are not available, the famous proposition that the famine led to "one million dead, one million fled" does not seem suspiciously inaccurate.

Irish emigrants during and after the famine went largely to four main destinations: the United States, Canada, Great Britain, and Australia. (However, numerous other destinations received smaller groups of Irish emigrant settlers.) The most important group of emigrants was likely those who went to the United States, for they created significant bodies of Irish in the major cities of the American Northeast, most notably in Boston and New York. These ethnic Irish enclaves encouraged other Irish to emigrate, as the later migrants could be reasonably certain of encountering people of similar backgrounds and culture in their new homeland. This was frequently a wishful dream, however; many Irish emigrants to the United States encountered hostility and outright prejudice upon their arrival. Yet their collective success contributed to the Irish becoming one of the most prominent, successful, and politically important ethnic identities in the United States.

Throughout the nineteenth and twentieth centuries, Irish emigrants went abroad for an enormous variety of reasons. Significant debates exist among historians as to whether the Irish emigrants of the period 1800–2000 did so because they were the most entrepreneurial and daring, or whether instead they left because they were simply the most disadvantaged, hopeless, and desperate. It is likely that a true understanding of Irish emigration must accommodate both intrepidity and despair: many left in the hope of better economic opportunities; others left to rejoin brothers, parents, or spouses already abroad; some presumably left simply for the sake of adventure; many fled because there was no viable alternative to departure; and a notably large number of artistic figures went into self-imposed exile. Yet most Irish emigrants were not prominent artists or accomplished individuals, and they simply left for years, or a lifetime, to work and settle outside Ireland. Only in the 1960s did this trend diminish significantly. By the late 1990s the improving economy of the Republic of Ireland, combined with the lessening of hostilities in Northern Ireland, rendered the urge to emigrate less necessitous than it had been for the two previous centuries. Today many Irish still choose to live abroad, yet such a choice has ceased to be felt as economically unavoidable or politically imperative.

If Ireland is famously a nation of emigrants, the United States is equally a nation of immigrants (people moving into a country). The significant majority of modern American citizenry is descended from immigrants. The foundations of the country's political organization and legal structure originate in European intellectual traditions and political ideals. Much of America's artistic and aesthetic work continues to reveal strong affiliations with European culture, and American artists have long found receptive audiences for their works in Europe.

The United States is, in many ways, the most generally successful nation of immigrants in the modern world. Yet, although the United States may reasonably express pride in the widespread acceptance of immigrants into its population (the famous melting pot of America metaphor), such assimilation has not been without difficulties. The initial overwhelming of Native Americans by outside settlers essentially destroyed the native ways of life and

almost invariably dispossessed the indigenous peoples of their traditional lands. Many modern African Americans are descended directly from the most pitiable of immigrants to America, the slaves. Ethnic prejudices have been widespread throughout the history of the United States; although these rarely reached the levels of organized hatred attained by the pogroms of Eastern Europe, large bodies of Americans have nonetheless been deprived of their dignity and opportunities because of ethnic bias. Immigration quotas have also denied potential immigrants or refugees the chance to reside in America. In the United States a widespread paradox remains regarding immigration: there is a strong sense of identification with the ethnicity of immigrant ancestors, combined with a politically volatile suspicion of modern immigrants, particularly of those who are not legally permitted to reside in the United States.

It is almost impossible to assess fully the influence of Irish immigrants to the United States and Canada. Irish immigrants to England and Australia certainly attained significant accomplishments, yet the achievements of the Irish in North America, and particularly in the United States, have been nation forming. The Irish remain one of the most recognizable ethnic elements in American culture, and their traditions have become essentially indistinguishable from American traditions. (The largest Saint Patrick's Day parade in the world is not in Dublin, but New York City.) The Irish have played an extensive role in American political life; the famed Irish Brigade of the American Civil War was combative and highly decorated, and the Kennedys of Massachusetts are one of the most politically prominent families in American history. Yet the major connections between the Irish and the North Americans have always been established by undistinguished, normal migrants and by the affections for "the old country" they have instilled in their descendants. Similarly, the economic prosperity that the Irish have for centuries found in North America has brought generation after generation of Irish emigrants, each of which establishes its own interrelations between Ireland and the Americas. To this day many Irish who have never visited Canada or the United States have friends or family who are Irish immigrants there.

Andrew Goodspeed

See also: BOSTON; GREAT FAMINE, The; NEW YORK CITY

References

Coogan, Tim Pat. *Wherever Green is Worn.* New York: Palgrave, 2001.

Drudy, P. J., ed. *The Irish in America: Emigration, Assimilation and Impact.* Cambridge: Cambridge University Press, 1985.

Houston, Cecil, and William Smyth. *Irish Emigration and Canadian Settlement.* Toronto: University of Toronto Press, 1990.

McCaffrey, Lawrence. *Textures of Irish America.* Syracuse, NY: Syracuse University Press, 1992.

Miller, Kirby. *Emigrants and Exiles.* New York: Oxford University Press, 1985.

Miller, Kirby, et al. *Irish Immigrants in the Land of Canaan.* New York: Oxford University Press, 2003.

EMMET, JOHN PATTEN (1796–1842)

Born in Dublin on April 8, 1796, Dr. John Patten Emmet was the second son of lawyer and United Irishman Thomas Addis Emmet (1764–1827). John's uncle and Thomas's brother was the famous revolutionary and United Irishman Robert Emmet (1778–1803), who was half hanged and beheaded by the British for sedition in September 1803. Furthermore, John's grandfather was the respected Dr. Robert Emmet, who served as the late eighteenth-century personal physician to Ireland's lord lieutenant, Britain's official representative in Ireland.

Because of Thomas Addis Emmet's anti-British activities in Ireland during the run-up to the Rebellion of 1798, John's father was imprisoned in Scotland from 1798 to 1802. Upon his release, the Emmet family first moved to Brussels, then Paris, during the following two years. In 1804, the Emmets immigrated to the United States. Thomas practiced law in New York City, often representing a growing and needy Irish immigrant population. He also served as New York state attorney general (1812–1813).

During his early years in America, John Patten Emmet received a classical education at a Long Island academy. After graduation, he entered the United States Military Academy at West Point, New York. His growing reputation as a mathematician earned him a position on the faculty while he was still pursuing his undergraduate degree.

In 1817, John's poor health forced him to leave school. (Emmet was plagued with chronic ill health throughout his life.) He spent most of the next two years in Italy studying music, sculpture, and painting. Returning to New York in 1819, he entered medical school. Upon graduation in 1822, Dr. Emmet practiced medicine for three years in Charleston, South Carolina.

His emergent reputation as a chemist and inventor attracted the interest of former president Thomas Jefferson. In 1825, Jefferson offered Emmet the chair of professor of natural history at the newly established University of Virginia in

Charlottesville. As a professor, Emmet lectured on a wide range of subjects, including zoology, botany, mineralogy, chemistry, geology, and rural economy. In addition to his students, Emmet's classes were often attended by fellow colleagues and curious townspeople.

Two years later, with his teaching responsibilities reduced to permit him more time for his special interests, Dr. Emmet became the university's first professor of chemistry and materia medica. During that same year, 1827, he married Mary Byrd Tucker, the daughter of a prominent Virginia family. Together, they had three children.

In 1831, Emmet purchased a 106-acre farm near the university. He wanted the land for building a family home and space for pursuing his silk-making, horticulture, and wine production ventures.

Three years later, Emmet began overseeing the construction of his family's new home. Completed a year later, at a cost of $2,500, the two-and-a-half-story brick vernacular structure incorporated many Jeffersonian architectural features. Emmet christened this new home Morea House, after the botanical name for the Chinese mulberry tree, *Morus multicaulis,* whose leaves form the staple diet of the silkworm. Located near the university's original Academical Village, on what is now Sprigg Lane, the house is the only surviving structure built by an original faculty member. Today, the building is owned and used by the University of Virginia.

Dr. Emmet lived only seven years in Morea House. He died suddenly on August 15, 1842, at the age of forty-six, while on a journey to New York. He was buried in New York City's Marble Cemetery.

That year, his fellow faculty members paid him special tribute. They recognized his 17 years of distinguished service to the University of Virginia, the community, and the world of science and learning. Later, Charlottesville further honored Emmet by naming one of its main thoroughfares after him.

As a postscript, the Emmet family's Irish heritage was actively pursued by John's third son, Dr. Thomas Addis Emmet (1829–1919). This younger Dr. Emmet became a noted physician, lawyer, and writer. Among his written efforts were a detailed family history and a comprehensive volume on Irish immigration. (Copies of his works are available in the University of Virginia library.)

Additionally, Dr. Emmet spent the later years of his life tracing Irish records, trying to locate the grave of his famous relative, Robert Emmet. In 1905, he found the headless skeleton of a man in Dublin's St. Michan's cemetery which was believed to be that of his great-uncle.

Thomas Emmet died on March 1, 1919. Three years after his death, the doctor's body was finally reinterred in Dublin's Glasnevin Cemetery. During the interval since his death, the British government had refused his family's request to have Thomas's body buried in Ireland. It was only after the establishment of the Irish Free State that Ireland welcomed home another of its noble champions.

Cathal Liam

See also: EMMET, Thomas Addis;
    NATIONALISM, IRISH-AMERICAN

References
Emmet, Thomas Addis. *The Emmet Family, with Some Incidents Relating to Irish History and a Biographical Sketch of Prof. John Patten Emmet, M.D., and Other Members.* New York: Bradstreet Press, 1898.
Emmet, Thomas Addis. *Incidents of My life; Professional—Literary—Social, with Service in the Cause of Ireland.* New York: G. P. Putman's Sons, 1911.

Emmet, Thomas Addis. *Ireland under English Rule; or, A Plea for the Plaintiff.* New York: Putnam, 1903.

Emmet, Thomas Addis. *Irish Emigration During the Seventeenth and Eighteenth Centuries.* New York: 1899.

Emmet, Thomas Addis. *A Memoir of John Patten Emmet, M.D., Formerly Professor of Chemistry and Materia Medica in the University of Virginia, with a Brief Outline of the Emmet Family History.* New York: Bradstreet Press, 1898.

Emmet, Thomas Addis. *Memoir of Thomas Addis and Robert Emmet, with their Ancestors and Immediate Family.* New York: The Emmet Press, 1915.

Liam, Cathal. *Forever Green: Ireland Now & Again.* Cincinnati, OH: St. Pádraic Press, 2003.

EMMET, THOMAS ADDIS (1764–1827)

Thomas Addis Emmet has often been ignored because of the enormous presence in Irish history of his brother, Robert Emmet. Thomas Emmet, however, was one of the

Portrait of political activist and lawyer Thomas Addis Emmet. (Library of Congress)

core members of the Dublin Society of the United Irishmen, and after the failed Rebellion of 1798, he had an extremely successful and influential public career in the United States. Like William Sampson, Thomas Addis Emmet started his career with the United Irishmen by representing them in law courts during the mid-1790s. He became a member of the Directory of the United Irishmen in 1797, but he was arrested just before the rebellion broke out and sent to Fort George in Scotland, where his cellmates included William Sampson and William James Macneven. Following Lord Cornwallis's policy of conciliation, the imprisoned United Irishman leadership struck a deal with the British authorities: in exchange for a full disclosure of the Revolution plans, and especially those involving Irish cooperation with the French, the prisoners would be allowed to immigrate to any country that was not at war with Great Britain at the time. Emmet immigrated to the United States. Emmet's success as a lawyer in Ireland followed him over the Atlantic, and after he landed in Philadelphia in late 1803, the city's mayor, DeWitt Clinton, personally asked him to take up practice in New York City, surpassing the residency restrictions of practicing law for Emmet and for William Sampson. With help from Clinton, Emmet launched his legal career in the United States. The law firm that Emmet founded is still operating in New York City under the name Emmet & Marvin; Theodore Roosevelt was a partner in the firm. Unlike the career of his friend, William Sampson, Thomas Addis Emmet's career was successful from the beginning. In 1806 Emmet was part of the successful defense team for William Smith and Samuel Ogden for violating the Neutrality Act of 1794; this ended in a not-guilty verdict. In 1809 Emmet was prosecuting a criminal conspiracy case against the Journeymen Cordwainers of New York, who were defended by William Sampson. Emmet narrowly won the heated case. By using very skilled and eloquent argumentation in the courtroom, Emmet had a string of successes, and from 1812 to 1813 he served as the attorney general for the State of New York. In 1815 he argued a case for his friend, the steamboat inventor Robert Fulton, before the Supreme Court. Emmet continued with his legal career until the end, as he died amidst legal proceedings in 1827.

In addition to his legal career, Emmet was closely involved with the Irish community in New York. He supported Daniel O'Connell's campaign for Catholic emancipation but fell out of favor with O'Connell over his denunciation of the United Irishmen and armed struggle. Emmet's status in the Irish community helped to make the concerted effort against Rufus King's campaigns for political office in 1807 into a personal vendetta, which destroyed King's campaign. He also had a close relationship with Theobald Wolfe Tone's widow Matilda, whom he held in high regard. When he died in 1827, Emmet's burial procession was one of the largest New York had ever seen at that time. He is buried at St. Paul's Chapel in the Bowery on Broadway. The monument for him, which was commissioned and paid for by the Irish community on the East Coast, still stands to this day by the chapel entrance.

Aki Kalliomäki

See also: EMMET, John Patten; O'CONNELL, Daniel; SAMPSON, William

References

Emmet, Thomas Addis. *Memoir of Thomas Addis Emmet and Robert Emmet.* New York: Emmet Press, 1915.
Madden, Richard R. *The United Irishmen, Their Lives and Times.* Dublin: James Duffy, 1887.
O'Donnell, Ruan. *Robert Emmet and the Rebellion of 1798.* Dublin: Irish Academic Press, 2003.
O'Donnell, Ruan. *Robert Emmet and the Rebellion of 1803.* Dublin: Irish Academic Press, 2003.
Wilson, David. *United Irishmen, United States: Immigrant Radicals in the Early Republic.* Ithaca, NY: Cornell University Press, 1998.

ETHNIC AND RACE RELATIONS, IRISH AND AFRICAN AMERICANS

The history of Irish and African-American relations in the United States includes much conflict, but it was not always as negative as has often been portrayed. It was in the Caribbean, rather than in what would become the United States, that the two peoples first encountered each other in substantial numbers in the New World. Most Irish immigrants to the Caribbean were impoverished Catholic peasants who had been deported or exiled for various crimes, or kidnapped or sold into servitude. With the introduction of sugar plantations in the Caribbean, voluntary indentured servants could not meet the demand for increased labor; consequently, prisoners from Oliver Cromwell's Scottish and Irish campaigns, as well as Africans, began to be imported for slave labor. Beginning as early as the 1650s, as many as 60,000 Irish were brought to the New World in this way. Many historians argue that both European and African slaves were treated so badly in the Caribbean that there was little appreciable distinction among them, regardless of differences in skin color and ethnicity.

When in the 1830s the Catholic Irish began immigrating to America in substantially greater numbers than previously, early indicators are that the Irish, if anything, got along better with African Americans than with native-born white Americans. Numerous neighborhoods and districts in large cities, such as New York City's Seneca Village and Five Points District, were well-known—sometimes infamous—for their large numbers of African Americans and Irish immigrants living side by side. There were several instances of African Americans and Irish immigrants marrying or cohabitating, although concrete numbers are hard to come by. In 1849, Quakers conducting an inquiry into the living conditions of African Americans in Philadelphia commented that African Americans frequently lived in the same houses, and often the same rooms, as Irish immigrants. Even as late as 1899, one study of African Americans in the same city noted that of black-white married couples in one neighborhood, the majority of immigrant women married to black men were Irish, significantly outnumbering women from any other country married to black men.

Blacks and the Irish, as they had in the Caribbean in previous centuries, also worked together frequently; for example, many canals were dug and railroad lines laid by African Americans and the Irish toiling side by side. However, although many historians and social scientists have suggested that Irish racism against African Americans was motivated mainly by competition for low-wage jobs as the number of Irish immigrants increased, more recent scholarship has challenged this notion. For one thing, the Irish in the South during the antebellum period tended to be as racist toward blacks, if not even more so, as their compatriots in the Northern states. Given that African Americans were enslaved in the South at this time, the Irish were not

in direct competition with them for paid work. However, the connection in the minds of higher-class whites between blacks and the Irish had begun long before the two peoples began to live and work together in great numbers. Popular magazines, novels, plays, and songs from the late eighteenth century contain examples of African and Irish characters cavorting together, with both portrayed as hilariously childlike buffoons. Even in the minds of sympathetic observers, the extreme poverty and degradation many African Americans and Irish immigrants shared tended to conflate the two peoples. The Quakers who conducted the 1849 Philadelphia study of black neighborhoods remarked that of the African Americans and Irish there, "it is hard to tell which has sunk the lowest in filth and misery."

These long-extant prejudices and stereotypes reached a peak in the mid-nineteenth century and made many Irish immigrants begin to distance themselves from the blacks they were often connected with not only literally in their neighborhoods and working quarters, but also in the minds of native-born white Americans. Many Irish recognized that they were linked with blacks, whether they liked it or not, in the perceptions of white Protestant Americans, so their antiblack racism has been viewed by many historians as a defense mechanism to ensure their place—however low—in the "white" strata of nineteenth-century American society. This led to many Irish adopting general American antiblack and pro-slavery beliefs with more fervor than even the most ardent native-born white racists. The Catholic Irish *Freedman's Journal,* an otherwise respectable publication, frequently printed articles disparaging African Americans. Even when the Irish patriot Daniel O'Connell denounced American slavery, several Irish immigrants rallied against him, penning public letters rebuking their hero. Undoubtedly, part of the distaste of many Irish for abolitionism was the movement's roots in Protestant evangelicalism, but that alone does not explain the wholesale support for slavery of so many Irish, especially given that many, though not all, abolitionists also decried prejudice and discrimination against Catholics and immigrants. Another reason many Irish immigrants strongly opposed abolitionism is that most white Americans, even those theoretically opposed to slavery, viewed abolitionists and their unsparing discourse with mistrust and dislike, at best. Even a few African Americans publicly declared that they were antislavery but "not necessarily abolitionists" as the historian Benjamin Quarles noted. By opposing abolitionism, Irish immigrants were arguably proclaiming their "Americanness" rather than trumpeting their racism.

Nevertheless, it is undeniable that many Irish, both men and women, were also among the most enthusiastic participants in riots targeting African Americans, the savagery of their attacks frequently horrifying other whites. (In one incident, both Irish men and women cut off pieces of the body of a crippled black lynching victim as gruesome souvenirs; in another, Irish female rioters beat to death, over a six-hour period, an Irish militiaman who tried to stop their attacks.) Not surprisingly, many antislavery novels of the period portray Irish characters as violent, uncouth "nagur" haters, in contrast to peaceful, good-natured blacks. By giving full vent to the worst racism of native-born whites, some Irish undoubtedly hoped to secure recognition of their own

"whiteness." They may have lacked money, education, and social status, but at least they possessed the "white" privilege of attacking blacks. One reason so many Irish treated African Americans horribly was simply because they, like other whites, could usually do so with impunity. Rioters who attacked blacks were seldom punished severely, even when they had committed the most horrific acts of violence against their victims. (Many policemen, firemen, and militia members in large cities were Irish Catholic themselves, which may have exacerbated matters.)

Irish immigrants could also show their hatred of blacks in nonviolent but equally blatant ways, as when Irish longshoremen campaigned in New Orleans for the right to work on an "all-white waterfront." As Irish immigrants made greater inroads in the workforce, Irish workers, like many other whites, sometimes refused to work alongside African Americans, forcing employers who otherwise would have hired blacks to change their practices. Because the actions of a minority of Irish immigrants against African Americans were so odious, the fact that many Irish did not share such racist attitudes has frequently been overlooked. Frederick Douglass recalled in his memoirs that during his childhood, Irish immigrants who learned he was a slave expressed genuine pity for him. During one riot targeting African Americans in New York in 1863, an Irish Catholic family took an African American family into their house and fed and sheltered them for several days, and there are many reports of similar occurrences. Given the often fearsome reprisals suffered by whites who tried to defend African Americans from attacks, it is no exaggeration to say such Irish immigrants acted heroically.

While they abhorred white Protestant Americans comparing them to blacks, the Irish in America were not reluctant to compare themselves to African Americans, or to slaves, to call attention to their own grievances. A play staged in New York around 1860 by Irish actors was entitled *Uncle Pat's Cabin, or Lights and Shades of Life in Ireland*, in an explicit reference to Harriet Beecher Stowe's famous antislavery novel *Uncle Tom's Cabin*. The play highlighted the oppression faced by the Catholic Irish in their native land at the hands of Protestant landowners. African Americans were also keenly aware of native-born whites' linking them to Irish immigrants, and they were no happier about this than the Irish. African-American journalists complained of the poorest, most ignorant European—and Catholic—immigrants being more welcome in America than native-born, Protestant residents of African descent. Many African Americans could not help resenting the often virulent prejudice against them that the Irish so readily adopted in the United States. Some, like Frederick Douglass and Marcus Garvey, perceived clearly that the two peoples in fact had much in common and hoped that the Irish, given their long history of oppression in their homeland and the discrimination and difficulties they continued to face in the United States, would show more solidarity with the plight of slaves and free blacks. The oppression of the Irish by the English for more than 500 years, though systematic and often brutal, was not the equal of American slavery and subsequent antiblack Jim Crow laws. However, there were numerous clear similarities between the oppression suffered by the two peoples: eviction or bodily removal from native lands; indiscriminate abuse; hellish Atlantic crossings on overcrowded, unsanitary ships; stereotyping in the media and popular literature as apelike brutes or childlike fools; and discrimination in employment and housing.

Some black and white observers were insightful enough to postulate that the racial conflict between the Irish and African Americans might in part have been created, or at least encouraged, by higher-class whites looking to maintain control over their social inferiors, whether African Americans or poor whites. One of the first novels published by an African American, Frank J. Webb's *The Garies and Their Friends*, portrays a wealthy, racist white lawyer who cunningly exploits the poverty and ignorance of Irish immigrants to enlist them in intimidating and even murdering African Americans. Webb's novel is notable for its relatively sympathetic treatment of the Irish and their exploitation. The famed English actress Fanny Kemble, who lived on a slaveholding plantation in Georgia during her brief marriage to a Southern planter, wrote in her widely read memoirs that wealthy whites in the South deliberately exacerbated tensions between African-American slavers and Irish immigrant laborers to prevent the two groups from developing a natural alliance with each other based on their shared experiences of oppression.

Gradually, relations between the Irish and African Americans began to improve, largely as a result of Irish Americans' slow acceptance by and assimilation into the dominant white American culture. Despite white Protestant Americans' general approbation of their Catholicism and culture, the Irish shared the most important factor in common with them: skin color. Although dislike of the Irish lingered into the twentieth century, they did not face the barriers African Americans did such as the Jim Crow laws in the South, which were not abolished until the 1960s. In addition, their sheer numbers, far higher than the African-American population, made it impossible for white Protestant Americans to continue to marginalize Irish Catholics completely. As Irish Americans felt more accepted as true Americans, they felt less need to differentiate themselves so vehemently from the African Americans with whom they had previously, and disparagingly, been conflated. Irish-American politicians, most notably President John F. Kennedy and his brother Robert Kennedy, stood up to white racist politicians and helped to implement civil rights for African Americans. Although racial tensions remained between many Irish and African Americans throughout the twentieth century, most notably the school busing protests that occurred in largely Irish-American South Boston during the early 1970s, these were mainly general white-black racial problems rather than specifically Irish-African conflicts. It is interesting to note, however, that despite the history of previously tense race relations between African and Irish Americans, the successes of the African American civil rights movement were a direct influence on Irish Nationalists who wished to gain full civil rights for Catholics in Northern Ireland in the 1960s and later.

Danielle Maze

See also: ABOLITIONISM AND SLAVERY; DOUGLASS, Frederick; DRAFT RIOTS; EMIGRATION; KENNEDY, John Fitzgerald; O'CONNELL, Daniel

References
Douglass, Frederick. *My Bondage and My Freedom*. 1855. Reprint, Urbana: University of Illinois Press, 1987.
DuBois, W. E. B. *The Philadelphia Negro*. New York: Lippincott, 1899.
Kemble, Frances Anne. *Journal of a Residence on a Georgian Plantation in 1838–1839*. London: Longman, Roberts and Green, 1863.
Osofsky, Gilbert. *Harlem: the Making of a Ghetto. Negro New York, 1890–1930*. New York: Harper Torchbooks, 1968.
Quarles, Benjamin. *Black Abolitionists*. New York: Oxford University Press, 1969.
Report of the Committee of Merchants for the Relief of Colored People Suffering from the Late Riots in the City of New York. New York: G. A. Whitehorne, 1863.
A Statistical Inquiry into the Condition of People of Colour, of the City and Districts of Philadelphia. Philadelphia: Kite and Walton, 1849.
Webb, Frank J. *The Garies and Their Friends*. 1857. Reprint, New York: Negro Universities Press, 1971.

ETHNIC AND RACE RELATIONS, IRISH AND FRENCH CANADIANS

Ethnic relations between Irish and French Canadians have been historically shaped by intense struggles for power within the Canadian Catholic Church among Irish and French Catholics and by sectarian sentiment, which has aroused conflict between Irish Protestants and the largely French Catholic population. Reaching their peak in the nineteenth century, such tensions have diminished markedly in the twentieth century, as Irish- and French-Canadian populations have become largely secularized and their conflicts have been subsumed within wider linguistic struggles between English and French Canada.

To focus on the frequent conflict between Protestants and Catholics both within the Irish immigrant cohort and in the wider context of British North American and Canadian society at the expense of intra-confessional conflicts would be to neglect a major dynamic within Canadian history. Although there were several families of Irish extraction in New France, after the conquest of New France in 1759, there was an influx both of Protestants and (largely Irish) Catholics. In the eastern parts of what is now Canada, a sizable French-speaking population, the Acadians, were subject to expulsion by an order in 1755, and the colonial legislature in Nova Scotia proscribed the Roman Catholic religion. The Church there and elsewhere in British North America through most of the first half of the nineteenth century remained dominated in its highest episcopal positions by French Canadians, though they ministered to an increasingly ethnically diverse Catholic population, comprising Scottish Catholics in the maritime colonies; large Irish Catholic populations in Upper Canada, especially in major urban centers such as Halifax, Montreal, and York; and sizable numbers of German and other Catholics. If the episcopacy remained in French-Canadian hands through the first decades of the nineteenth century in much of British North America, Irish Canadians developed a hold on parts of the Church in maritime Canada (especially in parts of Nova Scotia) to the exclusion of many Acadian church leaders until the early twentieth century.

In the first decades of the nineteenth century Catholics in the maritime colonies won full political rights, and the ethnic complexion of the clergy became more varied, but key positions within the Church remained in French-Canadian hands. In places such as New Brunswick and Quebec, conflict between English- and French-speaking Catholics centered on administrative control of the Church, schooling, and a range of disputes that revealed deep ethno-religious cleavages within the Church, especially as figures such as Bishop MacDonnell (the Scottish-born bishop of Kingston from 1826) and Bishop Michael Power (the Irish-born Bishop of Toronto in 1840) represented the changing face of the episcopacy in British North America. While English-speaking Catholics faced an adversarial Orange press and frequent outbursts of anti-Catholicism, their integration within the mainstream of British North American society was marked. Irish Protestants, meanwhile, found a frequent bête noir in ultramontane Catholicism, which in different but pronounced ways had influenced the development of French-Canadian and Irish-Canadian Catholicism in the Victorian era.

In colonial politics, too much stress has been placed on viewing the Rebellions of 1837–1838 as ethnic revolts of the French and Irish. In Lower Canada especially the Irish-born community was deeply split between those who allied themselves with the Patriot leader Louis-Joseph Papineau, and those who, in such groups as Saint Patrick's Society of Montreal (established 1834), offered robust support to colonial authorities in suppression of the rebellions. As French-Canadians' influence over the Church as a whole waned, confessionalism became intertwined with politics to produce a vessel of ethno-religious politics in places such as Lower Canada, from which Irish Catholics felt increasingly isolated. In Montreal, for instance, the influx of Famine Irish arrived in a city with a vibrant Irish-Catholic associational culture—and a church, Saint Patrick's, that served as the center of the English-speaking Catholic community. As the demographics of Canadian Catholicism changed, with influxes of French-speaking Catholics into

Ontario in the later nineteenth century, the growth of English- and French-speaking métis populations in the West, and the immigration of thousands of Catholics of other ethnic backgrounds, conflicts intensified over the control of dioceses in Ontario, languages of instruction in Catholic schools (this became especially virulent in the first decades of the twentieth century), and continuing tensions between congregations which served as effective custodians of ethno-religious identity within the Church. The Irish Catholics' propensity to decouple linguistic and confessional issues in education disputes, and continuing wrestling over episcopal control of some diocese, have colored relations between the Irish and French Canadians in the early twentieth century. From the 1930s, these conflicts have been much less pronounced: the Acadians have won considerable control over the Church in areas of high French-speaking populations, and Irish-Canadians in Quebec and elsewhere, while not generally supportive of Quebec nationalism, have professed a "special relationship" with French Canada on the basis of shared confessional ties. This representation of communal binds demands closer scholarly attention. We know much more now, thanks to the ongoing work of Sherry Olson and others, about the comparative demographic behavior and social position of Irish and French Canadians in urban centers; rural communities demand further attention as we expand our knowledge of the complex interactions between these populations.

Kevin James

See also: EMIGRATION

References

James, K. J. "Dynamics of Ethnic Associational Culture in a Nineteenth-Century City: Saint Patrick's Society of Montreal, 1834–56." *Canadian Journal of Irish Studies* 26, no. 1 (2001): 47–66.

Murphy, Terrence, and Gerald Stortz, eds. *Creed and Culture: The Place of English-Speaking Catholics in Canadian Society, 1750–1930.* Montreal: McGill-Queen's Press, 1993.

Olson, Sherry. Website of Professor Sherry Olson. www.geog.mcgill.ca/faculty/olson/welcome.html (accessed August 23, 2007).

Trigger, Rosalyn. 'The geopolitics of the Irish Catholic parish in nineteenth-century Montreal.' *Journal of Historical Geography* 27.4 (2001): 553–572.

ETHNIC AND RACE RELATIONS, IRISH AND INDIGENOUS PEOPLES

The relationship between the Irish and indigenous peoples has always been uneasy. From its beginnings in the sixteenth century to its demise in the twentieth century, Protestant and Catholic Irish have poured into all reaches of the British Empire. There is no one mold for the nature of Irish participation in colonial activities. Some immigrants became actively involved in dispossessing and slaughtering indigenous populations while others blended into well-established settler societies. Ultimately, these subjects of imperialism became agents as they pursued self or family interest and wealth. Their involvement has been referred to by Hiram Morgan as an "unwelcome heritage" where the Irish, "far from empathising with indigenous peoples overseas . . . were as brutal as any other white colonisers."

In the United States, Scotch-Irish immigrants first rose to prominence as they followed the promise of land ownership and greater religious freedom. They settled first in the middle colonies and then began a process of internal migration, using the main route for settling the interior southern colonies, the Great Philadelphia Road. The settlement behavior of the Protestant Irish in colonial American resembled that of their German, English, and Scots counterparts, all of whom shared the colonial outlook. Such settlers memorialize their role as frontiersmen and so-called Indian fighters. As a dominant pioneering group, their pattern of settlement and land use altered the landscape and brought them into conflict with indigenous populations whose subsistence base was increasingly undermined.

After the American War of Independence, Britain reacted to the loss of its colonies by staking a tighter claim on British North America. This involved formalizing land claims and subduing the indigenous population through restriction of movement and religious conversion. Throughout North America, the French had already taken the lead in converting Native Americans to Catholicism. Wherever Irish missionaries participated in missions, they brought to their work a combination of egalitarianism and cultural imperialism. As time progressed the influence of Irish Catholicism on Native Americans was increasingly felt through the number of lay Irish immigrants arriving and requiring increased church infrastructure, as occurred in nineteenth-century New Brunswick when an influx of Irish immigrants afforded the presence of resident priests to minister to the Irish, Acadian, and Micmac Indians in the area.

Elsewhere in America, similar processes were at work. The Catholic Church authorities made the fledgling nation of Texas a separate jurisdiction from the Catholic Church in 1840 and sent Jean Marie Odin, a Vincentian priest, to supervise the transition. He became the first vicar apostolic of Texas in 1842 and made efforts to recruit priests from Ireland. One such recruit was Father John Joseph Lynch, future archbishop of Toronto. In the Northwest Territories, administrational intervention was requested when a colony of Scotch Presbyterians and Irish Catholics at the junction of the Assiniboine and Red rivers, which the Earl of Selkirk founded in 1812, aroused the ire of the Northwest Company and resulted in the Battle of Seven Oaks (June 19, 1816). In response, Selkirk obtained from the bishop of Quebec two missionaries to found a church mission, the express purpose of which was to convert the local aborigines. As the nineteenth century progressed, such administrational tactics were increasingly relied on to subdue Indian nations of the Plains culture area, which included the territories of the Stoneys/Assiniboine, Sarcee, Blackfoot, Blood, Peigan, Plains Cree, Sioux tribes. Heavy-handed interference in Native American society was the norm at the time, and numerous individual Irish men and women were involved in the process as treaties were settled, reservations established, and Indian agents dispatched.

Other Irish individuals in contact with Native Americans became intermediaries who encouraged better European understanding of indigenous art and culture. John Mullanphy of Enniskillen (1758–1833), the so-called first millionaire of the American West, sent his son Bryan to be educated at Stonyhurst College, Lancashire, in 1825. The 16-year-old boy brought 15 Native American artworks to his new school, where they remained until 1977, when they were lent to the British Museum. They are now part of a touring collection on Native American art and Irish commerce. Bryan Mullanphy (1809–1851) would go on to become a successful entrepreneur and philanthropist in the Midwest, endowing a hospital and other charities. Paul Kane (1810–1871), originally of Co. Cork, was an Irish Canadian who became famous for his paintings of First Nations peoples in the Canadian West and in the Oregon Country. In his youth Kane met George Catlin, an American painter who had depicted the Native Americans in the prairies and who was on a promotion tour for his book, *Letters and Notes on the Manners, Customs and Conditions of the North American Indians.* Kane decided to similarly document the Canadian Native Americans and undertook two voyages through the Canadian Northwest in the 1840s. Upon his return to Toronto, he produced more than 100 oil paintings from sketches he made during the journeys. The oil paintings departed from the accuracy of his field sketches in favor of more dramatic scenes; however, Kane's field sketches have proven a valuable resource for ethnographers. He also brought back from his trips a collection of artifacts, including masks, pipe stems, and crafts. Kane's travel report, published originally in London in 1859, was condescending but a success in its time. It has since been reported that Kane's travel notes were written in a style very different from the published text, and the book seems to have been heavily edited by others in order to package Kane's notes as a typical Victorian travel account. It is difficult to ascribe racism to the artist himself.

Contact between the Irish and indigenous people could also result in intermarriage. The Canadian métis developed a social style that freely borrowed from their aboriginal and European—including Irish—backgrounds to provide them with the cultural fabric of a new and colorful culture. They caught the imagination of many early writers with their genius for creating unique patterns and solutions for meeting day-to-day needs. For example, they adopted the multicolored sashes of the coureur de bois, the fiddling and jigging of the French and Irish, and mixed these cultural icons with the haunting chants and songs of the First Nation peoples. They had built settlements and created a complex network of communication patterns sufficient for the successful interrelationship of their members and outsiders. The nineteenth century métis had established a coherent and cohesive community.

The Irish Potato Famine, which culminated in "Black '47," did not directly affect Irish-indigenous relations on a large scale, although it greatly increased the presence of Irish Catholics in North America. The response from North America gave rise to an exceptional instance of goodwill expressed by the Choctaw Indian Nation. In dire straits themselves, they empathized when they heard of the plight of the Irish and collected the considerable sum of US$710 to buy much needed food for the starving Irish. Sixteen years before this, the Choctaw and four other tribes, including the Cherokee, Chickasaw, Creek and Seminole, had endured the Trail of Tears, a devastating forced trek from their ancestral lands to Oklahoma, to make room for new settlers. More than half perished from the exposure, malnutrition and diseases.

New postcolonial conceptualizations have sought to readdress the understanding of the Irish in North America. American writer Fintan O'Toole has discussed the complex cultural entanglement between

Ireland and the Wild West. Racist depictions of the Irish in the nineteenth-century English press would offer unflattering comparisons of native Irish and Native Americans. It has been rightly acknowledged that the Irish would come to play a central role in the near extermination of Native Americans, in a new environment where "the Irish cease to be the Indians and become the cowboys." However, it is increasingly highlighted how the historical realities of the western lifestyle were more complex. Cowboys tended to be young men and, unlike in Hollywood representations, were a mix of ethnic groups that reflected American society, including African Americans and Hispanics as well as English, Irish, German, and French immigrants; near the top of the profession were indigenous peoples. This diverse grouping was bound together through the necessity of upholding the reputation of their employers, the teamwork and shared adversity of working cattle on roundups and trail drives, and personal pride in what they did.

Irish and aboriginal historians, heritage workers, and political activists are increasingly drawing parallels between the Irish experience and that of First Nations peoples. Vernon Bellecourt, member of the Chippewa tribe of the Lakota nation and a founding member of the American Indian Movement (AIM), has suggested that the many struggles facing his people echo the struggles of the Irish against British oppression. For example, he identifies similarities between the Heart of the Earth Survival schools the AIM has started and the Irish hedge schools of the colonial period. He has also conducted a mission to Ireland that included attending Sinn Féin's Ard Fheis and speaking and providing interviews on behalf of his organization. Such activities indicate the potential for a rapidly expanding new area of study dedicated to examining native-newcomer relationships in a variety of contexts.

Mike Cottrell

See also: LYNCH, Archbishop John Joseph

References

Akenson, Donald Harman. "Irish Migration to North America, 1800–1920." In *The Irish Diaspora,* edited by Andy Bielenberg. New York: Longman, 2000.

American Indian Movement website. www.aimovement.org/ (accessed July 28, 2007).

Bielenberg, Andy, ed. *The Irish Diaspora.* New York: Longman, 2000.

Bielenburg, Andy. "Irish Emigration to the British Empire, 1700–1914." In *The Irish Diaspora,* edited by Andy Bielenberg. New York: Longman, 2000.

British Museum. "Native American Art: Irish American Trade: The Stonyhurst Mullanphy Collection." www.thebritishmuseum.ac.uk/explore/online_tours/americas/native_north_america/native_north_america.aspx (accessed August 23, 2007).

Cinefocus Canada. "The Art of Paul Kane." www.paulkane.ca (accessed July 28, 2007).

Irish Famine Curriculum Committee. *The Great Irish Famine.* [curriculum guide] Moorestown, New Jersey. 1996; revised 1998. www.nde.state.ne.us/SS/pdf/irish.pdf (accessed July 28, 2007).

Kenny, Kevin. "The Irish in the Empire." In *Ireland and the British Empire,* edited by Kevin Kenny. Oxford: Oxford University Press, 2004.

Morgan, Hiram. "An Unwelcome Heritage: Ireland's Role in British Empire-Building." *History of European Ideas* 19 (1994): 619.

O'Toole, Fintan. *A Mass for Jesse James: A Journey through 1980's Ireland.* Dublin: Raven Arts, 1990: 134.

Tallgrass Prairie National Reserve website. "Cowboys and Cattle." U.S. Department of the Interior. www.nps.gov/tapr/cowboys.htm (accessed August 23, 2007).

ETHNIC AND RACE RELATIONS, IRISH AND ITALIANS

The history of Irish American and Italian American relations originates between 1880 and 1924, the period when more than 4.5 million Italians entered the United States. Not long after Italy became a nation in 1871, the poor people of the cities led the way to America, followed by the impoverished peasants of the rural, interior regions. Eighty percent of those who emigrated came from the South, or the Mezzogiorno. The exodus was partly precipitated by an agricultural crisis and the resultant widespread poverty. The Italian immigrants were *morti di fame*—dying of hunger. Just as it was in Ireland, hunger was the symptom of a larger issue: the people of the Mezzogiorno were subjected to a long history of colonization by Northern Italy: military occupation, racist oppression, economic and political disenfranchisement, and a corrupt system of absentee landlords, coupled with natural disasters, cholera epidemics, and famine. Despite the similar histories of oppression that led to mass migration, the relations between the Irish-American community and the immigrants from southern Italy were tense, and conflicts overshadowed the desire for alliance.

The massive influx of immigrants to the United States reignited not only widespread anti-Catholic nativism and xenophobia, but it also exacerbated tensions between the newly arrived immigrant groups and the prior immigrant groups that were already firmly established, particularly the Irish. By the time the Italians started immigrating in large numbers, around 1880, the Irish-American community had a certain amount of social stability, as many were making economic advances, moving from the working classes to the middle classes. For the most part, when the southern Italian immigrants began to compete with Irish laborers for jobs, a portion of the Irish were moved into the managerial ranks to make room for the cheap Italian labor. Because Irish Americans now controlled the managerial jobs, they had powerful networks and the necessary resources to offer economic advancement to their own Irish communities.

Even though many Irish Americans had moved up the economic ladder and now held many of the managerial posts, there was still a considerable Irish-American working class in direct competition with recently arrived southern Italian laborers. The clashes between the two groups were many and spanned different industries. The Italians would agree to work for less money than the Irish, thus making them more attractive as a group to capitalists looking to maximize profits. The Irish laborers harbored resentment toward this cheap labor pool and considered it a threat to their attempts to organize and empower rank-and-file workers. And, indeed, it did threaten their unionizing efforts on occasion, as many American companies used Italian immigrants as union busters. Thus, the Italians developed a deserved reputation as strikebreakers; when Irish laborers would go on strike, the Italians were considered a simple solution to the issue.

The tensions concerning labor often led to violence. Job competition led to fierce discrimination that eventually led to rioting. In 1874, the coal-mining region of Armstrong, Pennsylvania, was the site of a bloody confrontation between these two groups. The Irish laborers were on strike. As was common, Italian laborers were brought in as unwitting scabs, desperate for work. The 150 Italians were greeted with gunfire, killing four. The Irish miners proceeded to burn the huts that housed the Italians. Because of this violent episode, the employers chose to provide weapons to the Italian workers as a protective measure against aggressive Irish-American forces. Relations between the two laboring groups remained strained well into the twentieth century.

One of the most well-known conflicts between Irish Americans and Italian Americans took place in 1891 in New Orleans. At that time, the Irish monopolized the jobs on the waterfront as well as the police force. When the Italians arrived in the late 1880s, they started running a fish and fruit trade, providing unwelcome competition for the Irish and initiating a rivalry. In addition, animosities flared between the two groups when it became apparent that a number of Italians were members of antidiscrimination groups and had been making alliances and developing commercial relationships with the African-American community, a transgressive development in the white supremacist South.

The already strained relationship between the Irish and Italians in New Orleans rose to a fever pitch when the Irish police chief, 32-year-old David Hennessey, was gunned down on March 15, 1890. Hennessey was one of the youngest police chiefs in the country and was well known throughout the nation for having an aggressive reputation. On his deathbed, Hennessey allegedly told his friend, Bill O'Connor, that the Italians were responsible for the shooting. O'Connor, a former policeman and captain of the Boylan Protective Police, a powerful local group that patrolled the streets of New Orleans with vigilante authority, led the investigation that resulted in more than 100 Italians being arrested. Ultimately, 19 Italian men were indicted for Hennessey's murder and were found innocent by the jury. This verdict ignited a fury among the Irish of New Orleans. On March 14, 1891, a mob bombarded the prison and lynched every Italian they found, murdering 11. Vicious anti-Italian hysteria ensued for quite some time, continuing through 1892, when widows of those lynched filed a federal lawsuit claiming that city officials purposefully failed to protect the victims from the violent mob. The claims were dismissed and no one was ever prosecuted for the 11 murders.

In addition to the sometimes volatile labor relations between the groups, the Catholic Church was another contentious site where the Irish and Italians encountered each other. As the first Catholic immigrant group to come to the United States in great numbers, the Irish were positioned early on to dominate the American Catholic Church hierarchy. When the Catholic immigrants from southern and eastern Europe arrived on U.S. soil a long period of internal dissension within the Catholic Church ensued. Consequently, for the Italians, the Church was yet another location where they were forced to confront Irish domination.

The Irish stronghold in the Church confirmed Catholicism as an integral part of Irish-American identity. For the southern Italians, on the other hand, their nationalism and their Catholicism were not so linked. The Italians perceived themselves to be under Irish control, as many Italians were essentially blocked from making progress in the American Catholic hierarchy. Irish America was quickly identified as the American equivalent to the *latifondisti*, the group of people in league with the Catholic Church, whose goal was to exploit the southern Italians. Thus, Irish America was perceived as being part of the ruling class, who would, on occasion, become convenient allies with the Yankee elite. The perception that the Irish were part of the established power structure, in the church, the labor market, and allied with the Yankee elite, fueled the antagonism between the Irish and Italians in the most crucial areas of their lives.

When the southern Italians arrived in the United States there were no Italian churches. For the most part, the churches were controlled by Irish Americans who were not 100 percent welcoming of their fellow Catholics. The new immigrants had their own unique rituals and wanted to continue practicing their faith as they had done in their homeland. The church-related rituals of the Italians were suspect in the eyes of the Irish-American Catholic hierarchy. The rituals were perceived as pagan, and therefore threatening to the traditions being practiced in the United States. Of particular suspicion were the Italian tradition of processions, their perceived superstitions, the amount of attention paid to saints' feast days, and the importance of the Virgin Mary in their devotions. At the time, the church hierarchy did not approve of the special devotion to Mary, as they feared it took the focus away from the Blessed Trinity. Within the church and within the larger xenophobic U.S. context, the new immigrants' "Old World" traditions were perceived as being hindrances to their successful assimilation.

The religious and class-based animosities between the Irish Americans and the Italian Americans fueled massive anti-Italian discrimination, which was accompanied by a fierce racial discourse. As is widely noted, the Irish considered Italians a different race, and would call them "niggers," "dagoes," and "wops." It was during the economic calamities of the 1960s, coupled with the 1965 Immigration Act, that Italian Americans began to develop a "white" identity, joining the "white" ranks with Irish Americans, (whose ethnic and racial status had been consecrated with the election of John F. Kennedy as president). For Italian Americans it occurred as a transformation in their self-perception as a community originally organized around a national heritage began to understand itself by way of a new racialized white identity. This transformation marked a major shift in Irish- and Italian-American relations, as they were no longer firmly at odds with each other according to this system of racial codification. Consequently, the two groups forged a common identity based on their inclination to blame African Americans for the decline of their own living standards.

The hostilities that ensued reached their height in 1974 with the antibusing riots in Boston, Massachusetts. Busing occurred in 24 other cities that same year, but it was in Boston where the violence most severely erupted and where the antagonism continued for years. Common representations of the antibusing riots tend to lay the blame with the Irish Americans alone, depicting them as the epitome of white ethnic racists. Although the location of the riots and most of the controversy surrounded the Irish neighborhood of South Boston, the Irish were not alone in their opposition to busing; the Italian community, despite its history of interethnic conflict, worked together with the Irish against busing. Along with the Irish residents of South Boston and Charlestown, the Italians of East Boston and the North End constituted much of the membership of Restore Our Alienated Rights, the area's primary antibusing organization. In this context these two formerly antagonistic ethnic groups joined forces in blaming African Americans for their own economic hardships and poor standards of living, resulting in both Italian and Irish Americans being considered the epitome of white, ethnic, working-class, right-wing conservatism.

Liz Burke

See also: NATIVISM AND ANTI-CATHOLICISM; ETHNIC AND RACE RELATIONS, IRISH AND AFRICAN AMERICANS

References

Gambino, Richard. *Blood of My Blood: The Dilemma of the Italian-Americans.* New York: Doubleday and Co., 1974.

Gambino, Richard. *Vendetta: The True Story of the Largest Lynching in U.S. History.* Toronto: Guernica, 1998.

Guglielmo, Jennifer, and Salvatore Salerno, eds. *Are Italians White?: How Race is Made in America.* New York: Routledge, 2003.

Iorizzo, Luciano J., and Salvatore Mondello. *The Italian-Americans.* New York: Twayne Publishers, 1971.

Jacobsen, Matthew Frye. *Barbarian Virtues: The United States Encounters Foreign Peoples at Home and Abroad, 1876–1917.* New York: Farrar, Straus, and Giroux, 2000.

Mangione, Jerre, and Ben Morreale. *La Storia: Five Centuries of the Italian American Experience.* New York: Harper Collins, 1992.

Nelli, Humbert S. *From Immigrants to Ethnics: The Italian Americans.* New York: Oxford University Press, 1983.

Rolle, Andrew F. *The American Italians: Their History and Culture.* Belmont, CA: Wadsworth, 1972.

Tager, Jack. *Boston Riots: Three Centuries of Social Violence.* Boston: Northeastern University Press, 2001.

ETHNIC AND RACE RELATIONS, IRISH AND LATINOS

The vast majority of Latinos encountered by the Irish immigrants upon their arrival in Latin America belonged to societies with relatively high degrees of miscegenation. Three groups predominated, including Europeans (Spanish, Portuguese, and to a lesser extent, French, German, British, and others), Amerindians (a vague term to designate thousands of groups with a probable common origin in Asia), and Africans (diverse groups particularly from eastern Africa).

Traditionally, Paraguay and Mexico have been the most important mestizo countries in the region—the result of intense crossbreeding between Europeans and Amerindians. The most important Amerindian communities can be found in Central America and the Andean area, especially in Bolivia, Guatemala, Ecuador, and Peru. Argentina and Uruguay have the largest European populations in Latin America, although until the last decades of the nineteenth century mixed European-Amerindians predominated in both countries. Likewise, important African communities live in the Caribbean, Brazil, and Suriname, countries that up to the eighteenth century also included significant Amerindian groups.

In general terms, the Irish followed the same relational patterns as other British immigrants in Latin America, and the local residents in their destination countries received them as so-called *ingleses*. These patterns were determined by the demographic, social, and religious factors of the Irish and other ethnic categories.

In eighteenth- and early nineteenth-century emigration from Ireland to Latin America there was a remarkable absence of women. With the exception of certain soldiers in the expeditions to Venezuela and Brazil who were accompanied by their families, Irish female emigration almost always began several years after male emigration. Women were generally willing to emigrate only once men who were known to them became established in a potential settlement region. Passenger list records in Argentina show that the first Irish female immigrants landed in Buenos Aires in 1828 whereas the first men arrived in 1776. Furthermore, it was not until the 1880s that the percentage of women reached 40.4 percent of the total arrivals, and for this reason the proportion of women among Irish-born residents in Argentina was still only 41.2 percent in 1895.

The direct effect of this female shortage was that up to the mid-nineteenth century in Argentina and Uruguay, and before that time in Mexico, Venezuela, and Colombia, it was not uncommon for Irish men to marry members of other ethnic groups. Their offspring were therefore mixed between Irish and Hispano-Creoles or Irish and Amerindians; the former were more frequent among merchants and successful urban settlers, and the latter among poor and isolated Irish rural workers.

In the 1860s, with the arrival from Ireland of greater numbers of women, endogamy rates increased in the Irish community, particularly among rural middle classes with a Roman Catholic background. In Argentina, marriages between Irish immigrants reached uncommonly high peaks in the second half of the nineteenth century. In one place, the parish of Luján in Buenos Aires province, intermarriage among Irish-born settlers was 77 percent in the period 1850–1879, compared with 56 percent among French and 42 percent among Spanish. In the early twentieth century, preoccupied with the social isolation and biological risks derived from such a high endogamy, some Irish priests were recommending that their flock marry Italian, Spanish, or other women. However, it is known that some male youngsters preferred to remain celibate rather than marry outside the community.

Protestant immigrants from Ireland usually associated with Argentines up to the 1880s, and with Britons and Anglo-Argentines thereafter, but were particularly closer to the latter groups in the period of massive European immigration. From the marriage records of Anglican and Presbyterian churches in Argentina, it seems the relations of Protestant Irish settlers with other Protestants possibly followed more of a social stratification than any theological distinctions. Independently of their Church of Ireland common background, wealthy and well-established merchants and landowners often belonged to the local Anglican community while middle-class urban employees and rural workers tended to be connected with the Presbyterian Church. Nevertheless, a number of Irish Protestants married Irish and Irish-Argentine Catholic women.

County divisions were significant among settlers from different parts of Ireland, and this was another factor in their relations with the other ethnic groups. John Brabazon, a settler in Argentina from a Protestant family of Co. Westmeath who left a journal relating his experience in Buenos Aires province in 1842–1852, wrote that "some of the Westmeath and Longford people were respectable, . . . the Wexford people were all respectable people [but] Ballymore people were such divils as ever filled the Jail of Mullingar" (cited by McKenna 2000, 101). The emigrants from Ballymore and Ballinacarrigy (Westmeath) and Ballymahon (Longford) mixed with the gaucho class—mestizo from old Spanish and Amerindians—which was seen as an unforgivable sin among the Irish community. Irish Midlands immigrants drank and gambled with gauchos, and had the highest degrees of cultural transfers with them.

This was never heard of in "Wexfordians," who used to look down on "Ballinacarrias" (emigrants from Ballinacarrigy or from the Irish Midlands in general) in horse races, at Mass, or on other occasions. The perceived lower status of the Midlands immigrants may have been derived from the arrangements made between the merchant Thomas Armstrong of Buenos Aires and the authorities of the workhouse in Ballymahon for the purpose of securing working-class immigrants in Buenos Aires.

Whether in Mexican Texas or in Argentina, the relations between Irish and Amerindians were at least tense—and often violent. Although the Irish were rarely engaged in direct military campaigns against the Indians, before the 1880s many land-hungry immigrants from Ireland were residing outside the frontier lines. They supported, and sometimes actively engaged in, the fight against the Indians, and therefore ensured the settlement and later acquisition of cheap land. Land did not belong to the Indians, who did not conceive it as property but as a hunting ground to be used by everybody. The Irish, as well as the Argentine elites and other European immigrants, were conscious of the potential value of land, and invested in purchasing or long-term leasing their properties. Consequently, they perceived that they had all the rights to defend their newly acquired holdings from "the wild children of the pampas" (as the indigenous peoples were styled by the Irish Argentine *Southern Cross* newspaper in 1875). Indian raids of small groups—called *malónes* in Argentina—invaded the area of ranches and sacked the cattle and pillaged the houses. Sometimes the Irish people were taken captives for a number of years in the Indian *tolderías*. Certain accounts by first settlers show that both Indians and Irish had little respect for human life. James Gaynor, who acquired an enormous tract of land in the department of Nueve de Julio, west of Buenos Aires province, boasted of having killed several "savages" who invaded his property.

A counterexample to this rule of violent relations between the Amerindian and Irish is the number of unions—both legal and informal—that several Irish workmen and ranch hands consummated with Indian women. Often the men were unmarried laborers in large ranches who resided in isolated places, and the women were chiefs' daughters from docile Indian tribes. This was relatively frequent in the department of General Viamonte, where the Coliqueo Indian family was granted lands for service to the Argentine army, and along the Paraná and Uruguay rivers, with a number of unions between Irish males and Guaraní women. There are no accounts of Irish women marrying Indian males.

There is ample evidence of the Irish showing a marked contempt for mestizo natives, who often were viewed by the Irish and the local landed elites as barbarian savages belonging to an inferior race. However, there have been intense cultural transfers between the Irish *empresarios* and Mexicans in Texas, and the Irish sheep farmers and the gauchos of the pampas in the River Plate region. There were efficient alliances between both groups, from which the Irish learned to speak Spanish, could hire efficient workforces for gathering cotton or for shearing, and acquired specific technical skills in cattle-breeding and related businesses. In the mid-1860s John Murphy of Salto department in Buenos Aires described how the gauchos at his neighbor's ranch taught him and his Irish hands to extinguish enormous fires using the carcass of a recently killed mare. In Texas, some Irish colonists became Spanish/English bilinguals, and in the Mexican Revolution perceived themselves more as Mexicans than U.S. Americans.

The creolization of the Irish in their relations with Latin American societies was generally driven by class factors. In contrast to other immigrants from the British Isles, the Irish merchants and the most successful rural settlers struggled to be accepted sooner or later as members of the local landed elites. Examples of this are the marriages of Thomas Armstrong in Buenos Aires and John MacKenna in Santiago, Chile, with members of well-known traditional families of the local bourgeoisie, as well as the viceroy Ambrose O'Higgins's union with a young woman of the Chilean upper-class. In their turn, the Irish workers, both in the cities and the countryside, related with natives of the same social category, in particular when these were mixed race. However, there are no accounts of Irish immigrants relating with Africans or African-Creoles. In Trinidad Island the rank and file of Devereux's Irish Legion in Bolívar's army sacked the houses of Africans and terrorized their families. The families recruited by Col. William Cotter for the Brazilian army were called *escravos brancos* (white slaves) by the Africans of Rio de Janeiro. The Irish united with German mercenaries against the Brazilians.

In the last decades of the nineteenth century, when mass European immigration flooded over Argentina, Brazil, and Uruguay, tensions arose between the established local bourgeoisie and the immigrants, and among newly arrived immigrants of diverse ethnic origins. The immigration scheme of 1889 financed by the Argentine government and carried out by its Irish-Argentine agents in Ireland (that came to be known as the Dresden Affair), had its origins in a government policy conceived to offset what was considered to be the excessive influx of Italians of the poorer classes. The arrival of the Passionist order in Argentina represents an example of bigotry among members of the Irish Catholic community—an attitude that was not uncommon among the larger part of its middle classes. The Irish leaders considered that because the community had paid to establish the order, the priests should have been mostly Irish and should have worked exclusively with their Irish flock. They accused the Passionists of Italianization of the order, and even submitted their claims to Rome.

Another manifestation of the Irish-Argentine auto-exclusion from other immigrant communities was during the celebration of sports spectacles. Both in Buenos Aires in 1909 and in Pergamino in 1929 boxing matches were organized between Irish or Irish-Argentine boxers and their Italian opponents.

Edmundo Murray

See also: DRESDEN AFFAIR

References

Coghlan, Eduardo A. *Los Irlandeses en la Argentina: Su Actuación y Descendencia.* Buenos Aires: Author's Edition, 1987.

Graham-Yooll, Andrew. *The Forgotten Colony: A History of the English-Speaking Communities in Argentina.* Buenos Aires: Literature of Latin America, 1999.

McKenna, Patrick. "Irish Emigration to Argentina: A Different Model." In *The Irish Diaspora,* edited by Andy Bielenberg. Essex: Pearson Education Ltd., 2000.